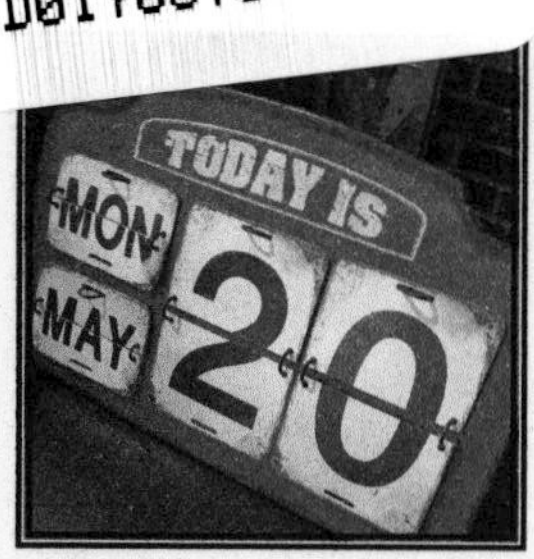
TODAY IS
MON
MAY
20

Yuto Tsukuda

Though the manga industry is changing with the times, no matter how much it and the world change, I'd like to continue to be involved somehow, someway with making manga.

Shun Saeki

Shake, shake, shake!

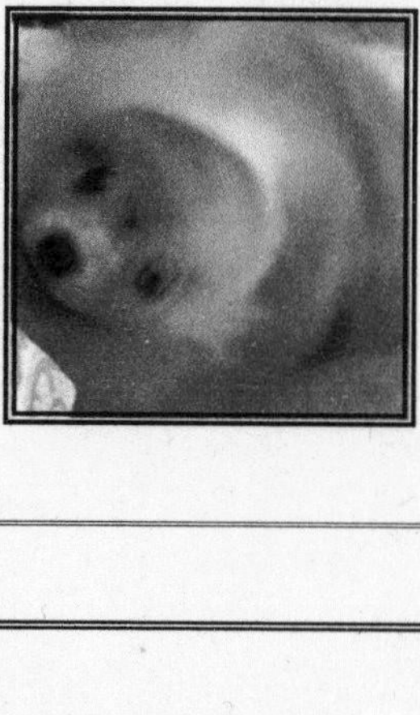

About the authors

Yuto Tsukuda won the 34th Jump Juniketsu Newcomers' Manga Award for his one-shot story *Kiba ni Naru*. He made his *Weekly Shonen Jump* debut in 2010 with the series *Shonen Shikku*. His follow-up series, *Food Wars!: Shokugeki no Soma*, is his first English-language release.

Shun Saeki made his *Jump NEXT!* debut in 2011 with the one-shot story *Kimi to Watashi no Renai Soudan*. *Food Wars!: Shokugeki no Soma* is his first *Shonen Jump* series.

Food Wars!
SHOKUGEKI NO SOMA

Volume 31
Shonen Jump Manga Edition
Story by Yuto Tsukuda, Art by Shun Saeki
Contributor Yuki Morisaki

Translation: Adrienne Beck
Touch-Up Art & Lettering: James Gaubatz, Mara Coman
Design: Alice Lewis
Editor: Jennifer LeBlanc

SHOKUGEKI NO SOMA © 2012 by Yuto Tsukuda, Shun Saeki
All rights reserved.
First published in Japan in 2012 by SHUEISHA Inc., Tokyo.
English translation rights arranged by SHUEISHA Inc.

The stories, characters and incidents mentioned in this publication
are entirely fictional.

No portion of this book may be reproduced or transmitted in
any form or by any means without written permission from the
copyright holders.

Printed in the U.S.A.

Published by VIZ Media, LLC
P.O. Box 77010
San Francisco, CA 94107

10 9 8 7 6 5 4 3 2 1
First printing, August 2019

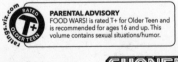

PARENTAL ADVISORY
FOOD WARS! is rated T+ for Older Teen and
is recommended for ages 16 and up. This
volume contains sexual situations/humor.

viz.com   shonenjump.com

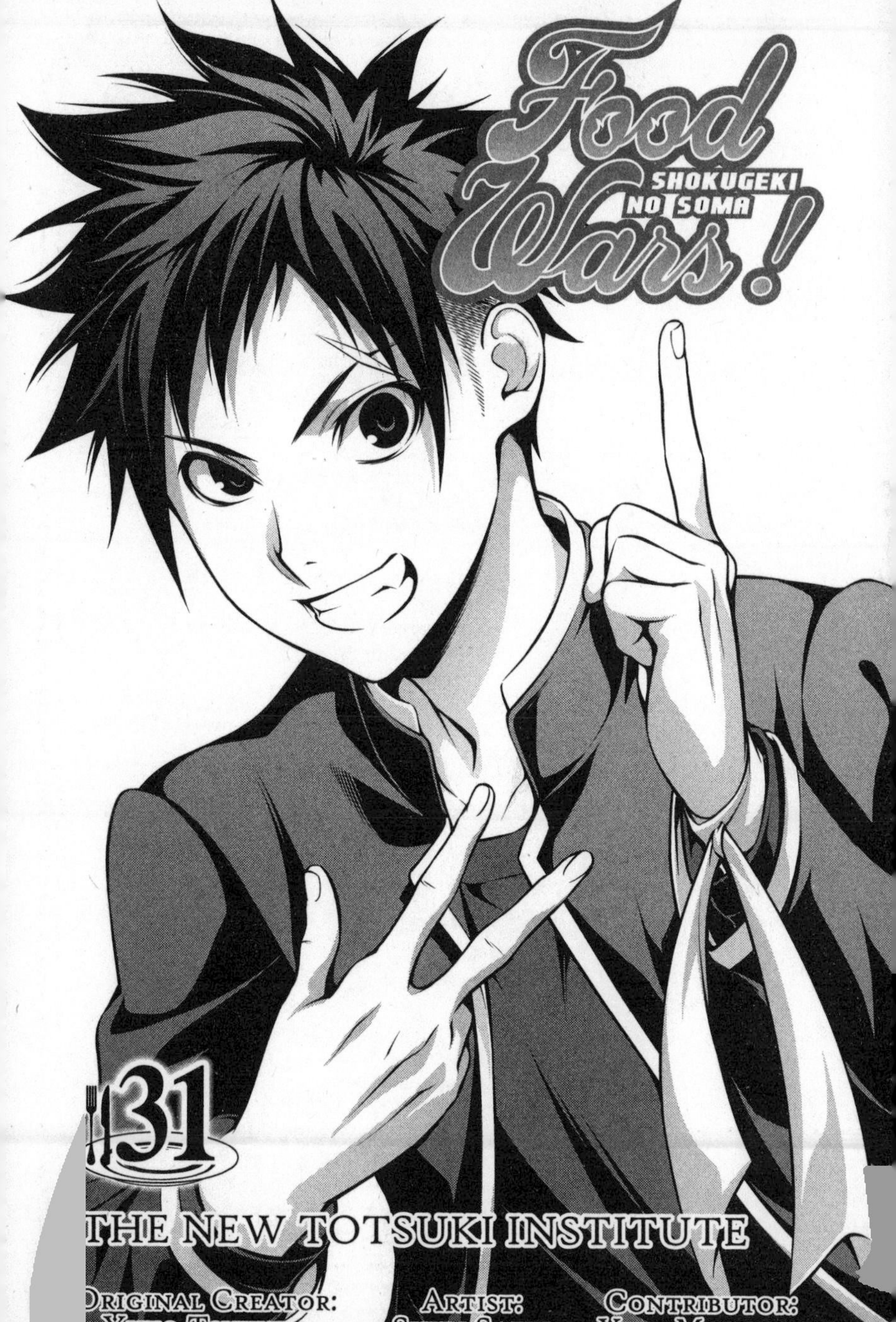

Food Wars!

Shokugeki no Soma

31

The New Totsuki Institute

Original Creator: Yuto Tsukuda

Artist: Shun Saeki

Contributor: Yuki Morisaki

CHARACTERS

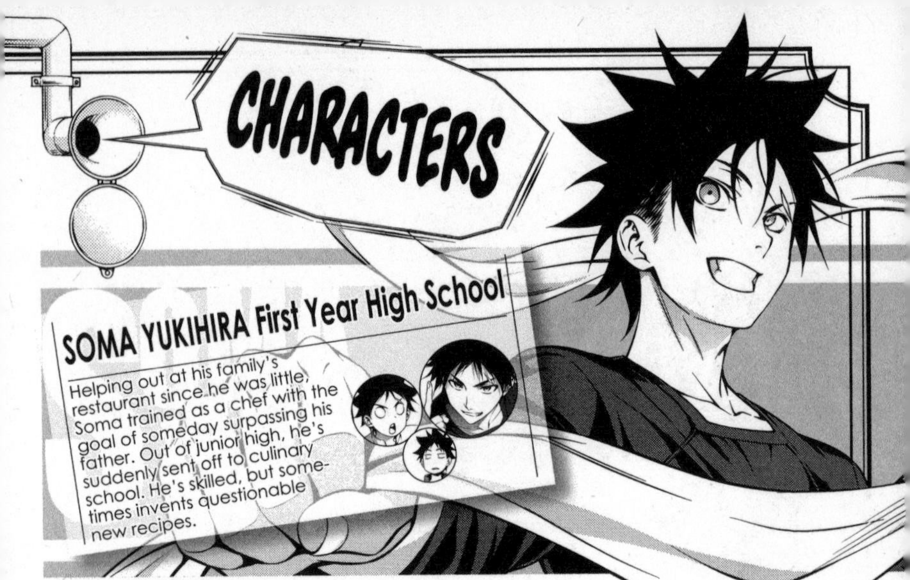

SOMA YUKIHIRA First Year High School

Helping out at his family's restaurant since he was little, Soma trained as a chef with the goal of someday surpassing his father. Out of junior high, he's suddenly sent off to culinary school. He's skilled, but sometimes invents questionable new recipes.

Shokugeki no SOMA

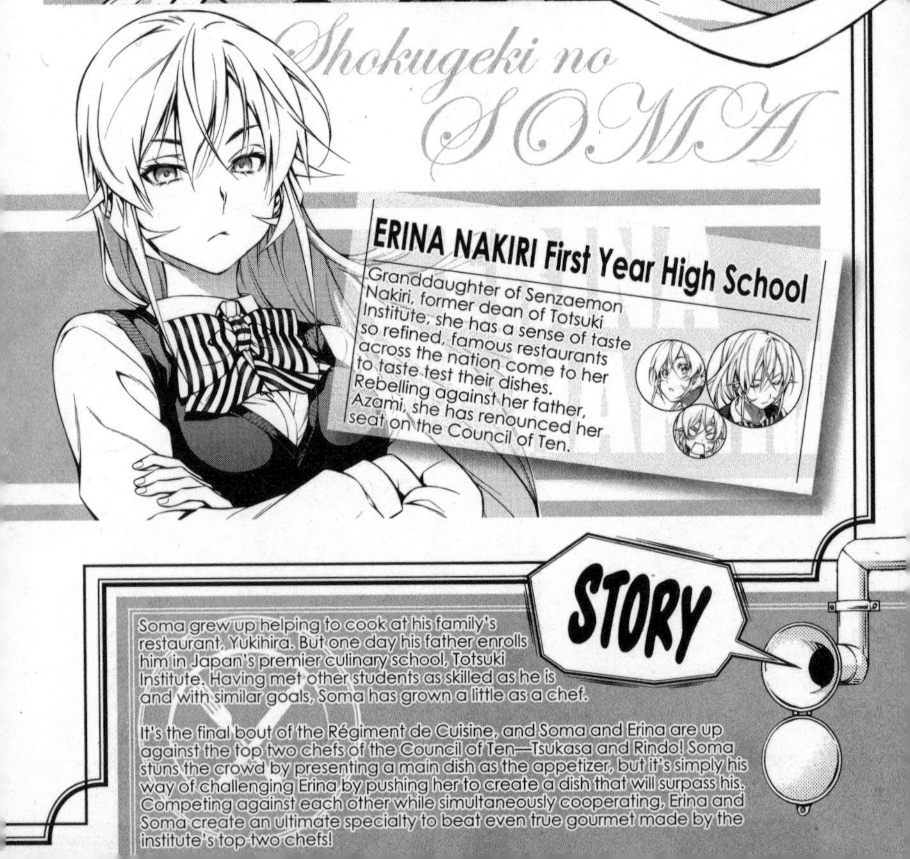

ERINA NAKIRI First Year High School

Granddaughter of Senzaemon Nakiri, former dean of Totsuki Institute, she has a sense of taste so refined, famous restaurants across the nation come to her to taste test their dishes. Rebelling against her father, Azami, she has renounced her seat on the Council of Ten.

STORY

Soma grew up helping to cook at his family's restaurant, Yukihira. But one day his father enrolls him in Japan's premier culinary school, Totsuki Institute. Having met other students as skilled as he is and with similar goals, Soma has grown a little as a chef.

It's the final bout of the Régiment de Cuisine, and Soma and Erina are up against the top two chefs of the Council of Ten—Tsukasa and Rindo! Soma stuns the crowd by presenting a main dish as the appetizer, but it's simply his way of challenging Erina by pushing her to create a dish that will surpass his. Competing against each other while simultaneously cooperating, Erina and Soma create an ultimate specialty to beat even true gourmet made by the institute's top two chefs!

Shokugeki no SOMA

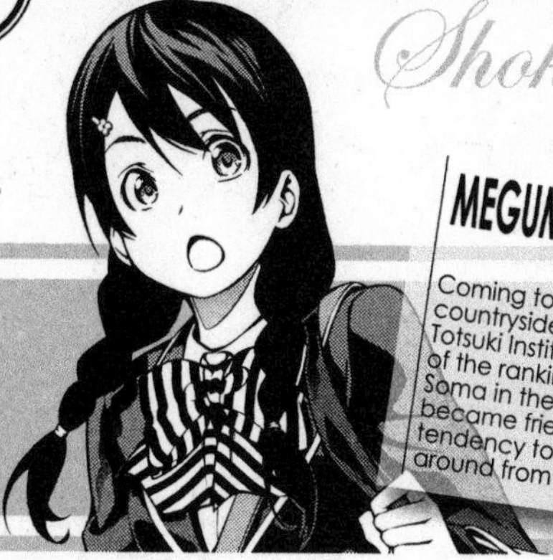

MEGUMI TADOKORO First Year High School

Coming to the big city from the countryside, Megumi made it into Totsuki Institute at the very bottom of the rankings. Partnered with Soma in their first class, the two became friends. However, he has a tendency to inadvertently yank her around from time to time.

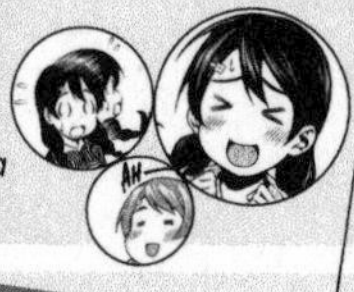
AH

TAKUMI ALDINI First Year High School

Working at his family's trattoria in Italy from a young age, he transferred into Totsuki Institute in junior high. Isami is his younger twin brother.

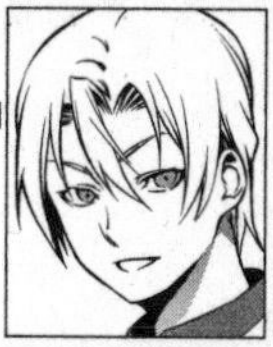

SATOSHI ISSHIKI Second Year High School

A Polaris resident and former seventh seat, he's responsible, caring and quick to change into an apron and nothing else before you know it.

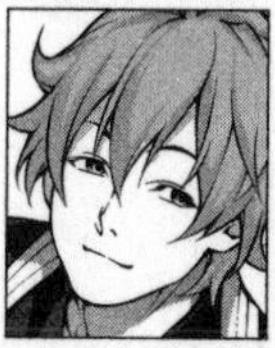

EISHI TSUKASA Third Year High School

The current first seat on Totsuki's Council of Ten. He comes off as meek and weak-willed at first, but he has absolute confidence in his skills as a chef.

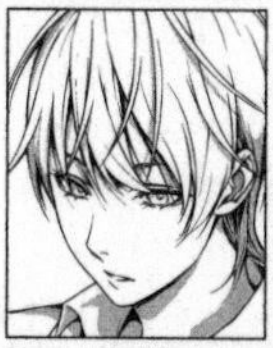

RINDO KOBAYASHI Third Year High School

The current second seat on Totsuki's Council of Ten, Rindo is friendly, sociable and easygoing. She's a master of handling unique ingredients.

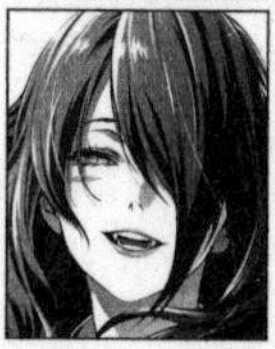

MOMO AKANEGAKUBO Third Year High School

The current third seat on the new Council of Ten, Momo specializes in baking and desserts. She is never without her stuffed animal named "Butchy."

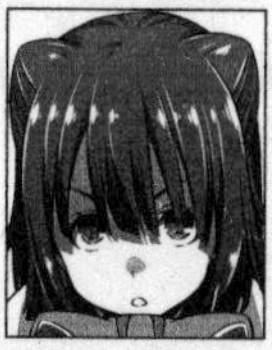

AZAMI NAKIRI

Erina's father, he convinced over half the Council of Ten to back him in staging a coup for taking control of the institute, forcing former dean Senzaemon Nakiri into retirement.

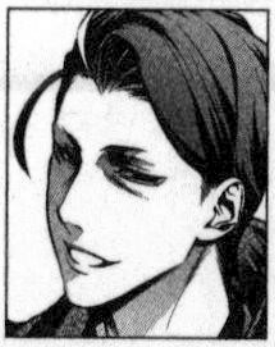

Food Wars!

SHOKUGEKI NO SOMA

31

Table of Contents

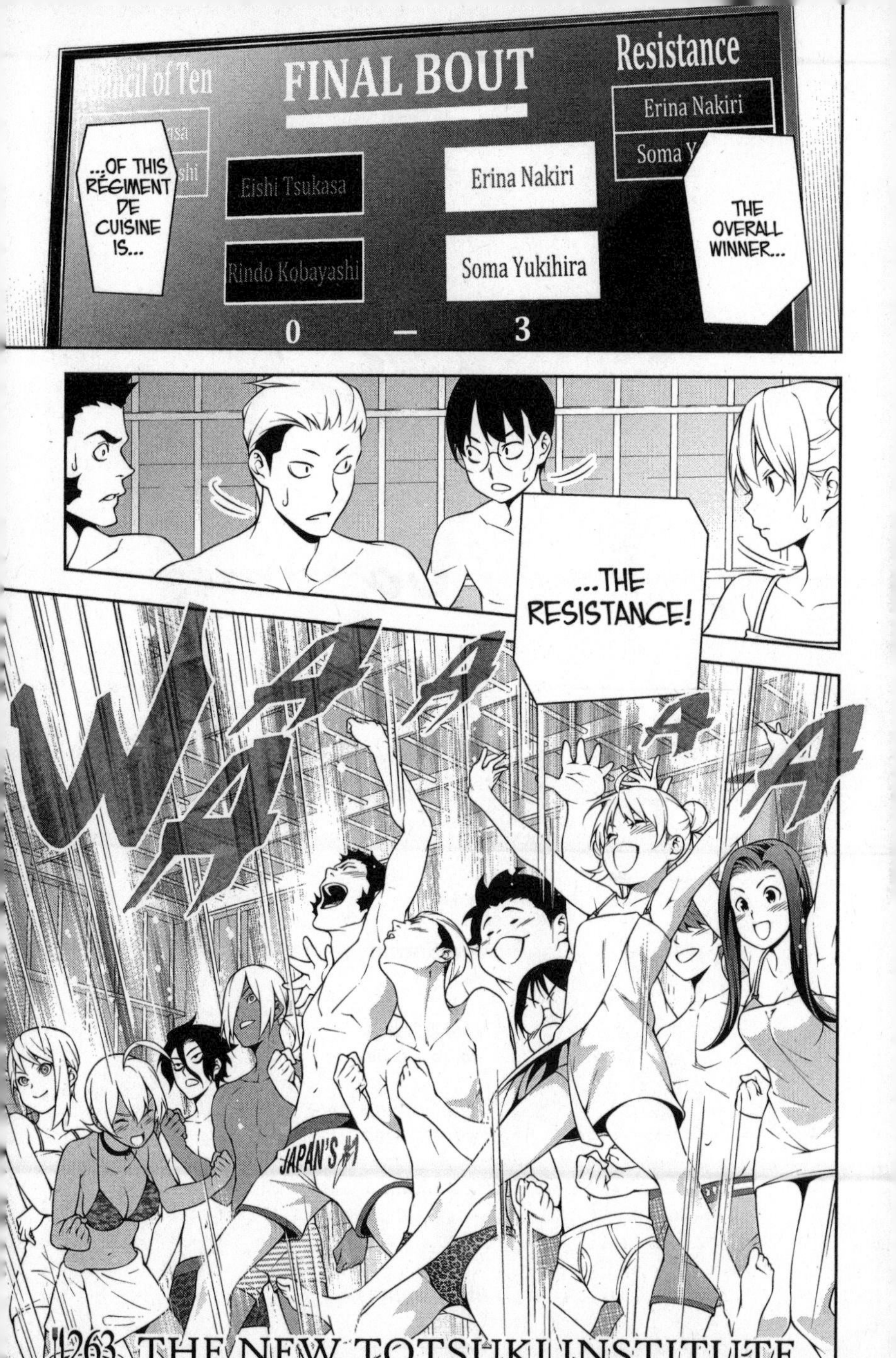
FINAL BOUT
Resistance
Erina Nakiri
Eishi Tsukasa
Erina Nakiri
Rindo Kobayashi
Soma Yukihira
0 – 3
THE OVERALL WINNER...
...OF THIS RÉGIMENT DE CUISINE IS...
...THE RESISTANCE!
WAAAAA
JAPAN'S #1

263 THE NEW TOTSUKI INSTITUTE

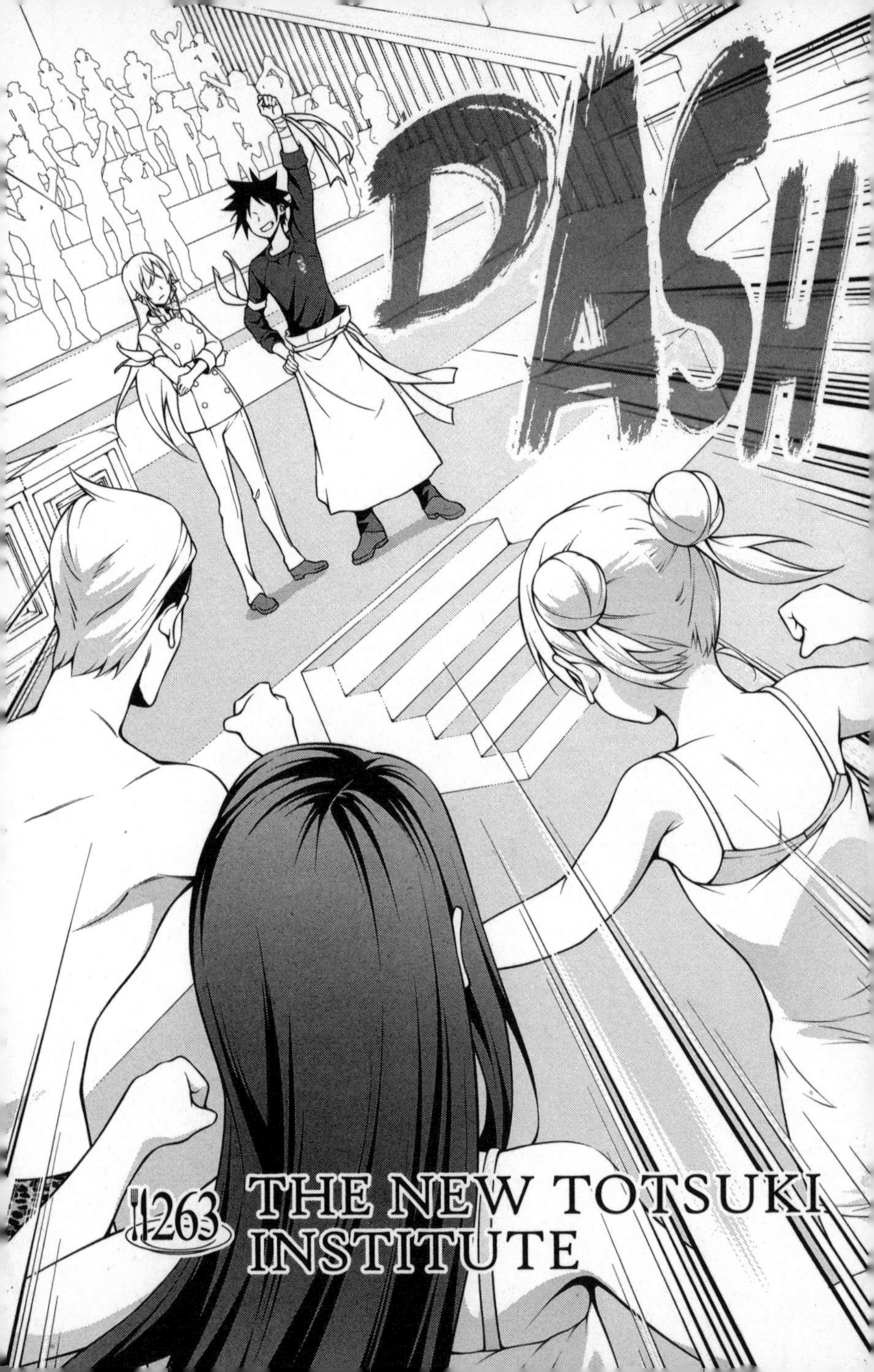
DASH
263
THE NEW TOTSUKI INSTITUTE

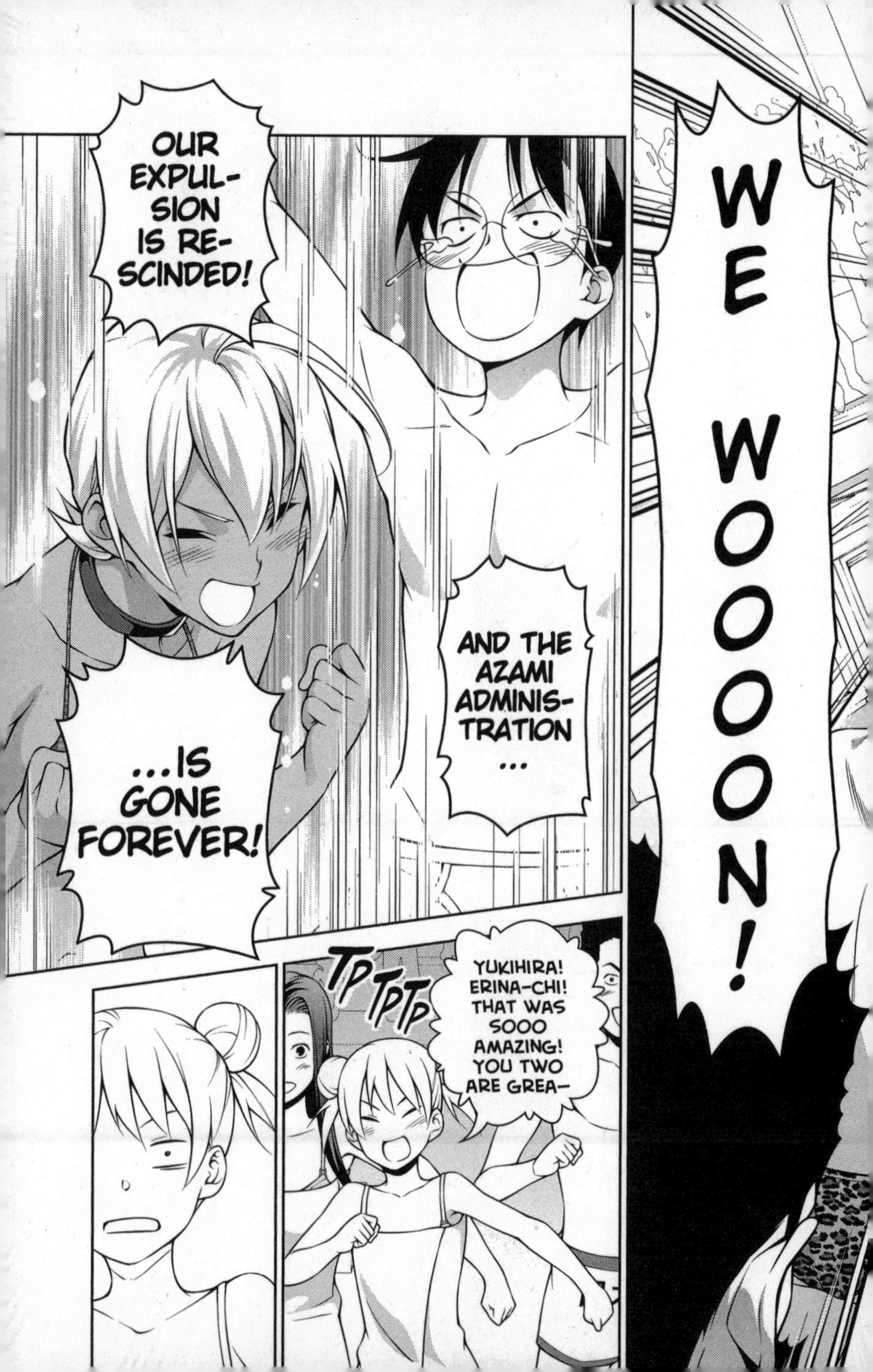
WE WOOOON!
OUR EXPUL-SION IS RE-SCINDED!
AND THE AZAMI ADMINIS-TRATION ...
...IS GONE FOREVER!
TP TPTP
YUKIHIRA! ERINA-CHI! THAT WAS SOOO AMAZING! YOU TWO ARE GREA-

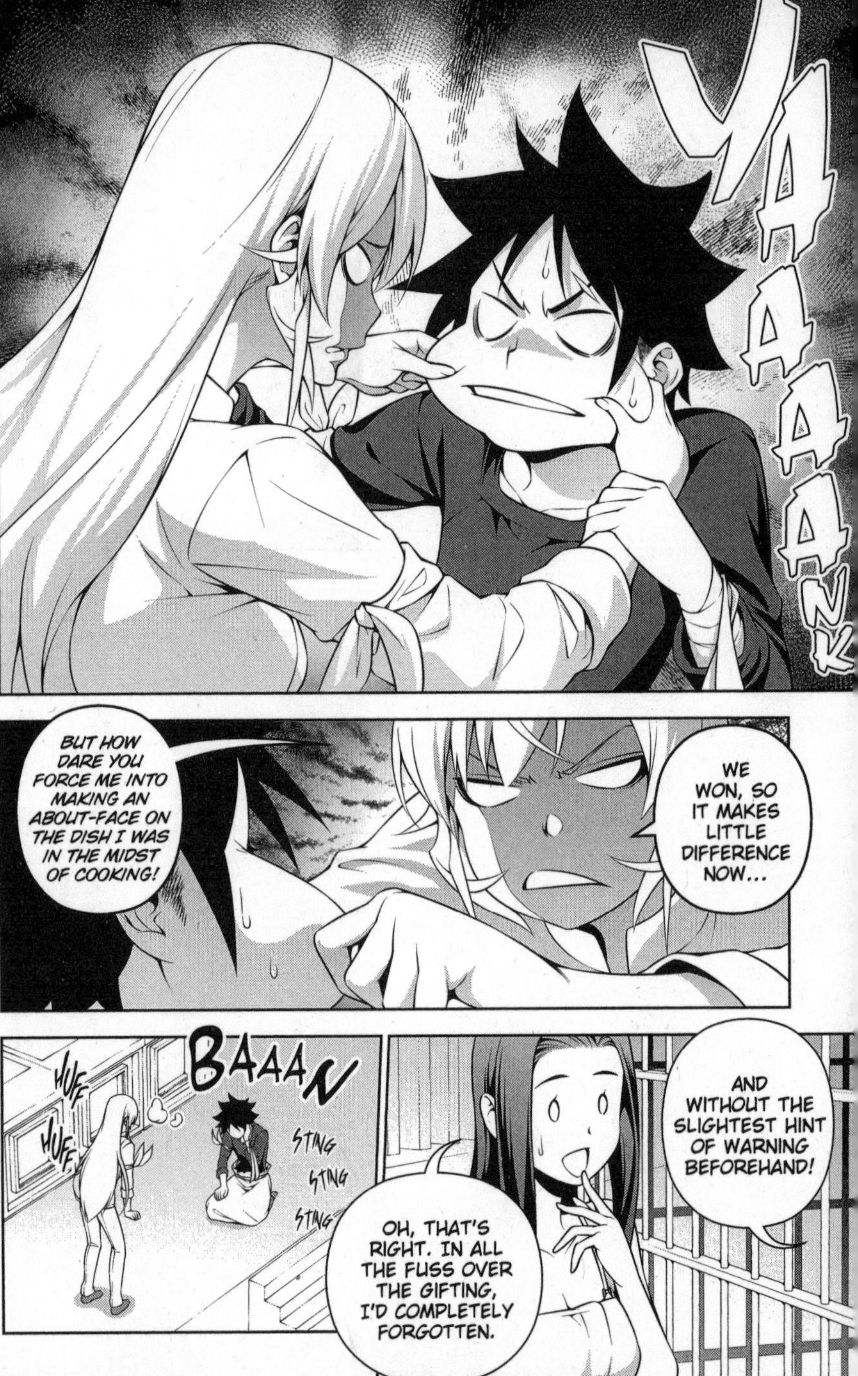
YAAAANK
WE WON, SO IT MAKES LITTLE DIFFERENCE NOW...
BUT HOW DARE YOU FORCE ME INTO MAKING AN ABOUT-FACE ON THE DISH I WAS IN THE MIDST OF COOKING!
AND WITHOUT THE SLIGHTEST HINT OF WARNING BEFOREHAND!
OH, THAT'S RIGHT. IN ALL THE FUSS OVER THE GIFTING, I'D COMPLETELY FORGOTTEN.
BAAAN
HUFF HUFF
STING STING STING

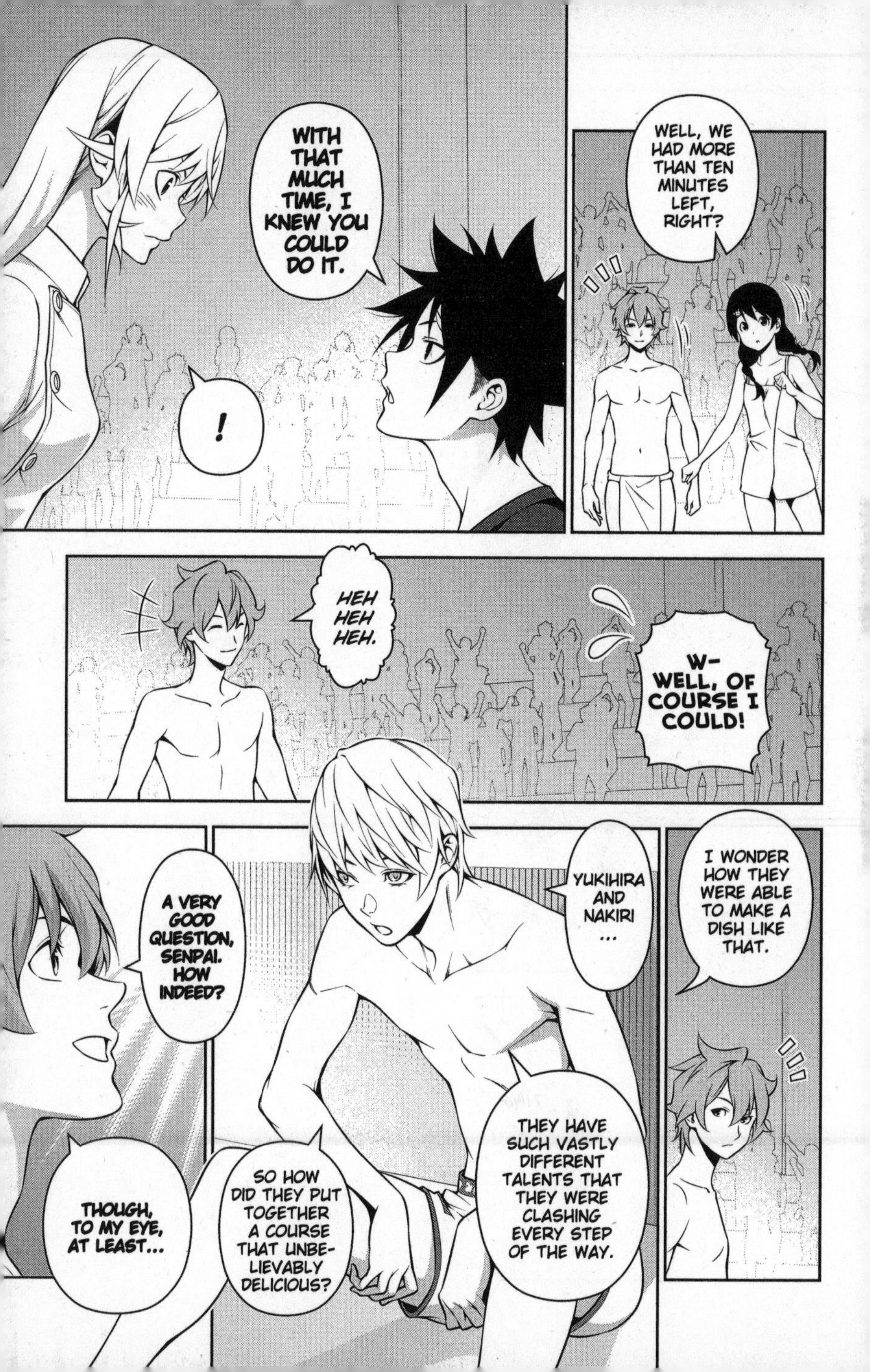

WELL, WE HAD MORE THAN TEN MINUTES LEFT, RIGHT?
WITH THAT MUCH TIME, I KNEW YOU COULD DO IT.
!
W- WELL, OF COURSE I COULD!
HEH HEH HEH.
I WONDER HOW THEY WERE ABLE TO MAKE A DISH LIKE THAT.
YUKIHIRA AND NAKIRI ...
THEY HAVE SUCH VASTLY DIFFERENT TALENTS THAT THEY WERE CLASHING EVERY STEP OF THE WAY.
SO HOW DID THEY PUT TOGETHER A COURSE THAT UNBE- LIEVABLY DELICIOUS?
A VERY GOOD QUESTION, SENPAI. HOW INDEED?
THOUGH, TO MY EYE, AT LEAST...

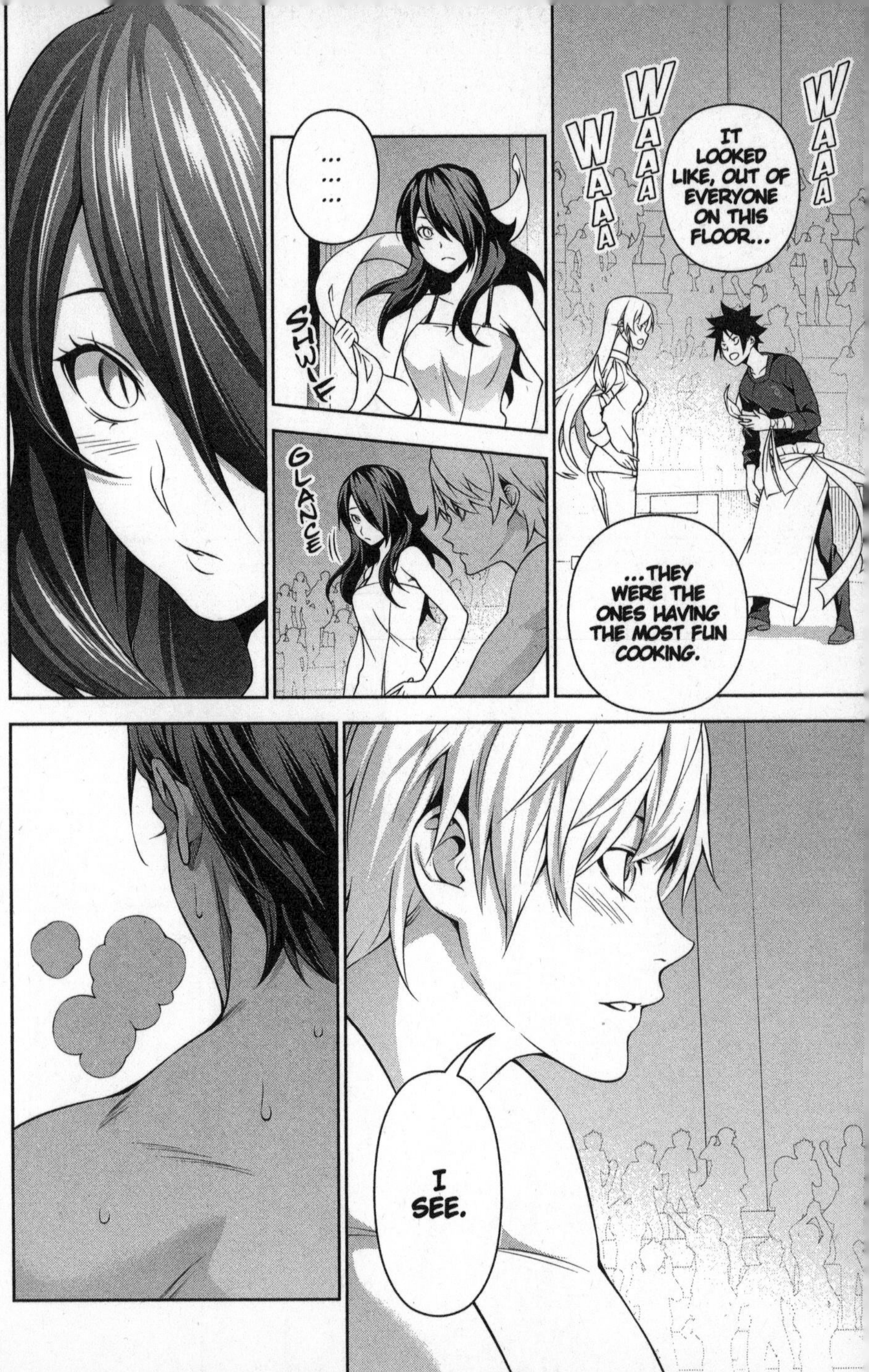
WAAA
WAAA
WAAA
IT LOOKED LIKE, OUT OF EVERYONE ON THIS FLOOR...
...THEY WERE THE ONES HAVING THE MOST FUN COOKING.
... ...
SHWIF
GLANCE
I SEE.

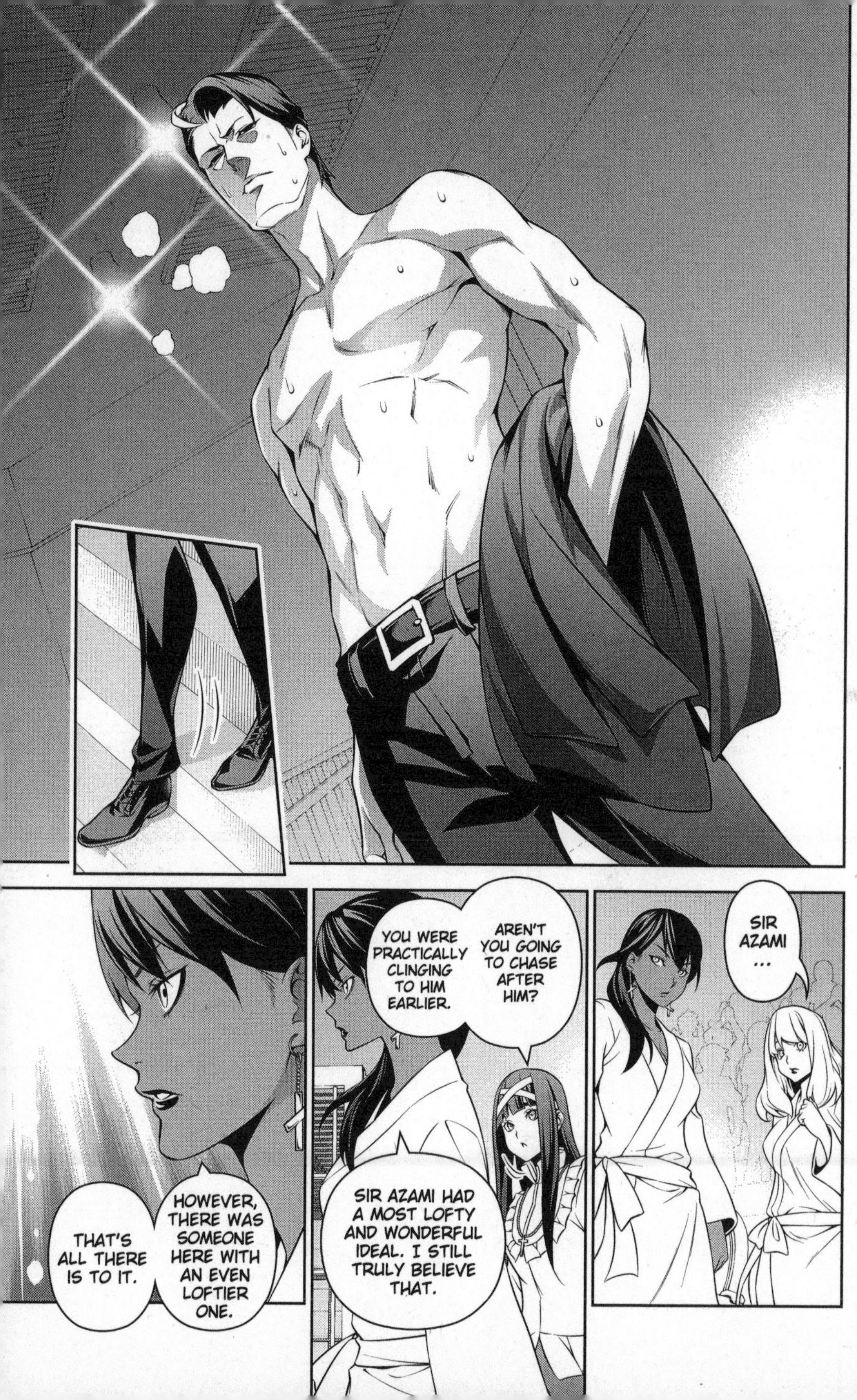
SIR AZAMI ...
AREN'T YOU GOING TO CHASE AFTER HIM?
YOU WERE PRACTICALLY CLINGING TO HIM EARLIER.
SIR AZAMI HAD A MOST LOFTY AND WONDERFUL IDEAL. I STILL TRULY BELIEVE THAT.
HOWEVER, THERE WAS SOMEONE HERE WITH AN EVEN LOFTIER ONE.
THAT'S ALL THERE IS TO IT.

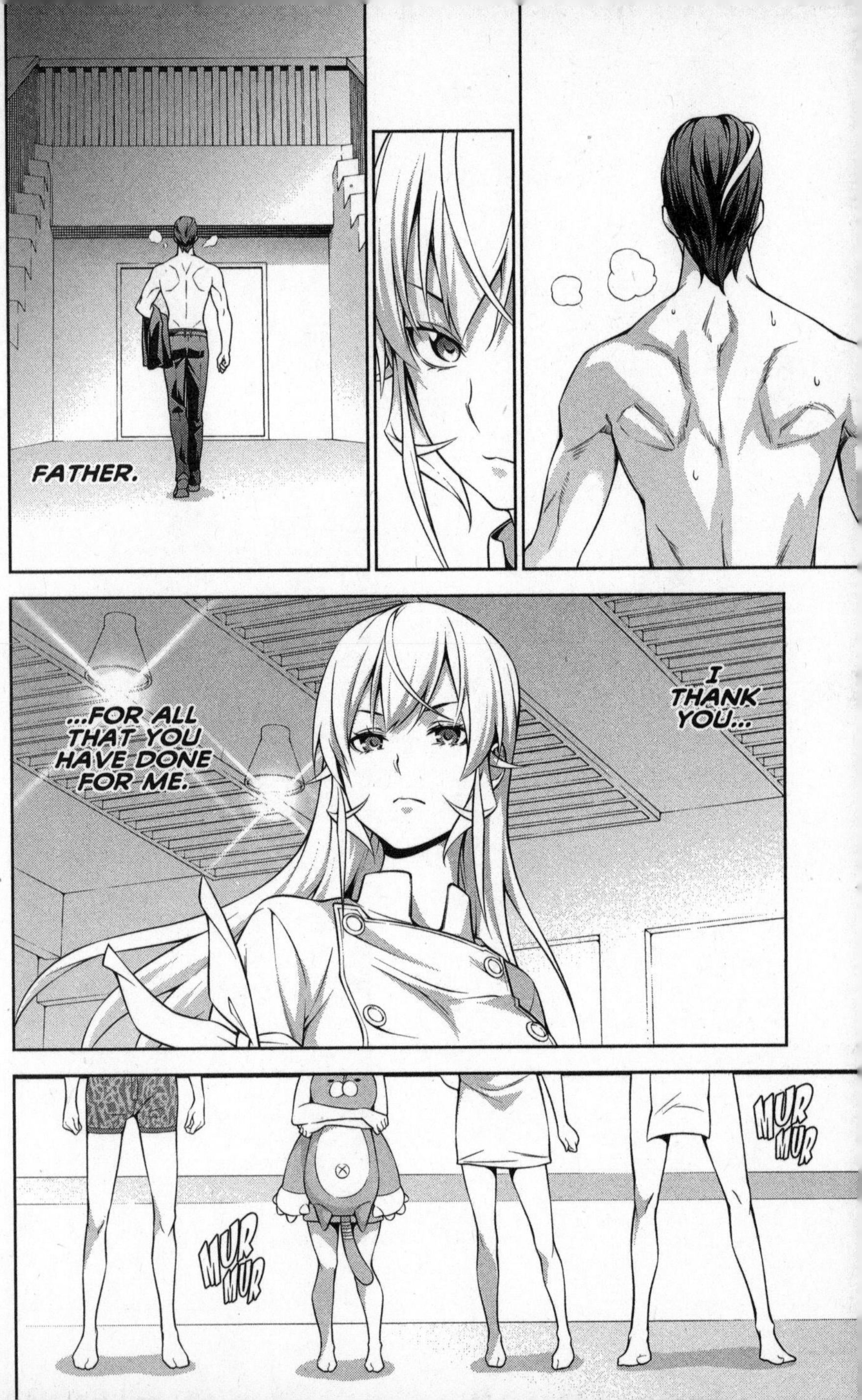
FATHER.
I THANK YOU...
...FOR ALL THAT YOU HAVE DONE FOR ME.
MUR MUR
MUR MUR

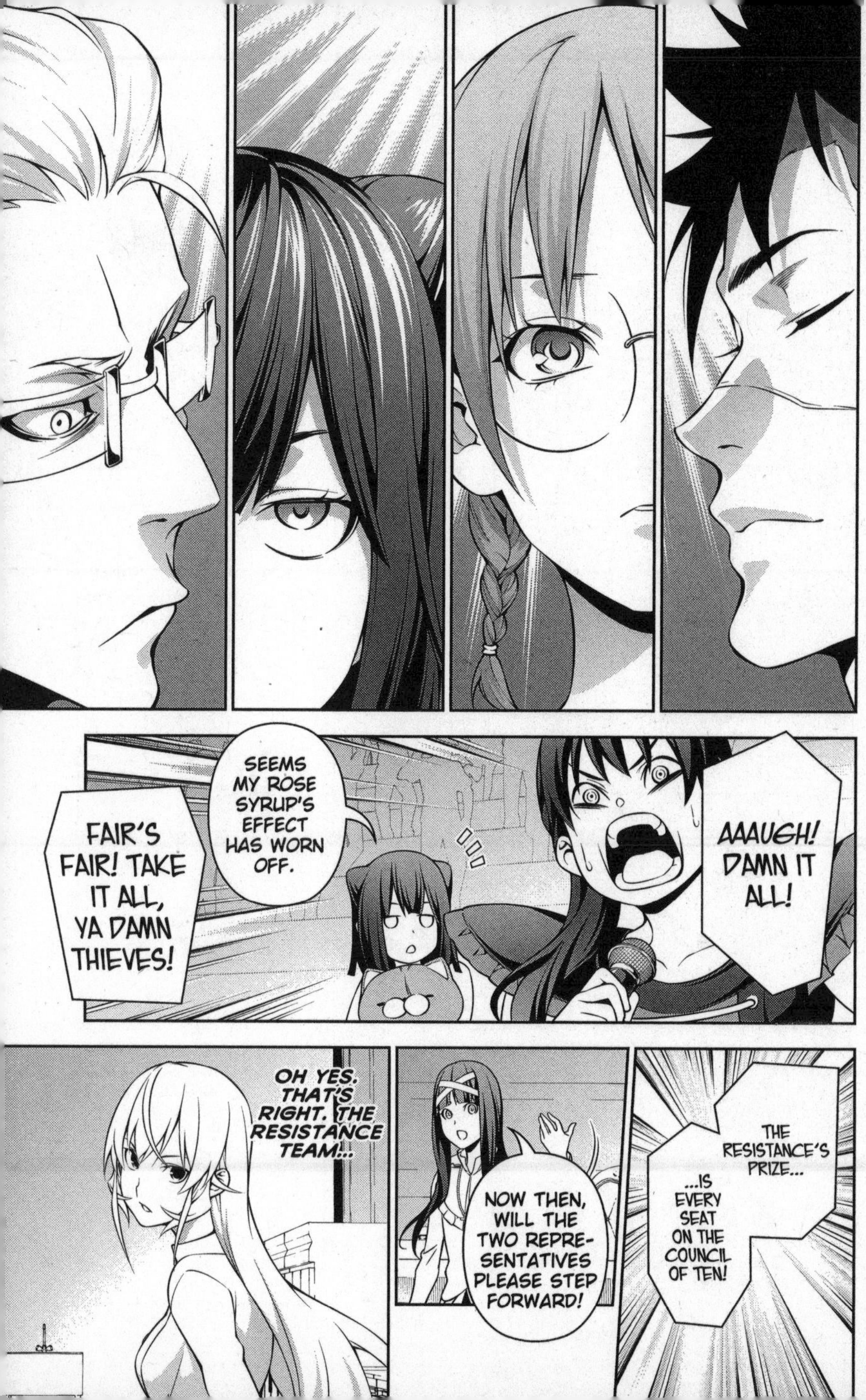

AAAUGH! DAMN IT ALL!
SEEMS MY ROSE SYRUP'S EFFECT HAS WORN OFF.
FAIR'S FAIR! TAKE IT ALL, YA DAMN THIEVES!
THE RESISTANCE'S PRIZE...
...IS EVERY SEAT ON THE COUNCIL OF TEN!
NOW THEN, WILL THE TWO REPRESENTATIVES PLEASE STEP FORWARD!
OH YES. THAT'S RIGHT. THE RESISTANCE TEAM...

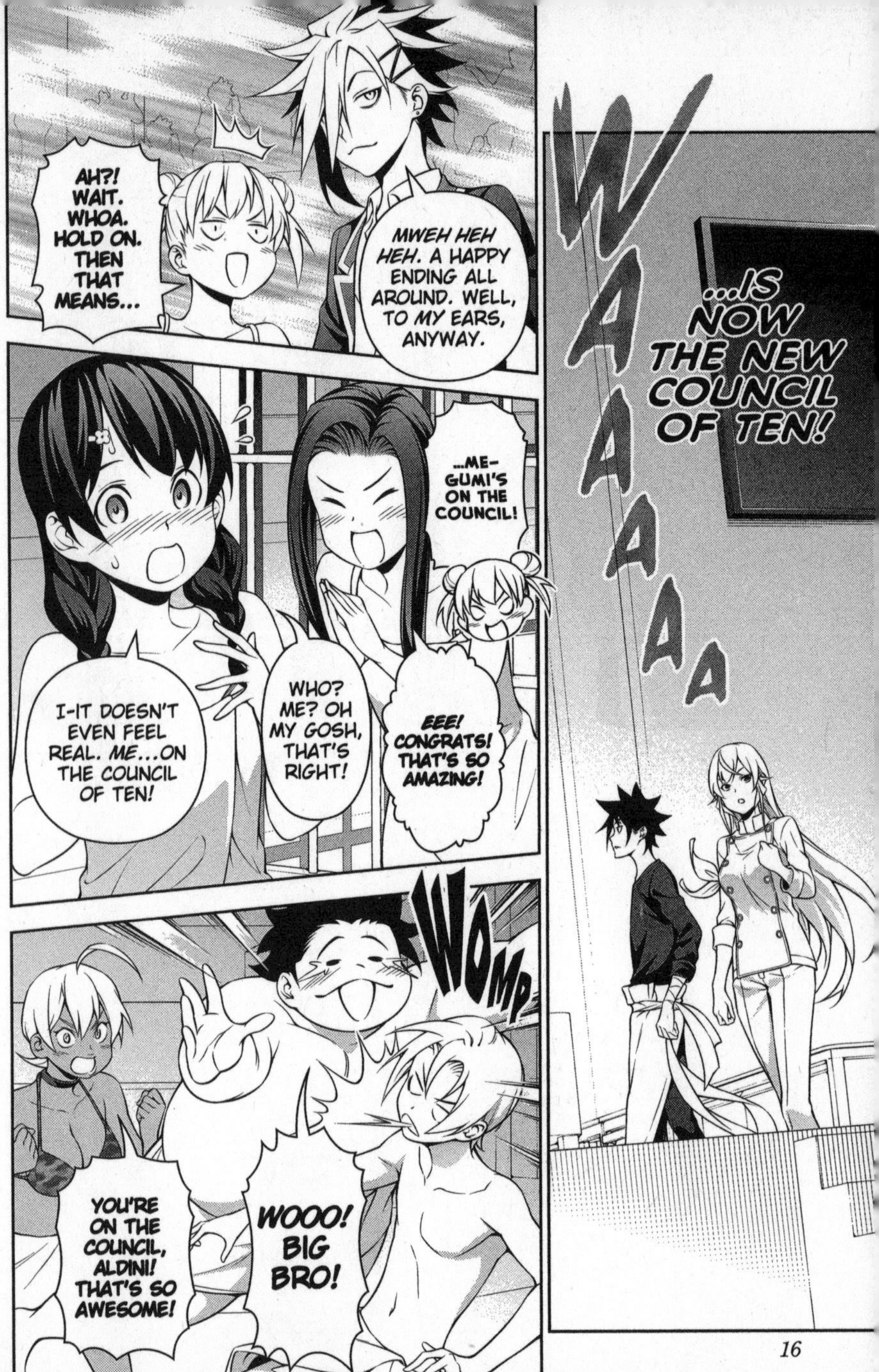
WAAAAAA
...IS NOW THE NEW COUNCIL OF TEN!
MWEH HEH HEH. A HAPPY ENDING ALL AROUND. WELL, TO MY EARS, ANYWAY.
AH?! WAIT. WHOA. HOLD ON. THEN THAT MEANS...
...ME-GUMI'S ON THE COUNCIL!
EEE! CONGRATS! THAT'S SO AMAZING!
WHO? ME? OH MY GOSH, THAT'S RIGHT!
I-IT DOESN'T EVEN FEEL REAL. ME...ON THE COUNCIL OF TEN!
WOMP
WOOO! BIG BRO!
YOU'RE ON THE COUNCIL, ALDINI! THAT'S SO AWESOME!

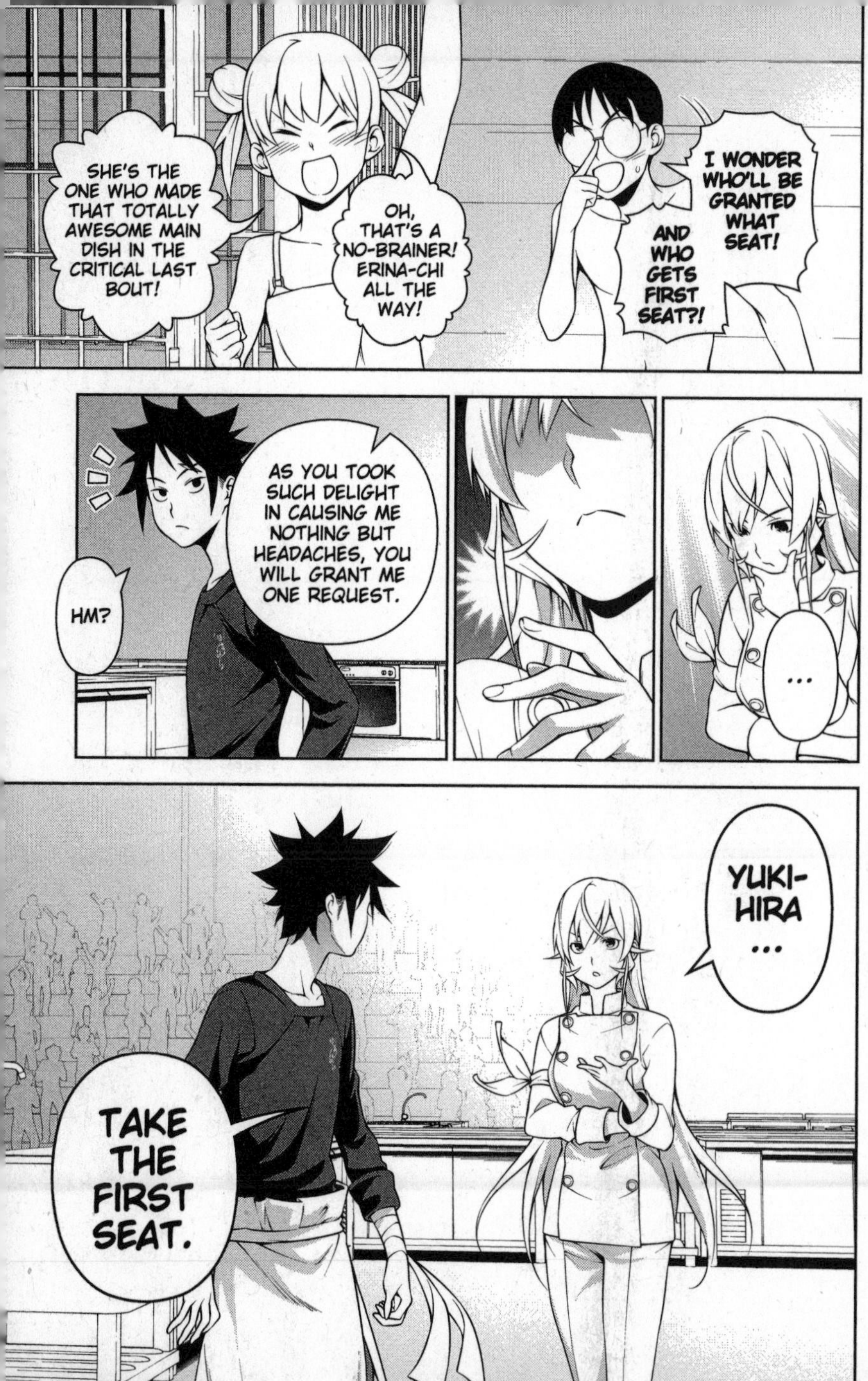
I WONDER WHO'LL BE GRANTED WHAT SEAT!
AND WHO GETS FIRST SEAT?!
OH, THAT'S A NO-BRAINER! ERINA-CHI ALL THE WAY!
SHE'S THE ONE WHO MADE THAT TOTALLY AWESOME MAIN DISH IN THE CRITICAL LAST BOUT!
...
AS YOU TOOK SUCH DELIGHT IN CAUSING ME NOTHING BUT HEADACHES, YOU WILL GRANT ME ONE REQUEST.
HM?
YUKI-HIRA...
TAKE THE FIRST SEAT.

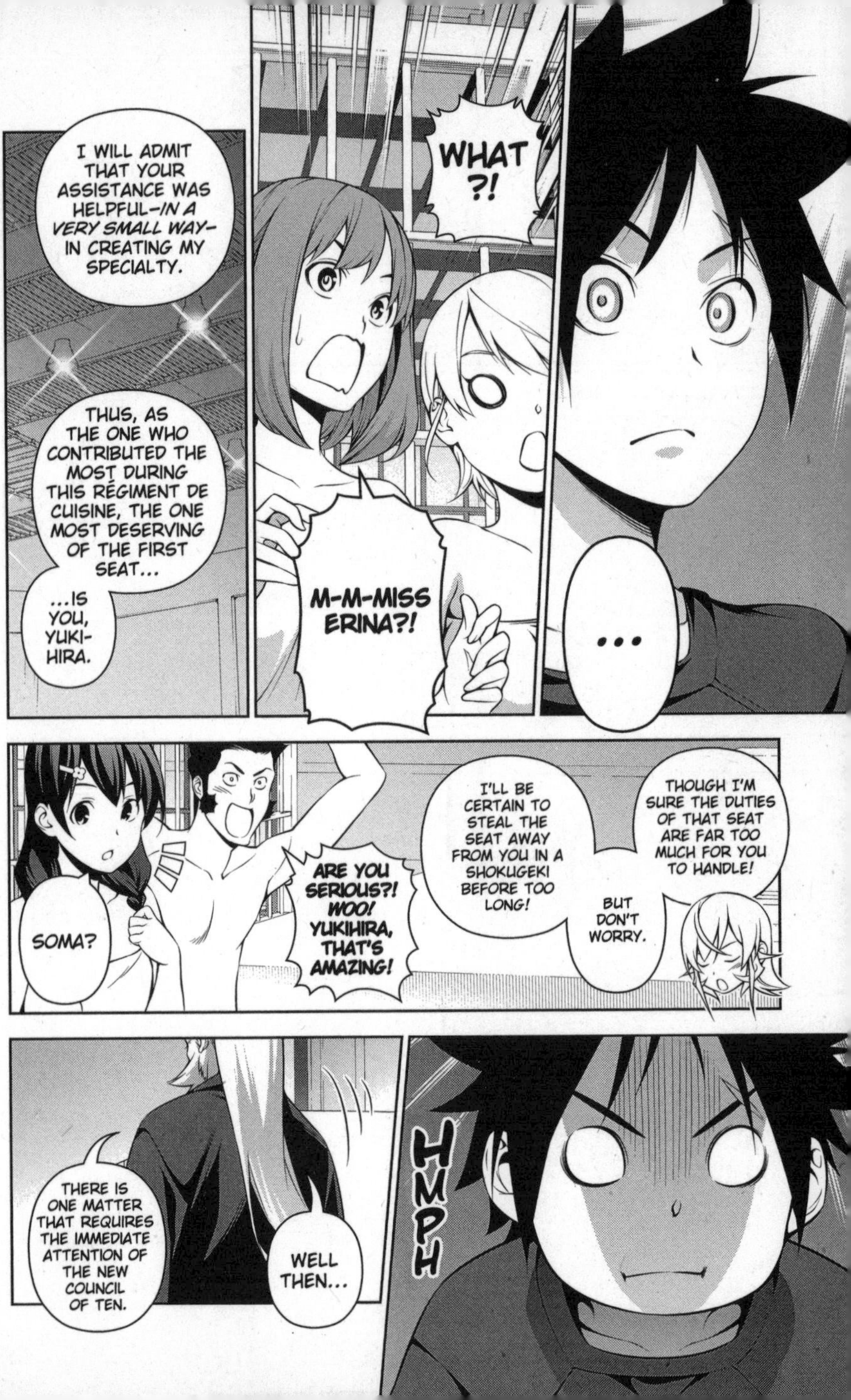
...
WHAT ?!
M-M-MISS ERINA?!
I WILL ADMIT THAT YOUR ASSISTANCE WAS HELPFUL—*IN A VERY SMALL WAY*—IN CREATING MY SPECIALTY.
THUS, AS THE ONE WHO CONTRIBUTED THE MOST DURING THIS RÉGIMENT DE CUISINE, THE ONE MOST DESERVING OF THE FIRST SEAT...
...IS YOU, YUKIHIRA.
THOUGH I'M SURE THE DUTIES OF THAT SEAT ARE FAR TOO MUCH FOR YOU TO HANDLE!
BUT DON'T WORRY.
I'LL BE CERTAIN TO STEAL THE SEAT AWAY FROM YOU IN A SHOKUGEKI BEFORE TOO LONG!
ARE YOU SERIOUS?! *WOO!* YUKIHIRA, THAT'S AMAZING!
SOMA?
HMPH
WELL THEN...
THERE IS ONE MATTER THAT REQUIRES THE IMMEDIATE ATTENTION OF THE NEW COUNCIL OF TEN.

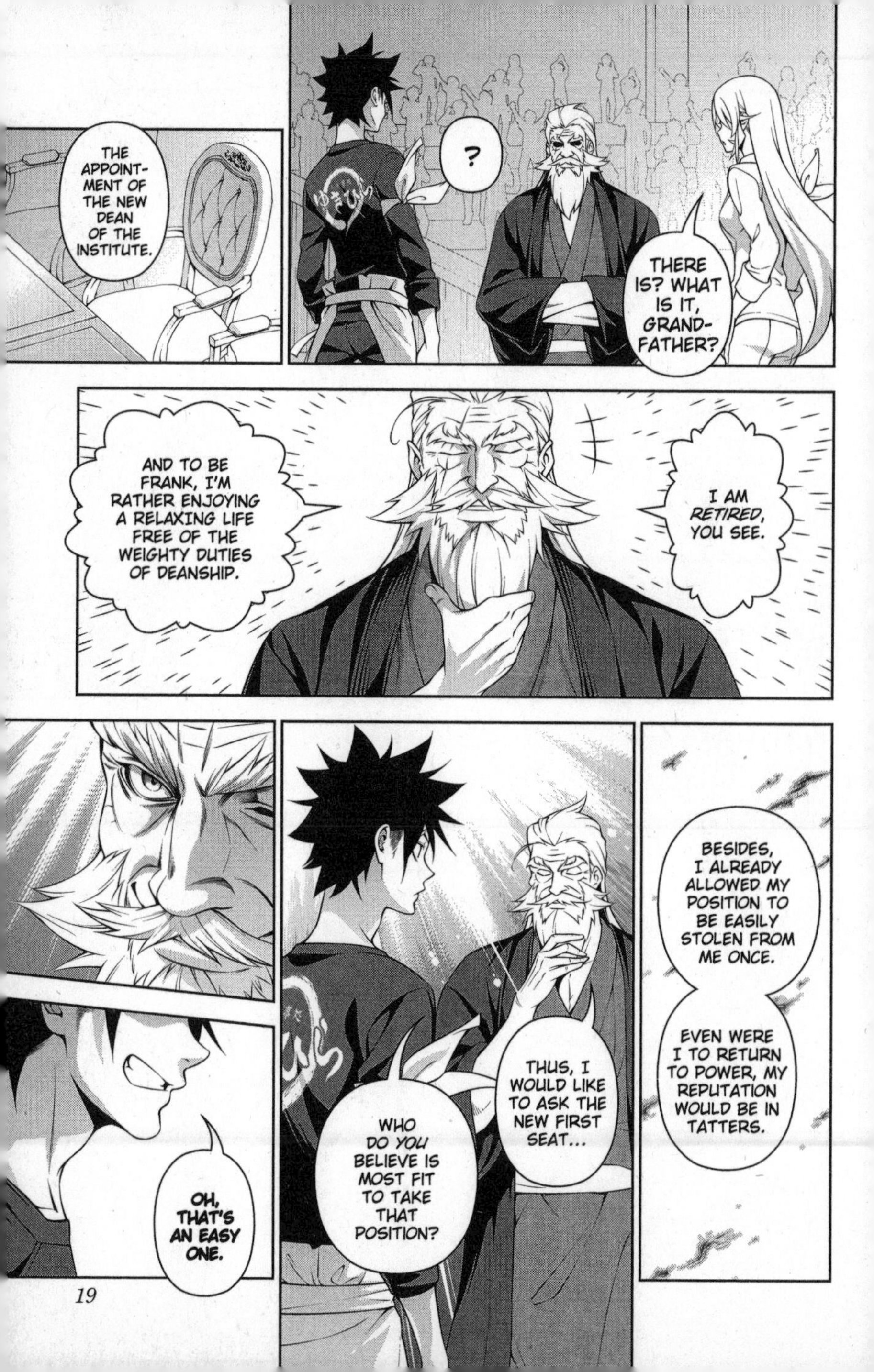
?
THERE IS? WHAT IS IT, GRANDFATHER?
THE APPOINTMENT OF THE NEW DEAN OF THE INSTITUTE.
I AM *RETIRED*, YOU SEE.
AND TO BE FRANK, I'M RATHER ENJOYING A RELAXING LIFE FREE OF THE WEIGHTY DUTIES OF DEANSHIP.
BESIDES, I ALREADY ALLOWED MY POSITION TO BE EASILY STOLEN FROM ME ONCE.
EVEN WERE I TO RETURN TO POWER, MY REPUTATION WOULD BE IN TATTERS.
THUS, I WOULD LIKE TO ASK THE NEW FIRST SEAT...
WHO DO *YOU* BELIEVE IS MOST FIT TO TAKE THAT POSITION?
OH, THAT'S AN EASY ONE.

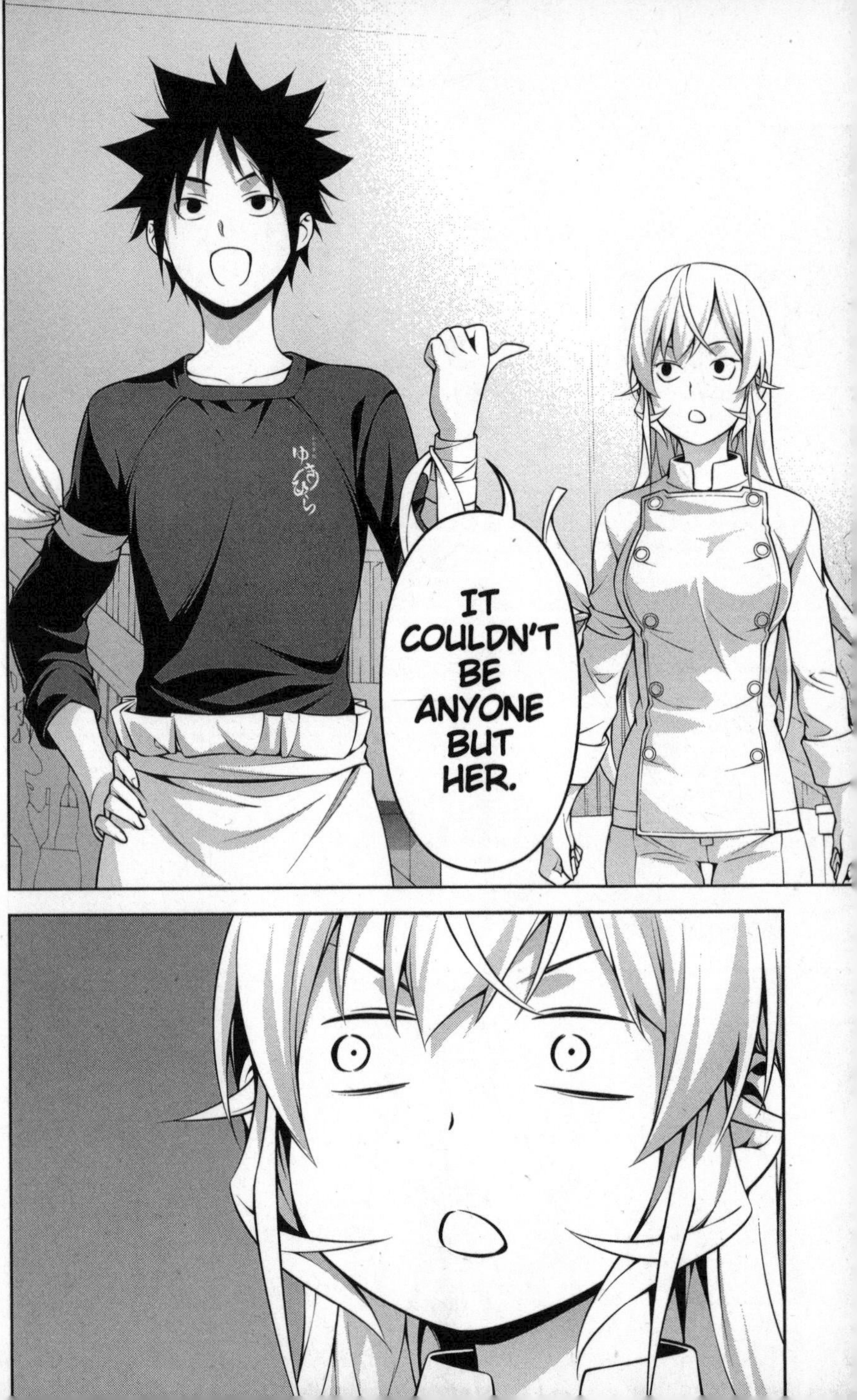
IT COULDN'T BE ANYONE BUT HER.

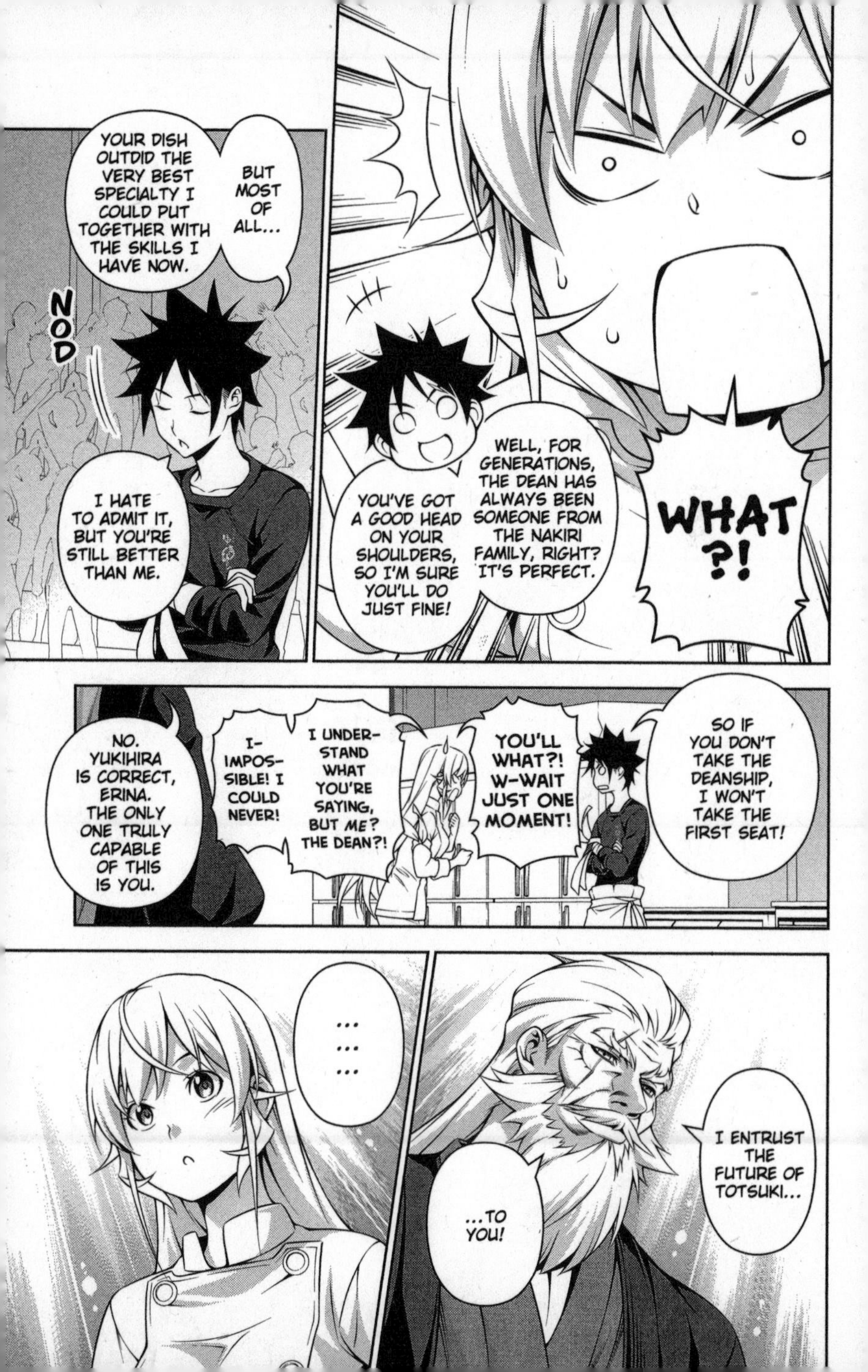
WHAT?!
WELL, FOR GENERATIONS, THE DEAN HAS ALWAYS BEEN SOMEONE FROM THE NAKIRI FAMILY, RIGHT? IT'S PERFECT.
YOU'VE GOT A GOOD HEAD ON YOUR SHOULDERS, SO I'M SURE YOU'LL DO JUST FINE!
BUT MOST OF ALL...
YOUR DISH OUTDID THE VERY BEST SPECIALTY I COULD PUT TOGETHER WITH THE SKILLS I HAVE NOW.
NOD
I HATE TO ADMIT IT, BUT YOU'RE STILL BETTER THAN ME.
SO IF YOU DON'T TAKE THE DEANSHIP, I WON'T TAKE THE FIRST SEAT!
YOU'LL WHAT?! W-WAIT JUST ONE MOMENT!
I UNDERSTAND WHAT YOU'RE SAYING, BUT ME? THE DEAN?!
I-IMPOSSIBLE! I COULD NEVER!
NO. YUKIHIRA IS CORRECT, ERINA. THE ONLY ONE TRULY CAPABLE OF THIS IS YOU.
I ENTRUST THE FUTURE OF TOTSUKI...
...TO YOU!
... ...

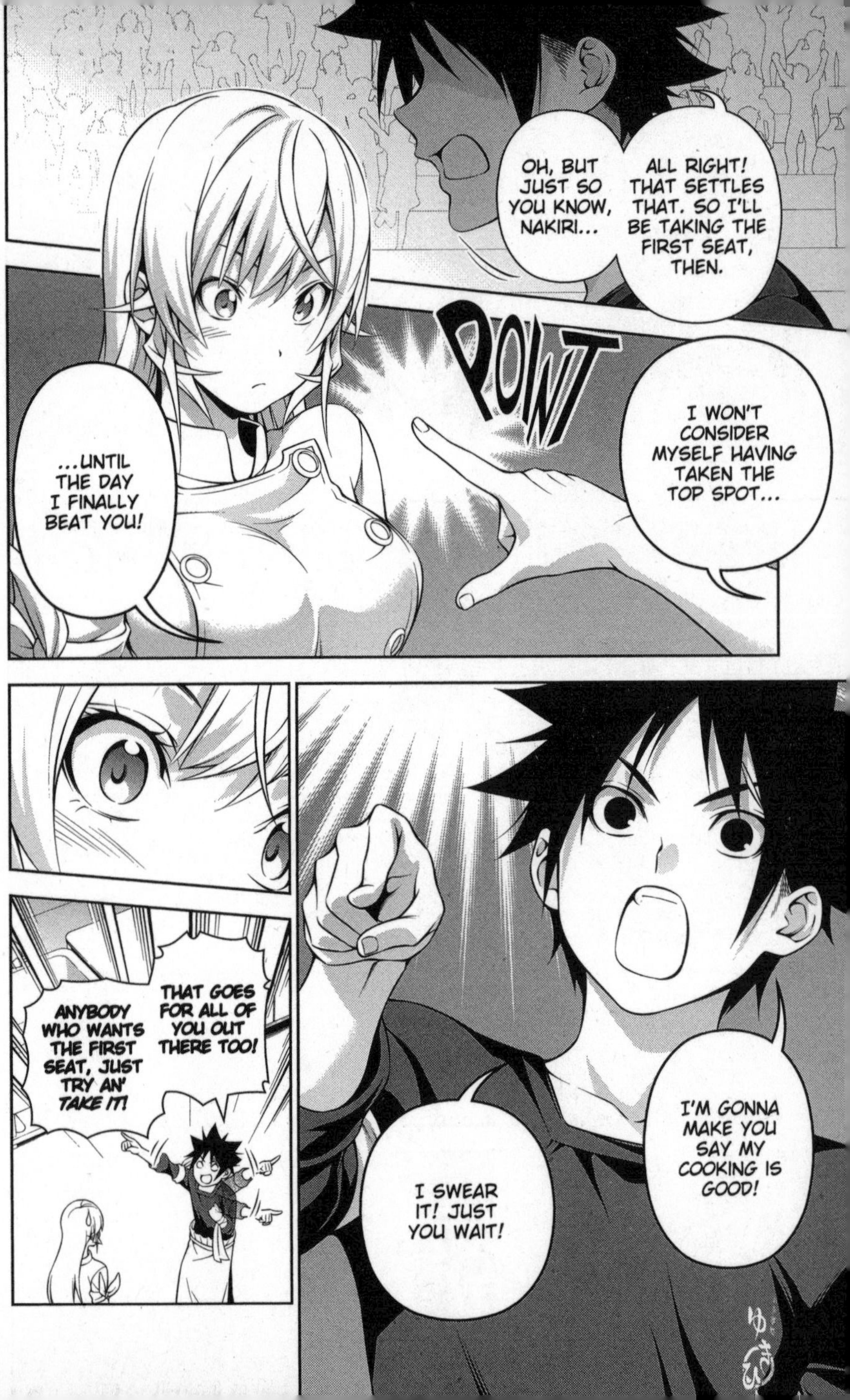
ALL RIGHT! THAT SETTLES THAT. SO I'LL BE TAKING THE FIRST SEAT, THEN.
OH, BUT JUST SO YOU KNOW, NAKIRI...
POINT
I WON'T CONSIDER MYSELF HAVING TAKEN THE TOP SPOT...
...UNTIL THE DAY I FINALLY BEAT YOU!
I'M GONNA MAKE YOU SAY MY COOKING IS GOOD!
I SWEAR IT! JUST YOU WAIT!
THAT GOES FOR ALL OF YOU OUT THERE TOO!
ANYBODY WHO WANTS THE FIRST SEAT, JUST TRY AN' *TAKE IT!*

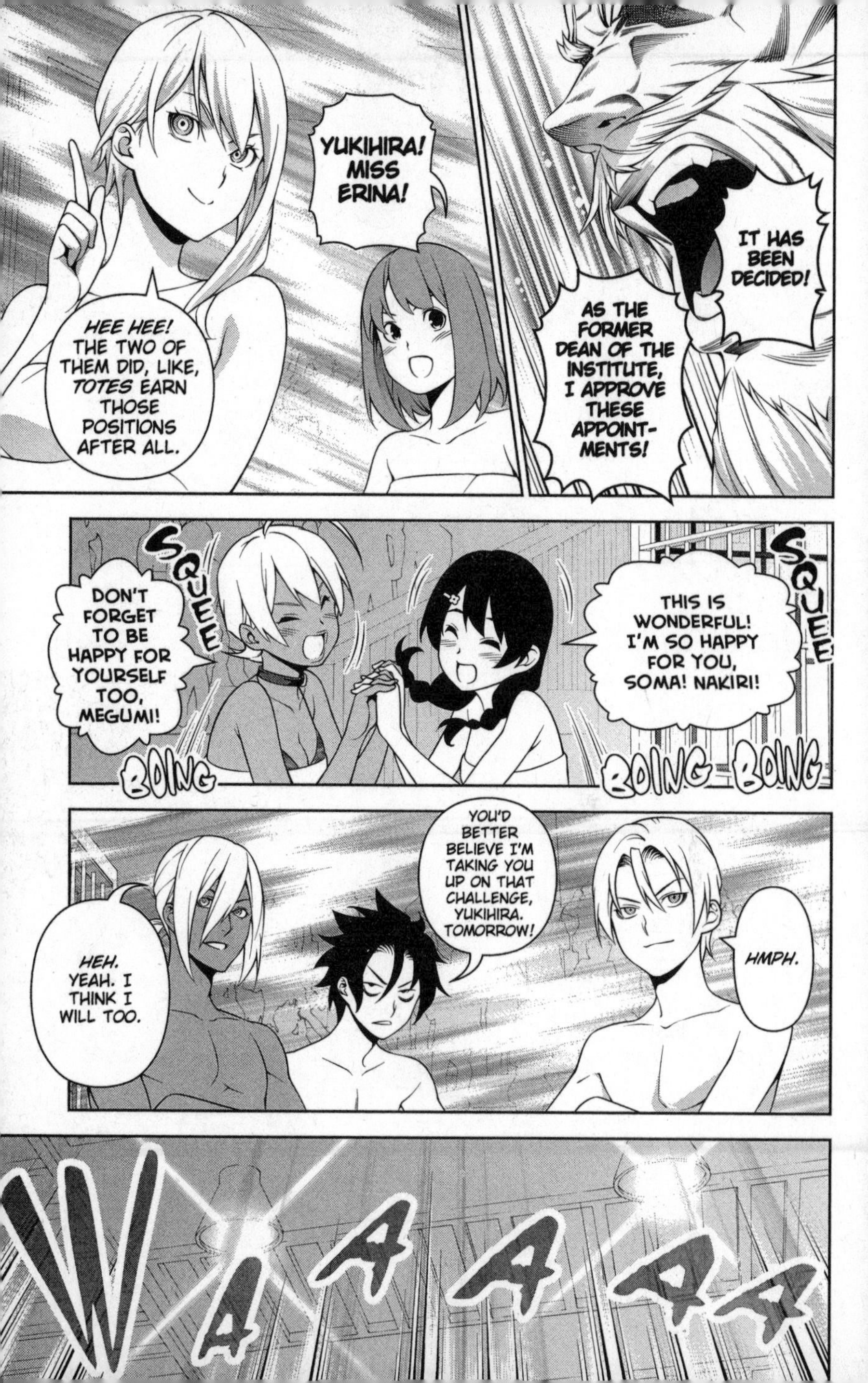
IT HAS BEEN DECIDED!
AS THE FORMER DEAN OF THE INSTITUTE, I APPROVE THESE APPOINT-MENTS!
YUKIHIRA! MISS ERINA!
HEE HEE! THE TWO OF THEM DID, LIKE, *TOTES* EARN THOSE POSITIONS AFTER ALL.
SQUEE
THIS IS WONDERFUL! I'M SO HAPPY FOR YOU, SOMA! NAKIRI!
SQUEE
DON'T FORGET TO BE HAPPY FOR YOURSELF TOO, MEGUMI!
BOING BOING
BOING
HMPH.
YOU'D BETTER BELIEVE I'M TAKING YOU UP ON THAT CHALLENGE, YUKIHIRA. TOMORROW!
HEH. YEAH. I THINK I WILL TOO.
WAAAAA

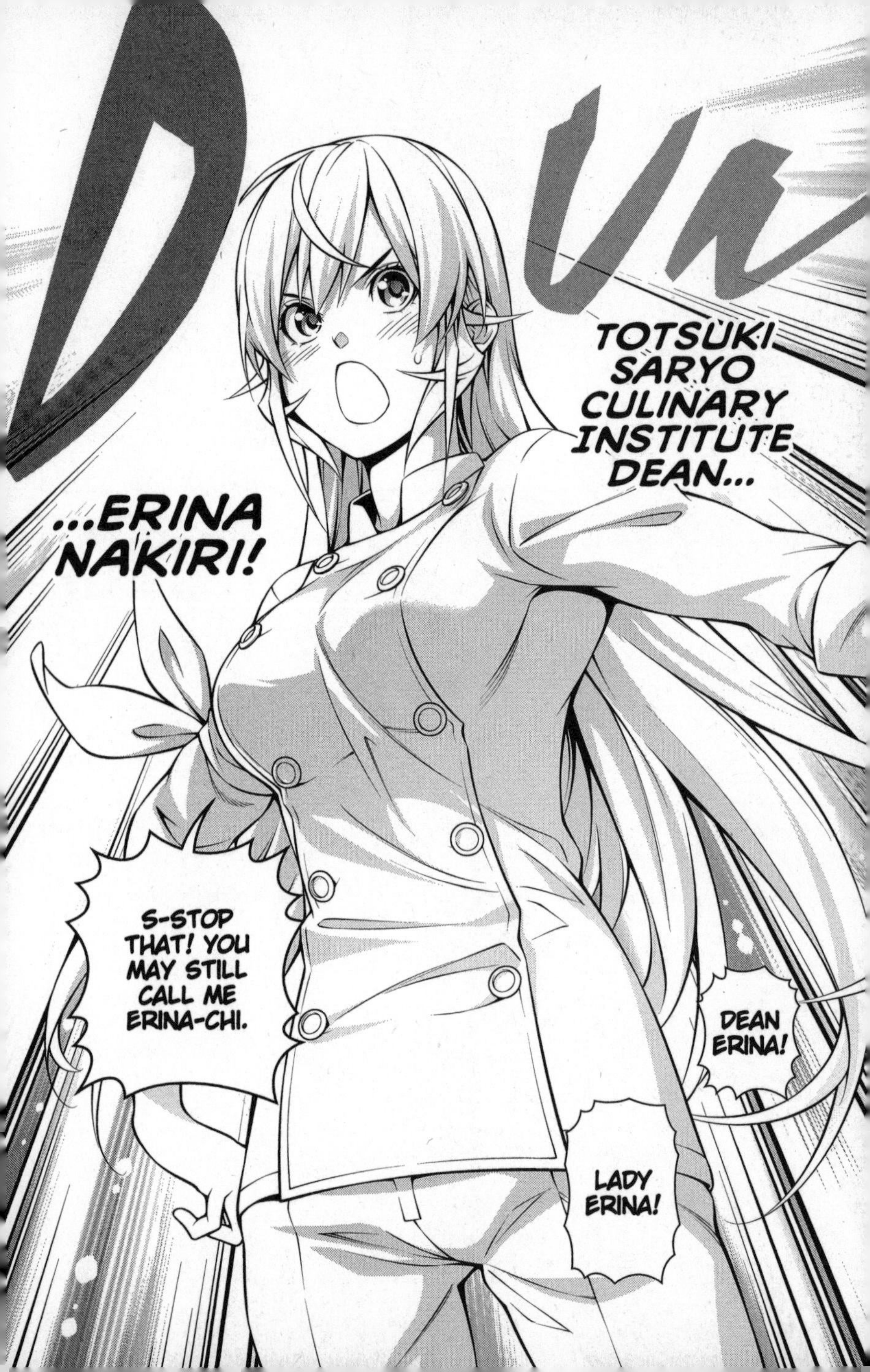
TOTSUKI SARYO CULINARY INSTITUTE DEAN...
...ERINA NAKIRI!
DEAN ERINA!
LADY ERINA!
S-STOP THAT! YOU MAY STILL CALL ME ERINA-CHI.

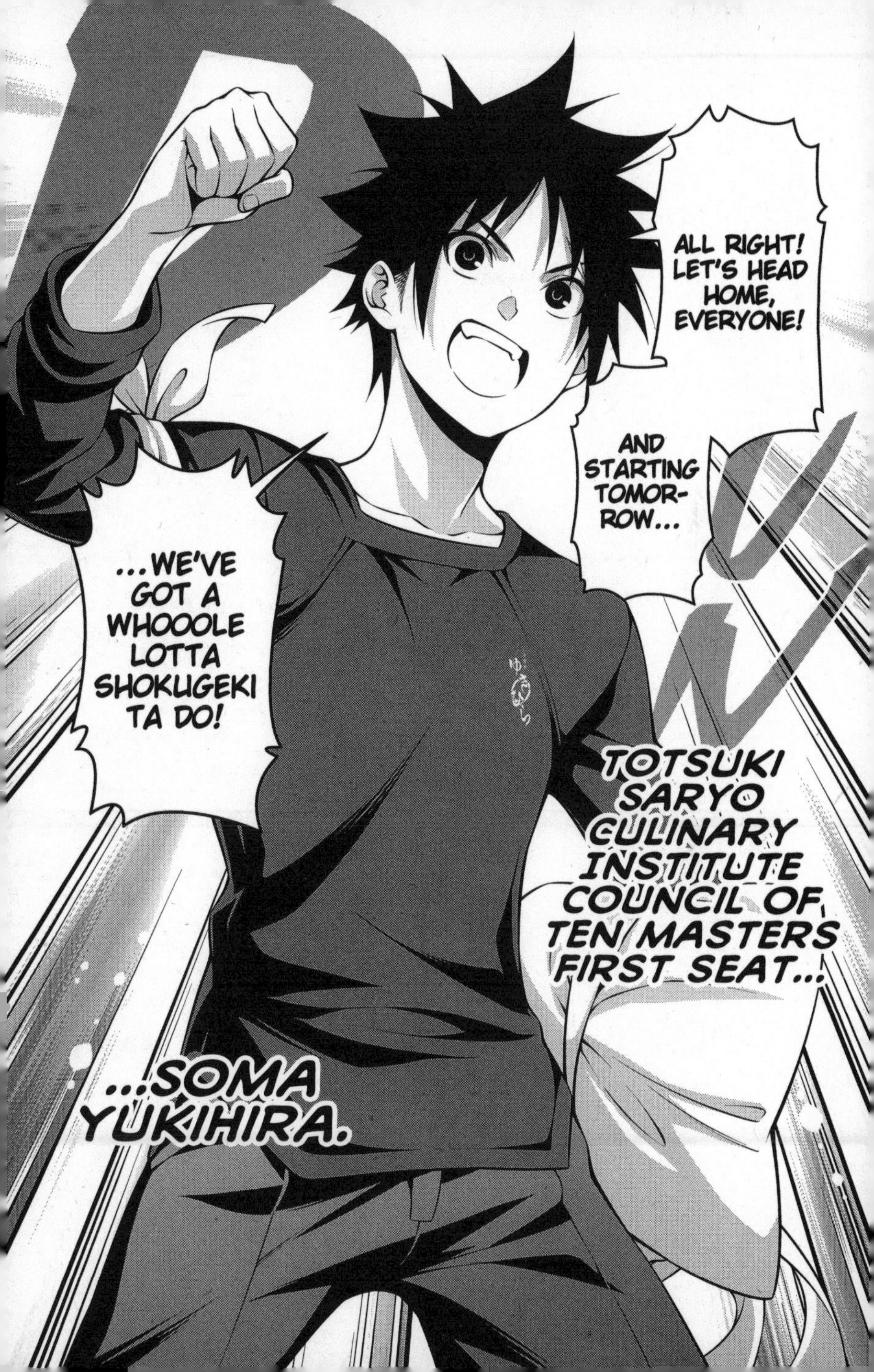
ALL RIGHT! LET'S HEAD HOME, EVERYONE!
AND STARTING TOMOR-ROW...
...WE'VE GOT A WHOOOLE LOTTA SHOKUGEKI TA DO!
TOTSUKI SARYO CULINARY INSTITUTE COUNCIL OF TEN MASTERS FIRST SEAT...
...SOMA YUKIHIRA.

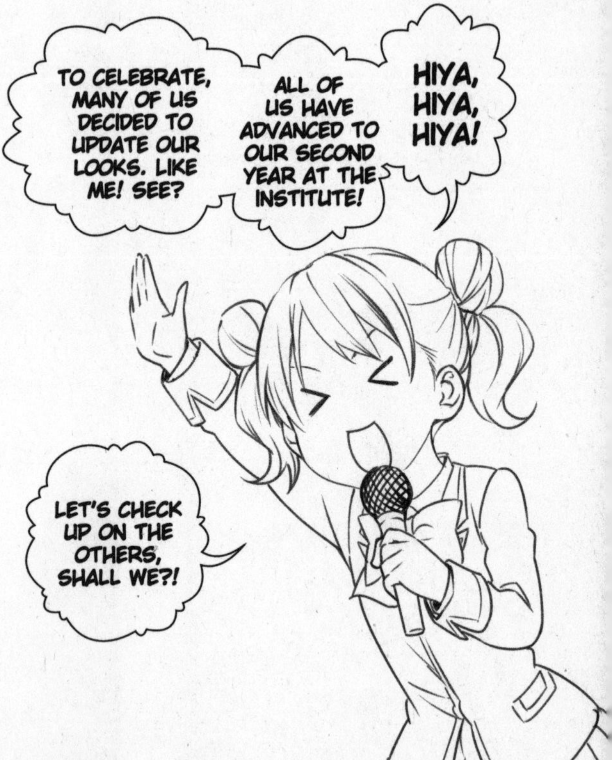
HIYA, HIYA, HIYA!
ALL OF US HAVE ADVANCED TO OUR SECOND YEAR AT THE INSTITUTE!
TO CELEBRATE, MANY OF US DECIDED TO UPDATE OUR LOOKS. LIKE ME! SEE?
LET'S CHECK UP ON THE OTHERS, SHALL WE?!

264 FROM: MEGUMI TADOKORO

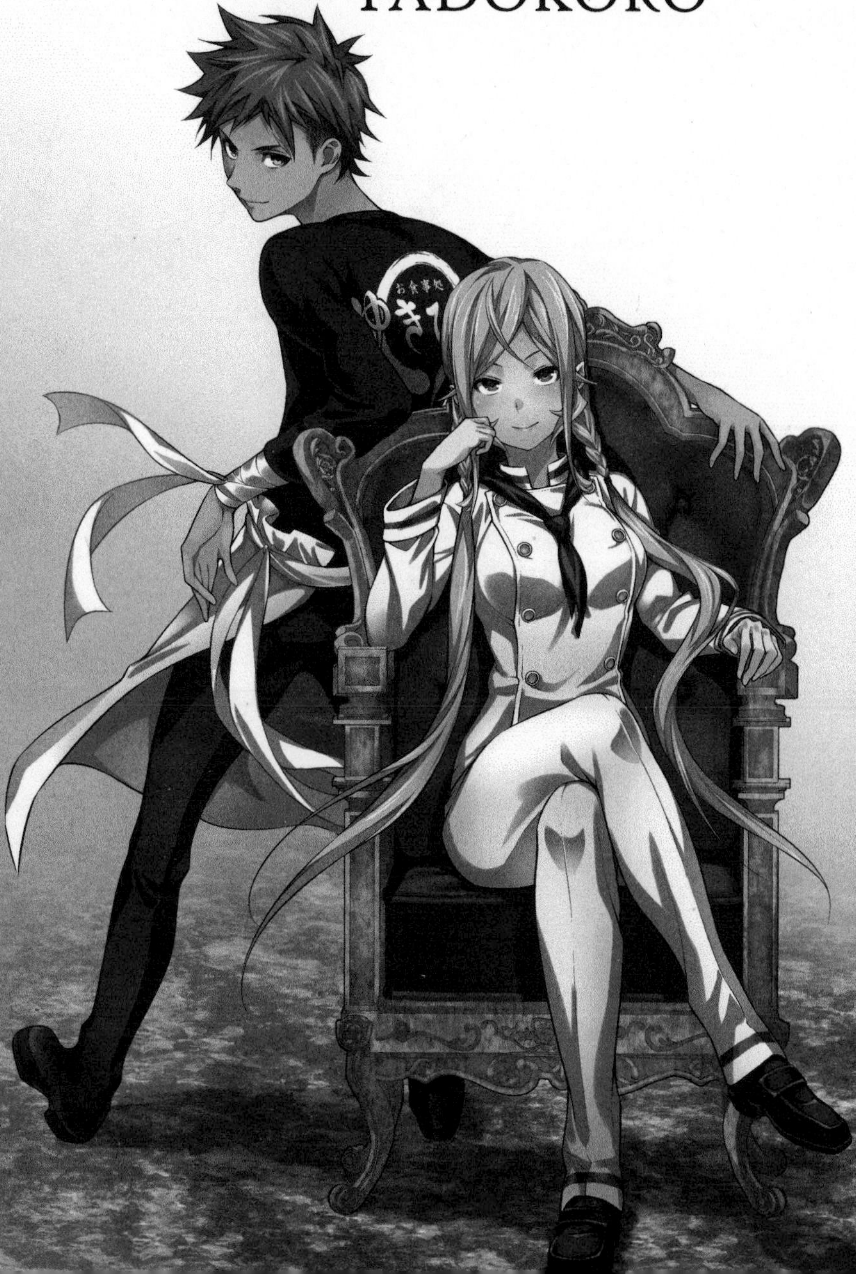

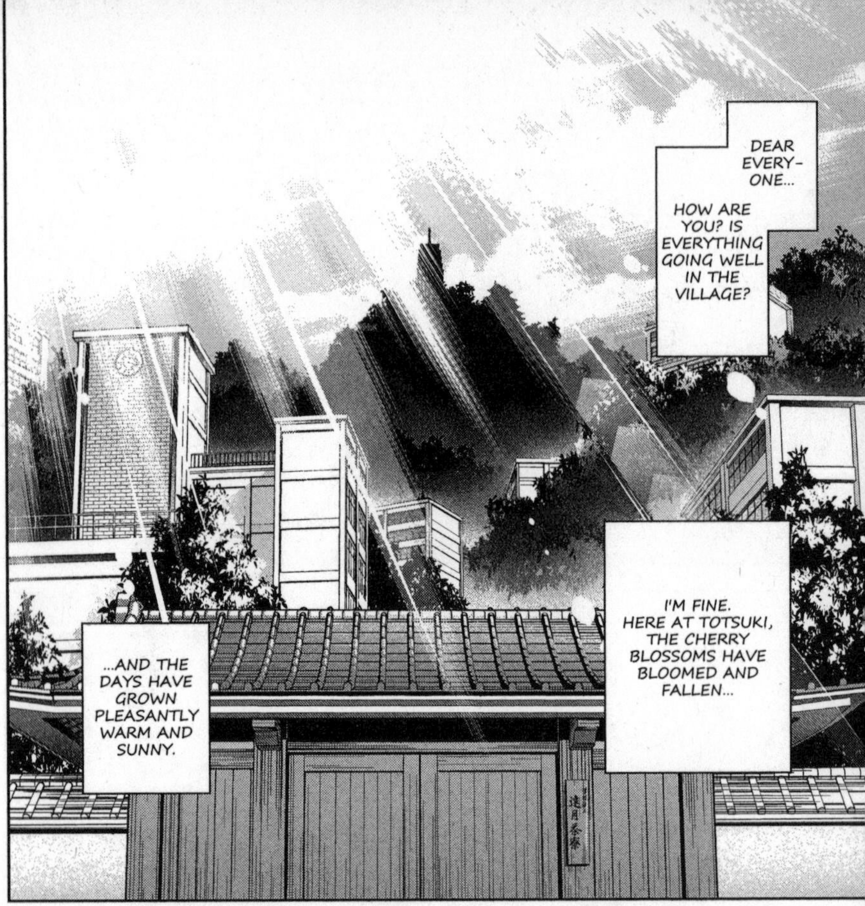
DEAR EVERY-ONE...
HOW ARE YOU? IS EVERYTHING GOING WELL IN THE VILLAGE?
I'M FINE. HERE AT TOTSUKI, THE CHERRY BLOSSOMS HAVE BLOOMED AND FALLEN...
...AND THE DAYS HAVE GROWN PLEASANTLY WARM AND SUNNY.
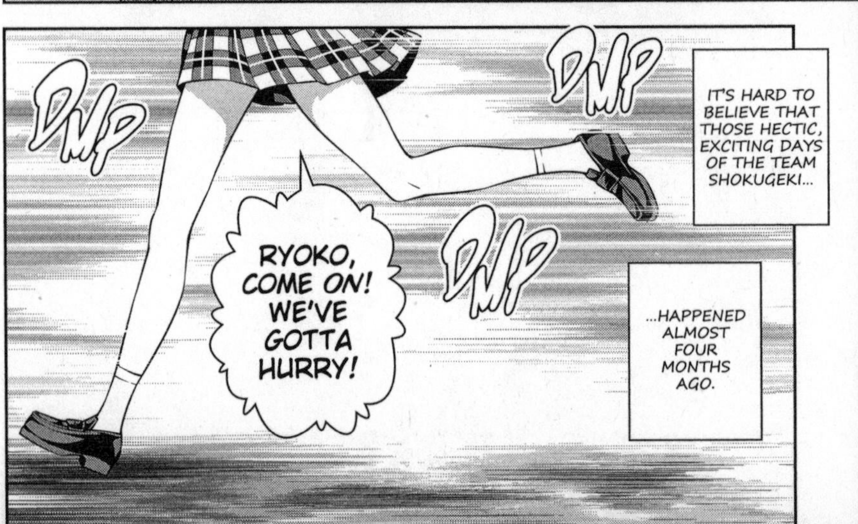
IT'S HARD TO BELIEVE THAT THOSE HECTIC, EXCITING DAYS OF THE TEAM SHOKUGEKI...
DMP
...HAPPENED ALMOST FOUR MONTHS AGO.
DMP
DMP
RYOKO, COME ON! WE'VE GOTTA HURRY!

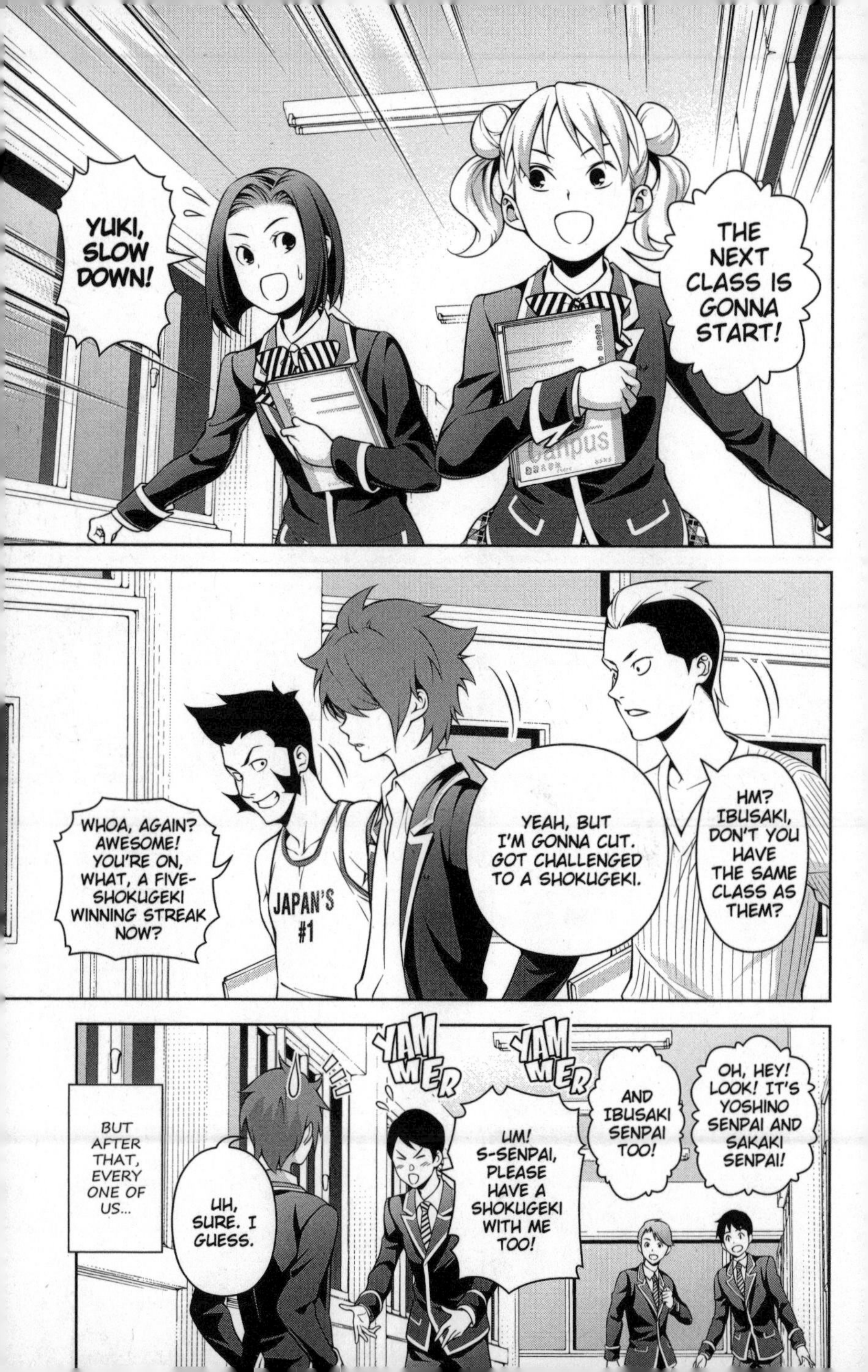
THE NEXT CLASS IS GONNA START!
YUKI, SLOW DOWN!
HM? IBUSAKI, DON'T YOU HAVE THE SAME CLASS AS THEM?
YEAH, BUT I'M GONNA CUT. GOT CHALLENGED TO A SHOKUGEKI.
WHOA, AGAIN? AWESOME! YOU'RE ON, WHAT, A FIVE-SHOKUGEKI WINNING STREAK NOW?
OH, HEY! LOOK! IT'S YOSHINO SENPAI AND SAKAKI SENPAI!
AND IBUSAKI SENPAI TOO!
YAMMER
YAMMER
UM! S-SENPAI, PLEASE HAVE A SHOKUGEKI WITH ME TOO!
UH, SURE. I GUESS.
BUT AFTER THAT, EVERY ONE OF US...

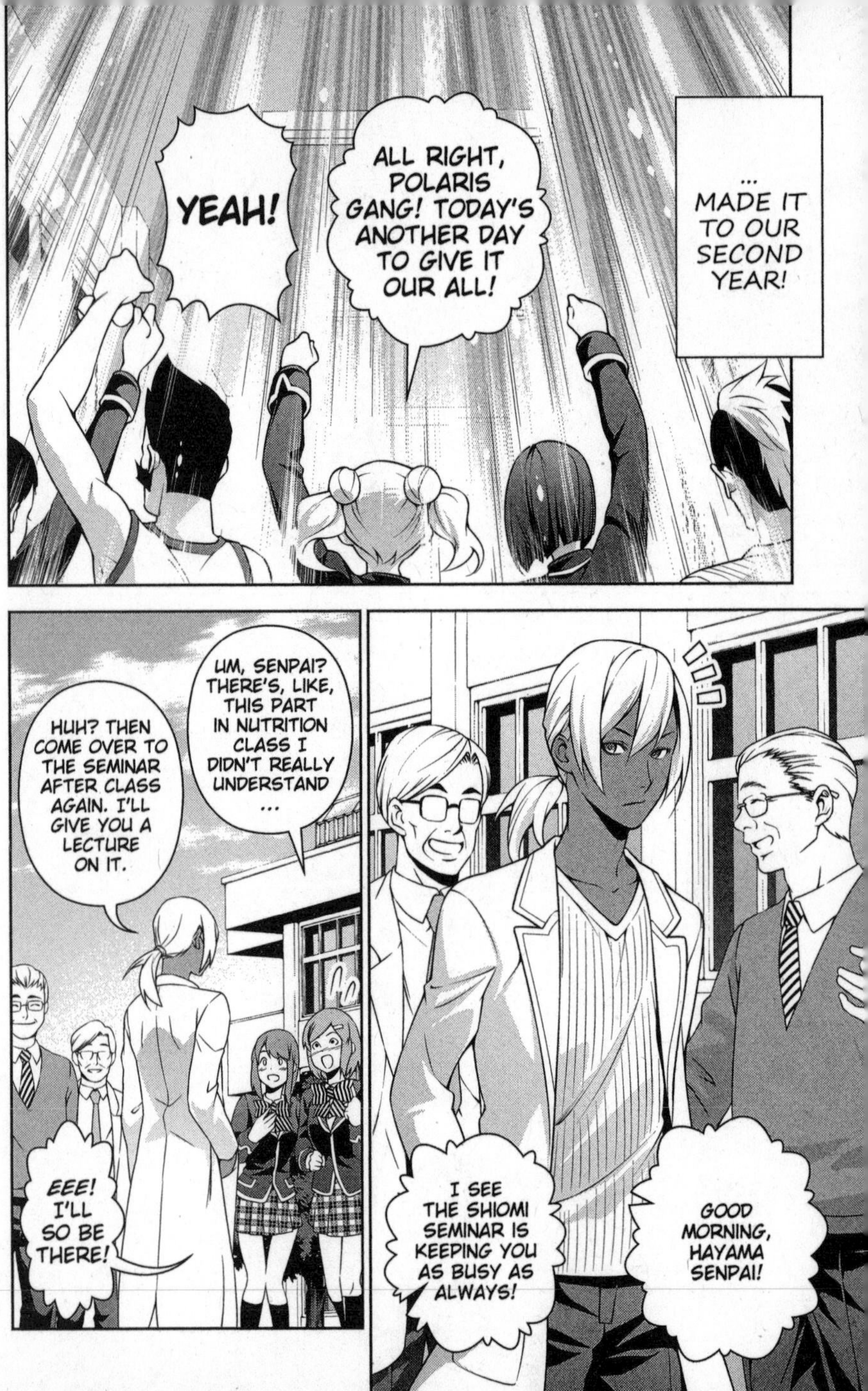
... MADE IT TO OUR SECOND YEAR!
ALL RIGHT, POLARIS GANG! TODAY'S ANOTHER DAY TO GIVE IT OUR ALL!
YEAH!
GOOD MORNING, HAYAMA SENPAI!
I SEE THE SHIOMI SEMINAR IS KEEPING YOU AS BUSY AS ALWAYS!
UM, SENPAI? THERE'S, LIKE, THIS PART IN NUTRITION CLASS I DIDN'T REALLY UNDERSTAND ...
HUH? THEN COME OVER TO THE SEMINAR AFTER CLASS AGAIN. I'LL GIVE YOU A LECTURE ON IT.
EEE! I'LL SO BE THERE!

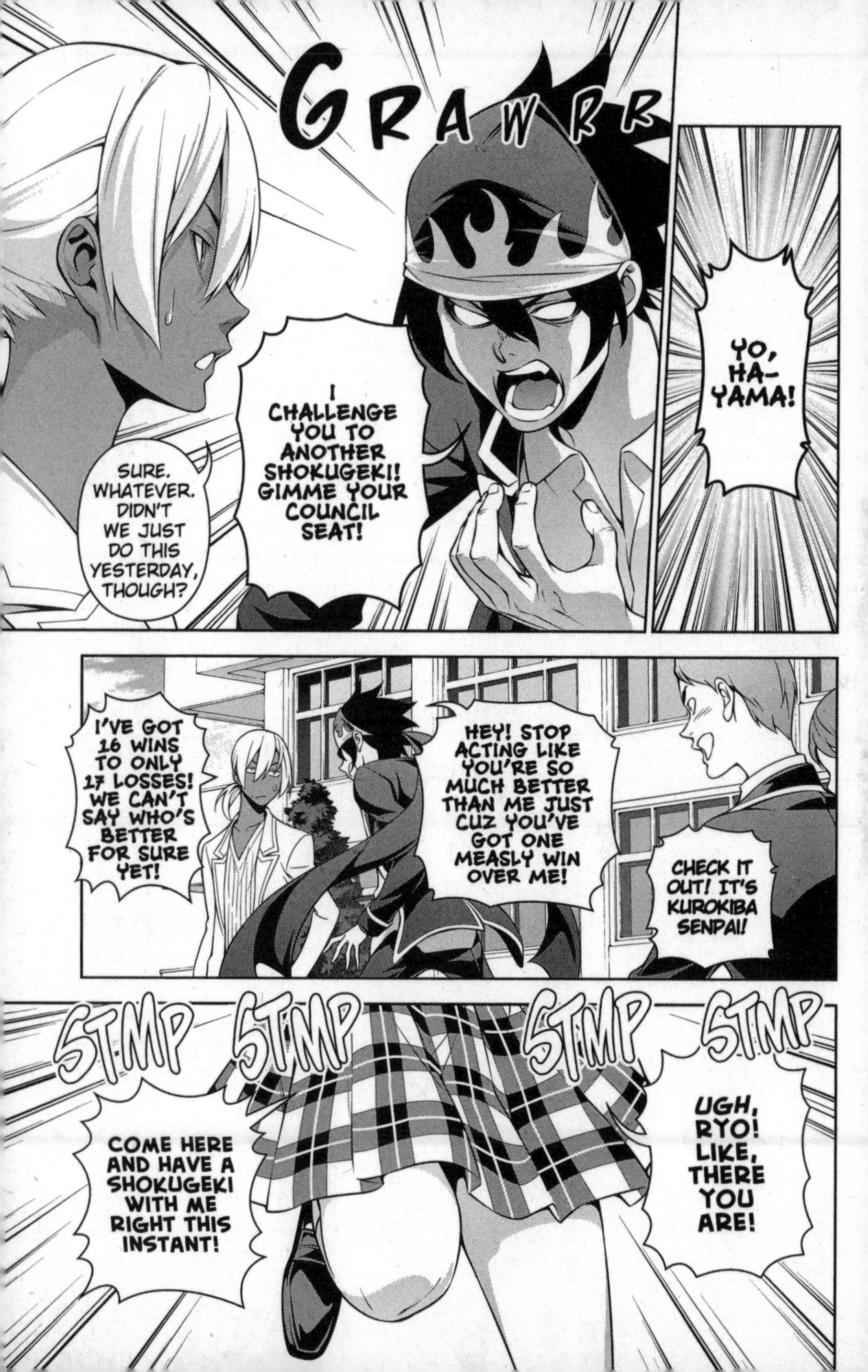
YO, HA-YAMA!
GRAWRR
I CHALLENGE YOU TO ANOTHER SHOKUGEKI! GIMME YOUR COUNCIL SEAT!
SURE. WHATEVER. DIDN'T WE JUST DO THIS YESTERDAY, THOUGH?
CHECK IT OUT! IT'S KUROKIBA SENPAI!
HEY! STOP ACTING LIKE YOU'RE SO MUCH BETTER THAN ME JUST CUZ YOU'VE GOT ONE MEASLY WIN OVER ME!
I'VE GOT 16 WINS TO ONLY 17 LOSSES! WE CAN'T SAY WHO'S BETTER FOR SURE YET!
STMP STMP STMP STMP
UGH, RYO! LIKE, THERE YOU ARE!
COME HERE AND HAVE A SHOKUGEKI WITH ME RIGHT THIS INSTANT!

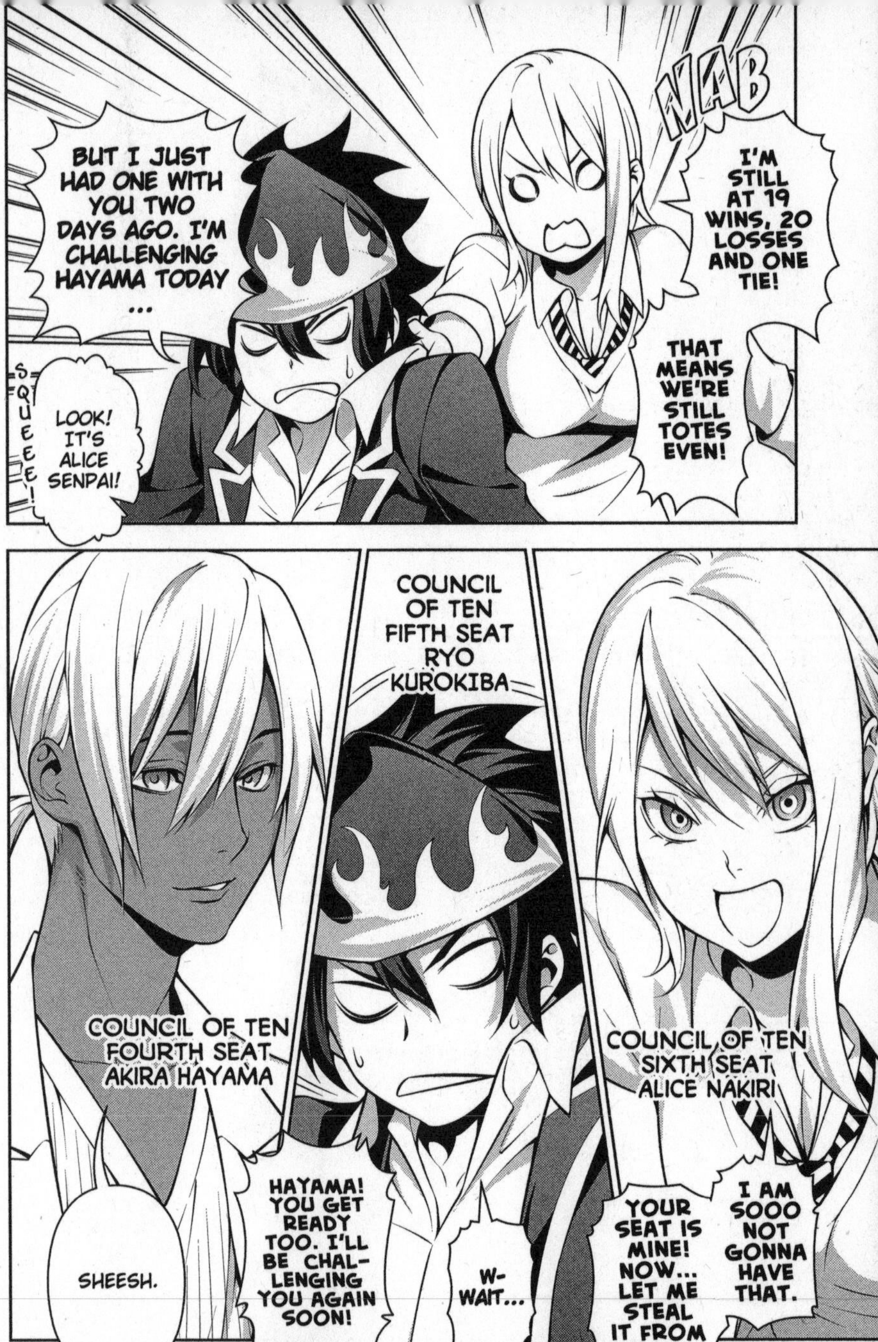
NAB
I'M STILL AT 19 WINS, 20 LOSSES AND ONE TIE!
THAT MEANS WE'RE STILL TOTES EVEN!
BUT I JUST HAD ONE WITH YOU TWO DAYS AGO. I'M CHALLENGING HAYAMA TODAY ...
LOOK! IT'S ALICE SENPAI!
SQUEEE!
COUNCIL OF TEN SIXTH SEAT ALICE NAKIRI
I AM SOOO NOT GONNA HAVE THAT.
YOUR SEAT IS MINE! NOW... LET ME STEAL IT FROM YOU!
COUNCIL OF TEN FIFTH SEAT RYO KUROKIBA
W-WAIT...
HAYAMA! YOU GET READY TOO. I'LL BE CHALLENGING YOU AGAIN SOON!
COUNCIL OF TEN FOURTH SEAT AKIRA HAYAMA
SHEESH.

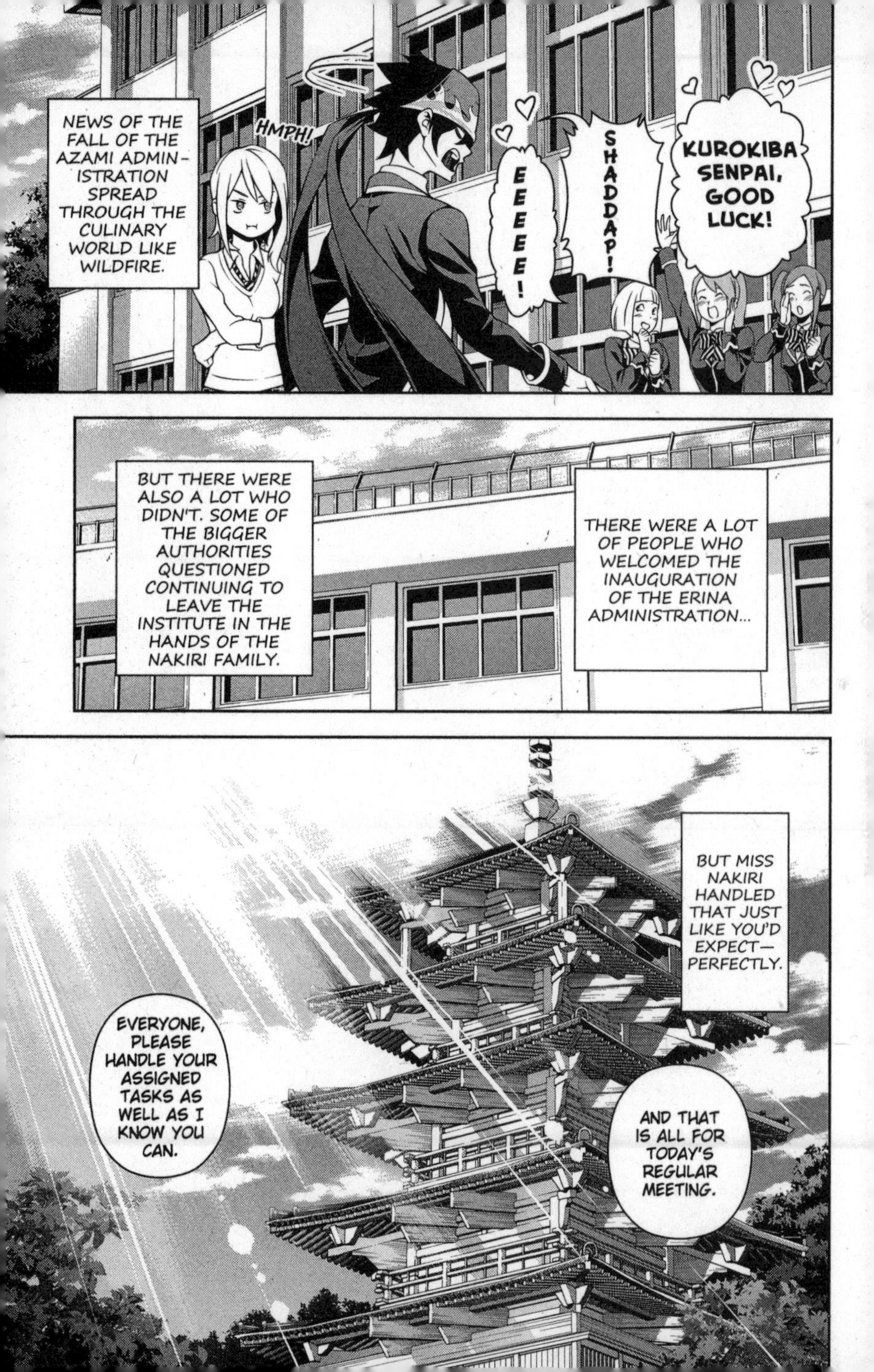
KUROKIBA SENPAI, GOOD LUCK!
SHADDAP!
EEEEEE!
HMPH!
NEWS OF THE FALL OF THE AZAMI ADMIN-ISTRATION SPREAD THROUGH THE CULINARY WORLD LIKE WILDFIRE.
THERE WERE A LOT OF PEOPLE WHO WELCOMED THE INAUGURATION OF THE ERINA ADMINISTRATION...
BUT THERE WERE ALSO A LOT WHO DIDN'T. SOME OF THE BIGGER AUTHORITIES QUESTIONED CONTINUING TO LEAVE THE INSTITUTE IN THE HANDS OF THE NAKIRI FAMILY.
BUT MISS NAKIRI HANDLED THAT JUST LIKE YOU'D EXPECT—PERFECTLY.
AND THAT IS ALL FOR TODAY'S REGULAR MEETING.
EVERYONE, PLEASE HANDLE YOUR ASSIGNED TASKS AS WELL AS I KNOW YOU CAN.

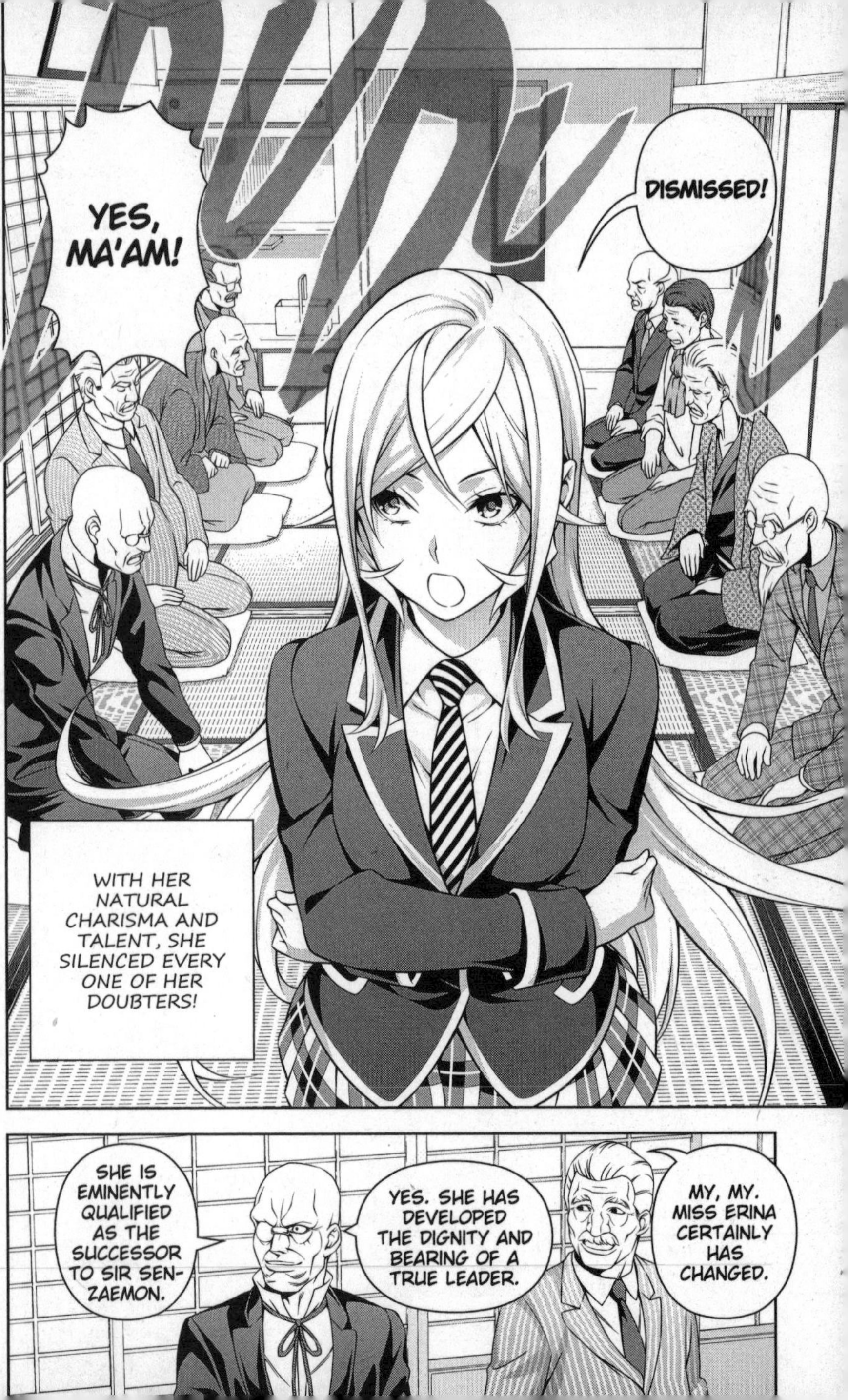
DISMISSED!
YES, MA'AM!
WITH HER NATURAL CHARISMA AND TALENT, SHE SILENCED EVERY ONE OF HER DOUBTERS!
MY, MY. MISS ERINA CERTAINLY HAS CHANGED.
YES. SHE HAS DEVELOPED THE DIGNITY AND BEARING OF A TRUE LEADER.
SHE IS EMINENTLY QUALIFIED AS THE SUCCESSOR TO SIR SEN-ZAEMON.

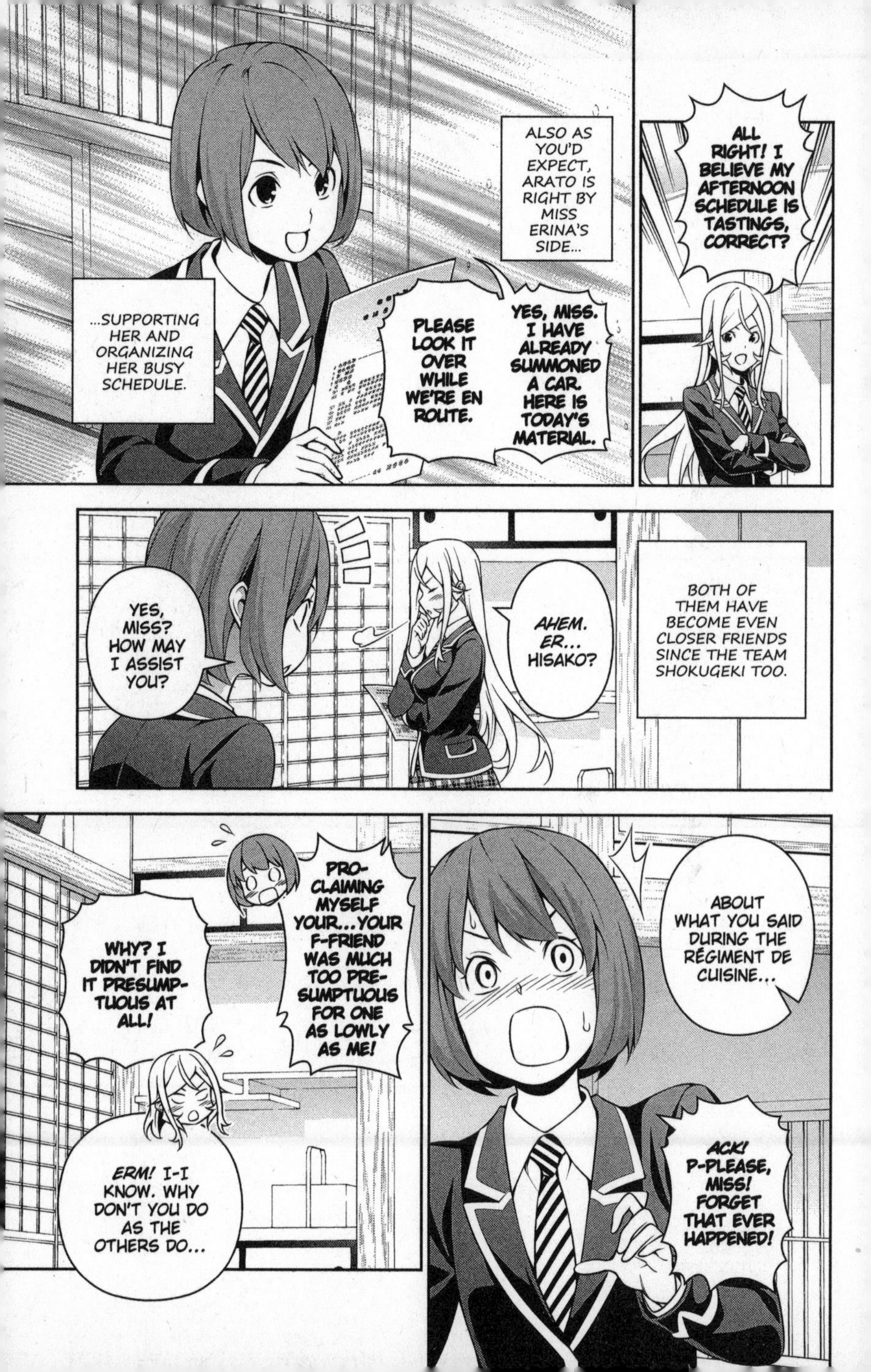
ALL RIGHT! I BELIEVE MY AFTERNOON SCHEDULE IS TASTINGS, CORRECT?
ALSO AS YOU'D EXPECT, ARATO IS RIGHT BY MISS ERINA'S SIDE...
YES, MISS. I HAVE ALREADY SUMMONED A CAR. HERE IS TODAY'S MATERIAL.
PLEASE LOOK IT OVER WHILE WE'RE EN ROUTE.
...SUPPORTING HER AND ORGANIZING HER BUSY SCHEDULE.
BOTH OF THEM HAVE BECOME EVEN CLOSER FRIENDS SINCE THE TEAM SHOKUGEKI TOO.
AHEM. ER... HISAKO?
YES, MISS? HOW MAY I ASSIST YOU?
ABOUT WHAT YOU SAID DURING THE RÉGIMENT DE CUISINE...
ACK! P-PLEASE, MISS! FORGET THAT EVER HAPPENED!
PRO-CLAIMING MYSELF YOUR...YOUR F-FRIEND WAS MUCH TOO PRE-SUMPTUOUS FOR ONE AS LOWLY AS ME!
WHY? I DIDN'T FIND IT PRESUMPTUOUS AT ALL!
ERM! I-I KNOW. WHY DON'T YOU DO AS THE OTHERS DO...

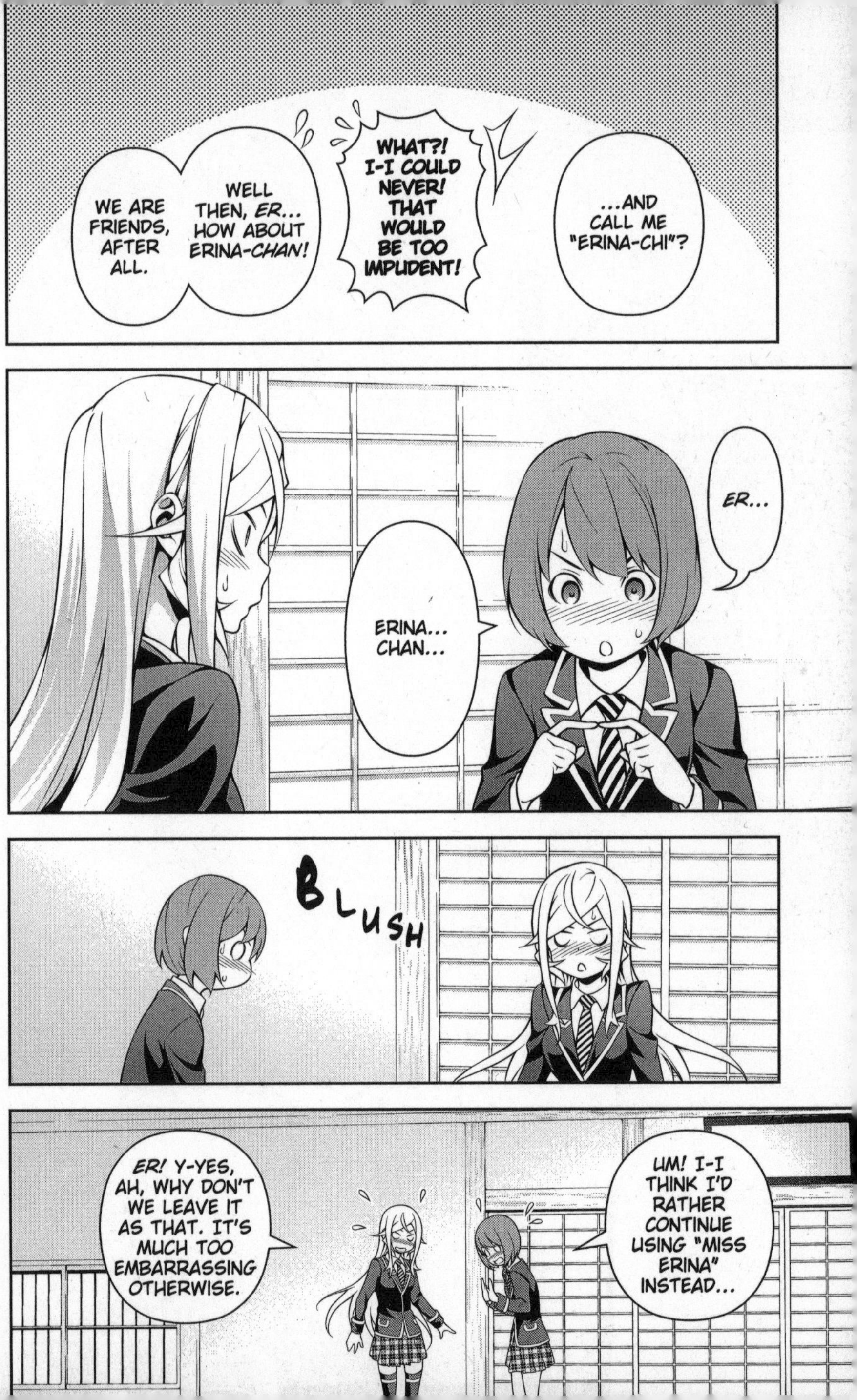
...AND CALL ME "ERINA-CHI"?
WHAT?! I-I COULD NEVER! THAT WOULD BE TOO IMPUDENT!
WELL THEN, *ER*... HOW ABOUT ERINA-*CHAN*!
WE ARE FRIENDS, AFTER ALL.
ER...
ERINA... CHAN...
BLUSH
UM! I-I THINK I'D RATHER CONTINUE USING "MISS ERINA" INSTEAD...
ER! Y-YES, AH, WHY DON'T WE LEAVE IT AS THAT. IT'S MUCH TOO EMBARRASSING OTHERWISE.

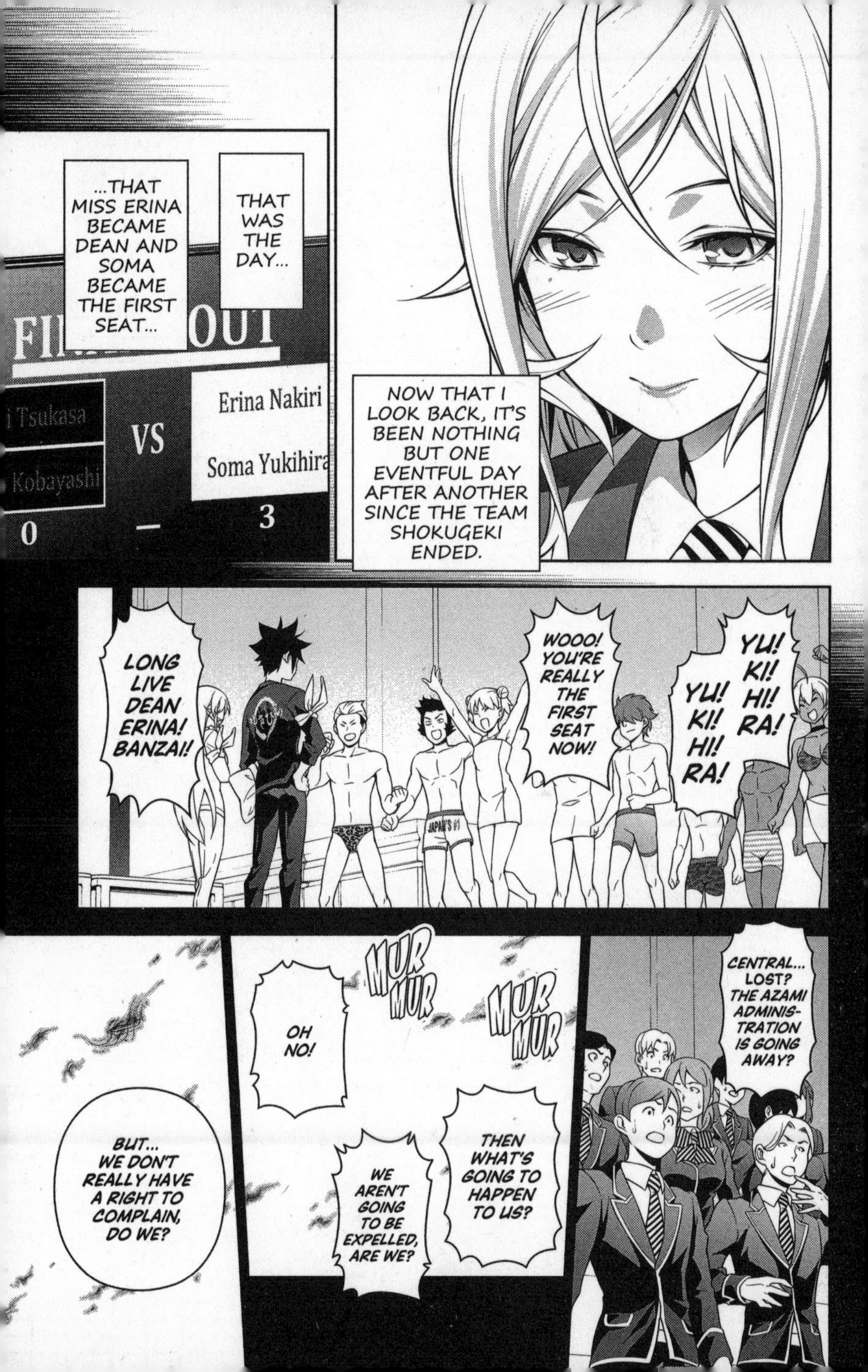
NOW THAT I LOOK BACK, IT'S BEEN NOTHING BUT ONE EVENTFUL DAY AFTER ANOTHER SINCE THE TEAM SHOKUGEKI ENDED.
THAT WAS THE DAY...
...THAT MISS ERINA BECAME DEAN AND SOMA BECAME THE FIRST SEAT...
Erina Nakiri
Soma Yukihira
VS
Kobayashi
0
3
YU! KI! HI! RA!
YU! KI! HI! RA!
WOOO! YOU'RE REALLY THE FIRST SEAT NOW!
JAPAN'S #1
LONG LIVE DEAN ERINA! BANZAI!
CENTRAL... LOST? THE AZAMI ADMINISTRATION IS GOING AWAY?
MUR MUR
MUR MUR
OH NO!
THEN WHAT'S GOING TO HAPPEN TO US?
WE AREN'T GOING TO BE EXPELLED, ARE WE?
BUT... WE DON'T REALLY HAVE A RIGHT TO COMPLAIN, DO WE?

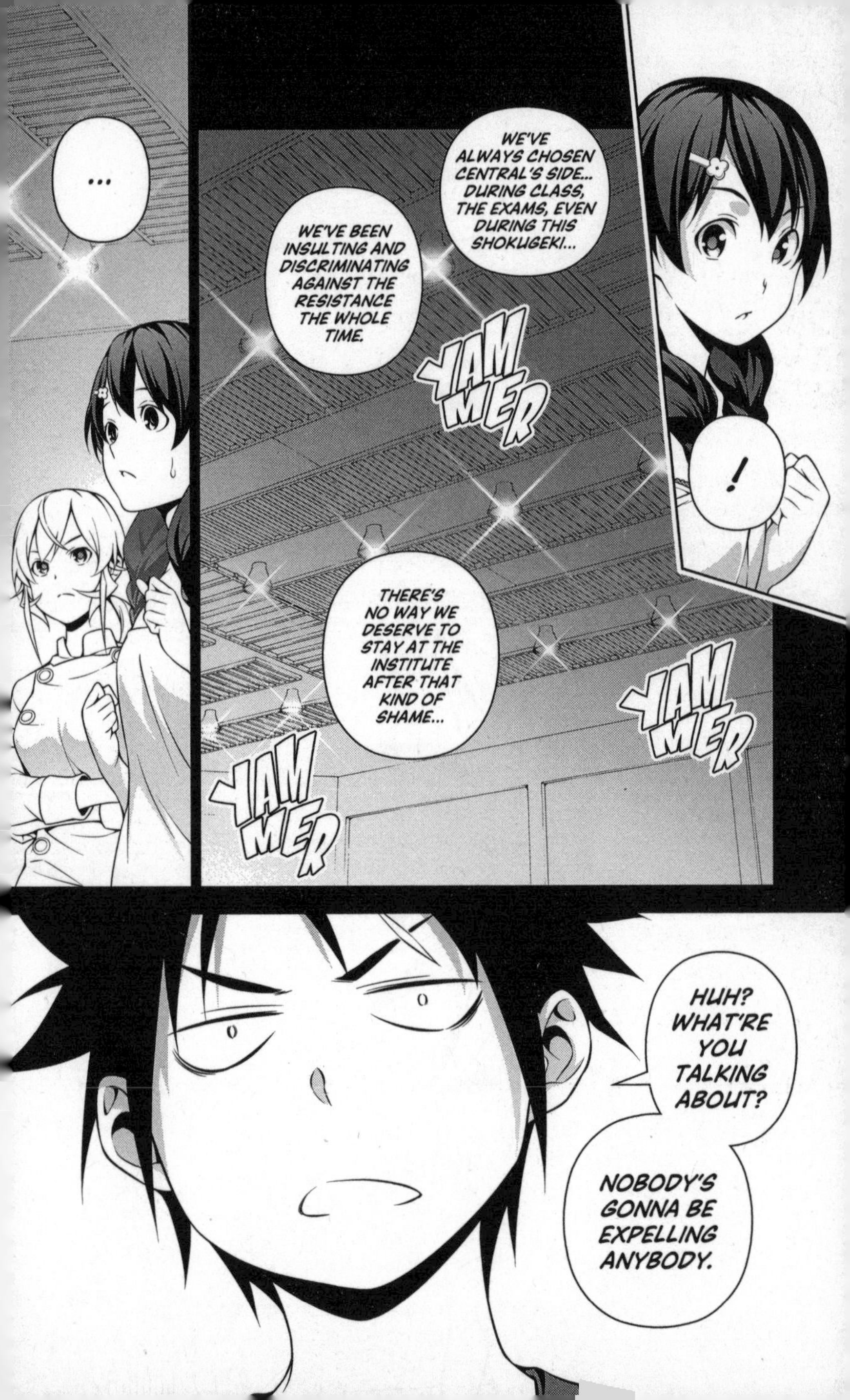
!
WE'VE ALWAYS CHOSEN CENTRAL'S SIDE... DURING CLASS, THE EXAMS, EVEN DURING THIS SHOKUGEKI...
WE'VE BEEN INSULTING AND DISCRIMINATING AGAINST THE RESISTANCE THE WHOLE TIME.
YAMMER
THERE'S NO WAY WE DESERVE TO STAY AT THE INSTITUTE AFTER THAT KIND OF SHAME...
YAMMER
YAMMER
...
HUH? WHAT'RE YOU TALKING ABOUT?
NOBODY'S GONNA BE EXPELLING ANYBODY.

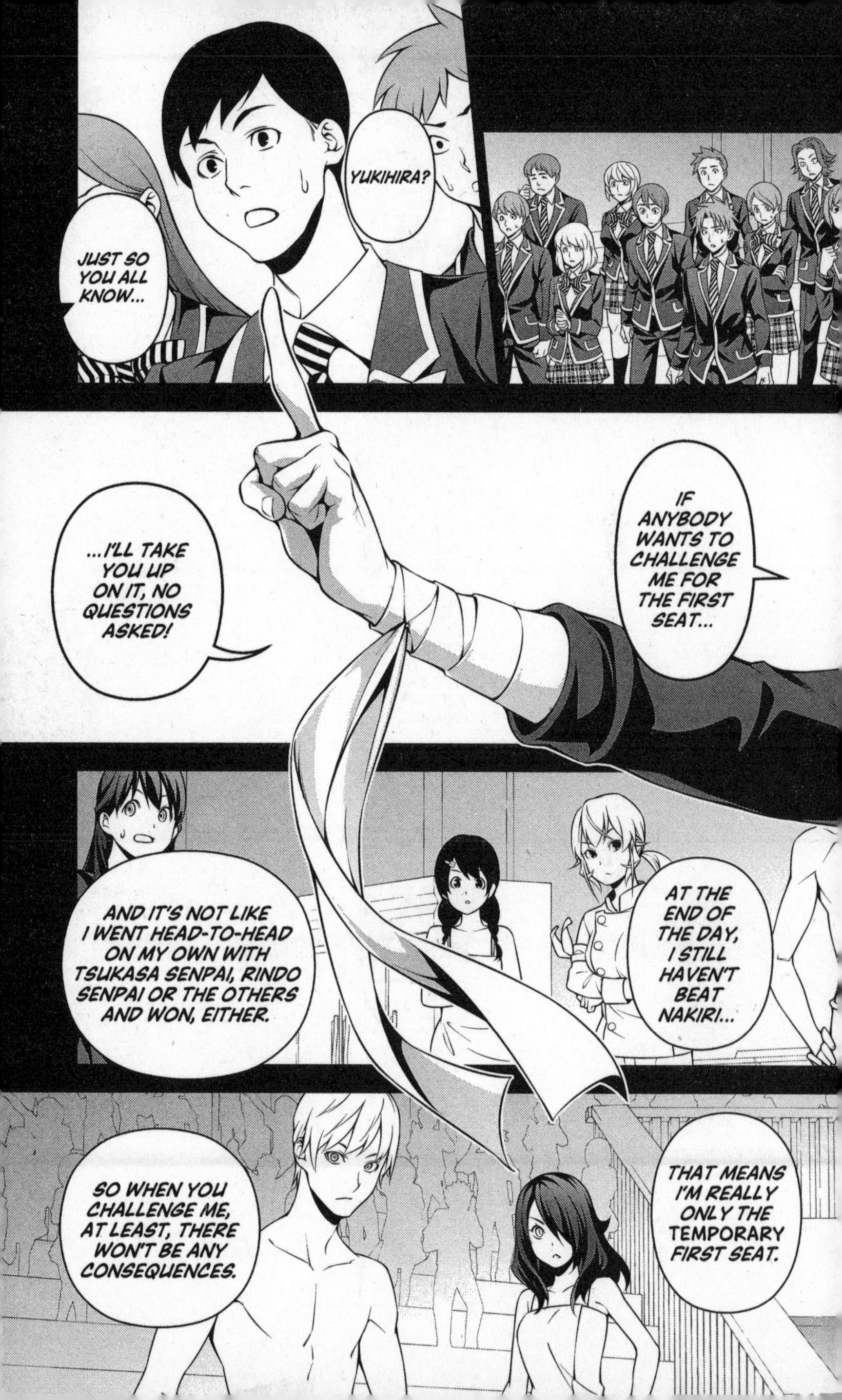
YUKIHIRA?
JUST SO YOU ALL KNOW...
IF ANYBODY WANTS TO CHALLENGE ME FOR THE FIRST SEAT...
...I'LL TAKE YOU UP ON IT, NO QUESTIONS ASKED!
AT THE END OF THE DAY, I STILL HAVEN'T BEAT NAKIRI...
AND IT'S NOT LIKE I WENT HEAD-TO-HEAD ON MY OWN WITH TSUKASA SENPAI, RINDO SENPAI OR THE OTHERS AND WON, EITHER.
THAT MEANS I'M REALLY ONLY THE TEMPORARY FIRST SEAT.
SO WHEN YOU CHALLENGE ME, AT LEAST, THERE WON'T BE ANY CONSEQUENCES.

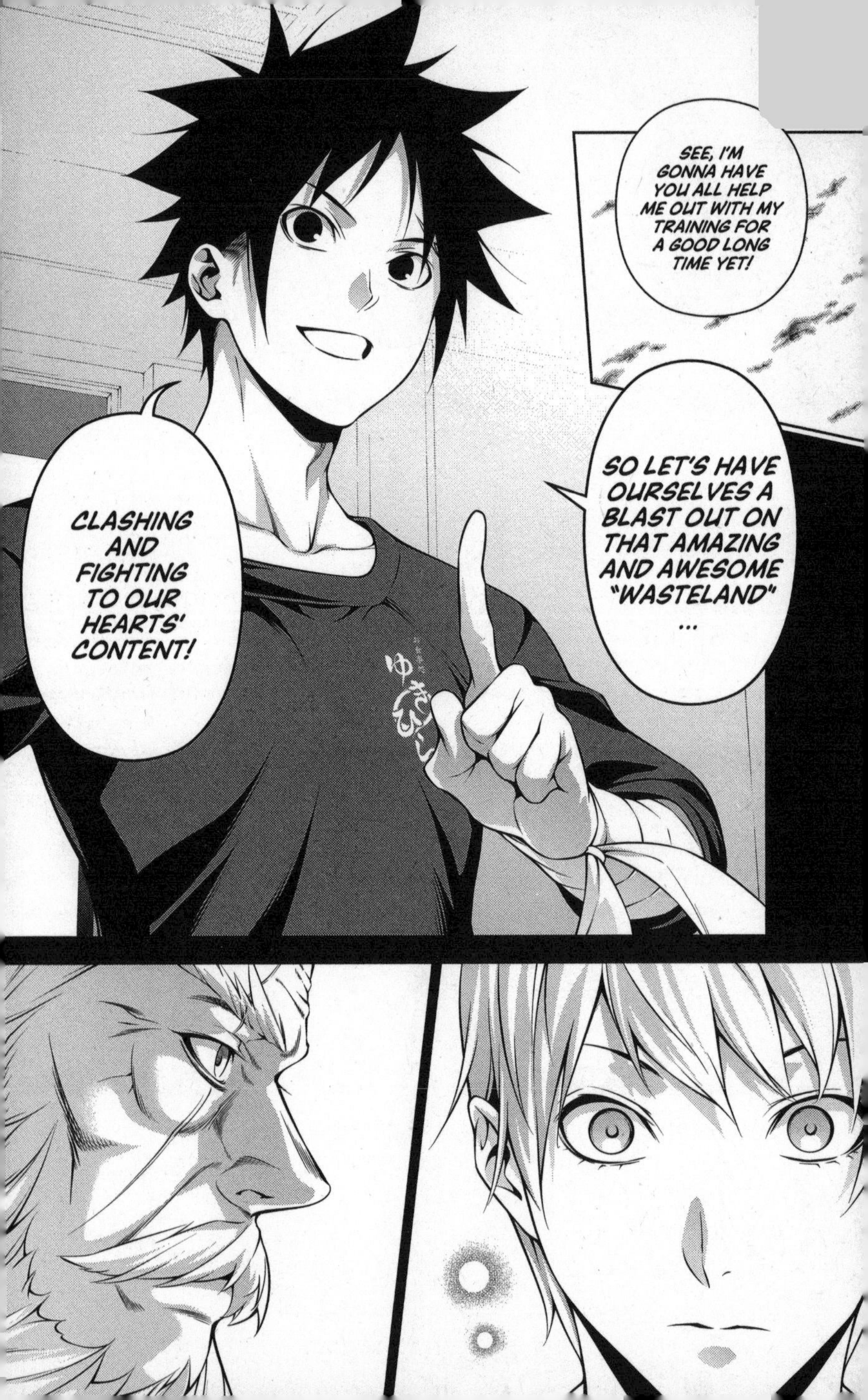
SEE, I'M GONNA HAVE YOU ALL HELP ME OUT WITH MY TRAINING FOR A GOOD LONG TIME YET!
SO LET'S HAVE OURSELVES A BLAST OUT ON THAT AMAZING AND AWESOME "WASTELAND"...
CLASHING AND FIGHTING TO OUR HEARTS' CONTENT!

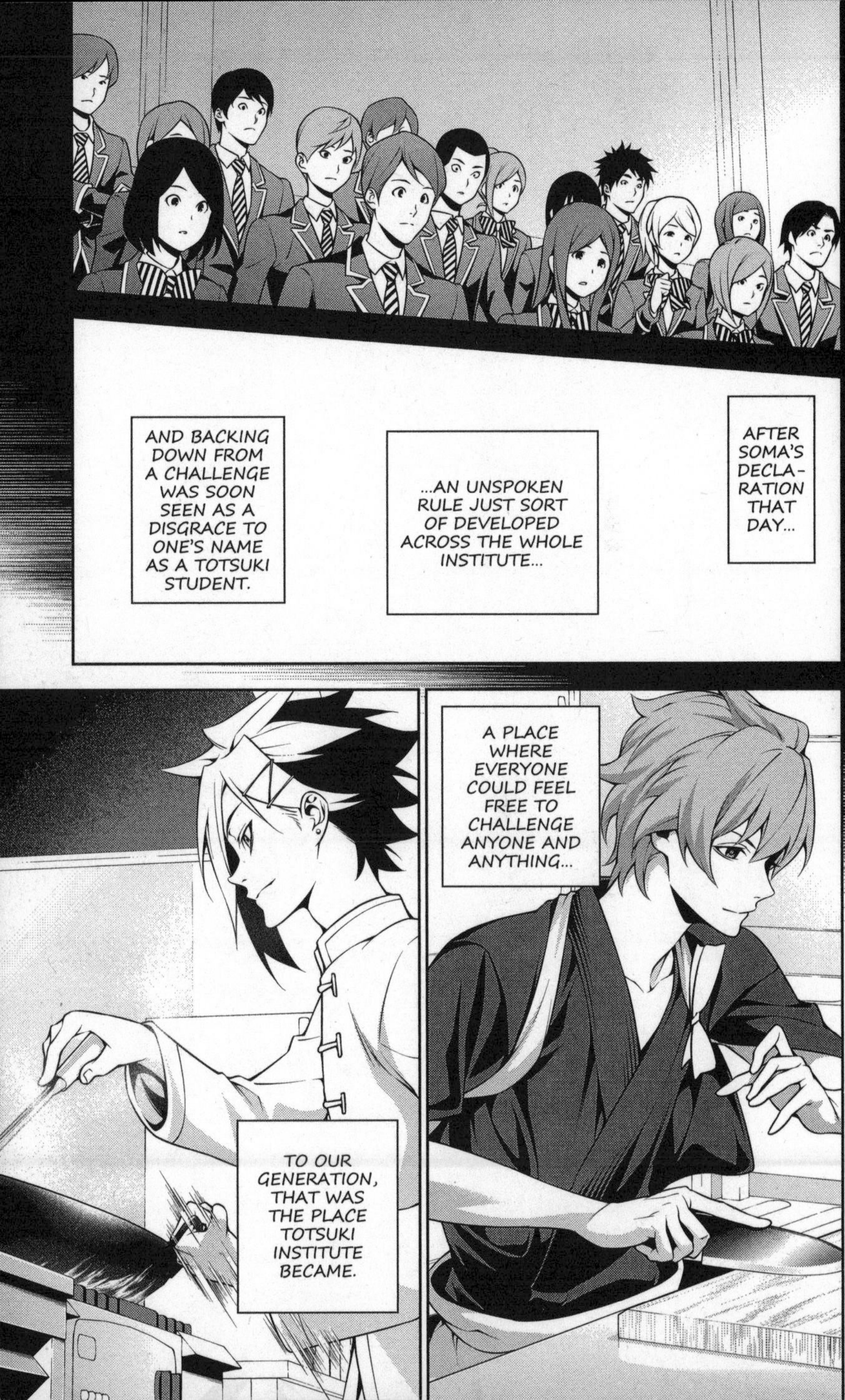
AFTER SOMA'S DECLA-RATION THAT DAY...
...AN UNSPOKEN RULE JUST SORT OF DEVELOPED ACROSS THE WHOLE INSTITUTE...
AND BACKING DOWN FROM A CHALLENGE WAS SOON SEEN AS A DISGRACE TO ONE'S NAME AS A TOTSUKI STUDENT.
A PLACE WHERE EVERYONE COULD FEEL FREE TO CHALLENGE ANYONE AND ANYTHING...
TO OUR GENERATION, THAT WAS THE PLACE TOTSUKI INSTITUTE BECAME.

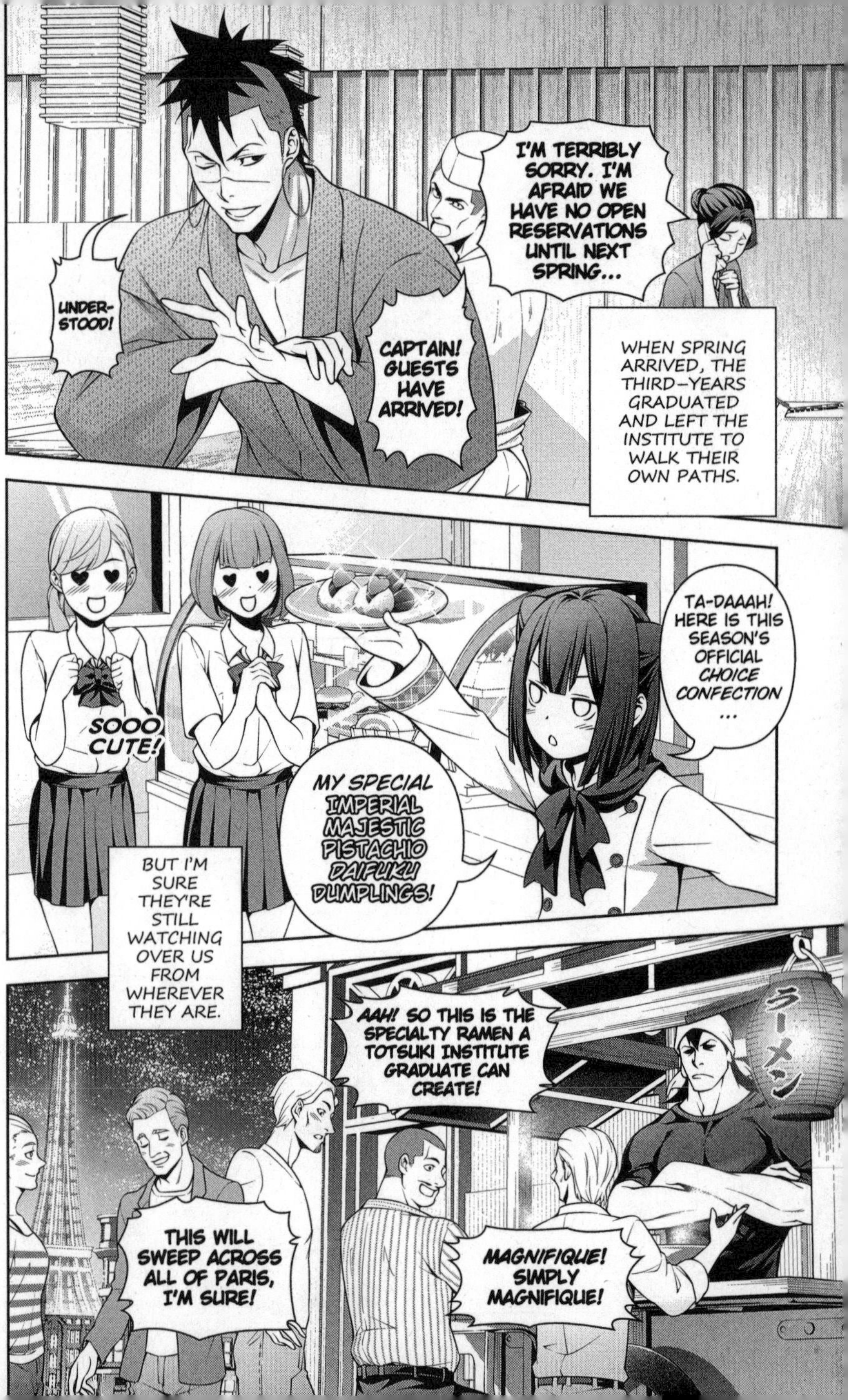
I'M TERRIBLY SORRY. I'M AFRAID WE HAVE NO OPEN RESERVATIONS UNTIL NEXT SPRING...
WHEN SPRING ARRIVED, THE THIRD-YEARS GRADUATED AND LEFT THE INSTITUTE TO WALK THEIR OWN PATHS.
CAPTAIN! GUESTS HAVE ARRIVED!
UNDER-STOOD!
TA-DAAAH! HERE IS THIS SEASON'S OFFICIAL *CHOICE CONFECTION*...
MY SPECIAL IMPERIAL MAJESTIC PISTACHIO *DAIFUKU* DUMPLINGS!
SOOO CUTE!
BUT I'M SURE THEY'RE STILL WATCHING OVER US FROM WHEREVER THEY ARE.
ラーメン
AAH! SO THIS IS THE SPECIALTY RAMEN A TOTSUKI INSTITUTE GRADUATE CAN CREATE!
MAGNIFIQUE! SIMPLY *MAGNIFIQUE!*
THIS WILL SWEEP ACROSS ALL OF PARIS, I'M SURE!

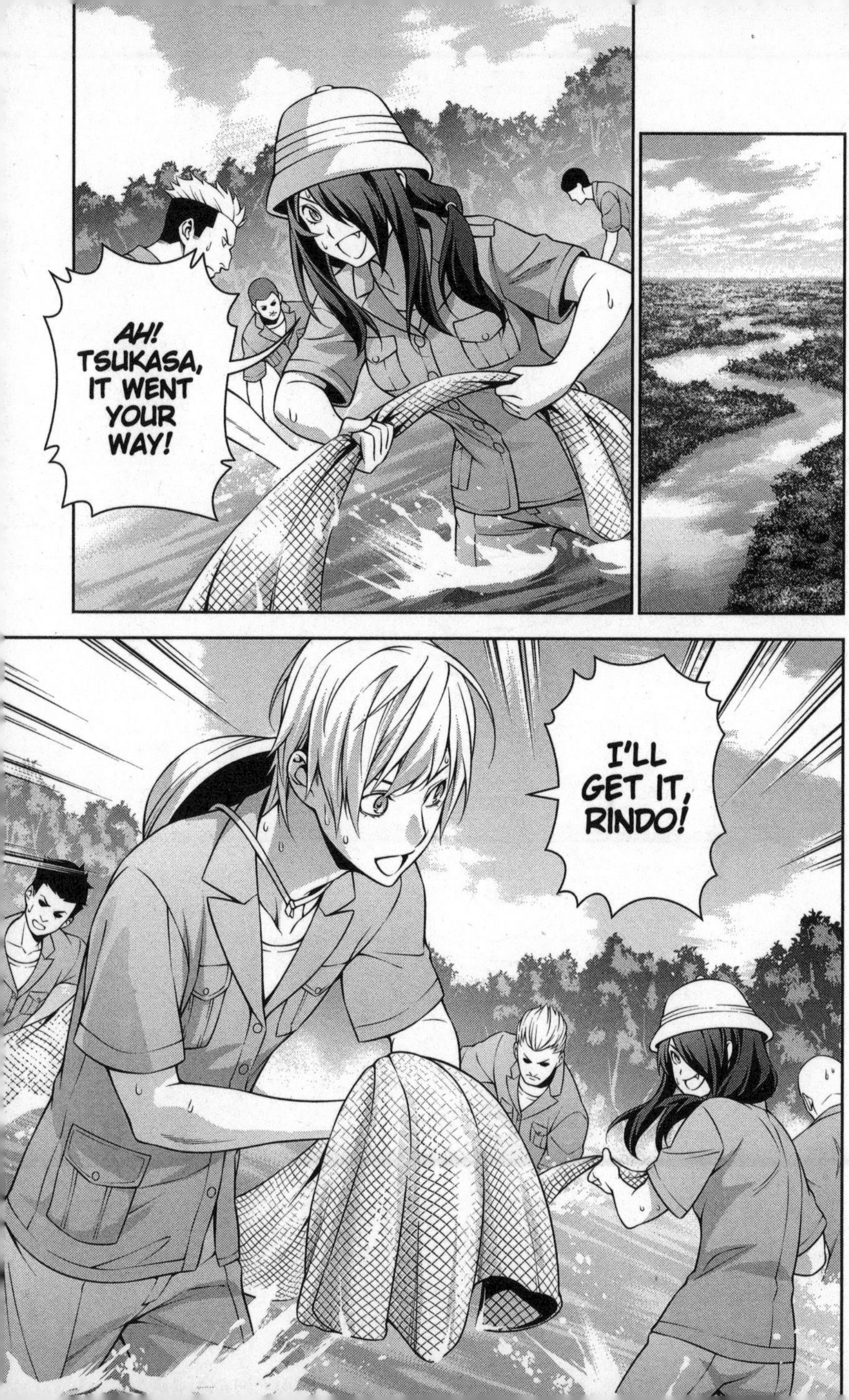
AH! TSUKASA, IT WENT YOUR WAY!
I'LL GET IT, RINDO!

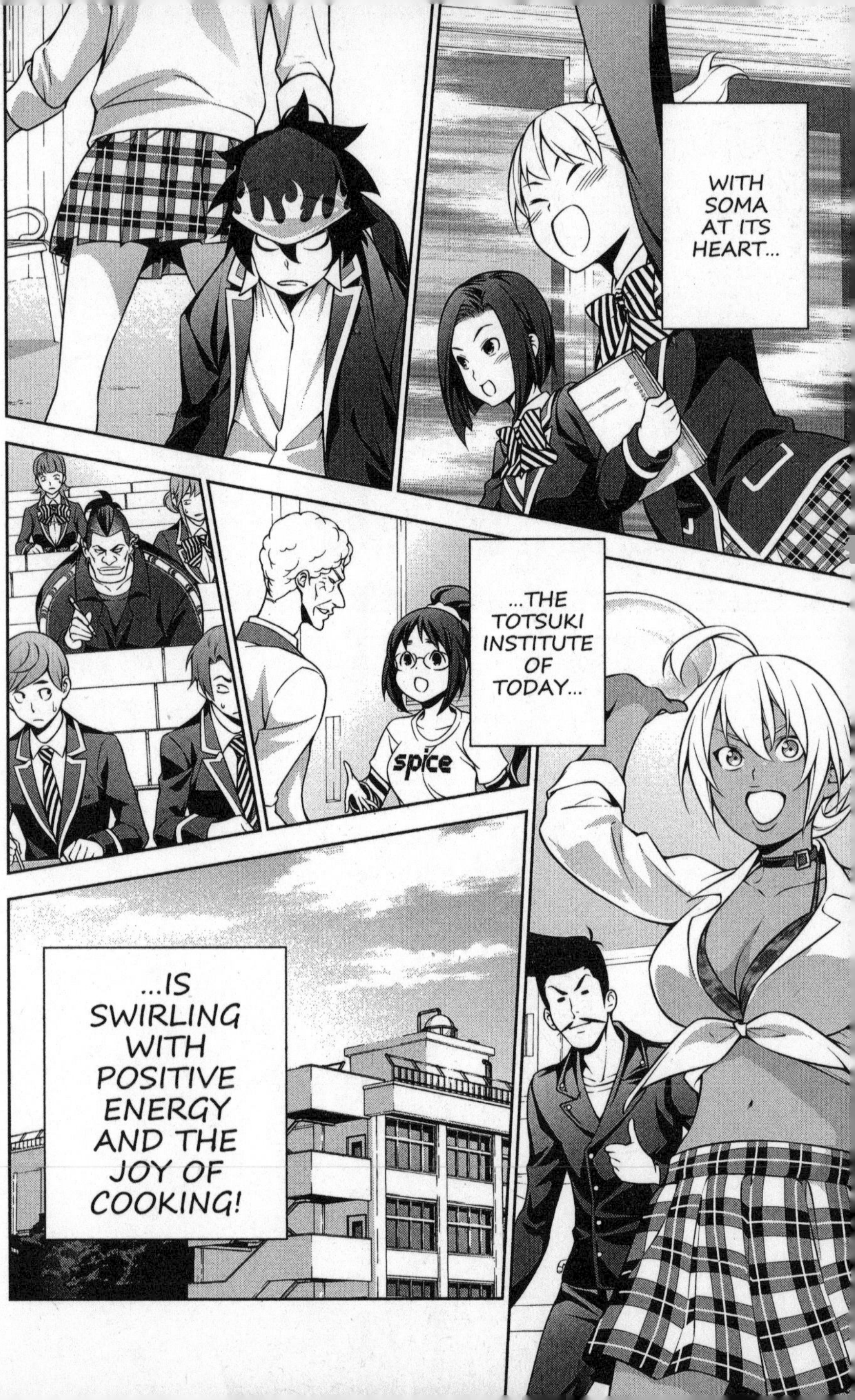
WITH SOMA AT ITS HEART...
...THE TOTSUKI INSTITUTE OF TODAY...
spice
...IS SWIRLING WITH POSITIVE ENERGY AND THE JOY OF COOKING!

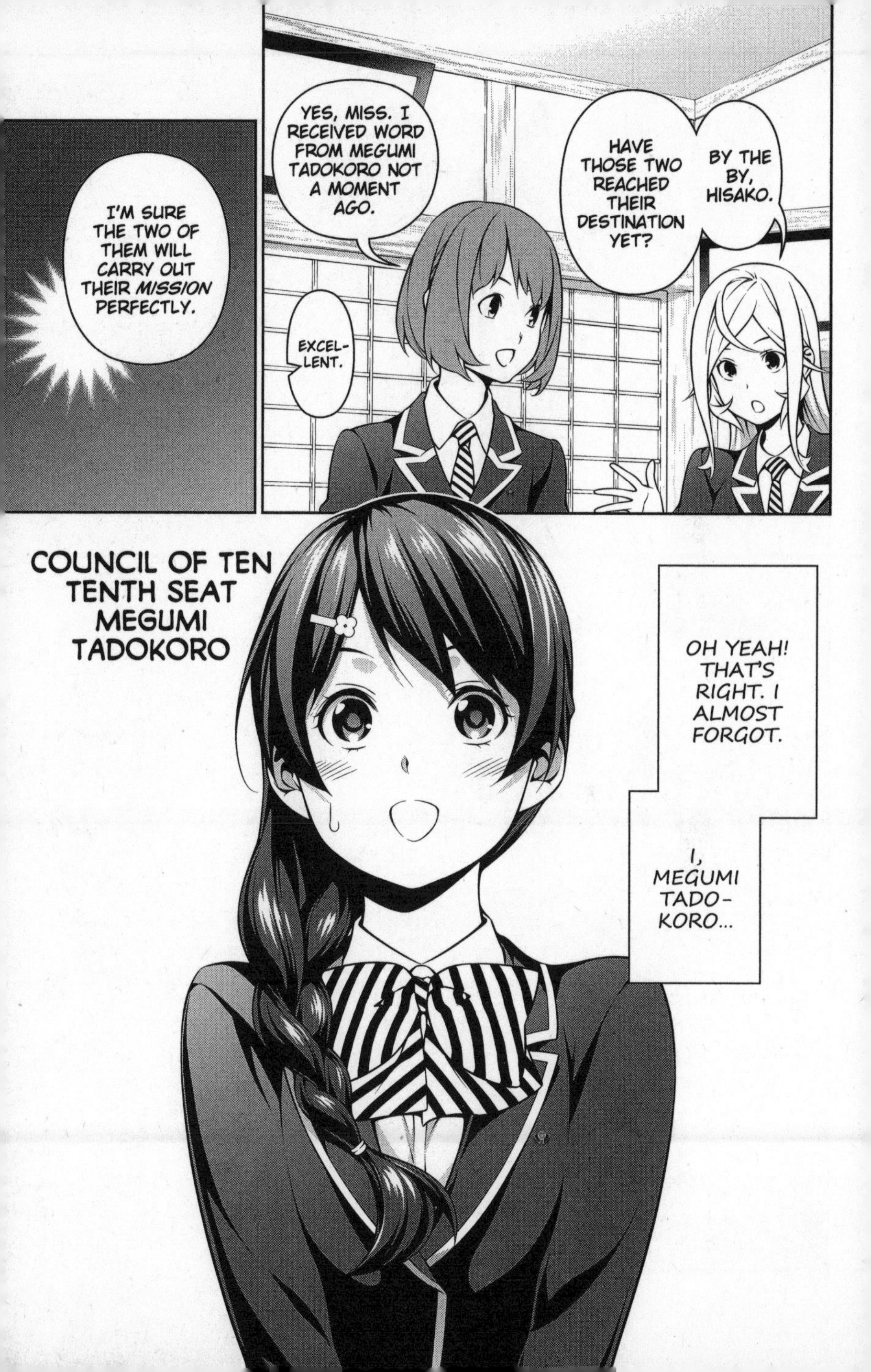
BY THE BY, HISAKO.
HAVE THOSE TWO REACHED THEIR DESTINATION YET?
YES, MISS. I RECEIVED WORD FROM MEGUMI TADOKORO NOT A MOMENT AGO.
EXCEL-LENT.
I'M SURE THE TWO OF THEM WILL CARRY OUT THEIR *MISSION* PERFECTLY.
OH YEAH! THAT'S RIGHT. I ALMOST FORGOT.
I, MEGUMI TADO-KORO...
COUNCIL OF TEN TENTH SEAT MEGUMI TADOKORO

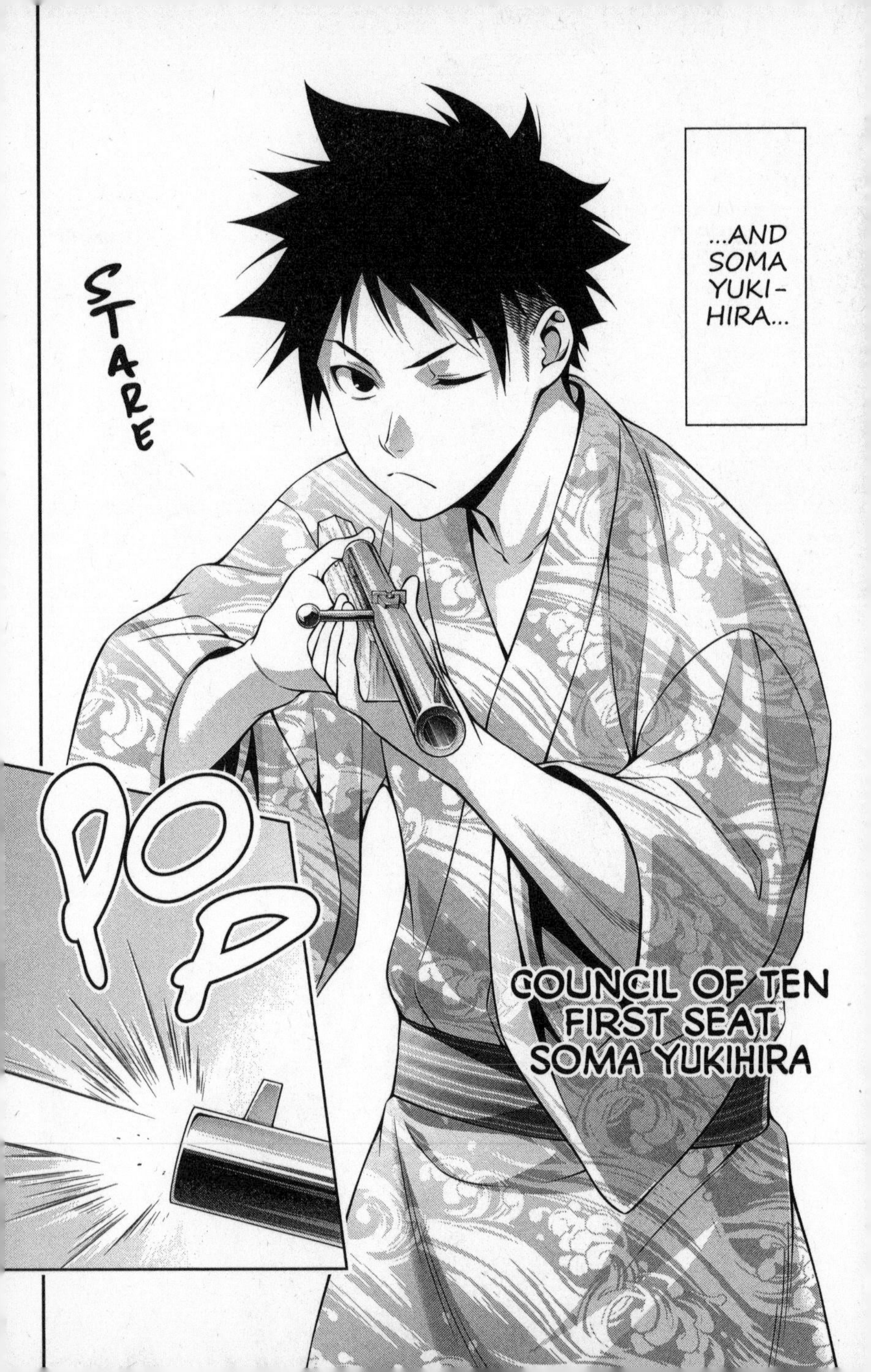
...AND SOMA YUKI-HIRA...
STARE
COUNCIL OF TEN FIRST SEAT SOMA YUKIHIRA
POP

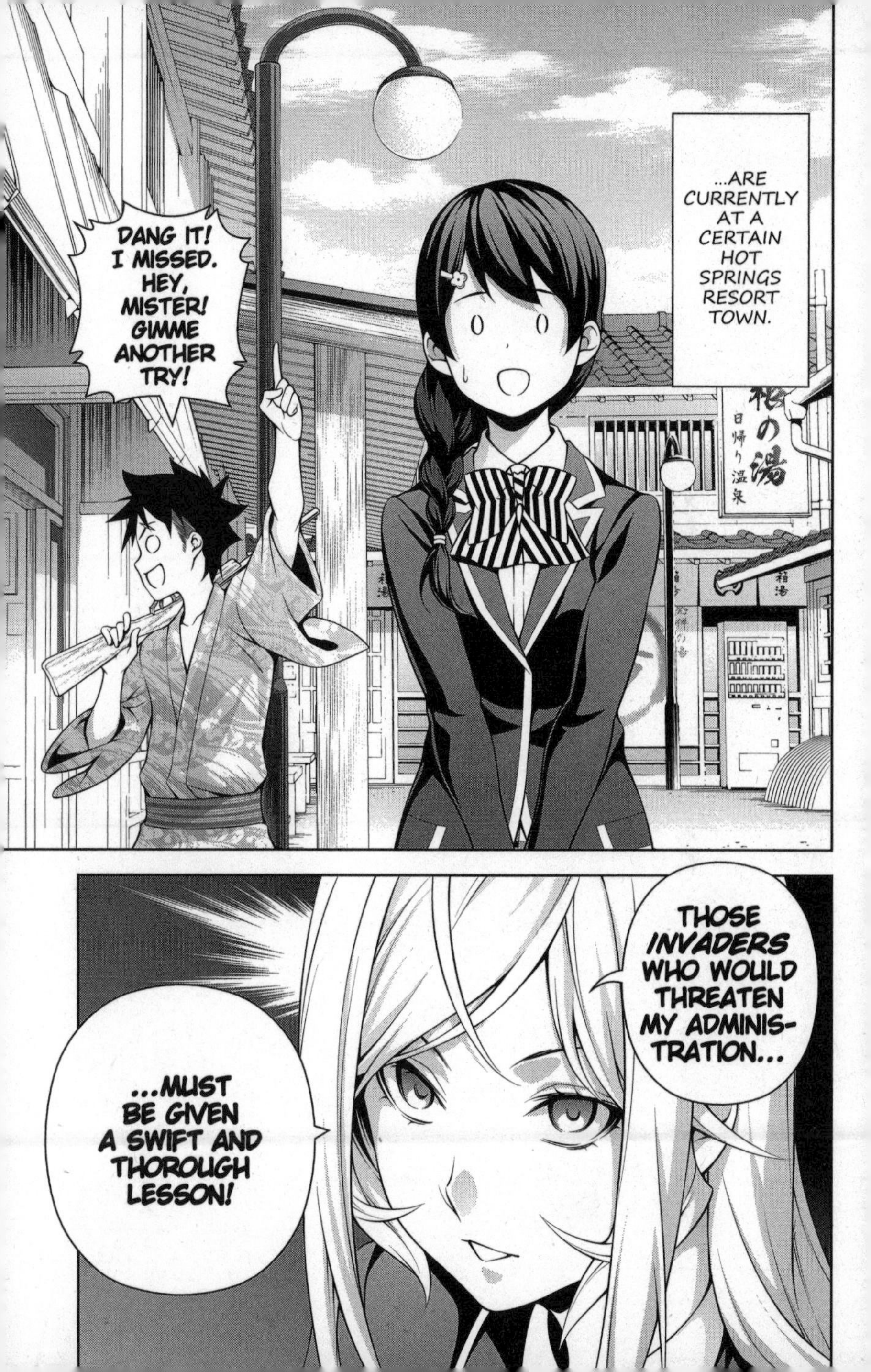
...ARE CURRENTLY AT A CERTAIN HOT SPRINGS RESORT TOWN.
日帰り温泉
DANG IT! I MISSED. HEY, MISTER! GIMME ANOTHER TRY!
THOSE *INVADERS* WHO WOULD THREATEN MY ADMINIS- TRATION...
...MUST BE GIVEN A SWIFT AND THOROUGH LESSON!

THE CASE OF RYOKO SAKAKI

UH, HELLO? SAY SOME-THING ALREADY!

WOW, UH, YOU LOOK EVEN MORE LIKE A MARRIED WOMAN THAN BEFORE.

WHO'RE YOU CALLING MARRIED ?!

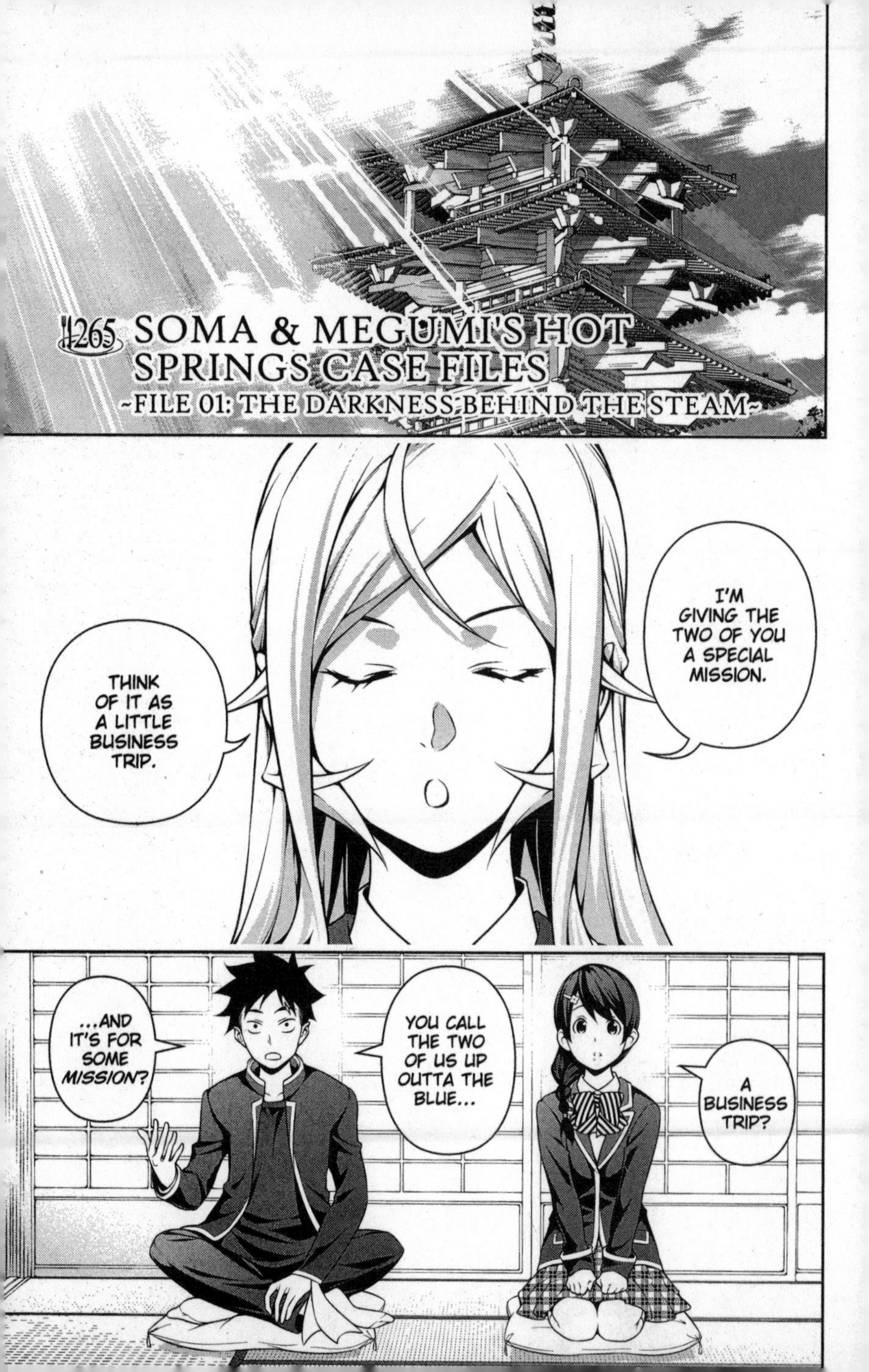
265 SOMA & MEGUMI'S HOT SPRINGS CASE FILES
~FILE 01: THE DARKNESS BEHIND THE STEAM~
I'M GIVING THE TWO OF YOU A SPECIAL MISSION.
THINK OF IT AS A LITTLE BUSINESS TRIP.
A BUSINESS TRIP?
YOU CALL THE TWO OF US UP OUTTA THE BLUE...
...AND IT'S FOR SOME *MISSION*?

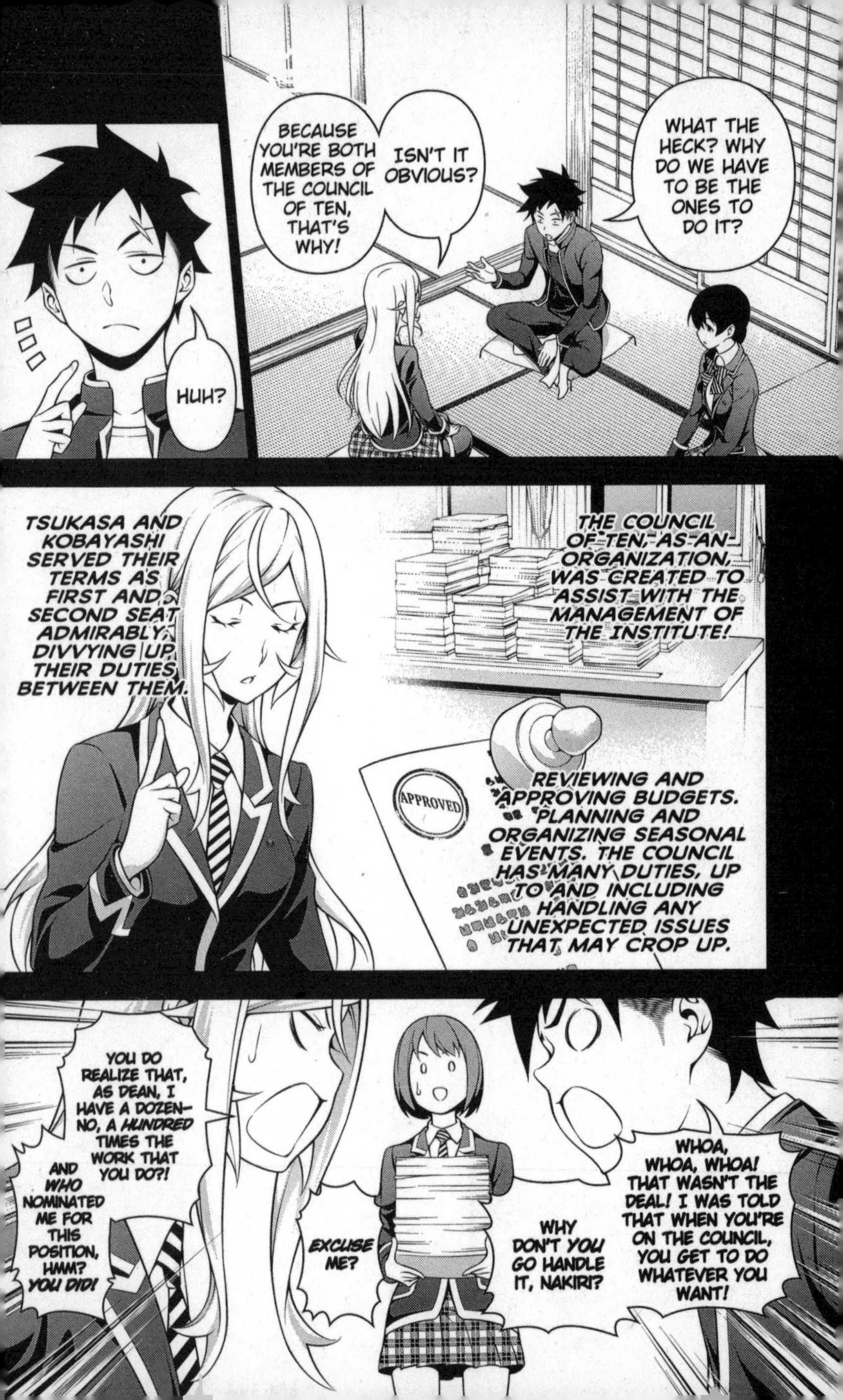
WHAT THE HECK? WHY DO WE HAVE TO BE THE ONES TO DO IT?
ISN'T IT OBVIOUS?
BECAUSE YOU'RE BOTH MEMBERS OF THE COUNCIL OF TEN, THAT'S WHY!
HUH?
THE COUNCIL OF TEN, AS AN ORGANIZATION, WAS CREATED TO ASSIST WITH THE MANAGEMENT OF THE INSTITUTE!
APPROVED
REVIEWING AND APPROVING BUDGETS. PLANNING AND ORGANIZING SEASONAL EVENTS. THE COUNCIL HAS MANY DUTIES, UP TO AND INCLUDING HANDLING ANY UNEXPECTED ISSUES THAT MAY CROP UP.
TSUKASA AND KOBAYASHI SERVED THEIR TERMS AS FIRST AND SECOND SEAT ADMIRABLY, DIVVYING UP THEIR DUTIES BETWEEN THEM.
WHOA, WHOA, WHOA! THAT WASN'T THE DEAL! I WAS TOLD THAT WHEN YOU'RE ON THE COUNCIL, YOU GET TO DO WHATEVER YOU WANT!
WHY DON'T YOU GO HANDLE IT, NAKIRI?
EXCUSE ME?
YOU DO REALIZE THAT, AS DEAN, I HAVE A DOZEN—NO, A HUNDRED TIMES THE WORK THAT YOU DO?!
AND WHO NOMINATED ME FOR THIS POSITION, HMM? YOU DID!

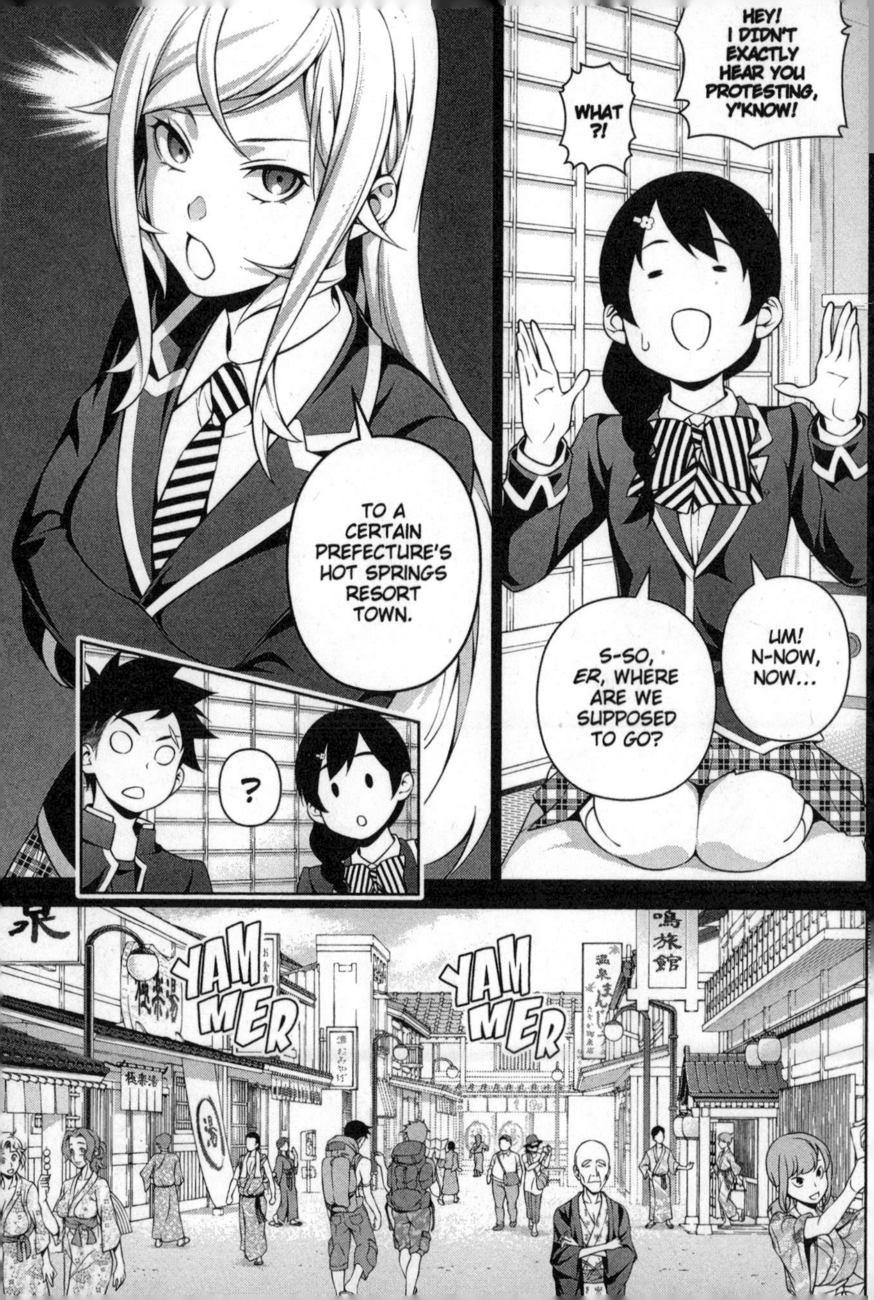
HEY! I DIDN'T EXACTLY HEAR YOU PROTESTING, Y'KNOW!
WHAT?!
UM! N-NOW, NOW...
S-SO, *ER*, WHERE ARE WE SUPPOSED TO GO?
TO A CERTAIN PREFECTURE'S HOT SPRINGS RESORT TOWN.
?
YAM MER
YAM MER

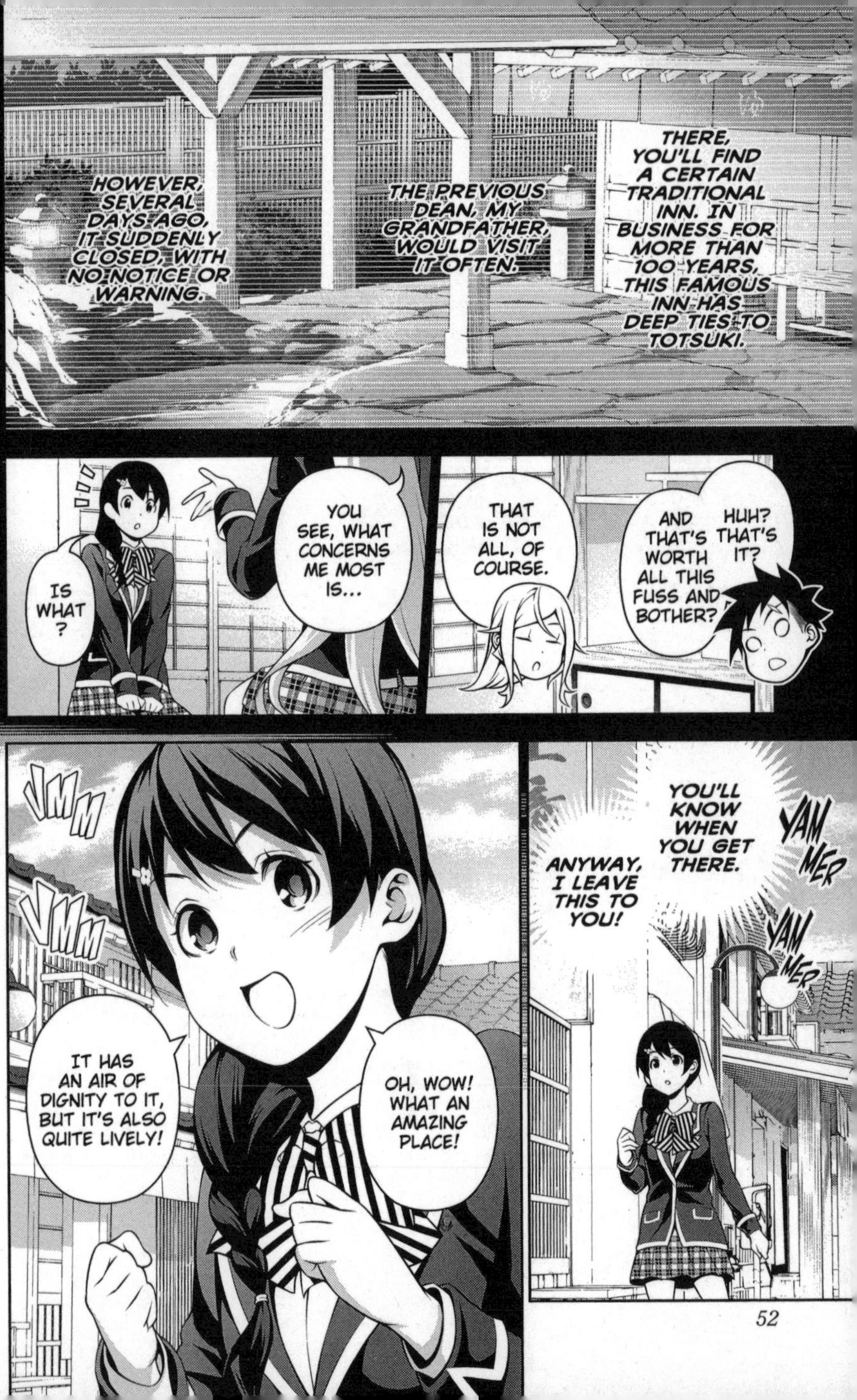
THERE, YOU'LL FIND A CERTAIN TRADITIONAL INN. IN BUSINESS FOR MORE THAN 100 YEARS, THIS FAMOUS INN HAS DEEP TIES TO TOTSUKI.
THE PREVIOUS DEAN, MY GRANDFATHER, WOULD VISIT IT OFTEN.
HOWEVER, SEVERAL DAYS AGO, IT SUDDENLY CLOSED, WITH NO NOTICE OR WARNING.
HUH? THAT'S IT?
AND THAT'S WORTH ALL THIS FUSS AND BOTHER?
THAT IS NOT ALL, OF COURSE.
YOU SEE, WHAT CONCERNS ME MOST IS...
IS WHAT?
YOU'LL KNOW WHEN YOU GET THERE.
ANYWAY, I LEAVE THIS TO YOU!
YAMMER
YAMMER
JMM
JMM
OH, WOW! WHAT AN AMAZING PLACE!
IT HAS AN AIR OF DIGNITY TO IT, BUT IT'S ALSO QUITE LIVELY!

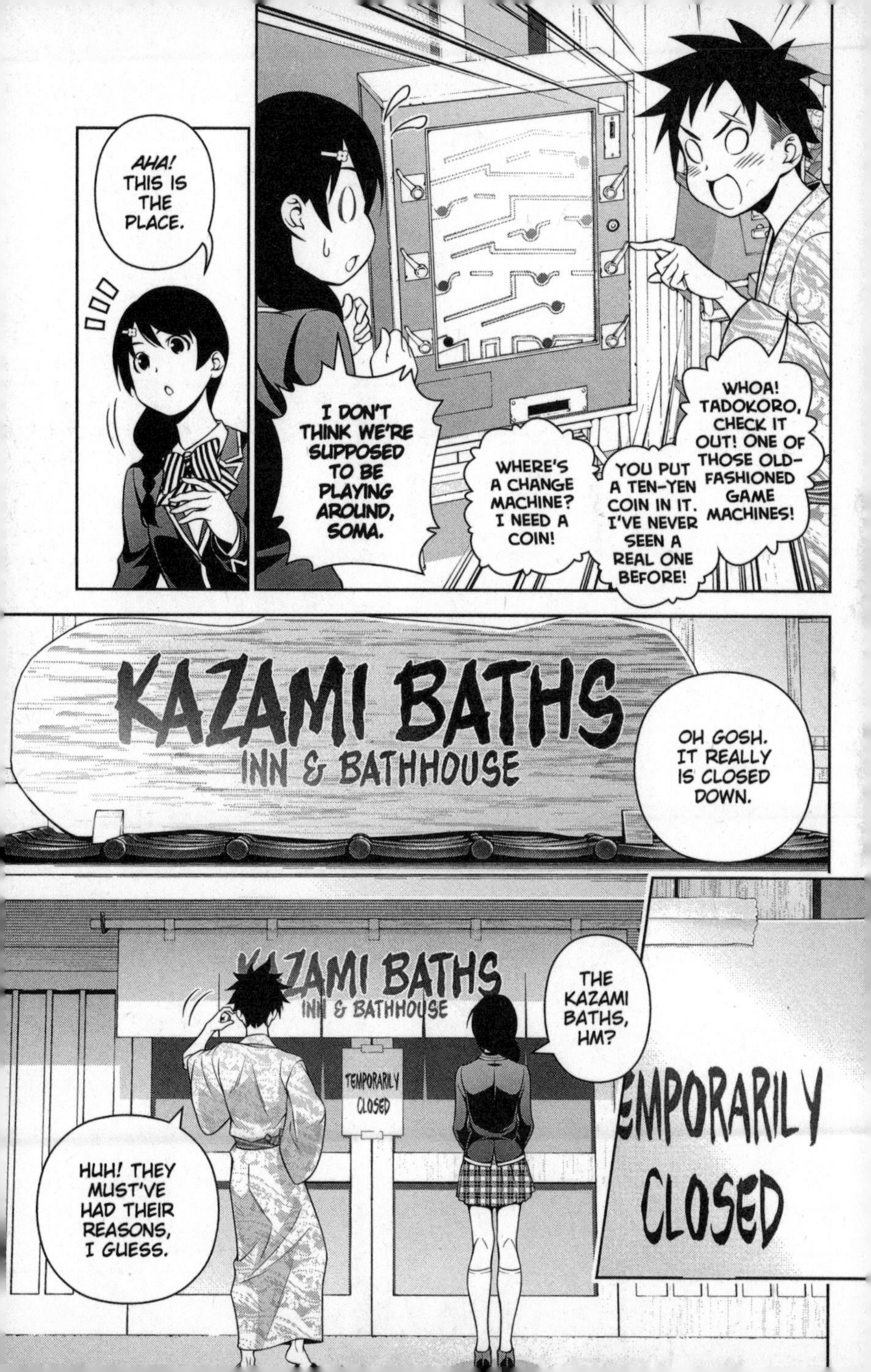
WHOA! TADOKORO, CHECK IT OUT! ONE OF THOSE OLD-FASHIONED GAME MACHINES!
YOU PUT A TEN-YEN COIN IN IT. I'VE NEVER SEEN A REAL ONE BEFORE!
WHERE'S A CHANGE MACHINE? I NEED A COIN!
I DON'T THINK WE'RE SUPPOSED TO BE PLAYING AROUND, SOMA.
AHA! THIS IS THE PLACE.
OH GOSH. IT REALLY IS CLOSED DOWN.
KAZAMI BATHS
INN & BATHHOUSE
EMPORARILY CLOSED
THE KAZAMI BATHS, HM?
KAZAMI BATHS
INN & BATHHOUSE
TEMPORARILY CLOSED
HUH! THEY MUST'VE HAD THEIR REASONS, I GUESS.

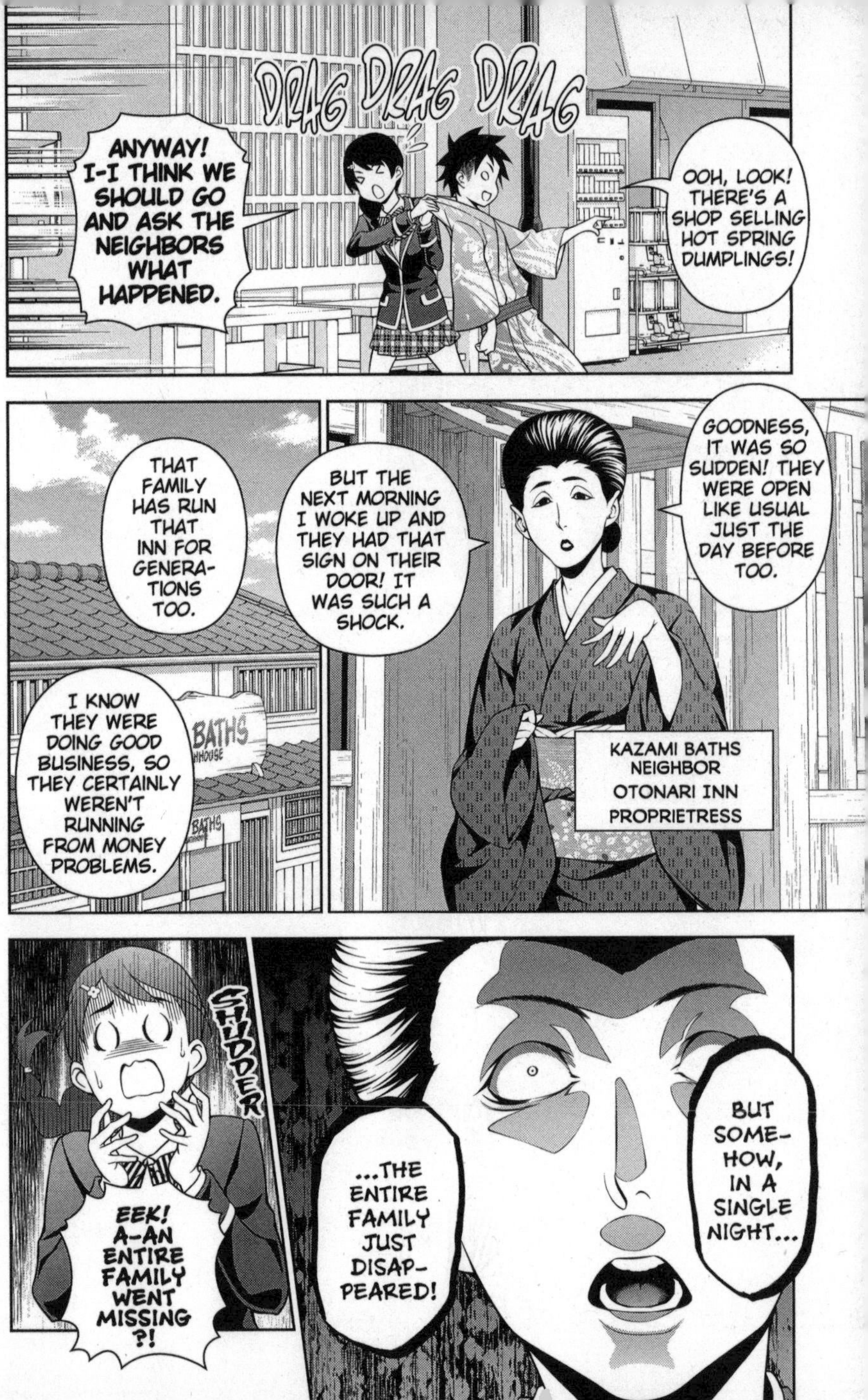
DRAG DRAG DRAG
OOH, LOOK! THERE'S A SHOP SELLING HOT SPRING DUMPLINGS!
ANYWAY! I-I THINK WE SHOULD GO AND ASK THE NEIGHBORS WHAT HAPPENED.
GOODNESS, IT WAS SO SUDDEN! THEY WERE OPEN LIKE USUAL JUST THE DAY BEFORE TOO.
BUT THE NEXT MORNING I WOKE UP AND THEY HAD THAT SIGN ON THEIR DOOR! IT WAS SUCH A SHOCK.
KAZAMI BATHS NEIGHBOR OTONARI INN PROPRIETRESS
THAT FAMILY HAS RUN THAT INN FOR GENERA-TIONS TOO.
BATHS
I KNOW THEY WERE DOING GOOD BUSINESS, SO THEY CERTAINLY WEREN'T RUNNING FROM MONEY PROBLEMS.
BUT SOME-HOW, IN A SINGLE NIGHT...
...THE ENTIRE FAMILY JUST DISAP-PEARED!
SHUDDER
EEK! A-AN ENTIRE FAMILY WENT MISSING ?!

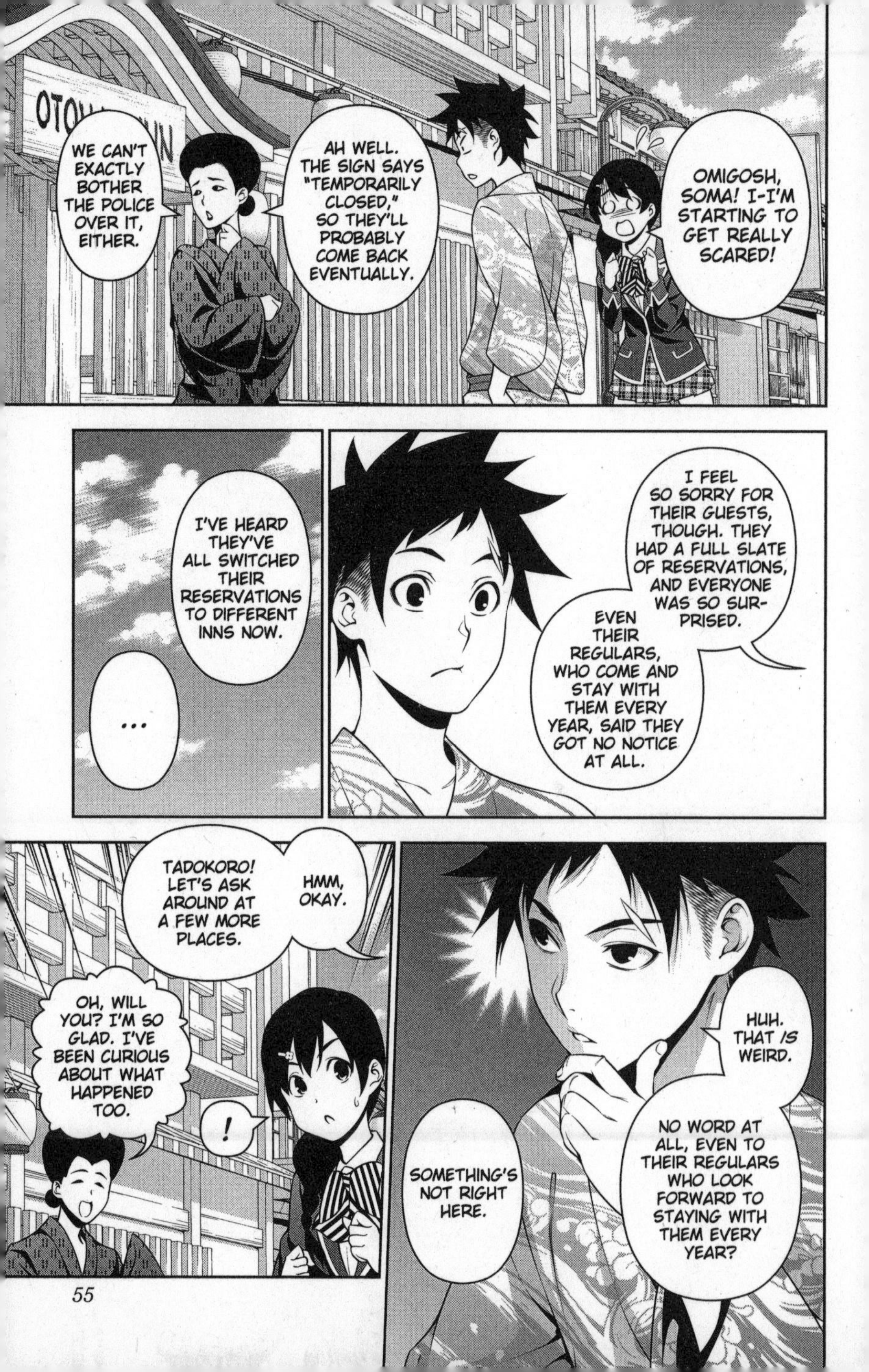
OMIGOSH, SOMA! I-I'M STARTING TO GET REALLY SCARED!
AH WELL. THE SIGN SAYS "TEMPORARILY CLOSED," SO THEY'LL PROBABLY COME BACK EVENTUALLY.
WE CAN'T EXACTLY BOTHER THE POLICE OVER IT, EITHER.
I FEEL SO SORRY FOR THEIR GUESTS, THOUGH. THEY HAD A FULL SLATE OF RESERVATIONS, AND EVERYONE WAS SO SURPRISED.
EVEN THEIR REGULARS, WHO COME AND STAY WITH THEM EVERY YEAR, SAID THEY GOT NO NOTICE AT ALL.
I'VE HEARD THEY'VE ALL SWITCHED THEIR RESERVATIONS TO DIFFERENT INNS NOW.
...
HUH. THAT *IS* WEIRD.
NO WORD AT ALL, EVEN TO THEIR REGULARS WHO LOOK FORWARD TO STAYING WITH THEM EVERY YEAR?
SOMETHING'S NOT RIGHT HERE.
HMM, OKAY.
TADOKORO! LET'S ASK AROUND AT A FEW MORE PLACES.
!
OH, WILL YOU? I'M SO GLAD. I'VE BEEN CURIOUS ABOUT WHAT HAPPENED TOO.

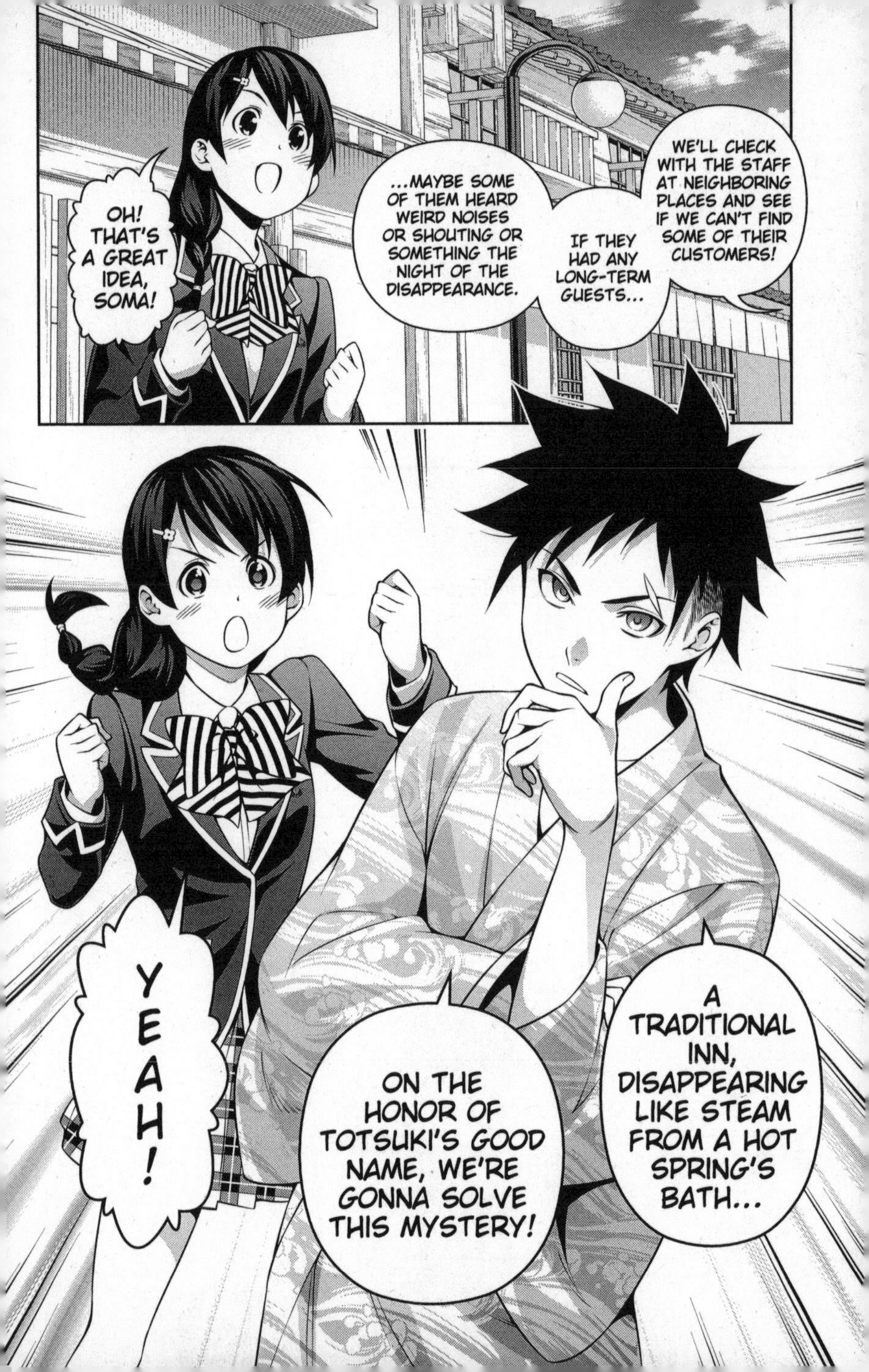
WE'LL CHECK WITH THE STAFF AT NEIGHBORING PLACES AND SEE IF WE CAN'T FIND SOME OF THEIR CUSTOMERS!
IF THEY HAD ANY LONG-TERM GUESTS...
...MAYBE SOME OF THEM HEARD WEIRD NOISES OR SHOUTING OR SOMETHING THE NIGHT OF THE DISAPPEARANCE.
OH! THAT'S A GREAT IDEA, SOMA!
A TRADITIONAL INN, DISAPPEARING LIKE STEAM FROM A HOT SPRING'S BATH...
ON THE HONOR OF TOTSUKI'S GOOD NAME, WE'RE GONNA SOLVE THIS MYSTERY!
YEAH!

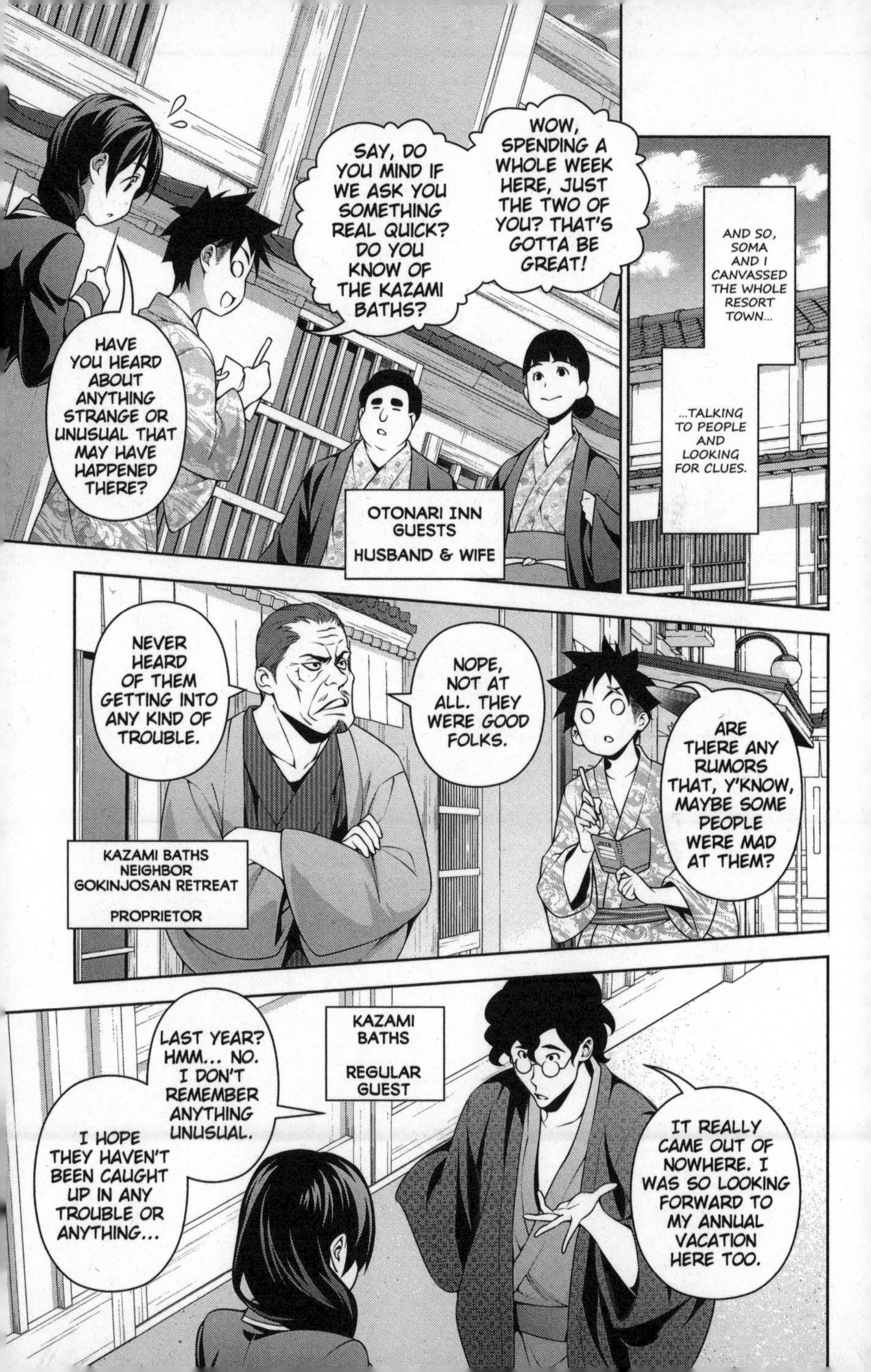
AND SO, SOMA AND I CANVASSED THE WHOLE RESORT TOWN...
...TALKING TO PEOPLE AND LOOKING FOR CLUES.
WOW, SPENDING A WHOLE WEEK HERE, JUST THE TWO OF YOU? THAT'S GOTTA BE GREAT!
SAY, DO YOU MIND IF WE ASK YOU SOMETHING REAL QUICK? DO YOU KNOW OF THE KAZAMI BATHS?
HAVE YOU HEARD ABOUT ANYTHING STRANGE OR UNUSUAL THAT MAY HAVE HAPPENED THERE?
OTONARI INN GUESTS
HUSBAND & WIFE
ARE THERE ANY RUMORS THAT, Y'KNOW, MAYBE SOME PEOPLE WERE MAD AT THEM?
NOPE, NOT AT ALL. THEY WERE GOOD FOLKS.
NEVER HEARD OF THEM GETTING INTO ANY KIND OF TROUBLE.
KAZAMI BATHS NEIGHBOR GOKINJOSAN RETREAT
PROPRIETOR
KAZAMI BATHS
REGULAR GUEST
LAST YEAR? HMM... NO. I DON'T REMEMBER ANYTHING UNUSUAL.
IT REALLY CAME OUT OF NOWHERE. I WAS SO LOOKING FORWARD TO MY ANNUAL VACATION HERE TOO.
I HOPE THEY HAVEN'T BEEN CAUGHT UP IN ANY TROUBLE OR ANYTHING...

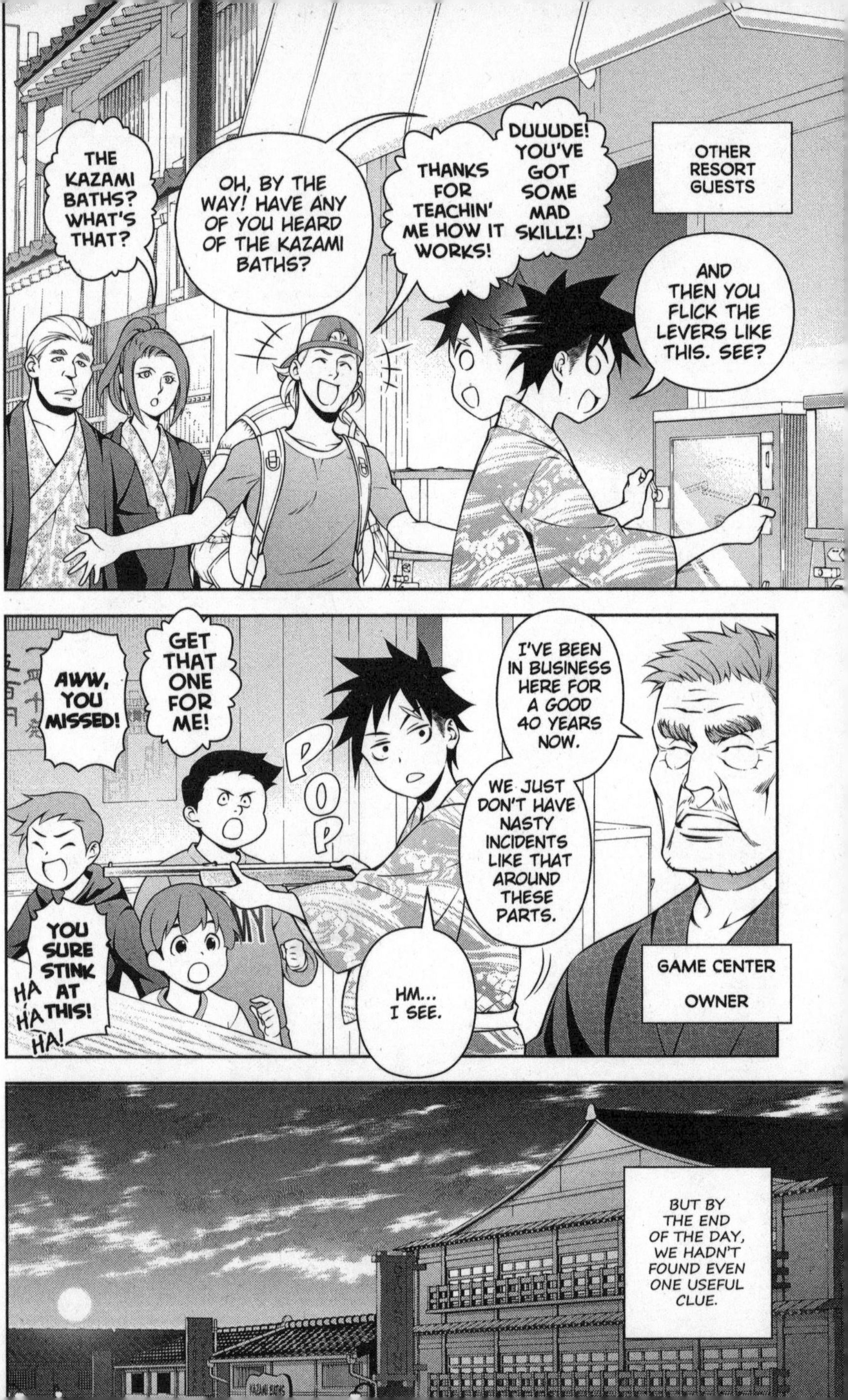
OTHER RESORT GUESTS
AND THEN YOU FLICK THE LEVERS LIKE THIS. SEE?
DUUUDE! YOU'VE GOT SOME MAD SKILLZ!
THANKS FOR TEACHIN' ME HOW IT WORKS!
OH, BY THE WAY! HAVE ANY OF YOU HEARD OF THE KAZAMI BATHS?
THE KAZAMI BATHS? WHAT'S THAT?
I'VE BEEN IN BUSINESS HERE FOR A GOOD 40 YEARS NOW.
WE JUST DON'T HAVE NASTY INCIDENTS LIKE THAT AROUND THESE PARTS.
GAME CENTER OWNER
HM... I SEE.
POP
POP
GET THAT ONE FOR ME!
AWW, YOU MISSED!
YOU SURE STINK AT THIS!
HA HA HA!
BUT BY THE END OF THE DAY, WE HADN'T FOUND EVEN ONE USEFUL CLUE.

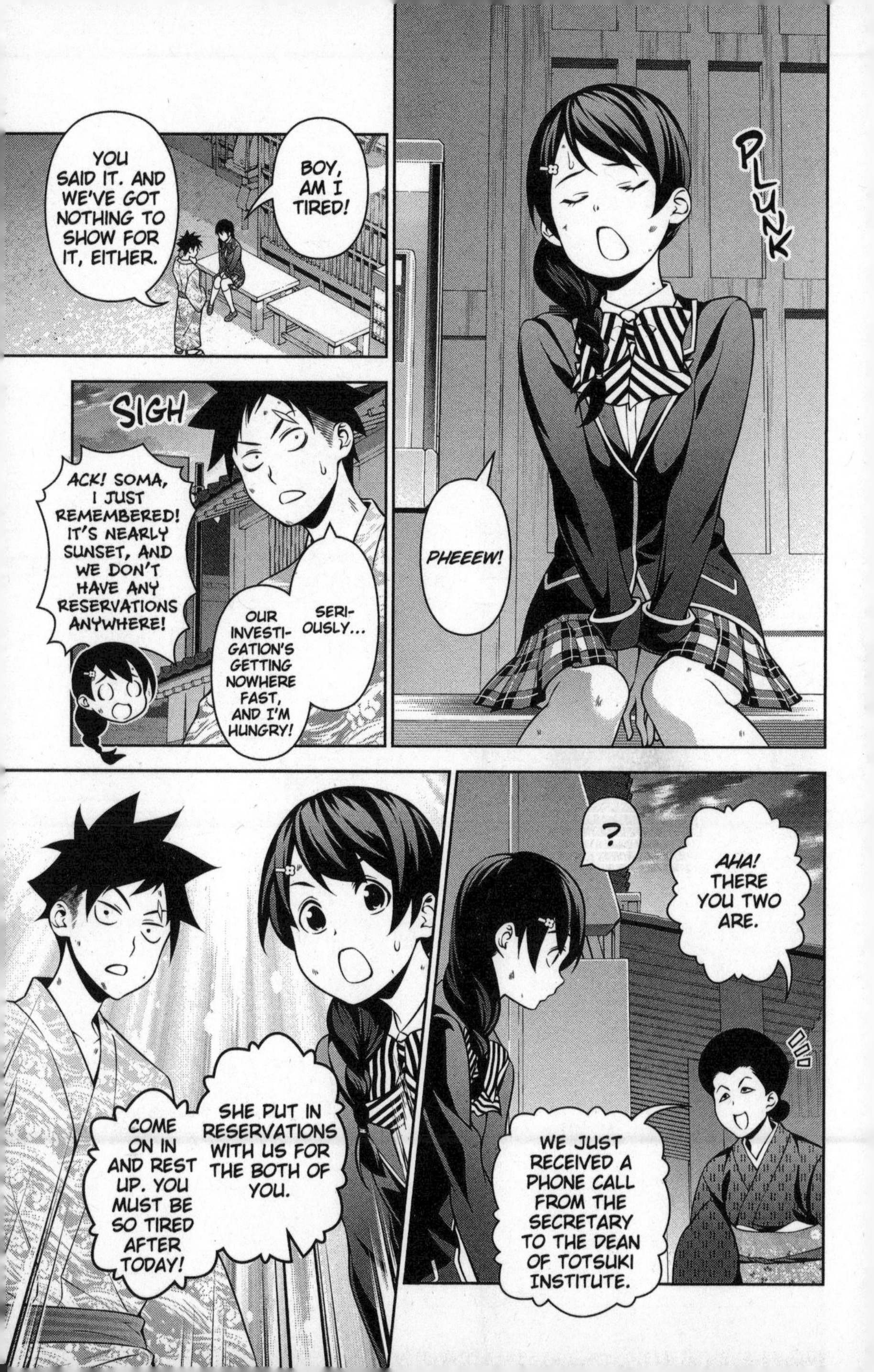
PLUNK
PHEEEW!
BOY, AM I TIRED!
YOU SAID IT. AND WE'VE GOT NOTHING TO SHOW FOR IT, EITHER.
SIGH
SERI-OUSLY...
OUR INVESTI-GATION'S GETTING NOWHERE FAST, AND I'M HUNGRY!
ACK! SOMA, I JUST REMEMBERED! IT'S NEARLY SUNSET, AND WE DON'T HAVE ANY RESERVATIONS ANYWHERE!
?
AHA! THERE YOU TWO ARE.
WE JUST RECEIVED A PHONE CALL FROM THE SECRETARY TO THE DEAN OF TOTSUKI INSTITUTE.
SHE PUT IN RESERVATIONS WITH US FOR THE BOTH OF YOU.
COME ON IN AND REST UP. YOU MUST BE SO TIRED AFTER TODAY!

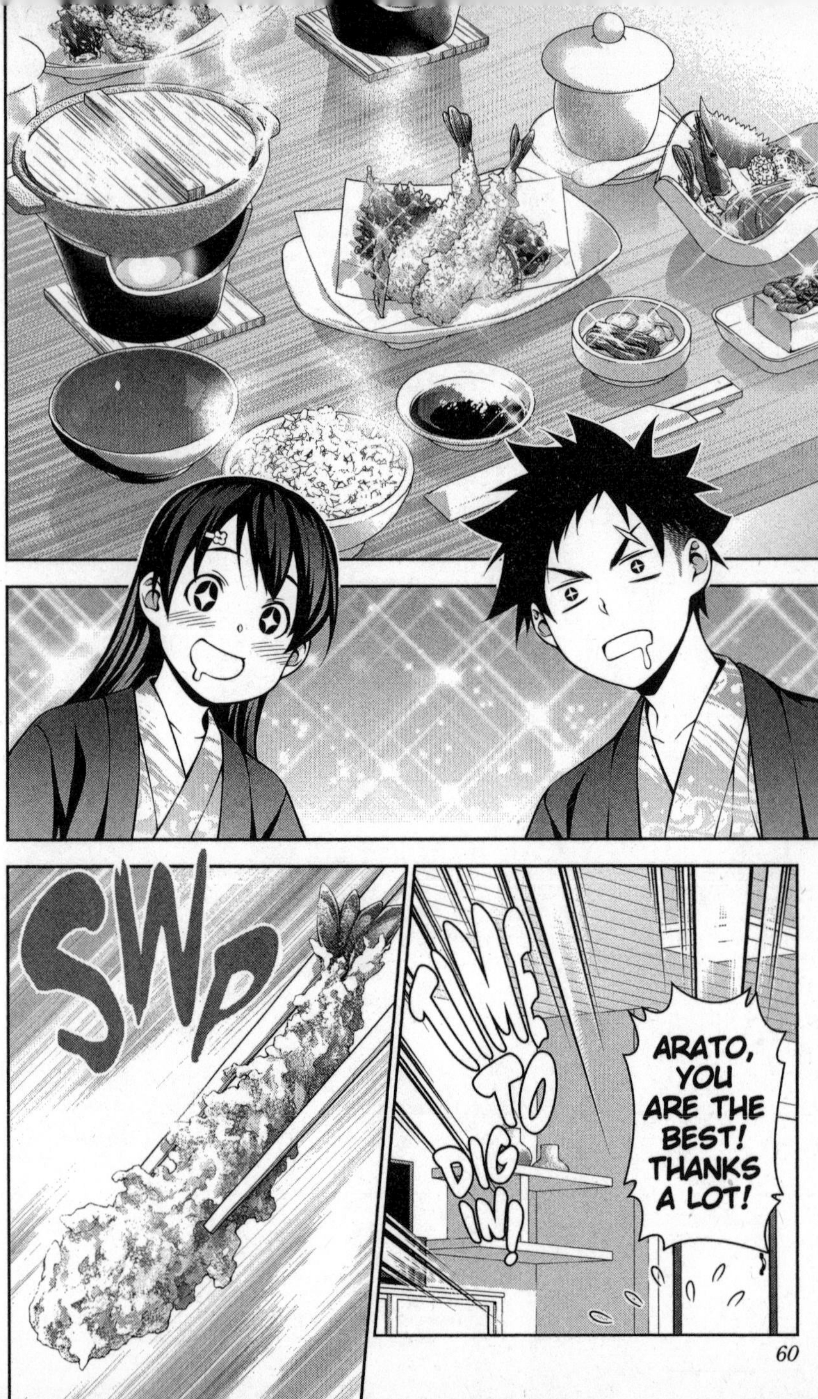
SWP
ARATO, YOU ARE THE BEST! THANKS A LOT!
TIME TO DIG IN!

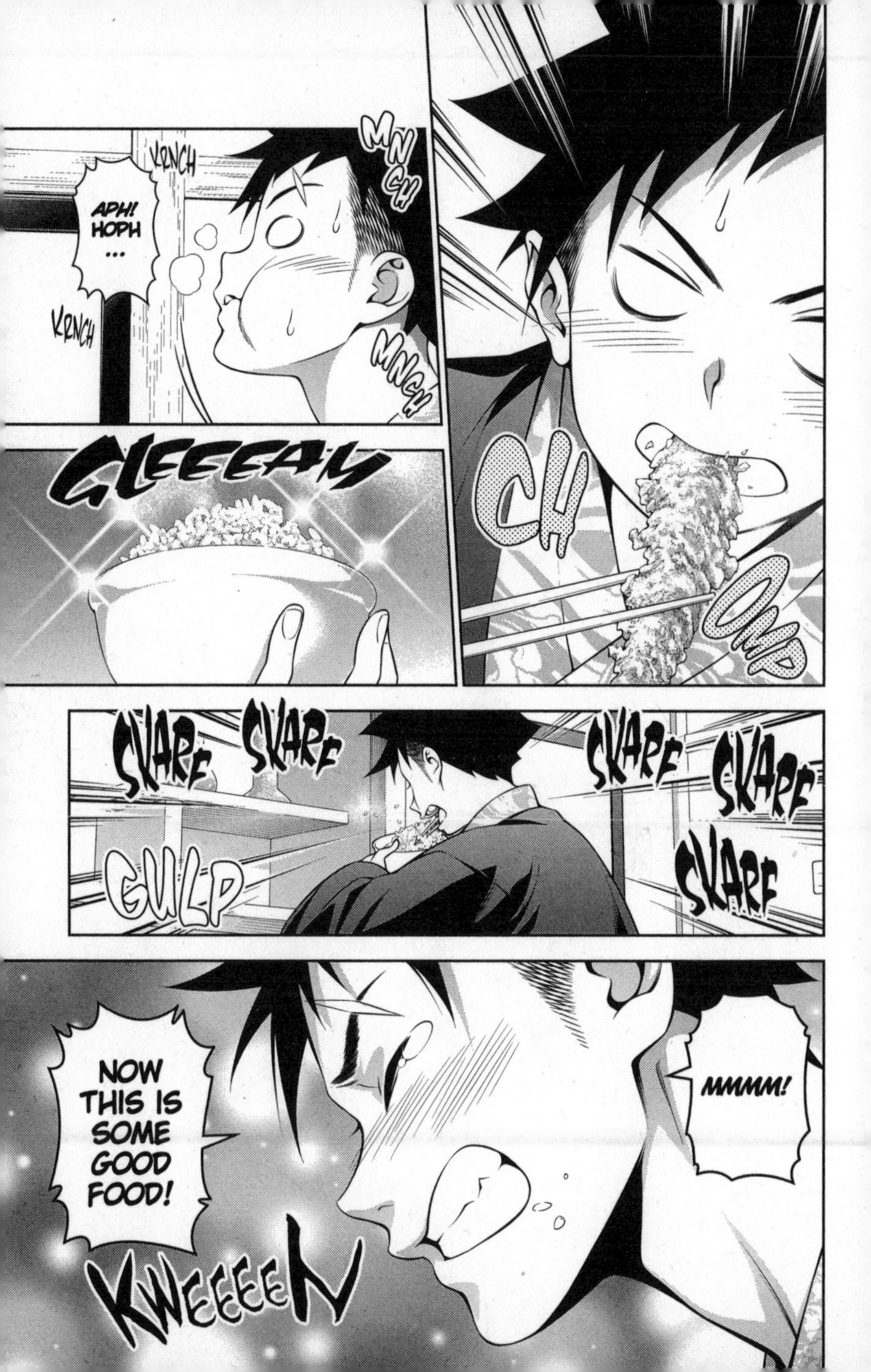
CH
OMP
MNCH
KRNCH
APH! HOPH ...
KRNCH
MNCH
GLEEEAM
SKARF
SKARF
SKARF
SKARF
SKARF
GULP
MMMM!
NOW THIS IS SOME GOOD FOOD!
KWEEEEN

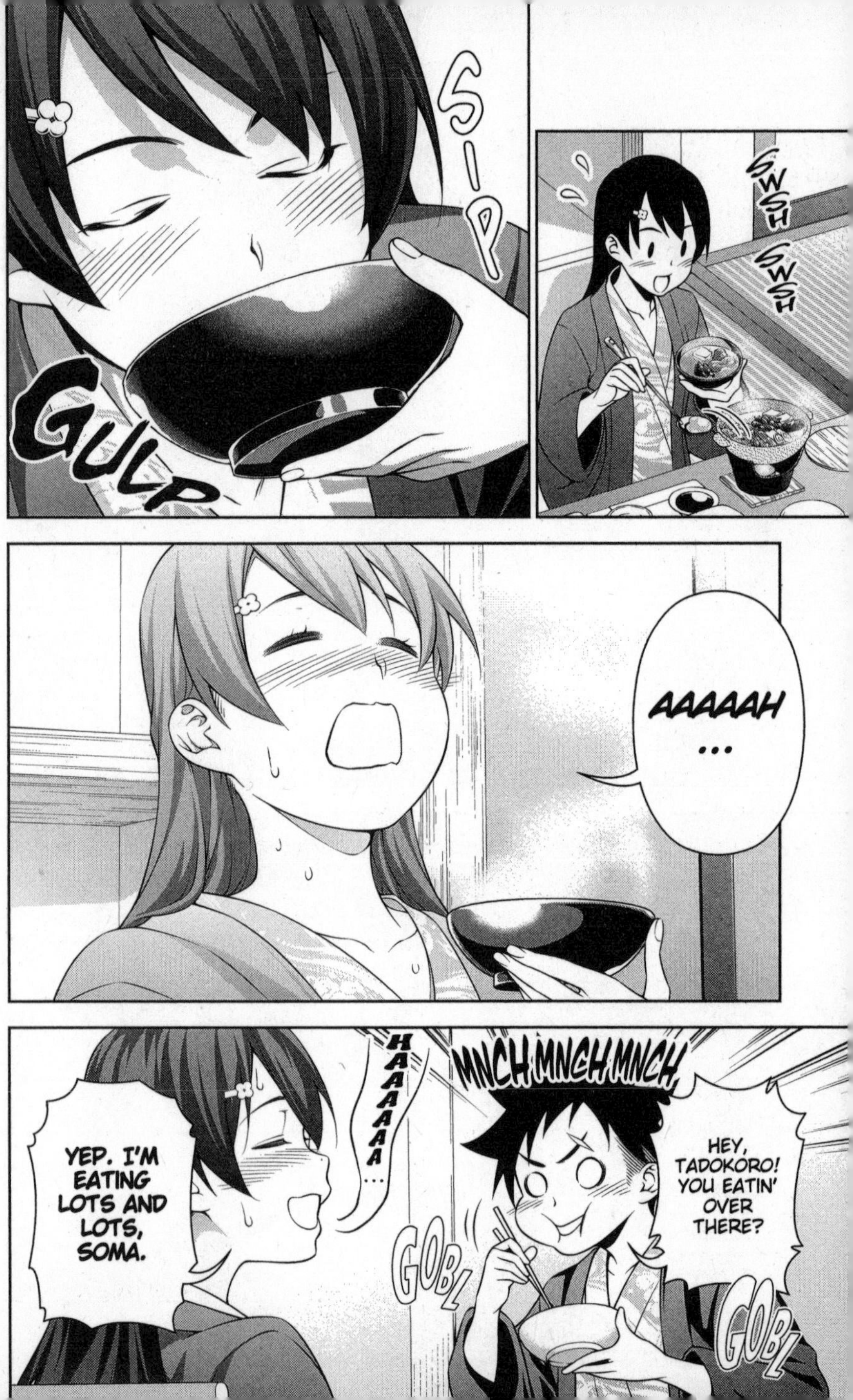
SWSH SWSH
SIP
GULP
AAAAAH ...
MNCH MNCH MNCH
HEY, TADOKORO! YOU EATIN' OVER THERE?
GOBL
GOBL
HAAAAAAA...
YEP. I'M EATING LOTS AND LOTS, SOMA.

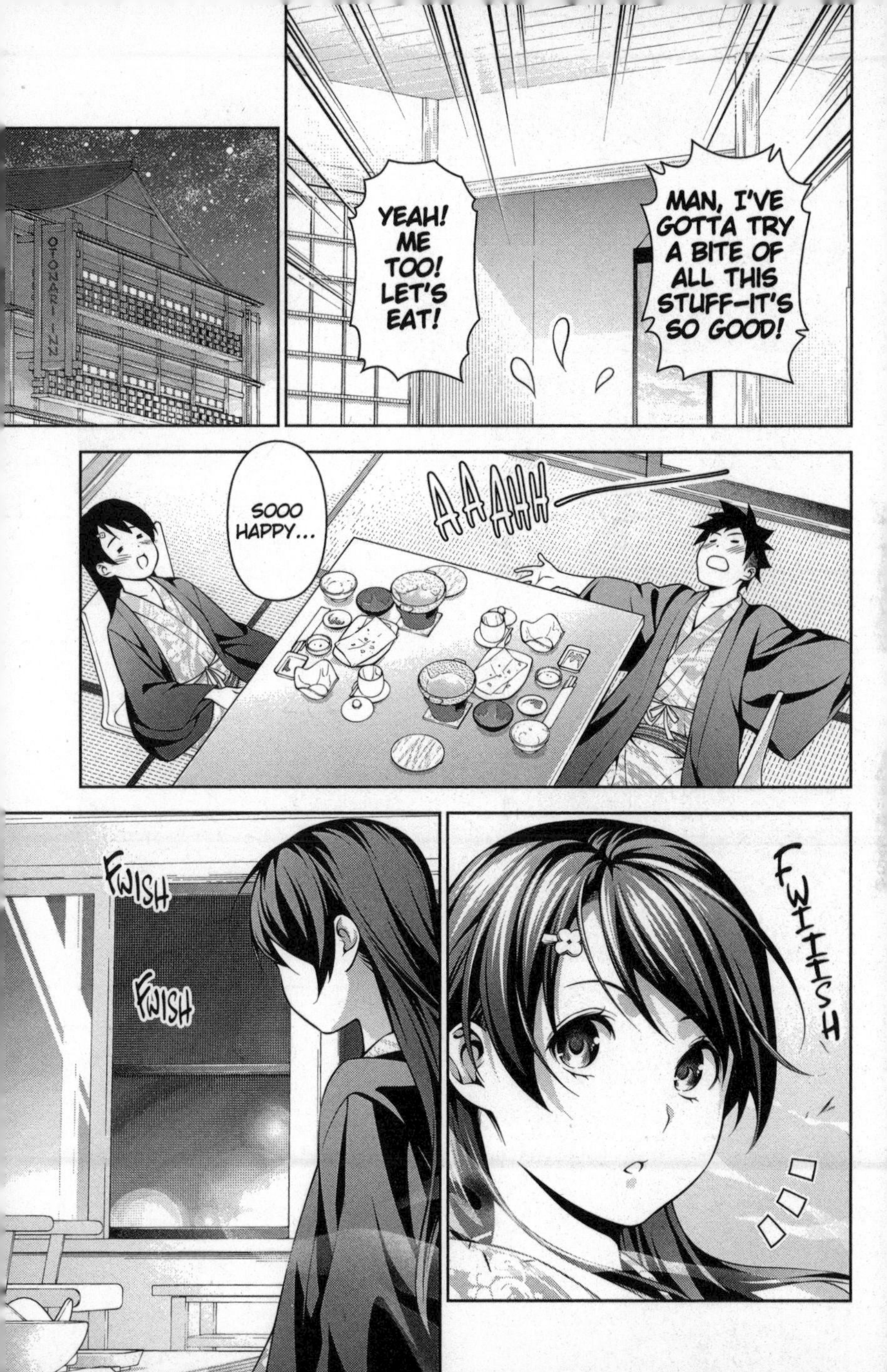
MAN, I'VE GOTTA TRY A BITE OF ALL THIS STUFF–IT'S SO GOOD!
YEAH! ME TOO! LET'S EAT!
OTONARI INN
AAAHH
SOOO HAPPY...
FWIIISH
FWISH
FWISH

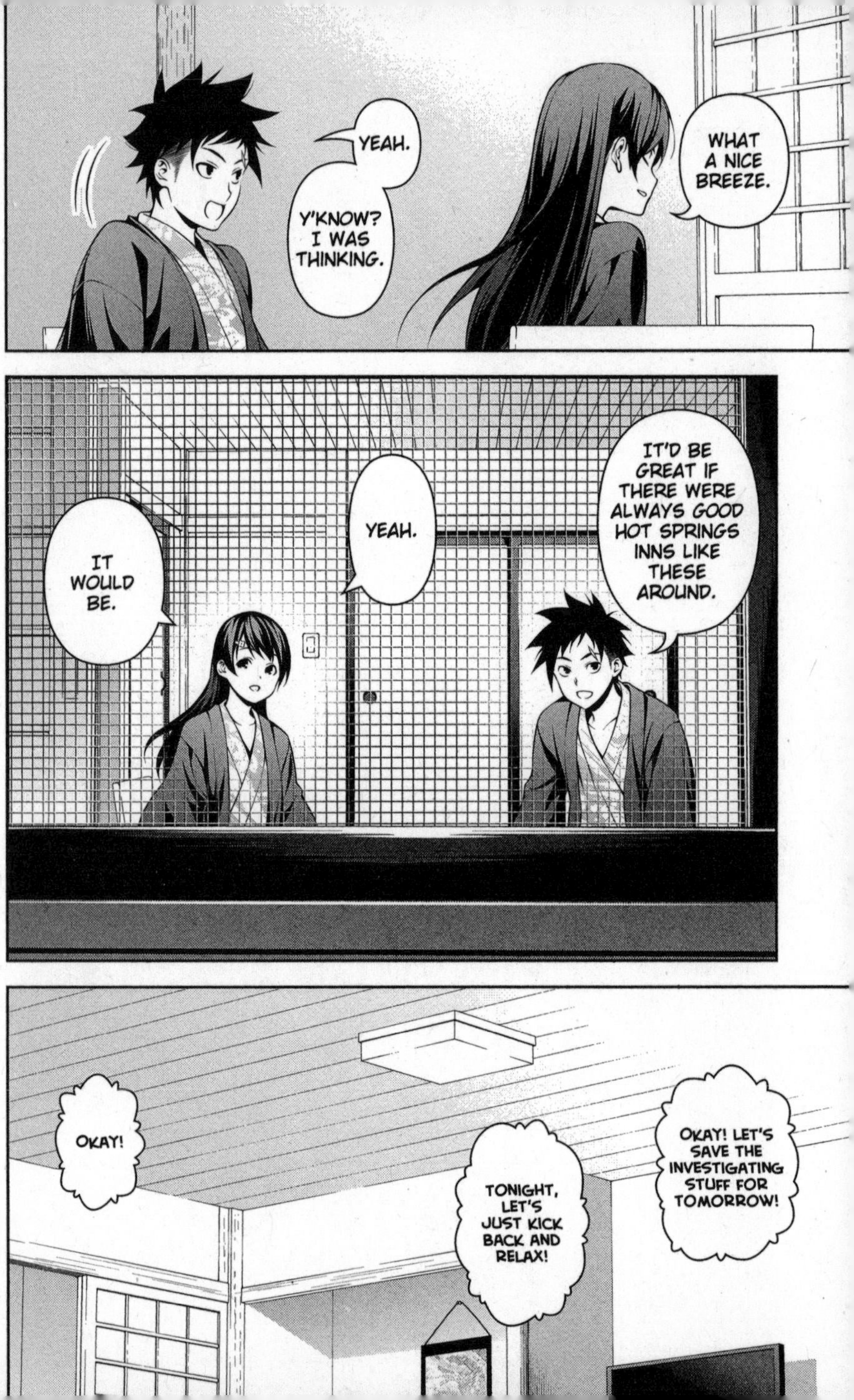
WHAT A NICE BREEZE.
YEAH.
Y'KNOW? I WAS THINKING.
IT'D BE GREAT IF THERE WERE ALWAYS GOOD HOT SPRINGS INNS LIKE THESE AROUND.
YEAH.
IT WOULD BE.
OKAY! LET'S SAVE THE INVESTIGATING STUFF FOR TOMORROW!
TONIGHT, LET'S JUST KICK BACK AND RELAX!
OKAY!

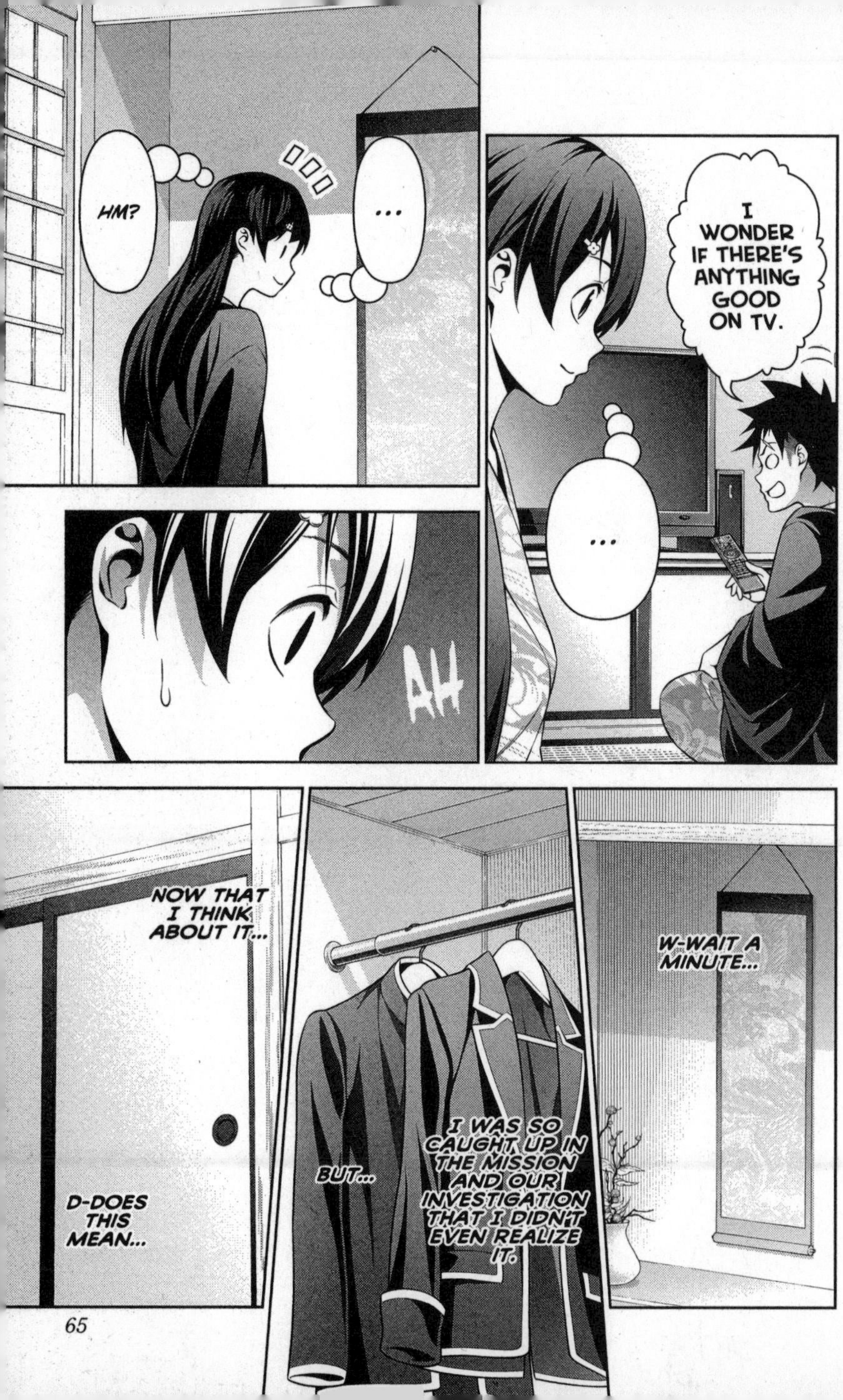
I WONDER IF THERE'S ANYTHING GOOD ON TV.
...
...
HM?
AH
W-WAIT A MINUTE...
I WAS SO CAUGHT UP IN THE MISSION AND OUR INVESTIGATION THAT I DIDN'T EVEN REALIZE IT.
BUT...
NOW THAT I THINK ABOUT IT...
D-DOES THIS MEAN...

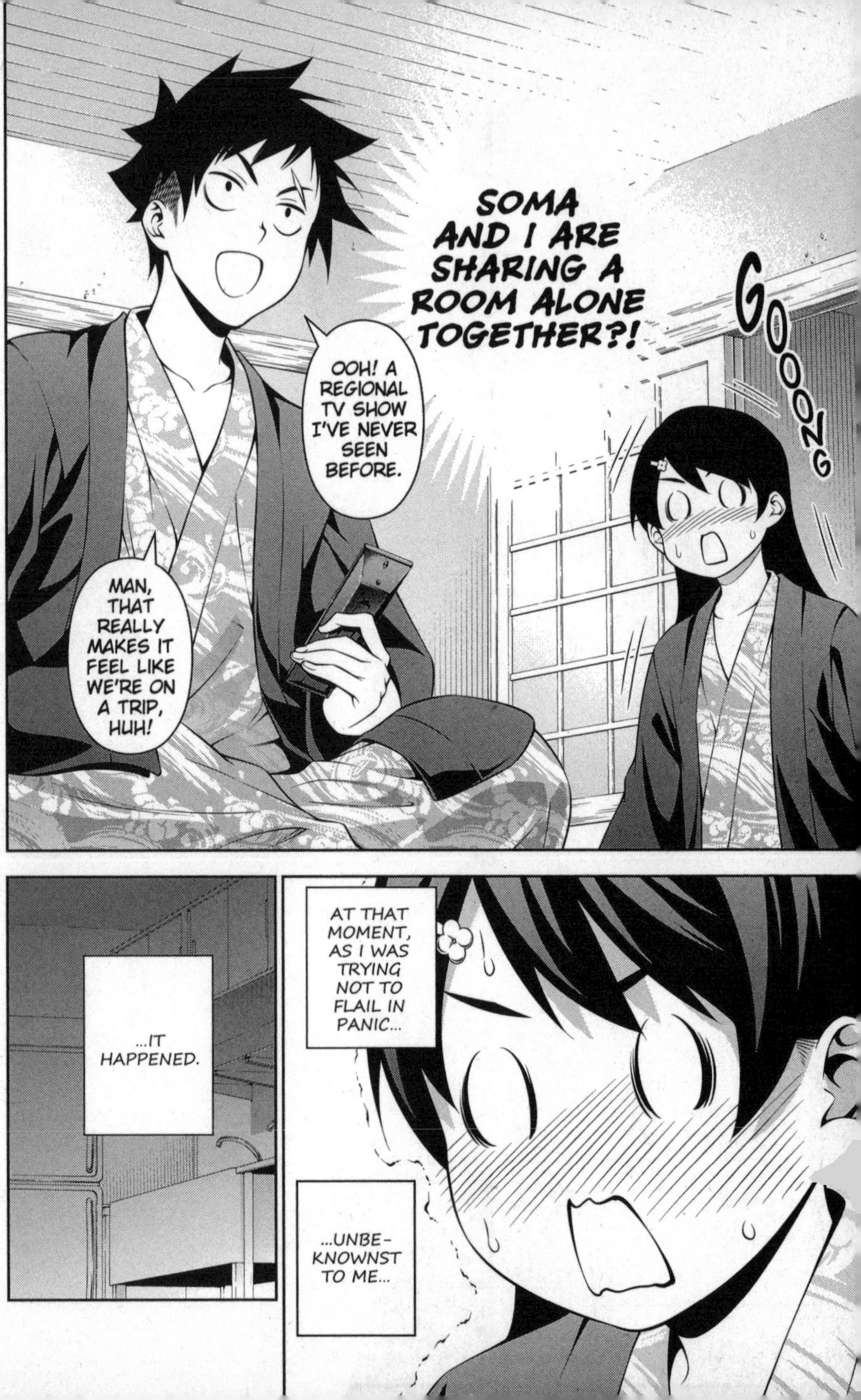
GOOOONG
SOMA AND I ARE SHARING A ROOM ALONE TOGETHER?!
OOH! A REGIONAL TV SHOW I'VE NEVER SEEN BEFORE.
MAN, THAT REALLY MAKES IT FEEL LIKE WE'RE ON A TRIP, HUH!
AT THAT MOMENT, AS I WAS TRYING NOT TO FLAIL IN PANIC...
...UNBE-KNOWNST TO ME...
...IT HAPPENED.

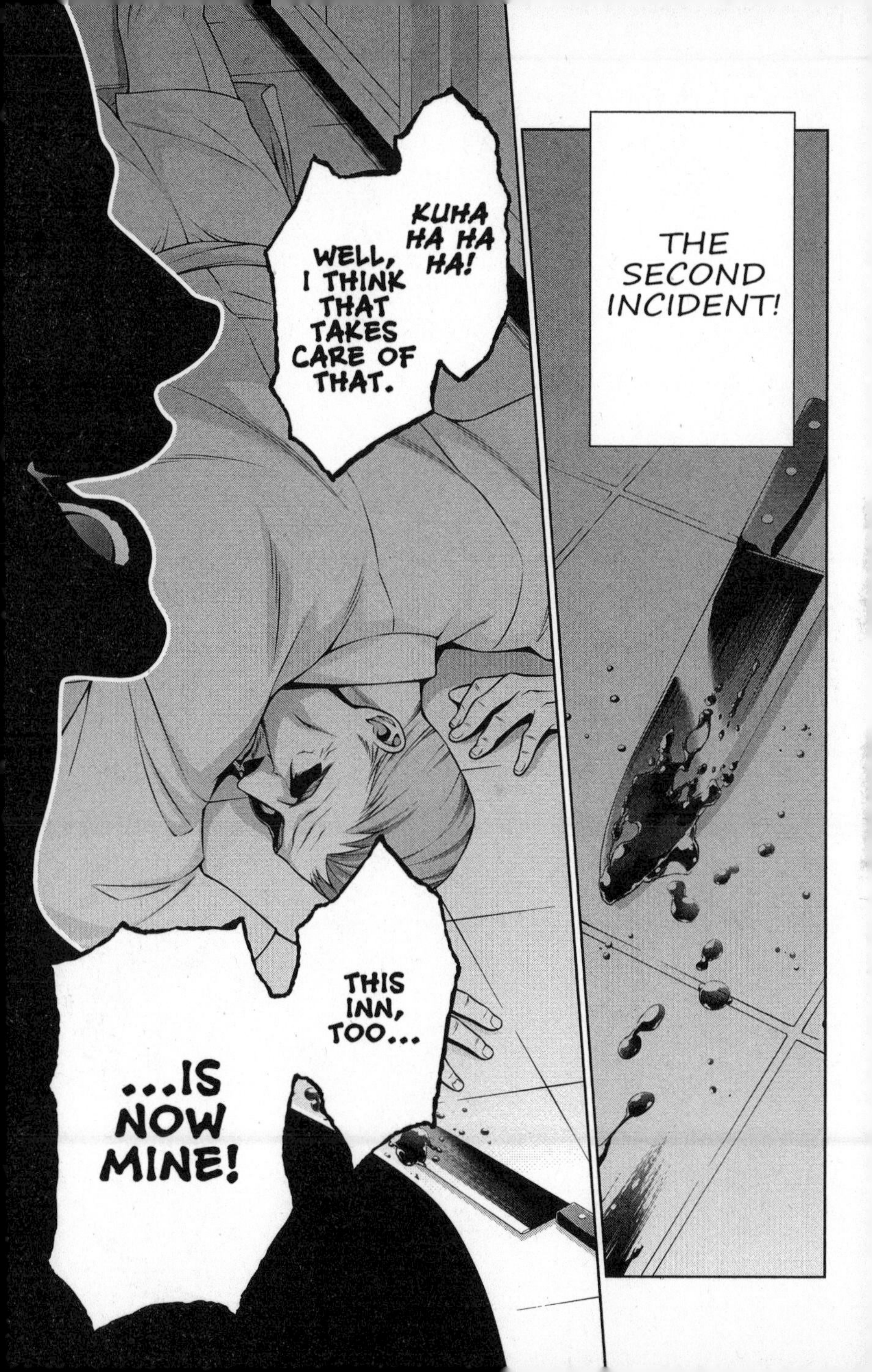
THE SECOND INCIDENT!
KUHA HA HA HA!
WELL, I THINK THAT TAKES CARE OF THAT.
THIS INN, TOO...
...IS NOW MINE!

THE CASE OF MEGUMI TADOKORO

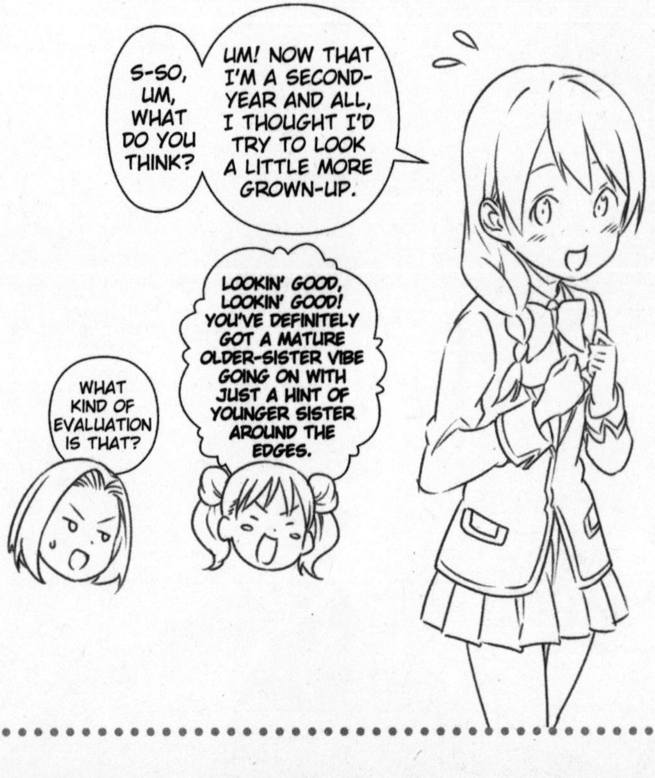
UM! NOW THAT I'M A SECOND-YEAR AND ALL, I THOUGHT I'D TRY TO LOOK A LITTLE MORE GROWN-UP.
S-SO, UM, WHAT DO YOU THINK?
LOOKIN' GOOD, LOOKIN' GOOD! YOU'VE DEFINITELY GOT A MATURE OLDER-SISTER VIBE GOING ON WITH JUST A HINT OF YOUNGER SISTER AROUND THE EDGES.
WHAT KIND OF EVALUATION IS THAT?

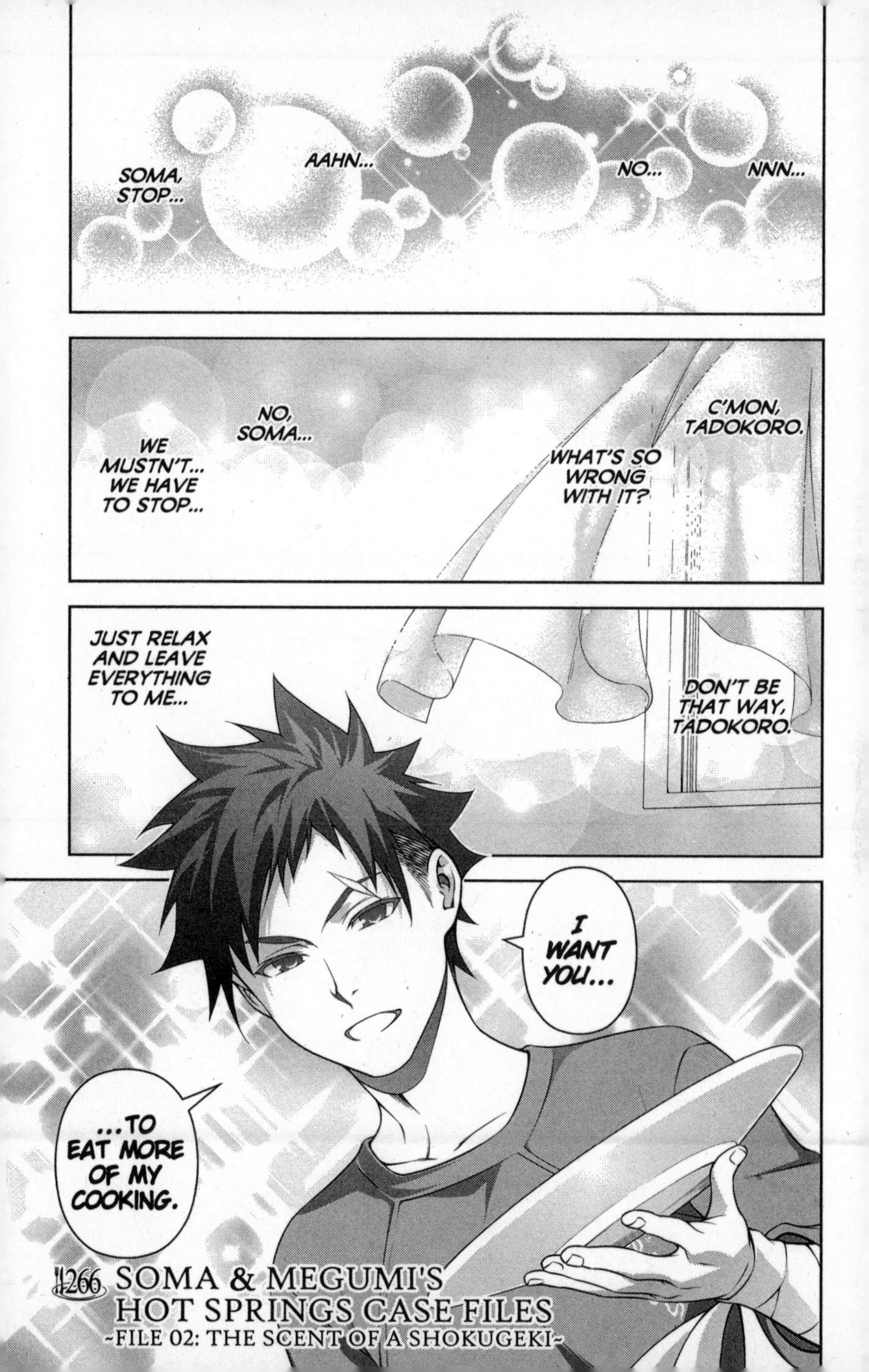
NNN...
NO...
AAHN...
SOMA, STOP...
C'MON, TADOKORO.
WHAT'S SO WRONG WITH IT?
NO, SOMA...
WE MUSTN'T... WE HAVE TO STOP...
DON'T BE THAT WAY, TADOKORO.
JUST RELAX AND LEAVE EVERYTHING TO ME...
I WANT YOU...
...TO EAT MORE OF MY COOKING.

1266 SOMA & MEGUMI'S HOT SPRINGS CASE FILES
~FILE 02: THE SCENT OF A SHOKUGEKI~

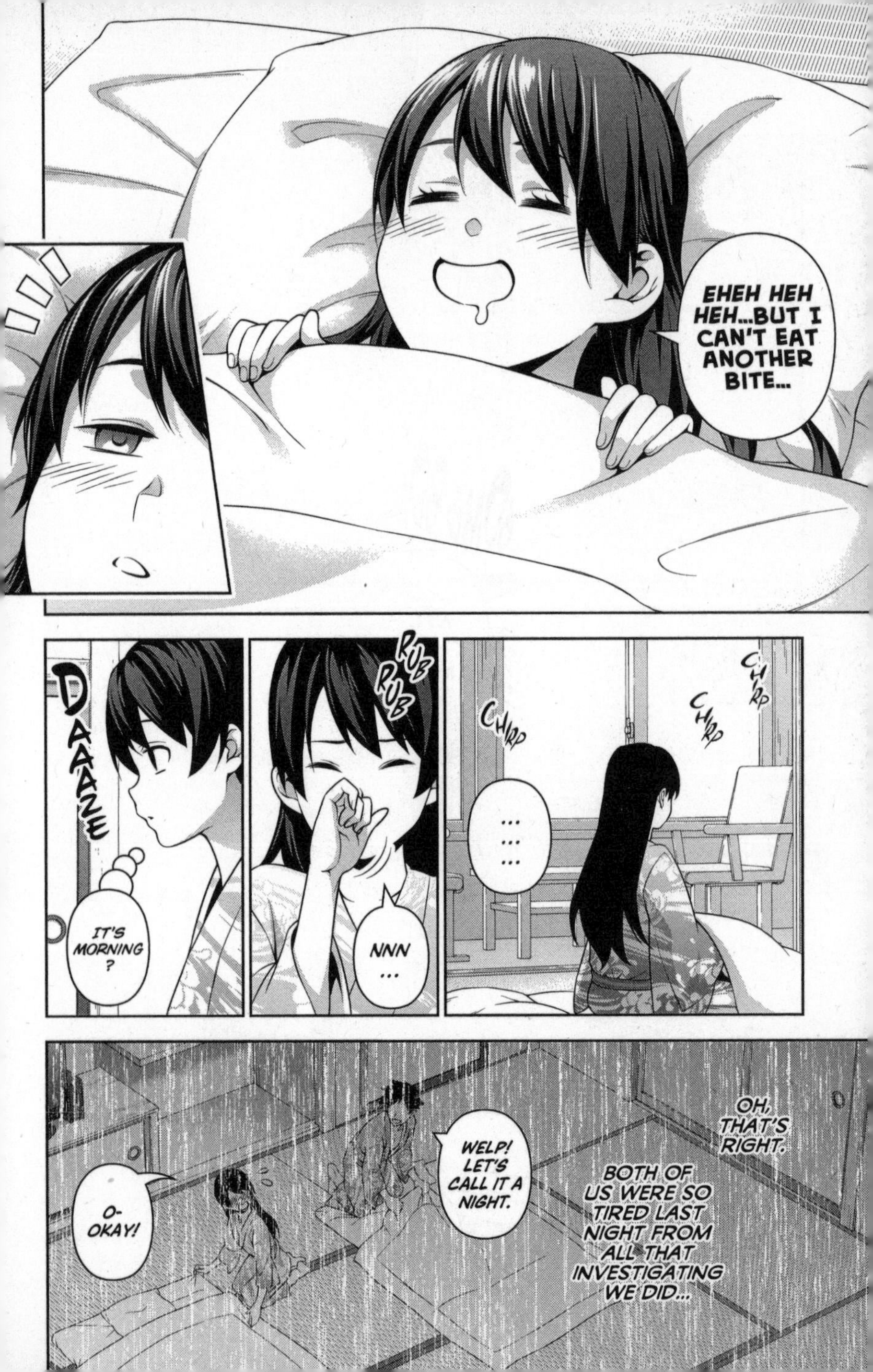
EHEH HEH HEH...BUT I CAN'T EAT ANOTHER BITE...
CHIRP
CHIRP
CHIRP
... ...
RUB RUB
NNN ...
DAAAZE
IT'S MORNING ?
OH, THAT'S RIGHT.
BOTH OF US WERE SO TIRED LAST NIGHT FROM ALL THAT INVESTIGATING WE DID...
WELP! LET'S CALL IT A NIGHT.
O-OKAY!

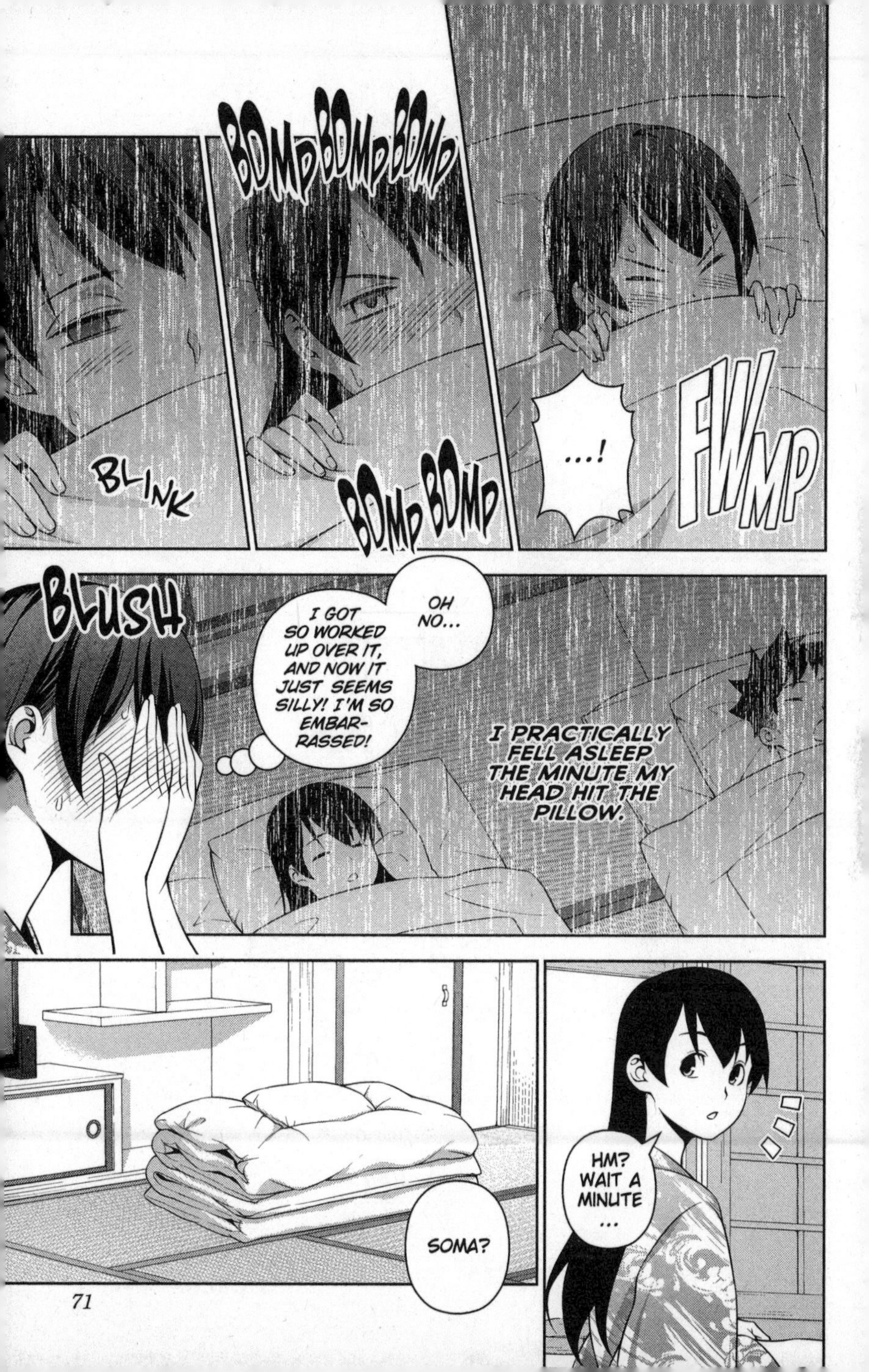

FWMP
...!
BOMP BOMP BOMP
BOMP BOMP
BLINK
I PRACTICALLY FELL ASLEEP THE MINUTE MY HEAD HIT THE PILLOW.
OH NO...
I GOT SO WORKED UP OVER IT, AND NOW IT JUST SEEMS SILLY! I'M SO EMBAR-RASSED!
BLUSH
HM? WAIT A MINUTE ...
SOMA?

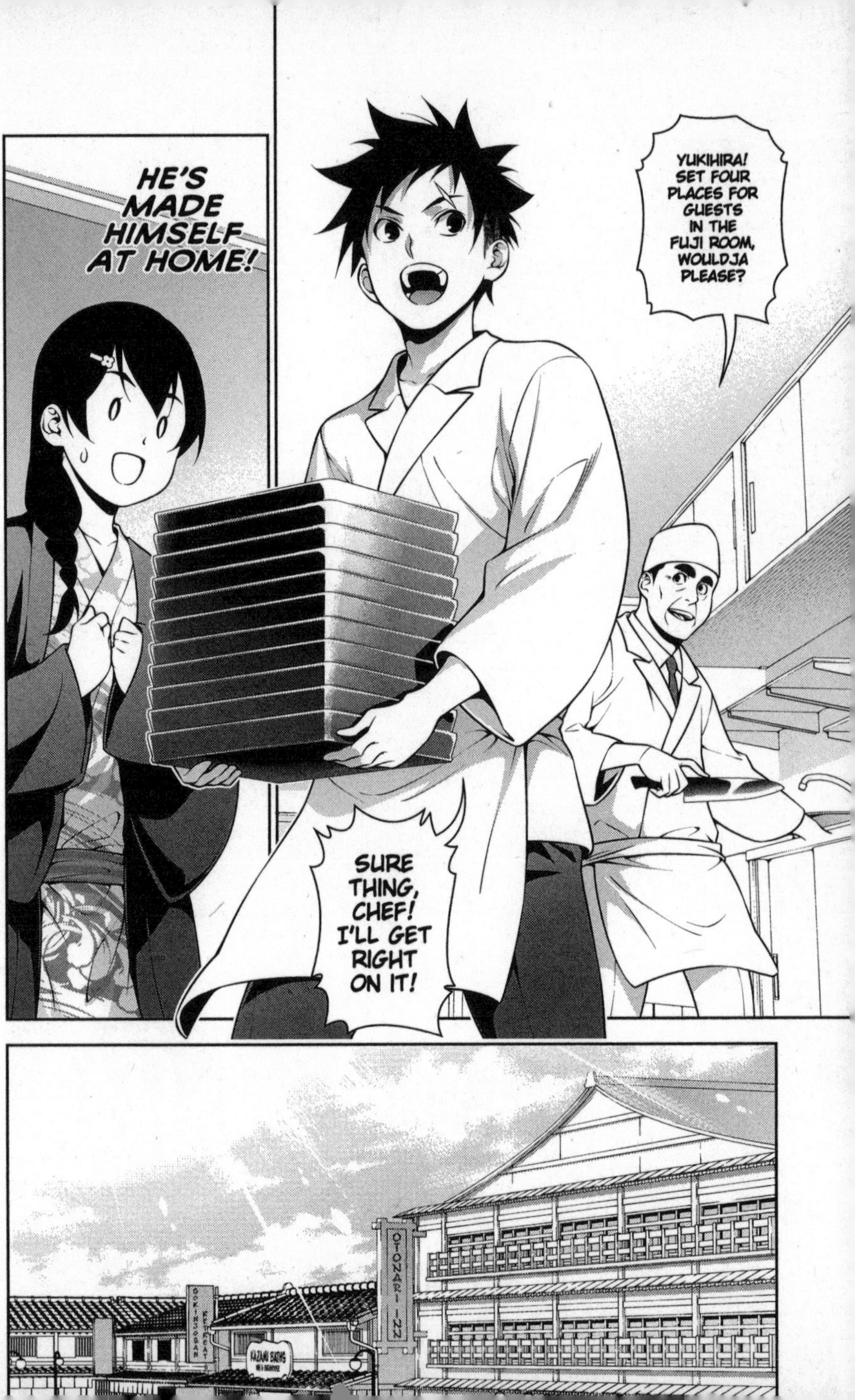
YUKIHIRA! SET FOUR PLACES FOR GUESTS IN THE FUJI ROOM, WOULDJA PLEASE?
SURE THING, CHEF! I'LL GET RIGHT ON IT!
HE'S MADE HIMSELF AT HOME!
OTONARI INN
KAZAMI BATHS
GOKINJOSAN RETREAT

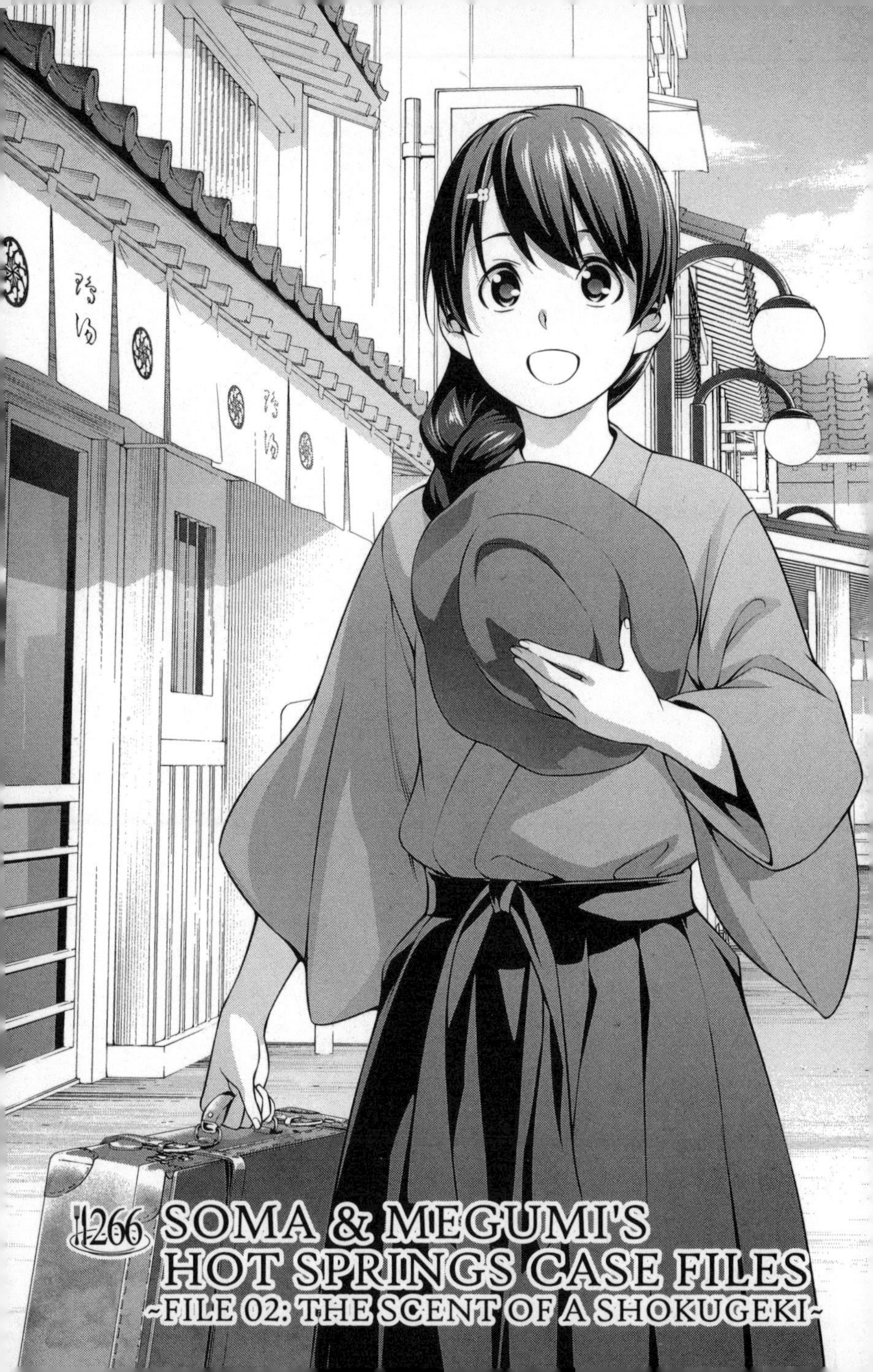
266
SOMA & MEGUMI'S HOT SPRINGS CASE FILES
~FILE 02: THE SCENT OF A SHOKUGEKI~

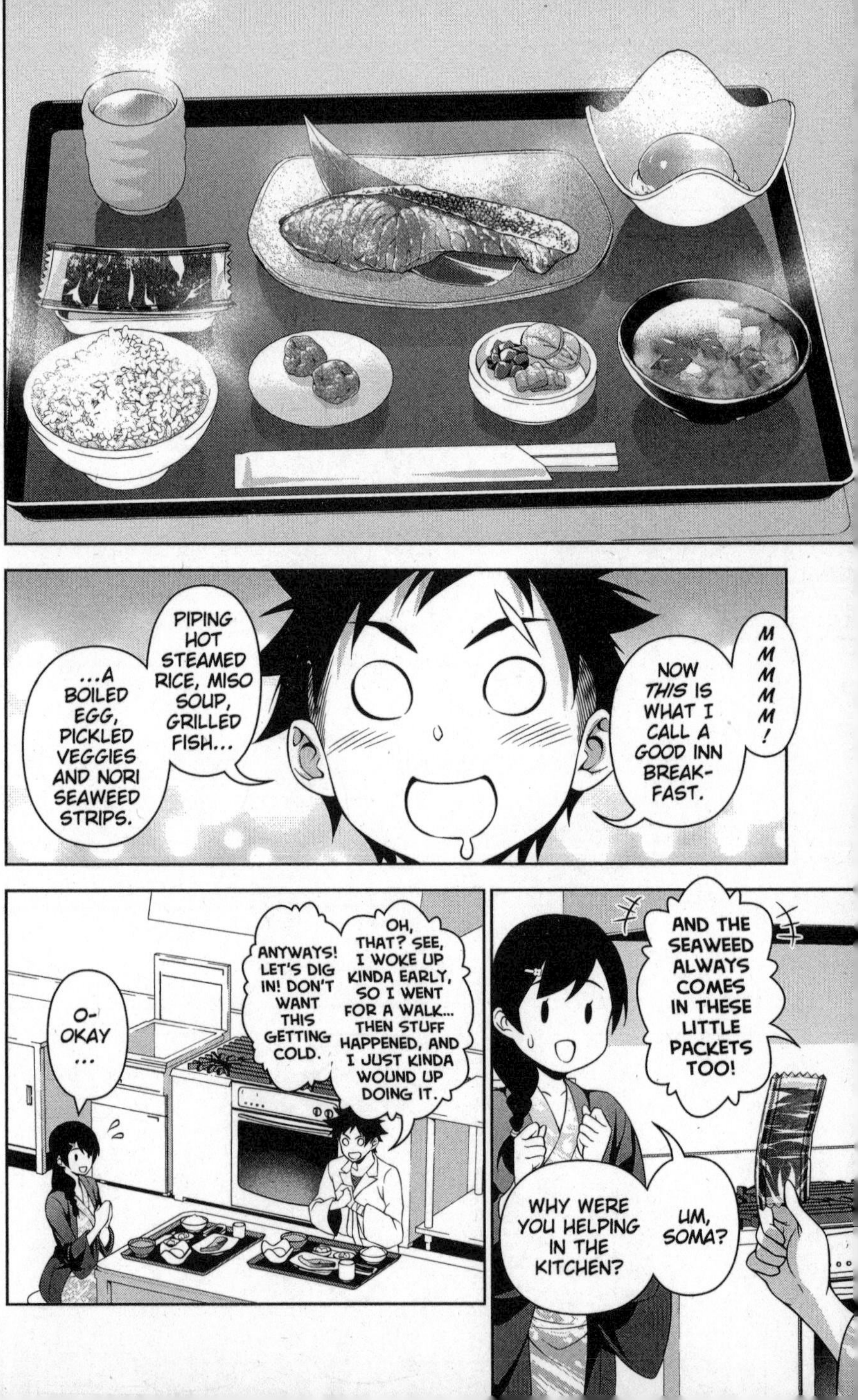
MMMMMM!
NOW THIS IS WHAT I CALL A GOOD INN BREAKFAST.
PIPING HOT STEAMED RICE, MISO SOUP, GRILLED FISH...
...A BOILED EGG, PICKLED VEGGIES AND NORI SEAWEED STRIPS.
AND THE SEAWEED ALWAYS COMES IN THESE LITTLE PACKETS TOO!
UM, SOMA?
WHY WERE YOU HELPING IN THE KITCHEN?
OH, THAT? SEE, I WOKE UP KINDA EARLY, SO I WENT FOR A WALK... THEN STUFF HAPPENED, AND I JUST KINDA WOUND UP DOING IT.
ANYWAYS! LET'S DIG IN! DON'T WANT THIS GETTING COLD.
O-OKAY...

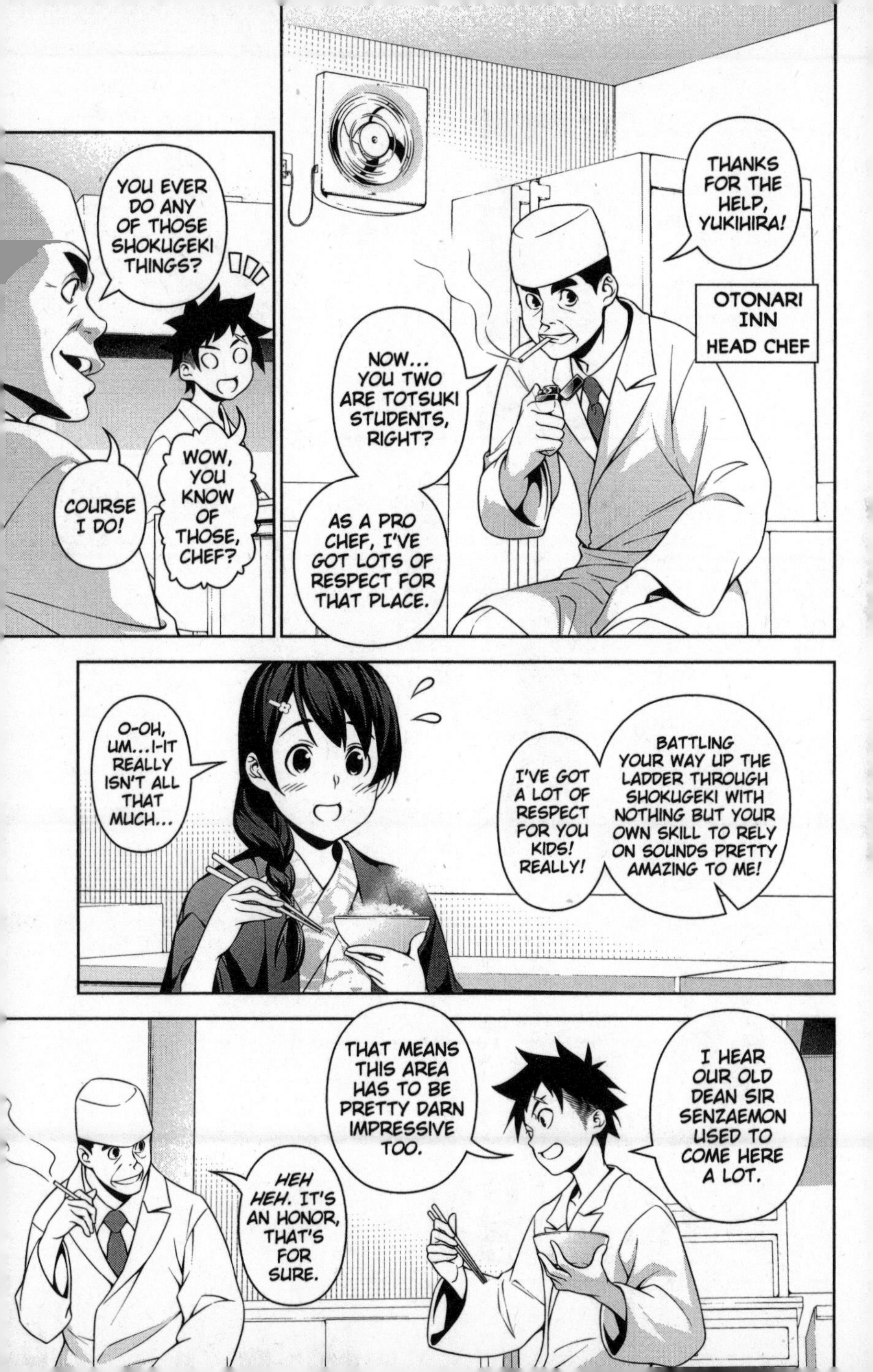
THANKS FOR THE HELP, YUKIHIRA!
OTONARI INN HEAD CHEF
NOW... YOU TWO ARE TOTSUKI STUDENTS, RIGHT?
AS A PRO CHEF, I'VE GOT LOTS OF RESPECT FOR THAT PLACE.
YOU EVER DO ANY OF THOSE SHOKUGEKI THINGS?
WOW, YOU KNOW OF THOSE, CHEF?
COURSE I DO!
BATTLING YOUR WAY UP THE LADDER THROUGH SHOKUGEKI WITH NOTHING BUT YOUR OWN SKILL TO RELY ON SOUNDS PRETTY AMAZING TO ME!
I'VE GOT A LOT OF RESPECT FOR YOU KIDS! REALLY!
O-OH, UM...I-IT REALLY ISN'T ALL THAT MUCH...
I HEAR OUR OLD DEAN SIR SENZAEMON USED TO COME HERE A LOT.
THAT MEANS THIS AREA HAS TO BE PRETTY DARN IMPRESSIVE TOO.
HEH HEH. IT'S AN HONOR, THAT'S FOR SURE.

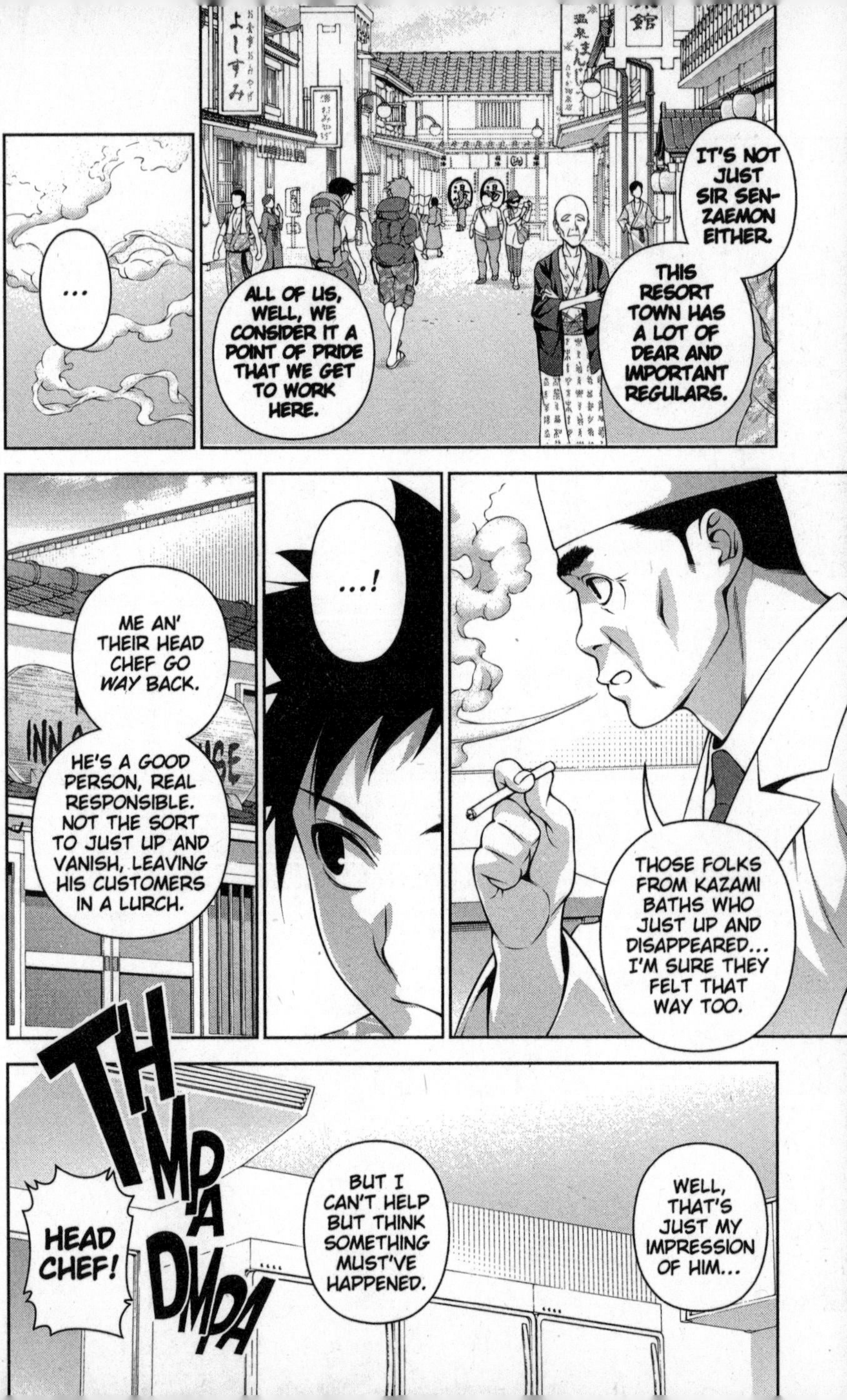
IT'S NOT JUST SIR SEN-ZAEMON EITHER.
THIS RESORT TOWN HAS A LOT OF DEAR AND IMPORTANT REGULARS.
ALL OF US, WELL, WE CONSIDER IT A POINT OF PRIDE THAT WE GET TO WORK HERE.
...
THOSE FOLKS FROM KAZAMI BATHS WHO JUST UP AND DISAPPEARED... I'M SURE THEY FELT THAT WAY TOO.
...!
ME AN' THEIR HEAD CHEF GO WAY BACK.
HE'S A GOOD PERSON, REAL RESPONSIBLE. NOT THE SORT TO JUST UP AND VANISH, LEAVING HIS CUSTOMERS IN A LURCH.
WELL, THAT'S JUST MY IMPRESSION OF HIM...
BUT I CAN'T HELP BUT THINK SOMETHING MUST'VE HAPPENED.
THMPA DMPA
HEAD CHEF!

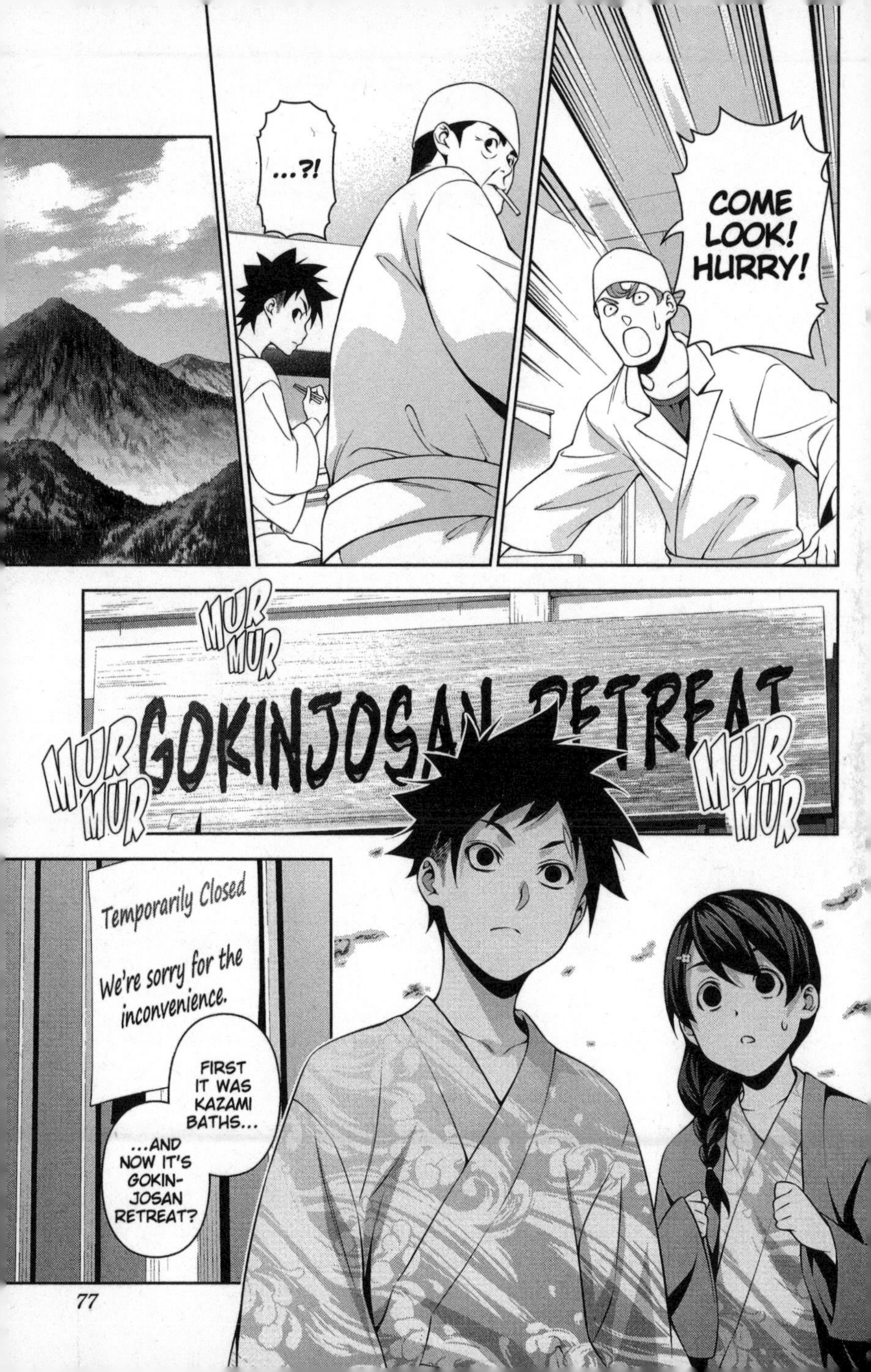
COME LOOK! HURRY!
...?!
MUR MUR
GOKINJOSAN RETREAT
MUR MUR
MUR MUR
Temporarily Closed
We're sorry for the inconvenience.
FIRST IT WAS KAZAMI BATHS...
...AND NOW IT'S GOKIN-JOSAN RETREAT?

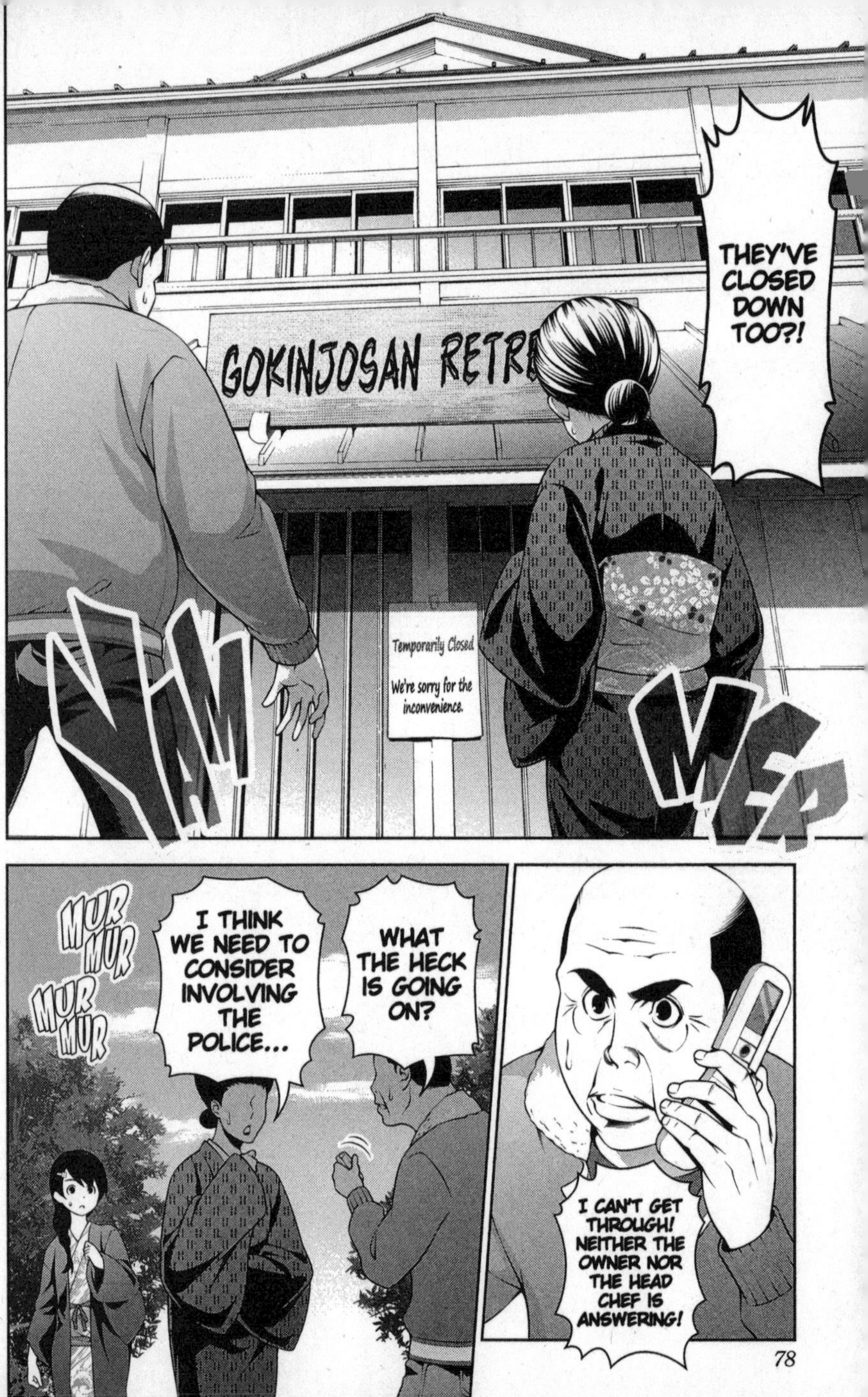
THEY'VE CLOSED DOWN TOO?!
GOKINJOSAN RETRE
Temporarily Closed
We're sorry for the inconvenience.
I CAN'T GET THROUGH! NEITHER THE OWNER NOR THE HEAD CHEF IS ANSWERING!
WHAT THE HECK IS GOING ON?
I THINK WE NEED TO CONSIDER INVOLVING THE POLICE...
MUR MUR
MUR MUR

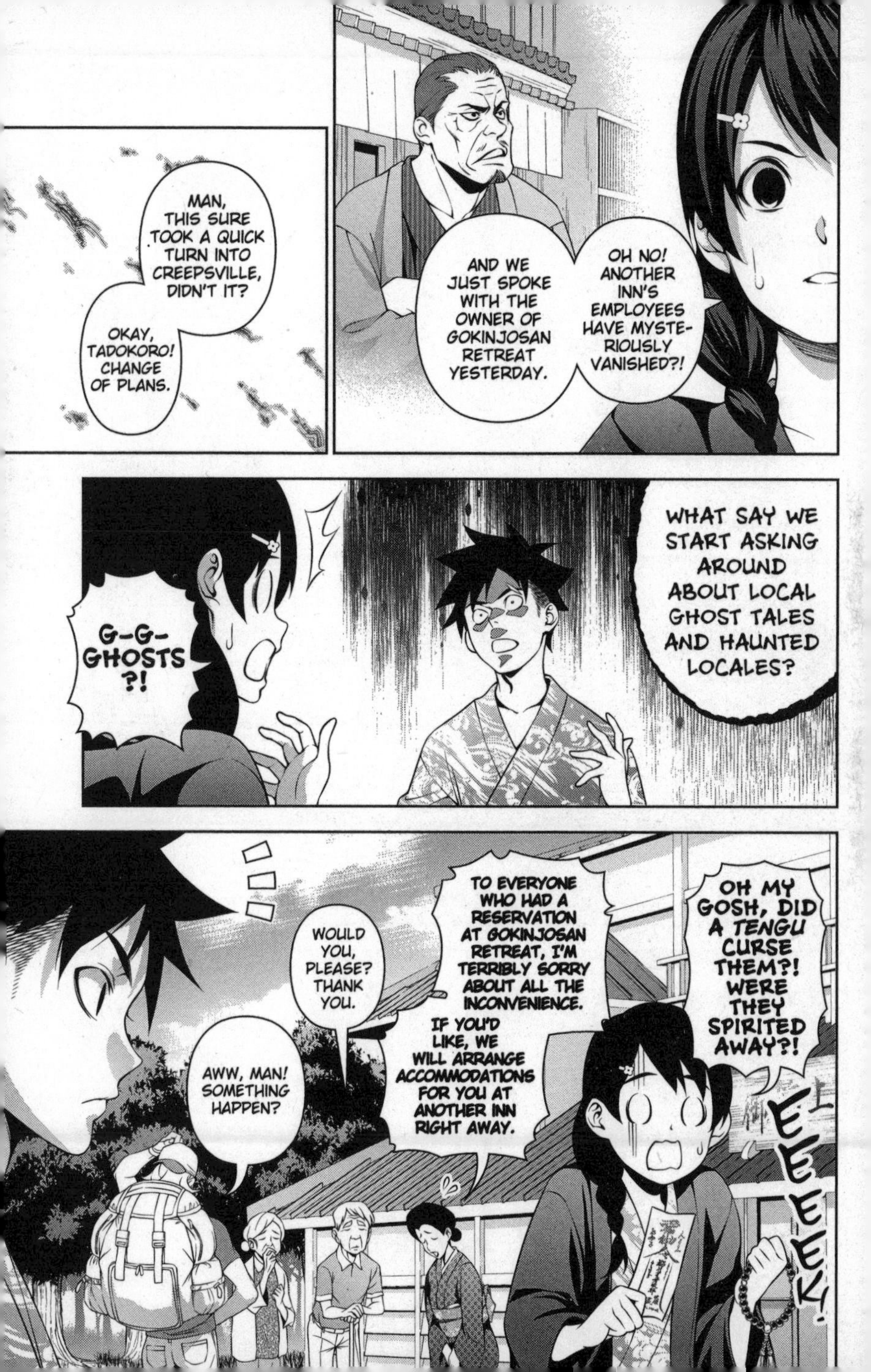
OH NO! ANOTHER INN'S EMPLOYEES HAVE MYSTERIOUSLY VANISHED?!
AND WE JUST SPOKE WITH THE OWNER OF GOKINJOSAN RETREAT YESTERDAY.
MAN, THIS SURE TOOK A QUICK TURN INTO CREEPSVILLE, DIDN'T IT?
OKAY, TADOKORO! CHANGE OF PLANS.
WHAT SAY WE START ASKING AROUND ABOUT LOCAL GHOST TALES AND HAUNTED LOCALES?
G-G-GHOSTS?!
OH MY GOSH, DID A *TENGU* CURSE THEM?! WERE THEY SPIRITED AWAY?!
EEEEEK!
TO EVERYONE WHO HAD A RESERVATION AT GOKINJOSAN RETREAT, I'M TERRIBLY SORRY ABOUT ALL THE INCONVENIENCE.
IF YOU'D LIKE, WE WILL ARRANGE ACCOMMODATIONS FOR YOU AT ANOTHER INN RIGHT AWAY.
WOULD YOU, PLEASE? THANK YOU.
AWW, MAN! SOMETHING HAPPEN?

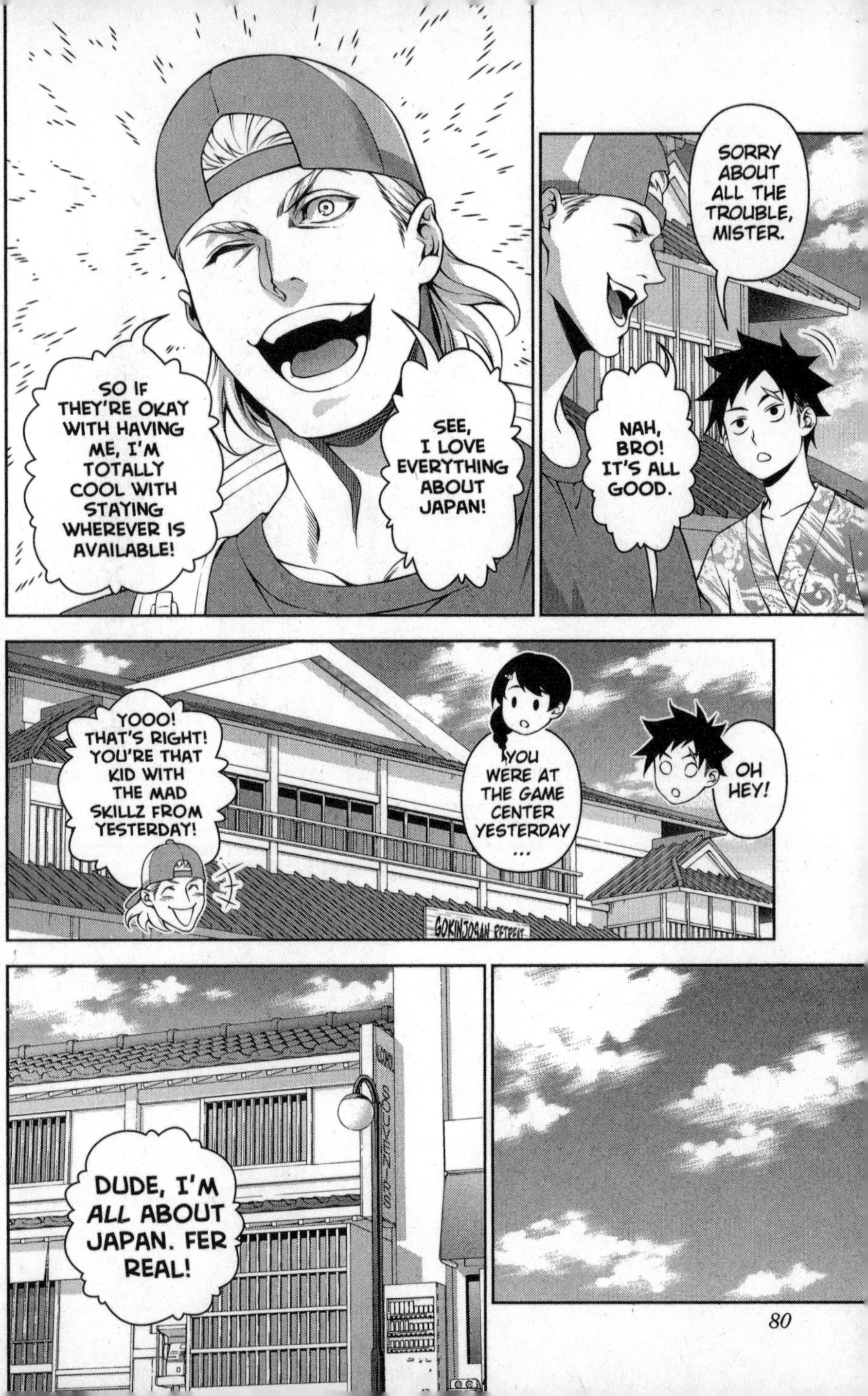
SORRY ABOUT ALL THE TROUBLE, MISTER.
NAH, BRO! IT'S ALL GOOD.
SEE, I LOVE EVERYTHING ABOUT JAPAN!
SO IF THEY'RE OKAY WITH HAVING ME, I'M TOTALLY COOL WITH STAYING WHEREVER IS AVAILABLE!
OH HEY!
YOU WERE AT THE GAME CENTER YESTERDAY ...
YOOO! THAT'S RIGHT! YOU'RE THAT KID WITH THE MAD SKILLZ FROM YESTERDAY!
GOKINJOGAN RETREAT
DUDE, I'M *ALL* ABOUT JAPAN. FER REAL!

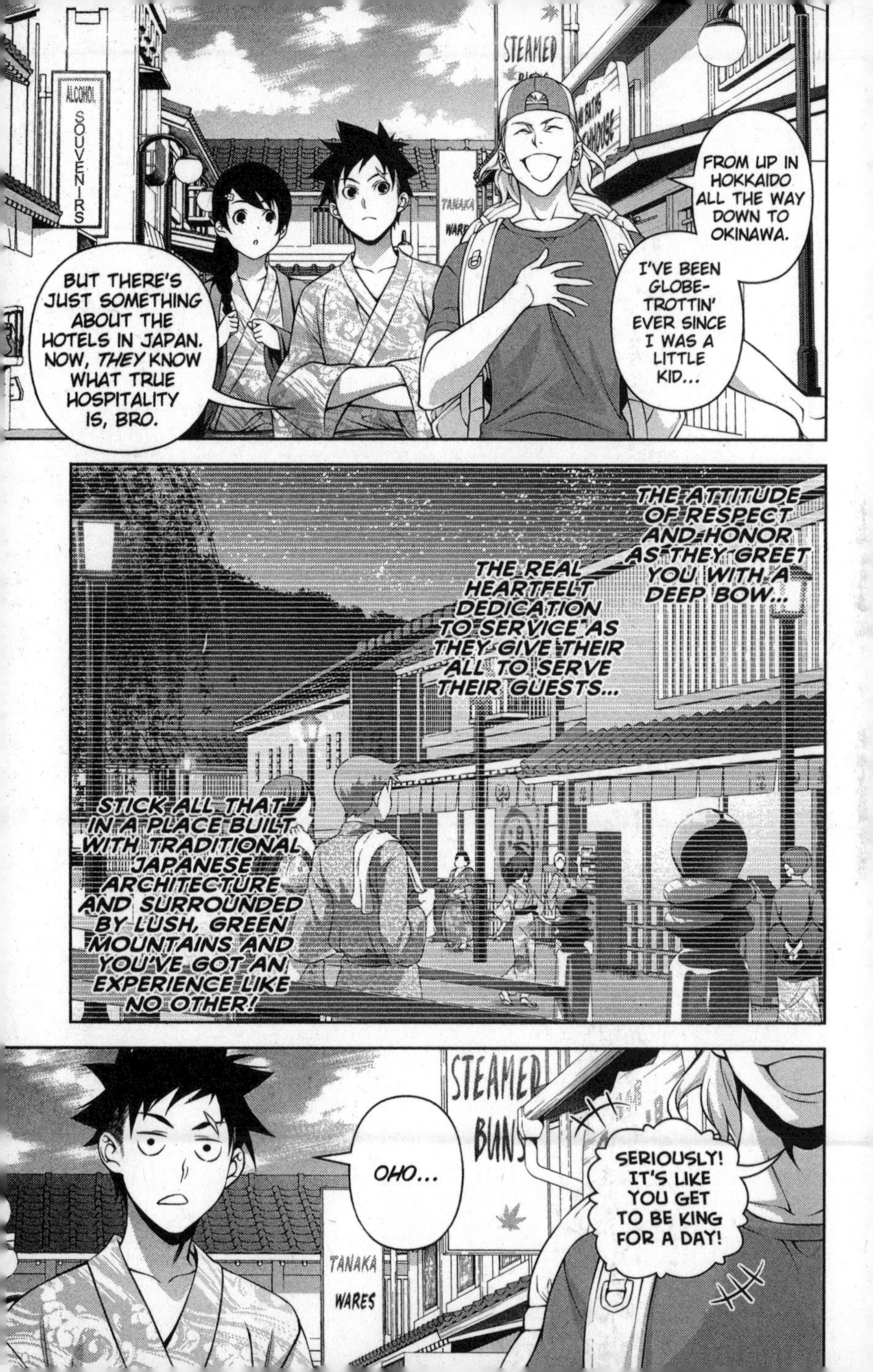
STEAMED
ALCOHOL
SOUVENIRS
TANAKA WARE
FROM UP IN HOKKAIDO ALL THE WAY DOWN TO OKINAWA.
I'VE BEEN GLOBE-TROTTIN' EVER SINCE I WAS A LITTLE KID...
BUT THERE'S JUST SOMETHING ABOUT THE HOTELS IN JAPAN. NOW, *THEY* KNOW WHAT TRUE HOSPITALITY IS, BRO.
THE ATTITUDE OF RESPECT AND HONOR AS THEY GREET YOU WITH A DEEP BOW...
THE REAL HEARTFELT DEDICATION TO SERVICE AS THEY GIVE THEIR ALL TO SERVE THEIR GUESTS...
STICK ALL THAT IN A PLACE BUILT WITH TRADITIONAL JAPANESE ARCHITECTURE AND SURROUNDED BY LUSH, GREEN MOUNTAINS AND YOU'VE GOT AN EXPERIENCE LIKE NO OTHER!
STEAMED BUNS
SERIOUSLY! IT'S LIKE YOU GET TO BE KING FOR A DAY!
OHO...
TANAKA WARES

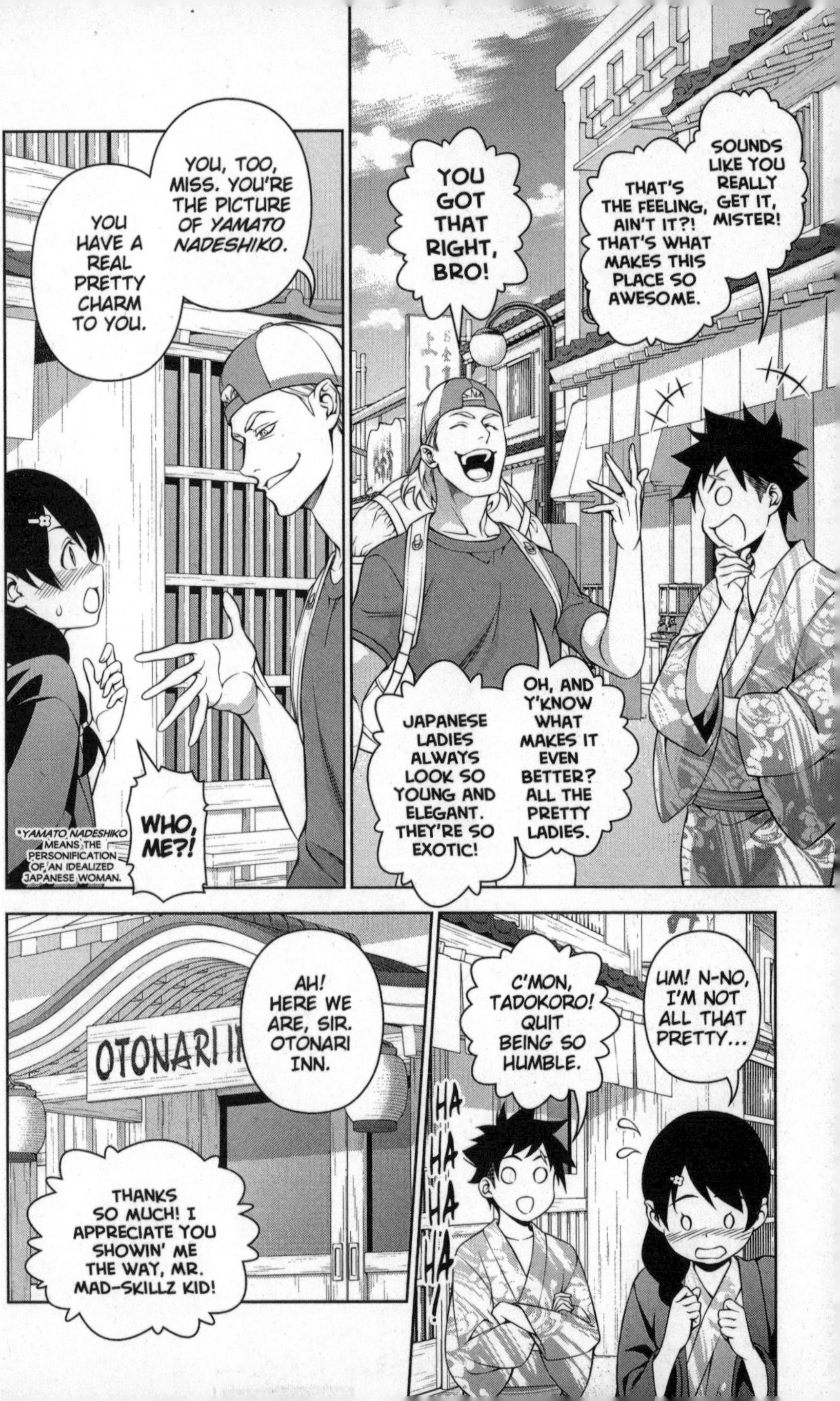
SOUNDS LIKE YOU REALLY GET IT, MISTER!
THAT'S THE FEELING, AIN'T IT?! THAT'S WHAT MAKES THIS PLACE SO AWESOME.
YOU GOT THAT RIGHT, BRO!
OH, AND Y'KNOW WHAT MAKES IT EVEN BETTER? ALL THE PRETTY LADIES.
JAPANESE LADIES ALWAYS LOOK SO YOUNG AND ELEGANT. THEY'RE SO EXOTIC!
YOU, TOO, MISS. YOU'RE THE PICTURE OF *YAMATO NADESHIKO*.
YOU HAVE A REAL PRETTY CHARM TO YOU.
WHO, ME?!
*YAMATO NADESHIKO MEANS THE PERSONIFICATION OF AN IDEALIZED JAPANESE WOMAN.
UM! N-NO, I'M NOT ALL THAT PRETTY...
C'MON, TADOKORO! QUIT BEING SO HUMBLE.
HA HA HA HA HA!
AH! HERE WE ARE, SIR. OTONARI INN.
OTONARI I
THANKS SO MUCH! I APPRECIATE YOU SHOWIN' ME THE WAY, MR. MAD-SKILLZ KID!

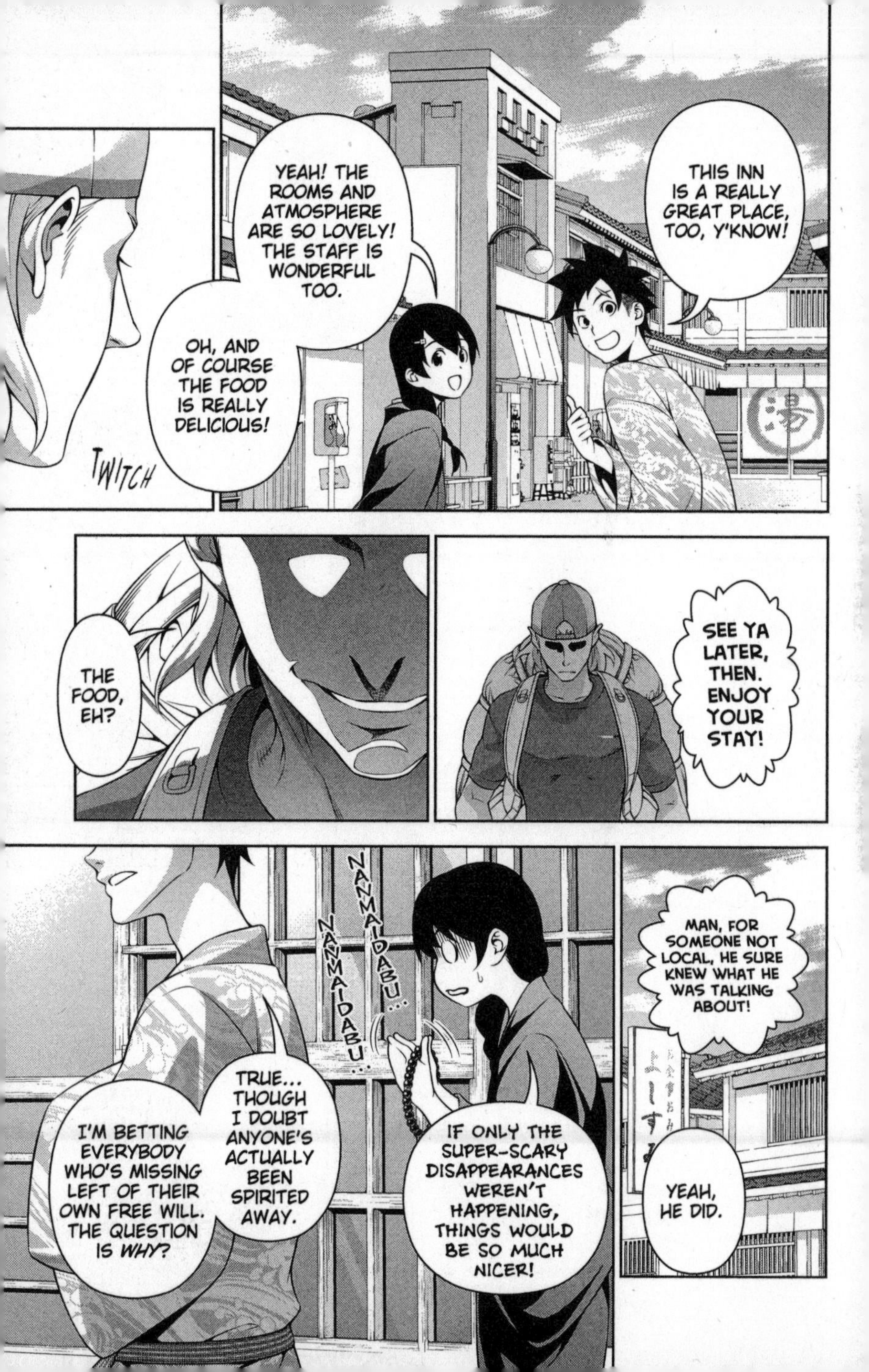
THIS INN IS A REALLY GREAT PLACE, TOO, Y'KNOW!
YEAH! THE ROOMS AND ATMOSPHERE ARE SO LOVELY! THE STAFF IS WONDERFUL TOO.
OH, AND OF COURSE THE FOOD IS REALLY DELICIOUS!
TWITCH
SEE YA LATER, THEN. ENJOY YOUR STAY!
THE FOOD, EH?
MAN, FOR SOMEONE NOT LOCAL, HE SURE KNEW WHAT HE WAS TALKING ABOUT!
YEAH, HE DID.
NANMAIDABU... NANMAIDABU...
IF ONLY THE SUPER-SCARY DISAPPEARANCES WEREN'T HAPPENING, THINGS WOULD BE SO MUCH NICER!
TRUE... THOUGH I DOUBT ANYONE'S ACTUALLY BEEN SPIRITED AWAY.
I'M BETTING EVERYBODY WHO'S MISSING LEFT OF THEIR OWN FREE WILL. THE QUESTION IS *WHY*?

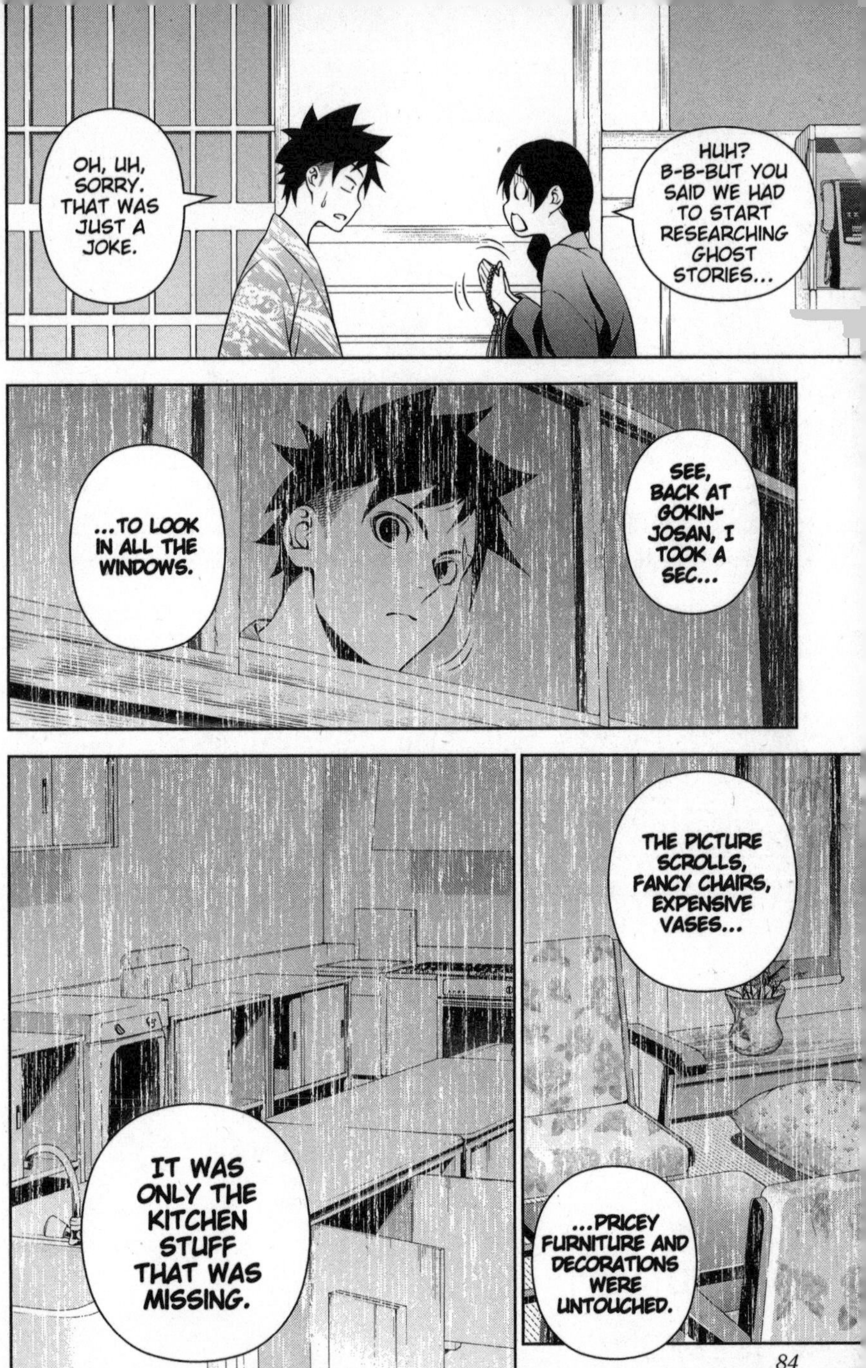
HUH? B-B-BUT YOU SAID WE HAD TO START RESEARCHING GHOST STORIES...
OH, UH, SORRY. THAT WAS JUST A JOKE.
SEE, BACK AT GOKIN-JOSAN, I TOOK A SEC...
...TO LOOK IN ALL THE WINDOWS.
THE PICTURE SCROLLS, FANCY CHAIRS, EXPENSIVE VASES...
...PRICEY FURNITURE AND DECORATIONS WERE UNTOUCHED.
IT WAS ONLY THE KITCHEN STUFF THAT WAS MISSING.

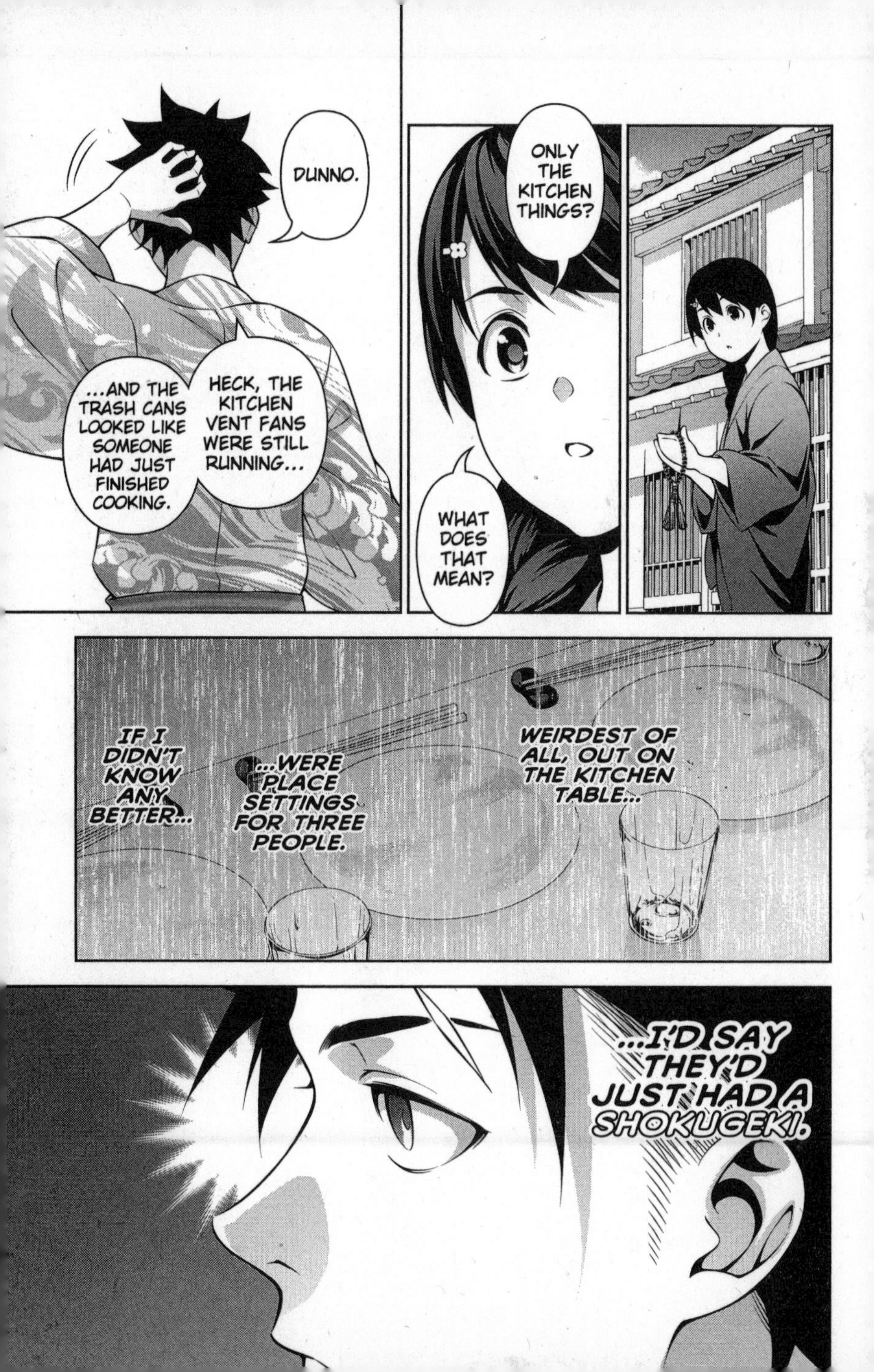
ONLY THE KITCHEN THINGS?
WHAT DOES THAT MEAN?
DUNNO.
HECK, THE KITCHEN VENT FANS WERE STILL RUNNING...
...AND THE TRASH CANS LOOKED LIKE SOMEONE HAD JUST FINISHED COOKING.
WEIRDEST OF ALL, OUT ON THE KITCHEN TABLE...
...WERE PLACE SETTINGS FOR THREE PEOPLE.
IF I DIDN'T KNOW ANY BETTER...
...I'D SAY THEY'D JUST HAD A SHOKUGEKI.

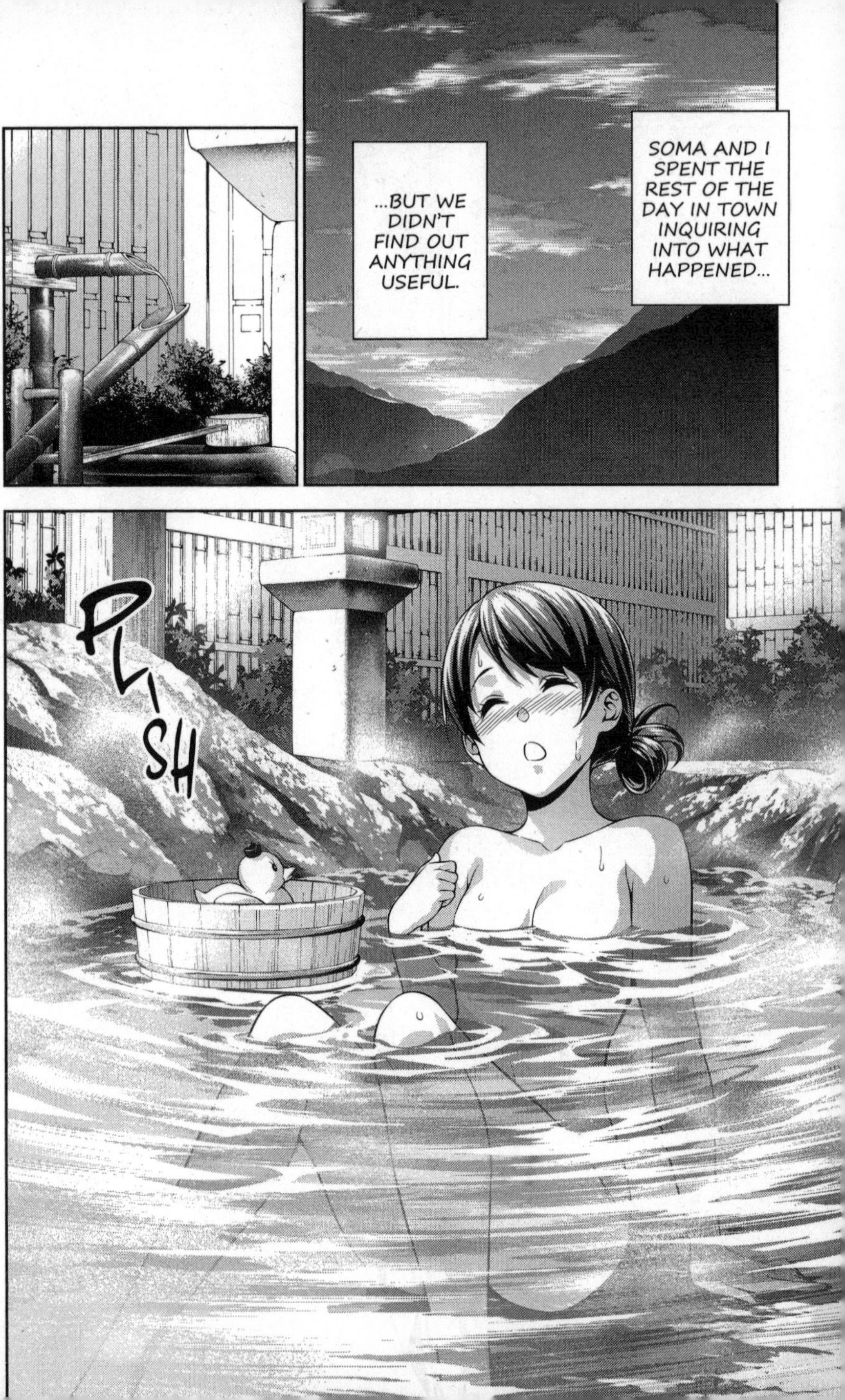
SOMA AND I SPENT THE REST OF THE DAY IN TOWN INQUIRING INTO WHAT HAPPENED...
...BUT WE DIDN'T FIND OUT ANYTHING USEFUL.
PLISH

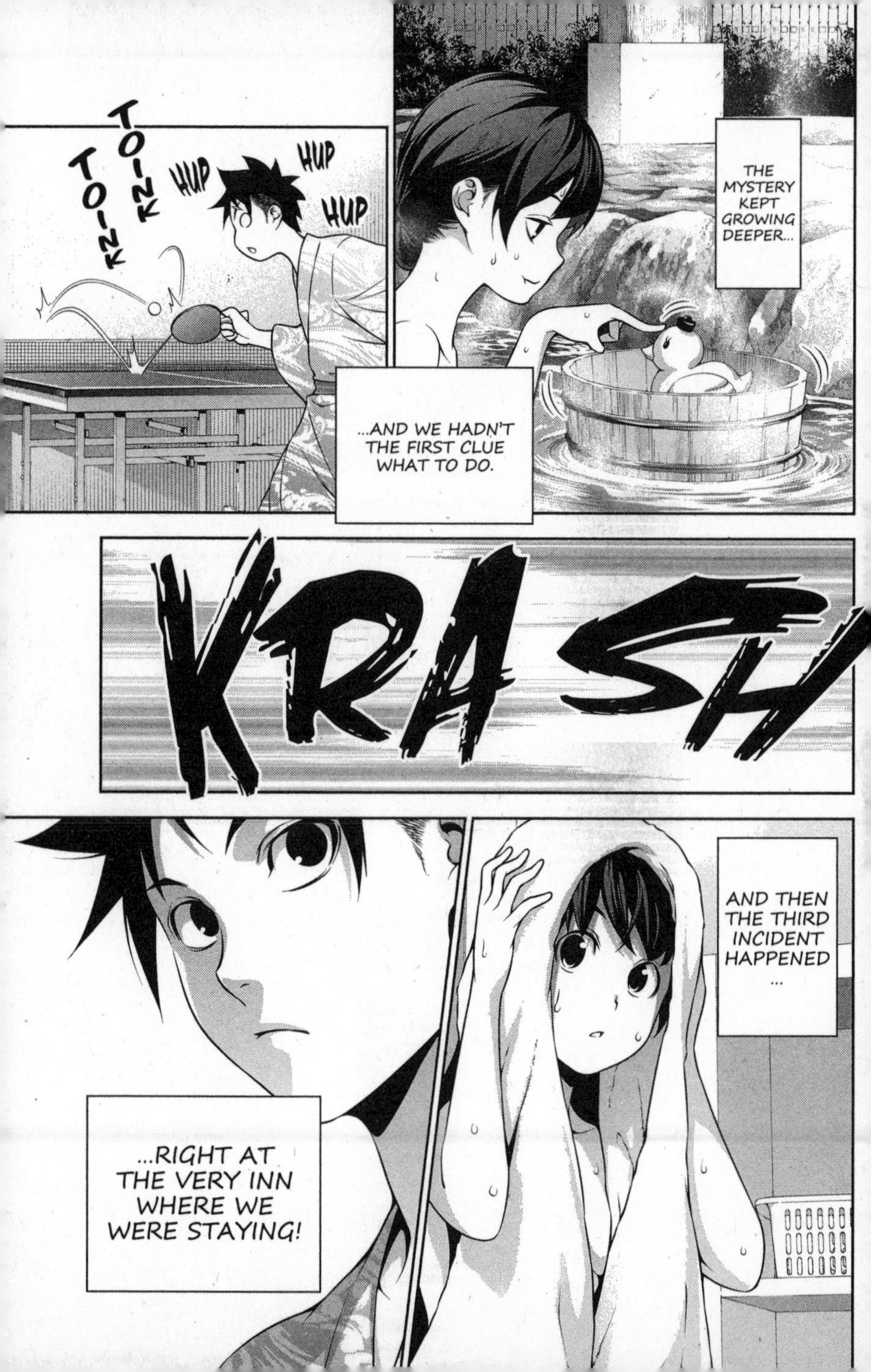
THE MYSTERY KEPT GROWING DEEPER...
...AND WE HADN'T THE FIRST CLUE WHAT TO DO.
TOINK
TOINK
HUP
HUP
HUP
KRASH
AND THEN THE THIRD INCIDENT HAPPENED ...
...RIGHT AT THE VERY INN WHERE WE WERE STAYING!

THE CASE OF MISS ALICE

ME? I KEEP DEBATING WHETHER TO LET MY HAIR GROW OUT OR NOT...

YOU DON'T SAY. WHY IS IT I'M GETTING A WHIFF OF MAIDENLY CHARM, HMM?

H-HEY! IT'S NOT LIKE THAT! I SWEAR!

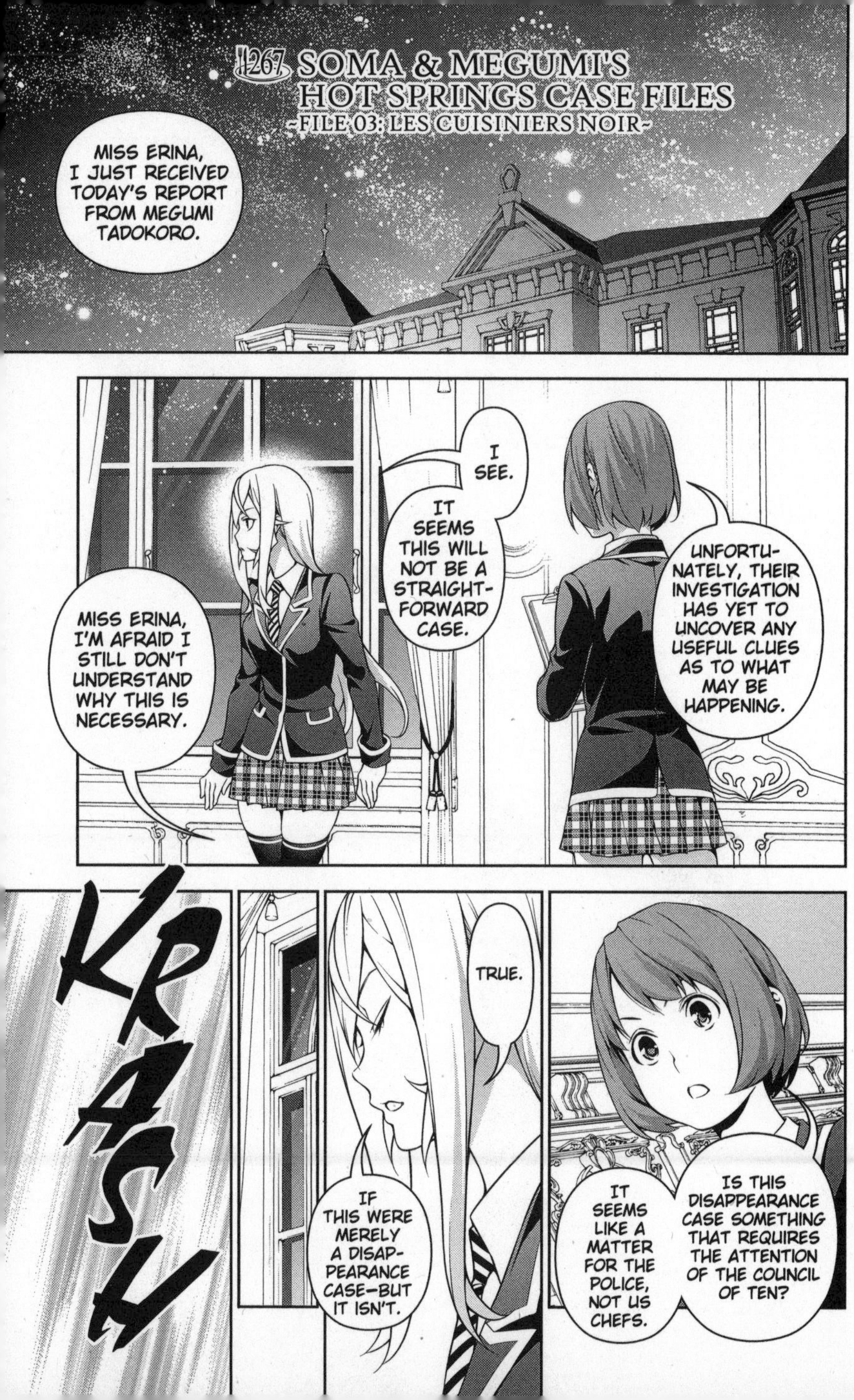

#267 SOMA & MEGUMI'S HOT SPRINGS CASE FILES
~FILE 03: LES CUISINIERS NOIR~
MISS ERINA, I JUST RECEIVED TODAY'S REPORT FROM MEGUMI TADOKORO.
UNFORTU-NATELY, THEIR INVESTIGATION HAS YET TO UNCOVER ANY USEFUL CLUES AS TO WHAT MAY BE HAPPENING.
I SEE.
IT SEEMS THIS WILL NOT BE A STRAIGHT-FORWARD CASE.
MISS ERINA, I'M AFRAID I STILL DON'T UNDERSTAND WHY THIS IS NECESSARY.
IS THIS DISAPPEARANCE CASE SOMETHING THAT REQUIRES THE ATTENTION OF THE COUNCIL OF TEN?
IT SEEMS LIKE A MATTER FOR THE POLICE, NOT US CHEFS.
TRUE.
IF THIS WERE MERELY A DISAP-PEARANCE CASE—BUT IT ISN'T.
KRASH

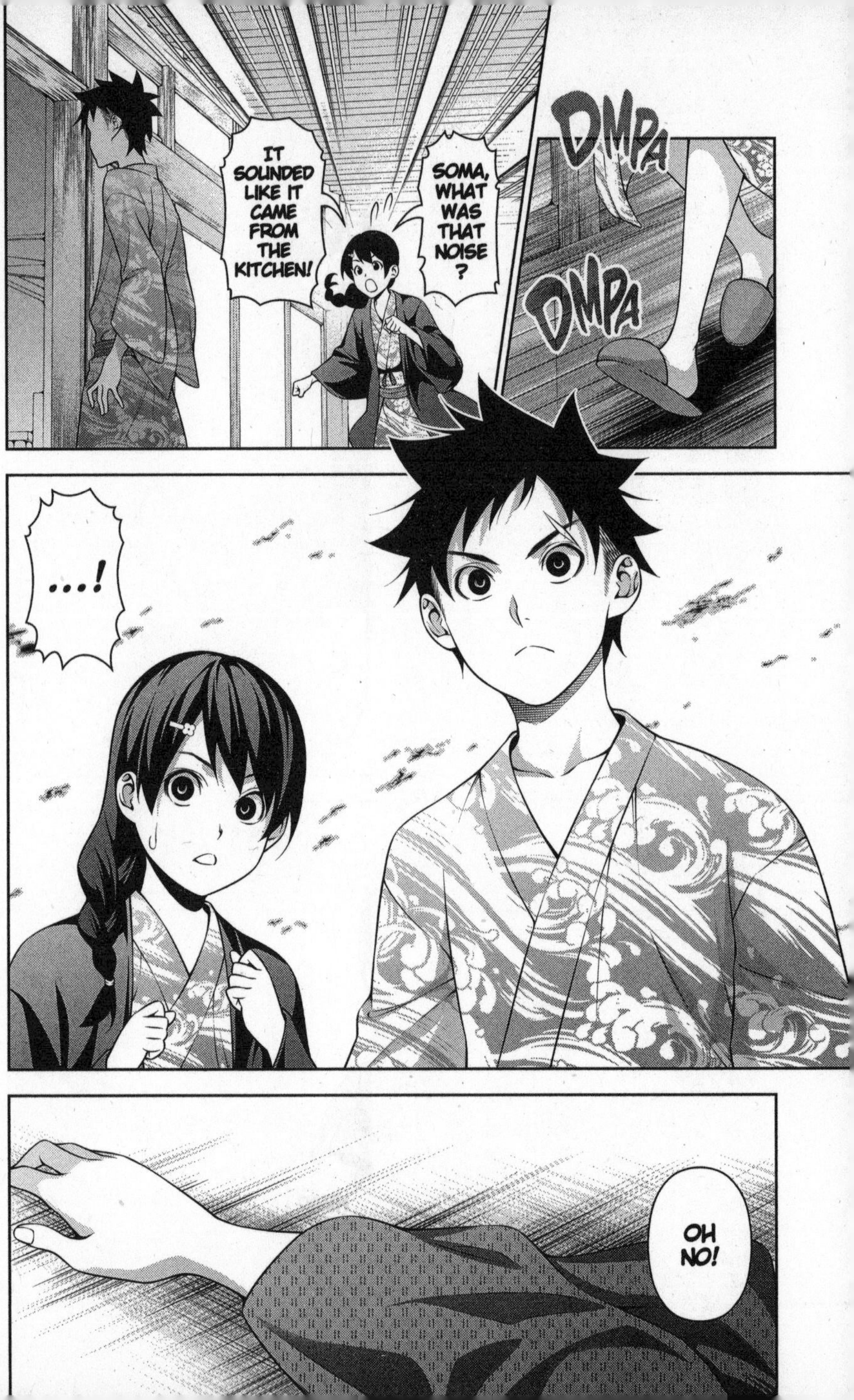
DMPA
DMPA
SOMA, WHAT WAS THAT NOISE?
IT SOUNDED LIKE IT CAME FROM THE KITCHEN!
...!
OH NO!

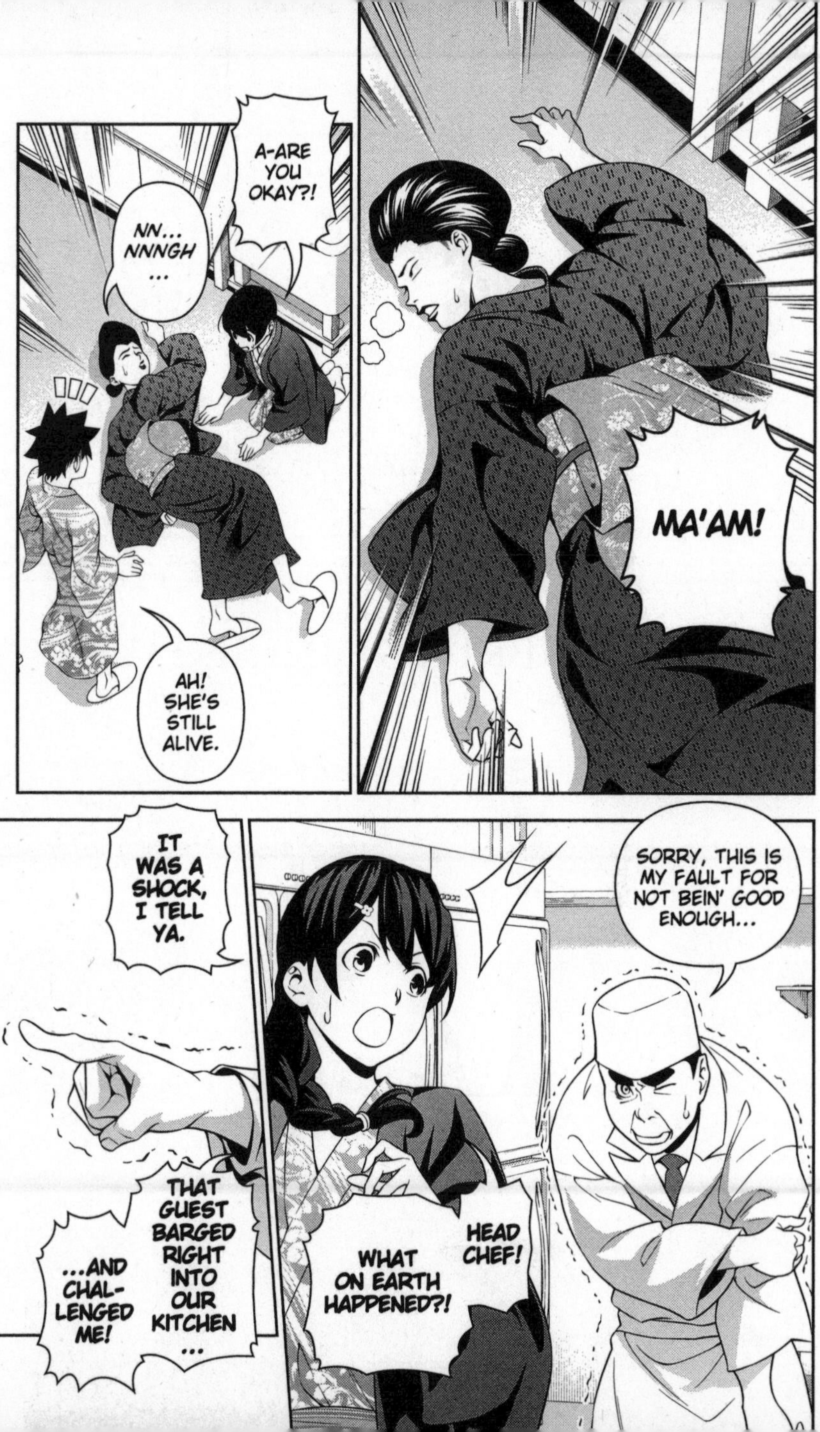
MA'AM!
A-ARE YOU OKAY?!
NN... NNNGH ...
AH! SHE'S STILL ALIVE.
SORRY, THIS IS MY FAULT FOR NOT BEIN' GOOD ENOUGH...
HEAD CHEF!
WHAT ON EARTH HAPPENED?!
IT WAS A SHOCK, I TELL YA.
THAT GUEST BARGED RIGHT INTO OUR KITCHEN ...
...AND CHAL-LENGED ME!

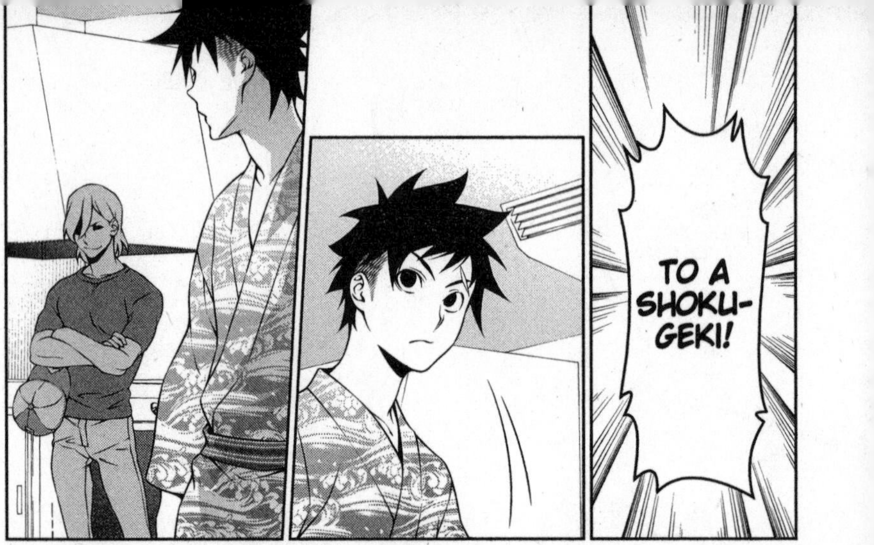
TO A SHOKUGEKI!

267 SOMA & MEGUMI'S HOT SPRINGS CASE FILES
~FILE 03: LES CUISINIERS NOIR~

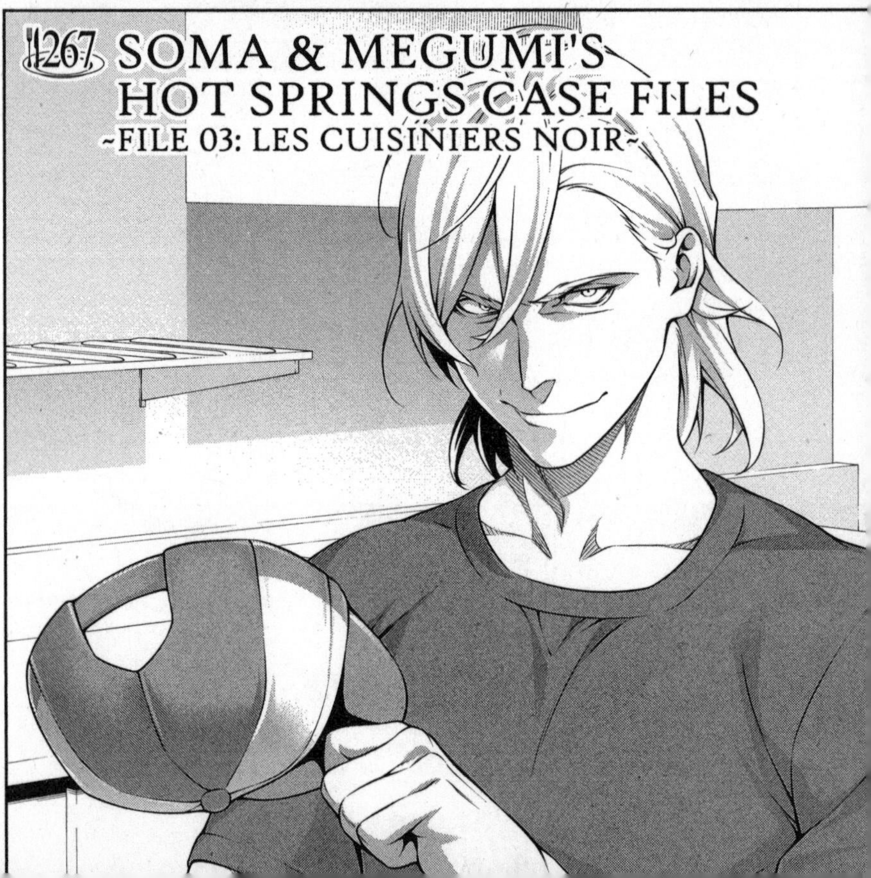

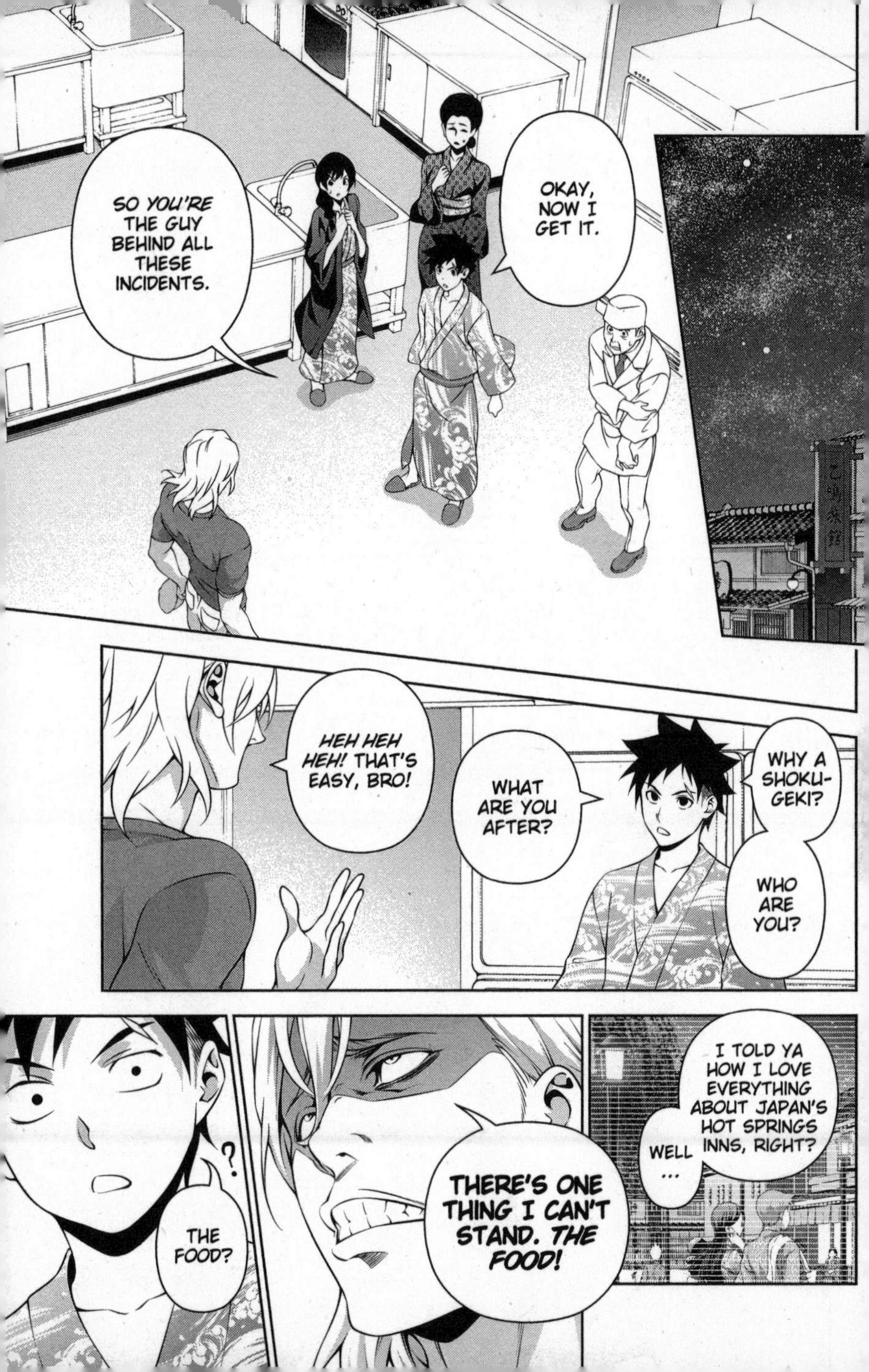
OKAY, NOW I GET IT.
SO *YOU'RE* THE GUY BEHIND ALL THESE INCIDENTS.
WHY A SHOKU-GEKI?
WHO ARE YOU?
WHAT ARE YOU AFTER?
HEH HEH HEH! THAT'S EASY, BRO!
WELL...
I TOLD YA HOW I LOVE EVERYTHING ABOUT JAPAN'S HOT SPRINGS INNS, RIGHT?
THERE'S ONE THING I CAN'T STAND. *THE FOOD!*
?
THE FOOD?

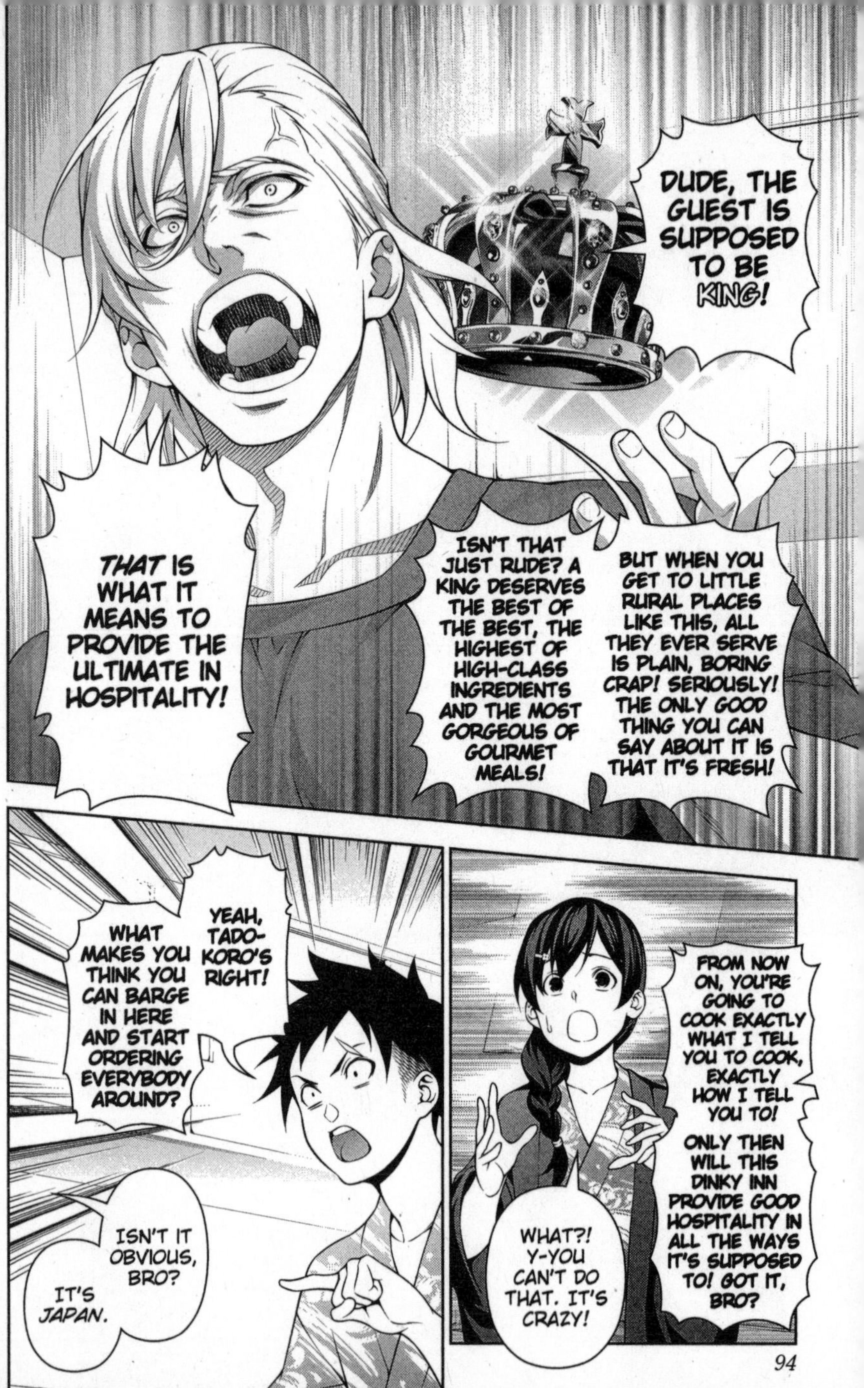
DUDE, THE GUEST IS SUPPOSED TO BE KING!
BUT WHEN YOU GET TO LITTLE RURAL PLACES LIKE THIS, ALL THEY EVER SERVE IS PLAIN, BORING CRAP! SERIOUSLY! THE ONLY GOOD THING YOU CAN SAY ABOUT IT IS THAT IT'S FRESH!
ISN'T THAT JUST RUDE? A KING DESERVES THE BEST OF THE BEST, THE HIGHEST OF HIGH-CLASS INGREDIENTS AND THE MOST GORGEOUS OF GOURMET MEALS!
THAT IS WHAT IT MEANS TO PROVIDE THE ULTIMATE IN HOSPITALITY!
FROM NOW ON, YOU'RE GOING TO COOK EXACTLY WHAT I TELL YOU TO COOK, EXACTLY HOW I TELL YOU TO!
ONLY THEN WILL THIS DINKY INN PROVIDE GOOD HOSPITALITY IN ALL THE WAYS IT'S SUPPOSED TO! GOT IT, BRO?
WHAT?! Y-YOU CAN'T DO THAT. IT'S CRAZY!
YEAH, TADOKORO'S RIGHT!
WHAT MAKES YOU THINK YOU CAN BARGE IN HERE AND START ORDERING EVERYBODY AROUND?
ISN'T IT OBVIOUS, BRO?
IT'S JAPAN.

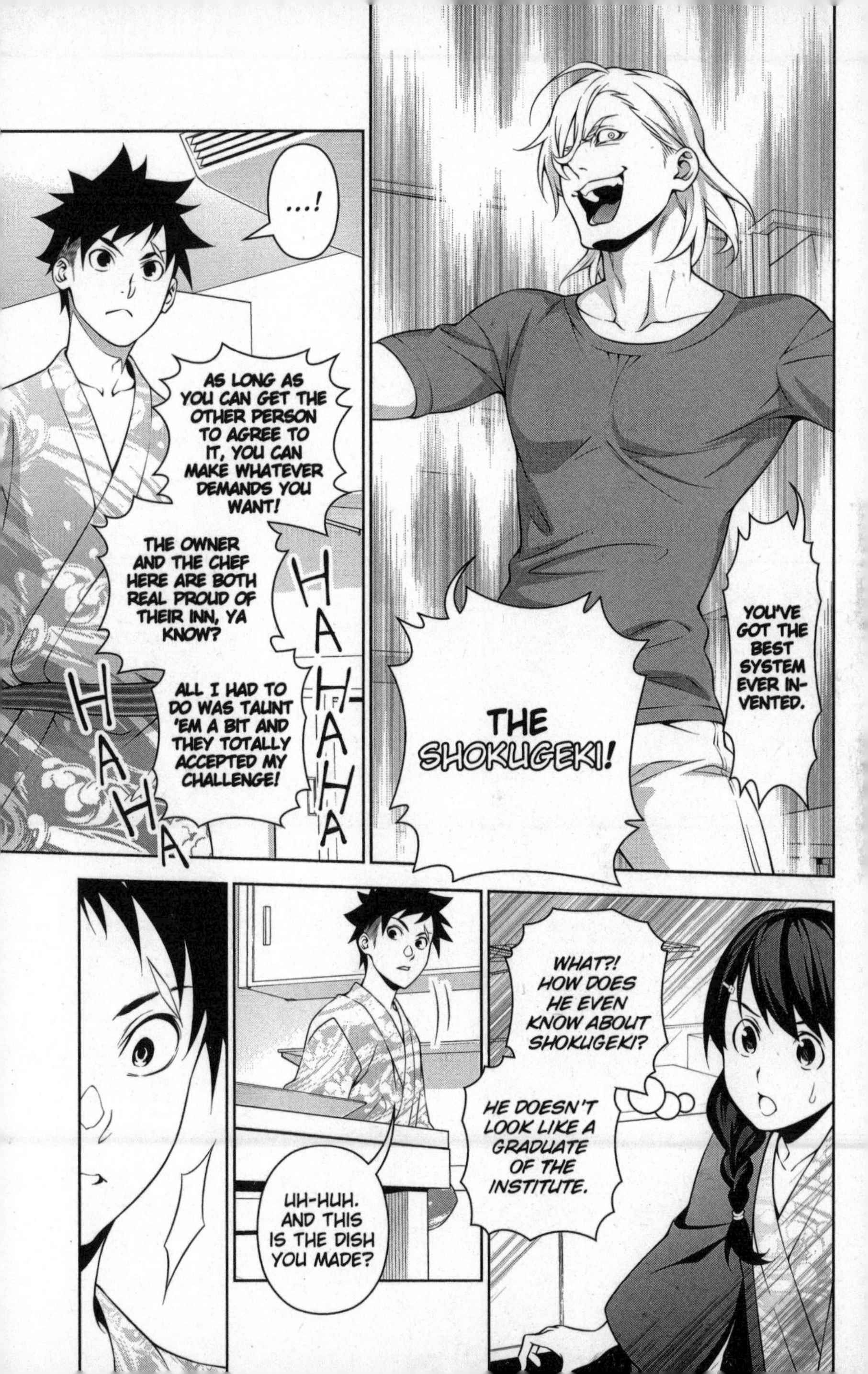
YOU'VE GOT THE BEST SYSTEM EVER IN-VENTED.
THE SHOKUGEKI!
...!
AS LONG AS YOU CAN GET THE OTHER PERSON TO AGREE TO IT, YOU CAN MAKE WHATEVER DEMANDS YOU WANT!
THE OWNER AND THE CHEF HERE ARE BOTH REAL PROUD OF THEIR INN, YA KNOW?
ALL I HAD TO DO WAS TAUNT 'EM A BIT AND THEY TOTALLY ACCEPTED MY CHALLENGE!
HAHAHA
HAHAHA
WHAT?! HOW DOES HE EVEN KNOW ABOUT SHOKUGEKI?
HE DOESN'T LOOK LIKE A GRADUATE OF THE INSTITUTE.
UH-HUH. AND THIS IS THE DISH YOU MADE?

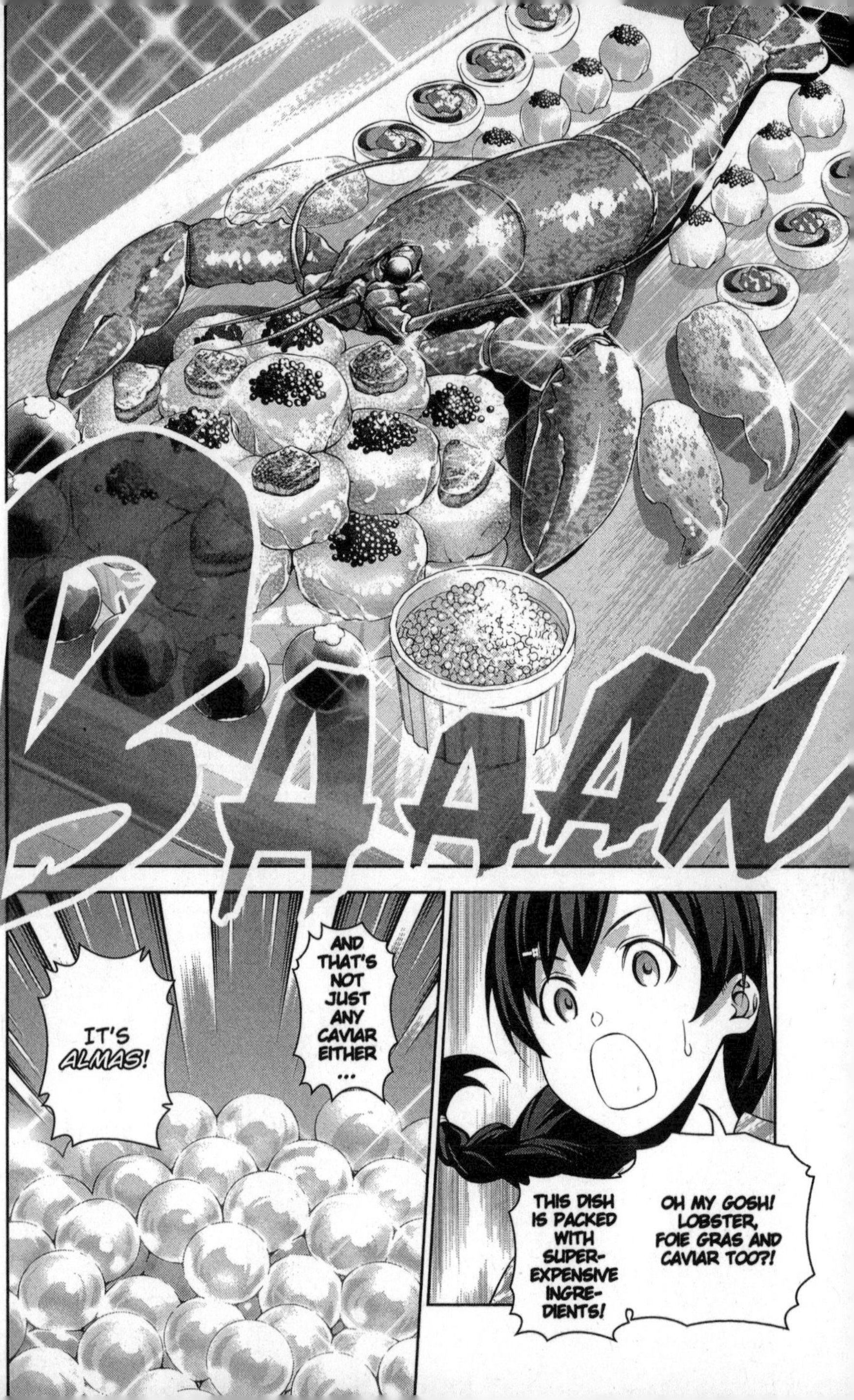
OH MY GOSH! LOBSTER, FOIE GRAS AND CAVIAR TOO?!
THIS DISH IS PACKED WITH SUPER-EXPENSIVE INGREDIENTS!
AND THAT'S NOT JUST ANY CAVIAR EITHER...
IT'S ALMAS!

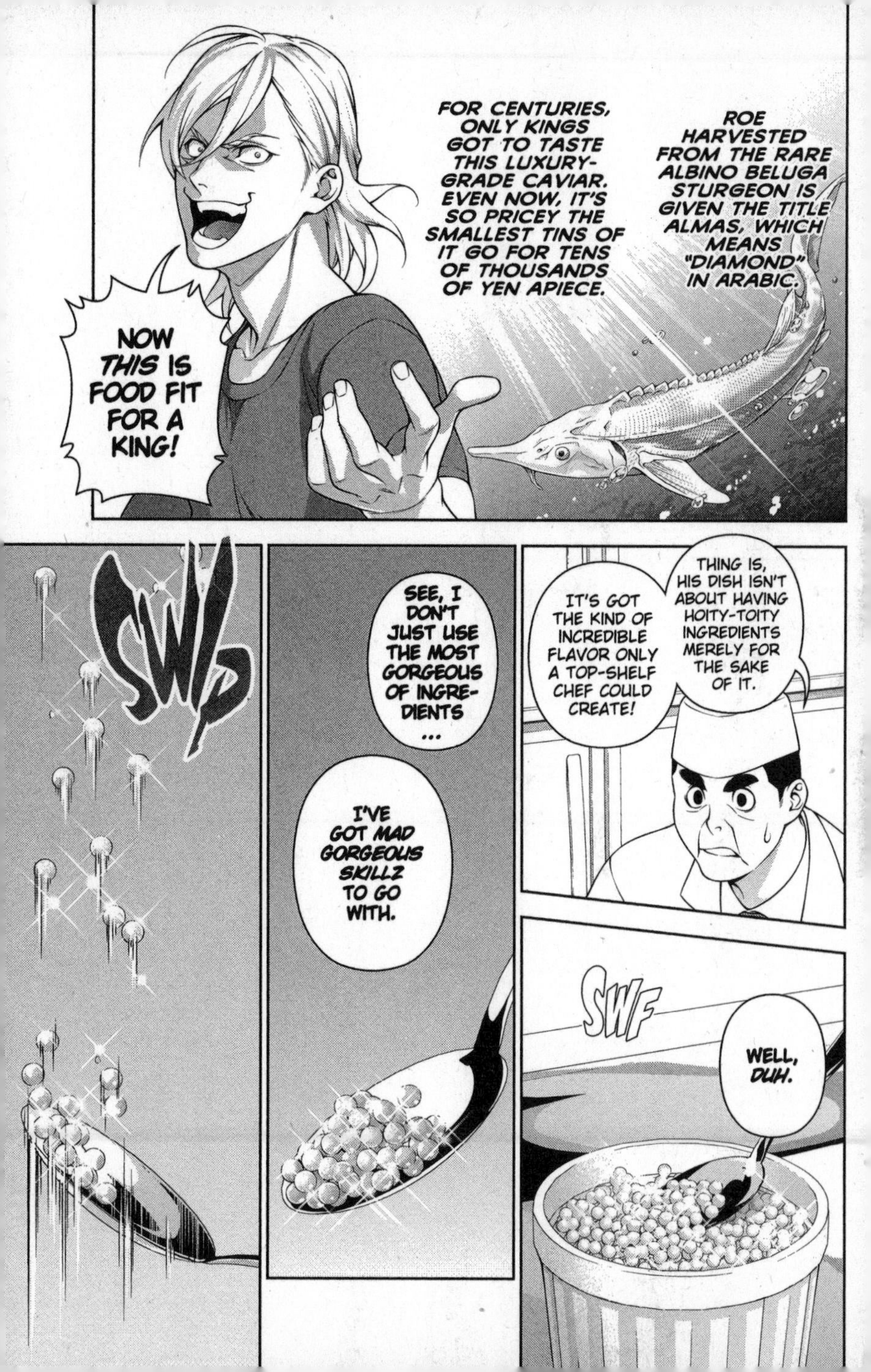
ROE HARVESTED FROM THE RARE ALBINO BELUGA STURGEON IS GIVEN THE TITLE ALMAS, WHICH MEANS "DIAMOND" IN ARABIC.
FOR CENTURIES, ONLY KINGS GOT TO TASTE THIS LUXURY-GRADE CAVIAR. EVEN NOW, IT'S SO PRICEY THE SMALLEST TINS OF IT GO FOR TENS OF THOUSANDS OF YEN APIECE.
NOW *THIS* IS FOOD FIT FOR A KING!
THING IS, HIS DISH ISN'T ABOUT HAVING HOITY-TOITY INGREDIENTS MERELY FOR THE SAKE OF IT.
IT'S GOT THE KIND OF INCREDIBLE FLAVOR ONLY A TOP-SHELF CHEF COULD CREATE!
SWF
WELL, DUH.
SEE, I DON'T JUST USE THE MOST GORGEOUS OF INGREDIENTS...
I'VE GOT MAD GORGEOUS SKILLZ TO GO WITH.
SWP

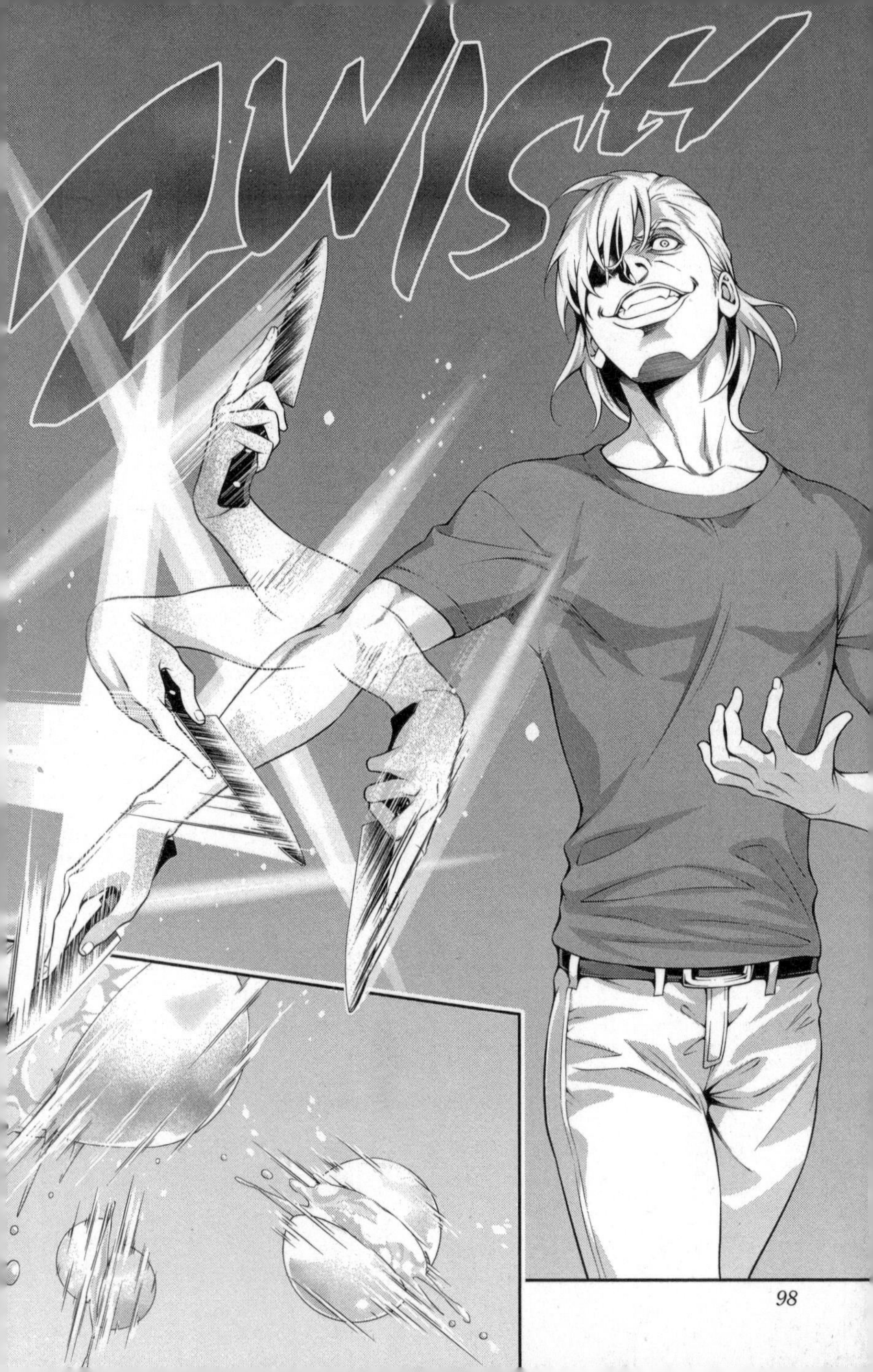
SWISH

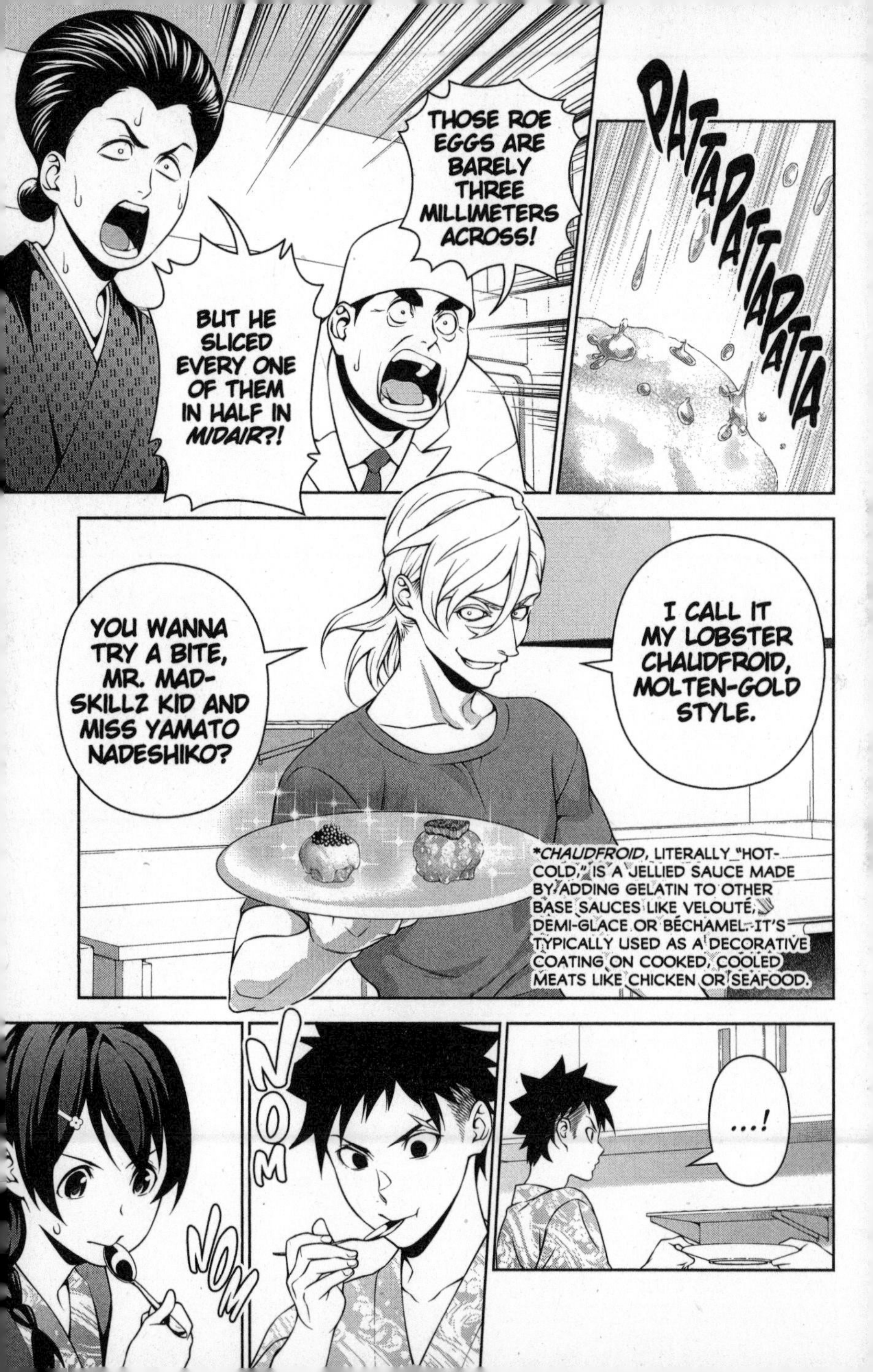
PATTAPATTAPATTA
THOSE ROE EGGS ARE BARELY THREE MILLIMETERS ACROSS!
BUT HE SLICED EVERY ONE OF THEM IN HALF IN *MIDAIR*?!
I CALL IT MY LOBSTER CHAUDFROID, MOLTEN-GOLD STYLE.
YOU WANNA TRY A BITE, MR. MAD-SKILLZ KID AND MISS YAMATO NADESHIKO?
**CHAUDFROID*, LITERALLY "HOT-COLD," IS A JELLIED SAUCE MADE BY ADDING GELATIN TO OTHER BASE SAUCES LIKE VELOUTÉ, DEMI-GLACE OR BÉCHAMEL. IT'S TYPICALLY USED AS A DECORATIVE COATING ON COOKED, COOLED MEATS LIKE CHICKEN OR SEAFOOD.
...!
NOM
NOM

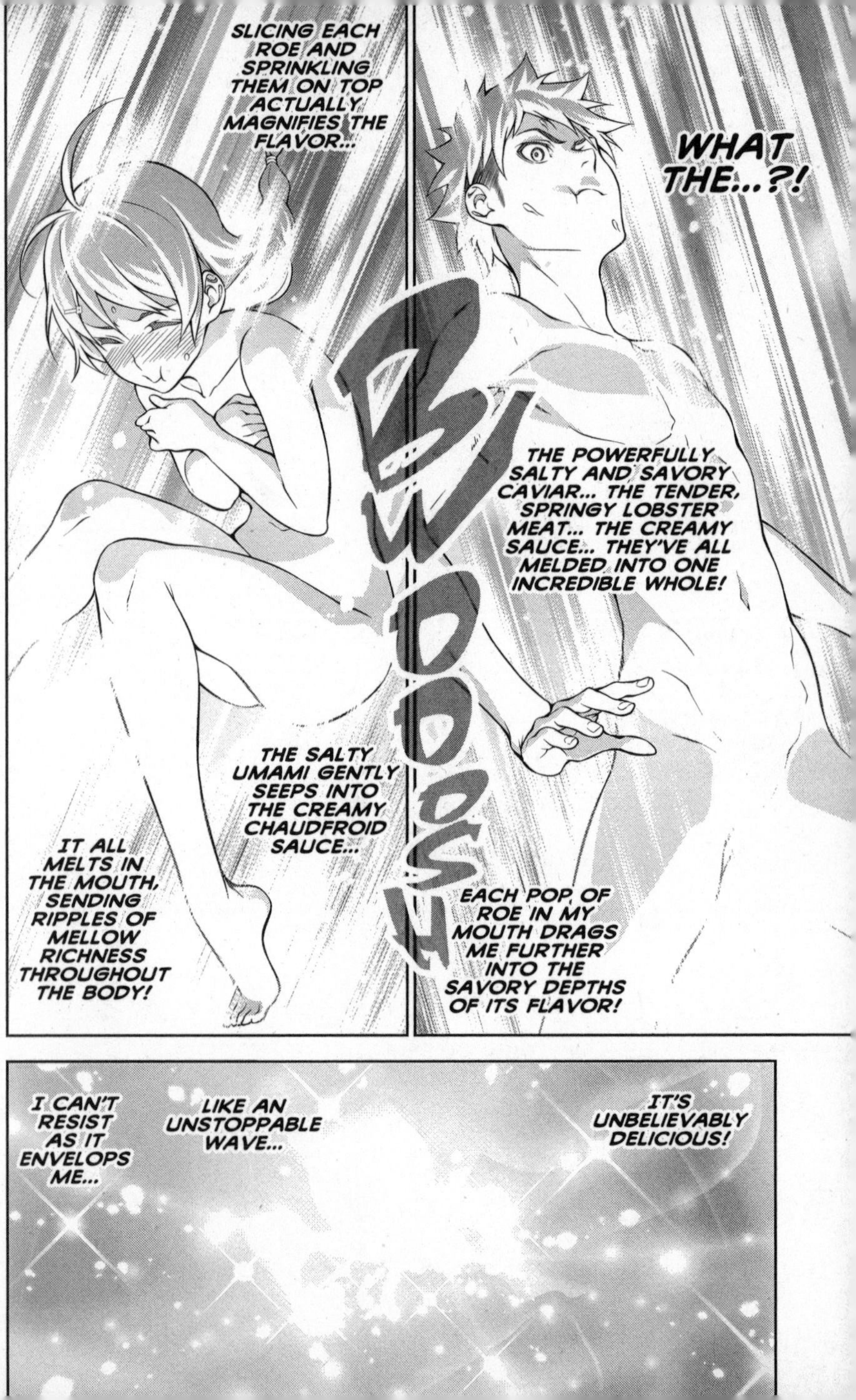
WHAT THE...?!
THE POWERFULLY SALTY AND SAVORY CAVIAR... THE TENDER, SPRINGY LOBSTER MEAT... THE CREAMY SAUCE... THEY'VE ALL MELDED INTO ONE INCREDIBLE WHOLE!
EACH POP OF ROE IN MY MOUTH DRAGS ME FURTHER INTO THE SAVORY DEPTHS OF ITS FLAVOR!
SLICING EACH ROE AND SPRINKLING THEM ON TOP ACTUALLY MAGNIFIES THE FLAVOR...
THE SALTY UMAMI GENTLY SEEPS INTO THE CREAMY CHAUDFROID SAUCE...
IT ALL MELTS IN THE MOUTH, SENDING RIPPLES OF MELLOW RICHNESS THROUGHOUT THE BODY!
IT'S UNBELIEVABLY DELICIOUS!
LIKE AN UNSTOPPABLE WAVE...
I CAN'T RESIST AS IT ENVELOPS ME...

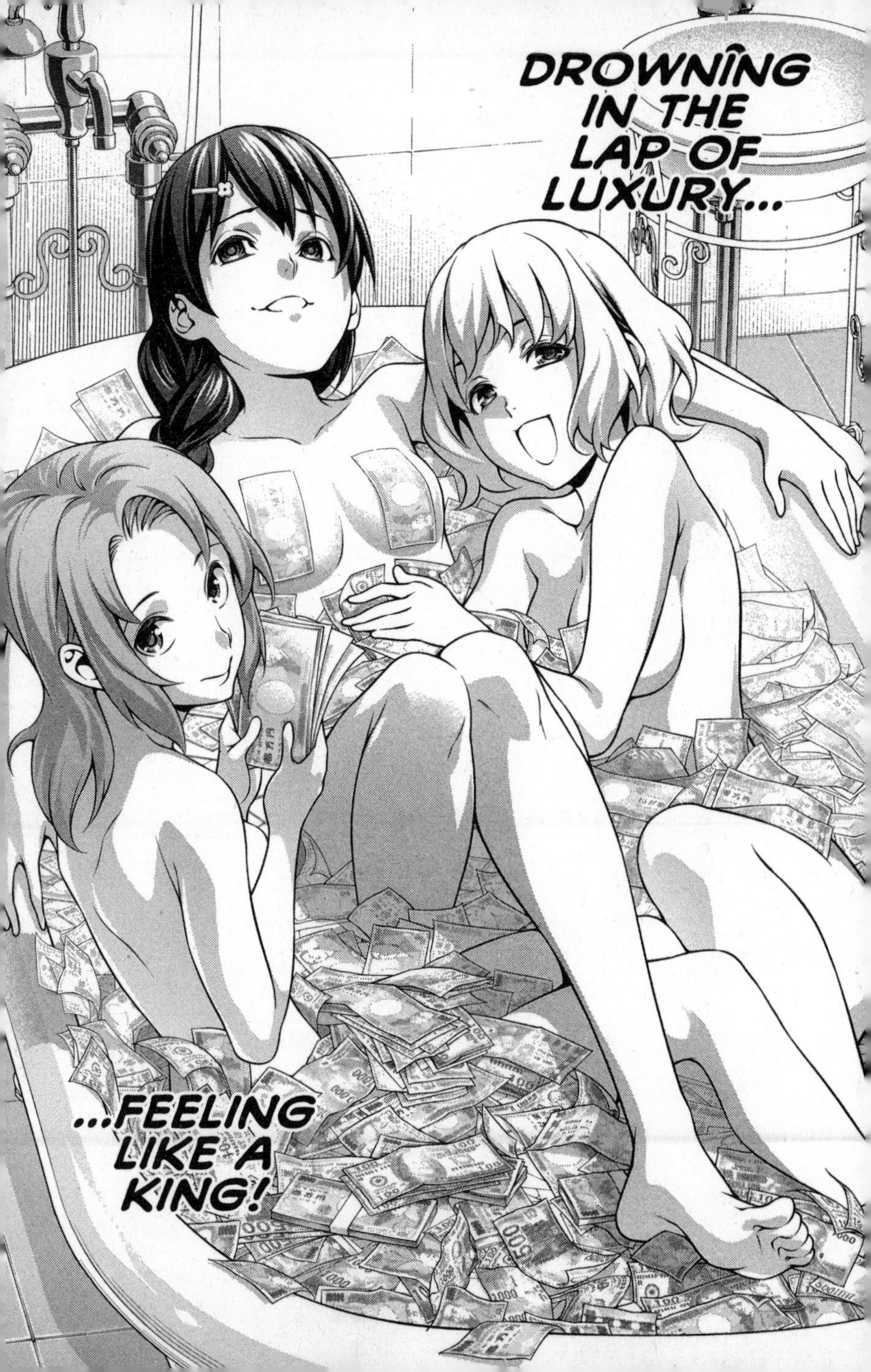
DROWNING IN THE LAP OF LUXURY...
...FEELING LIKE A KING!

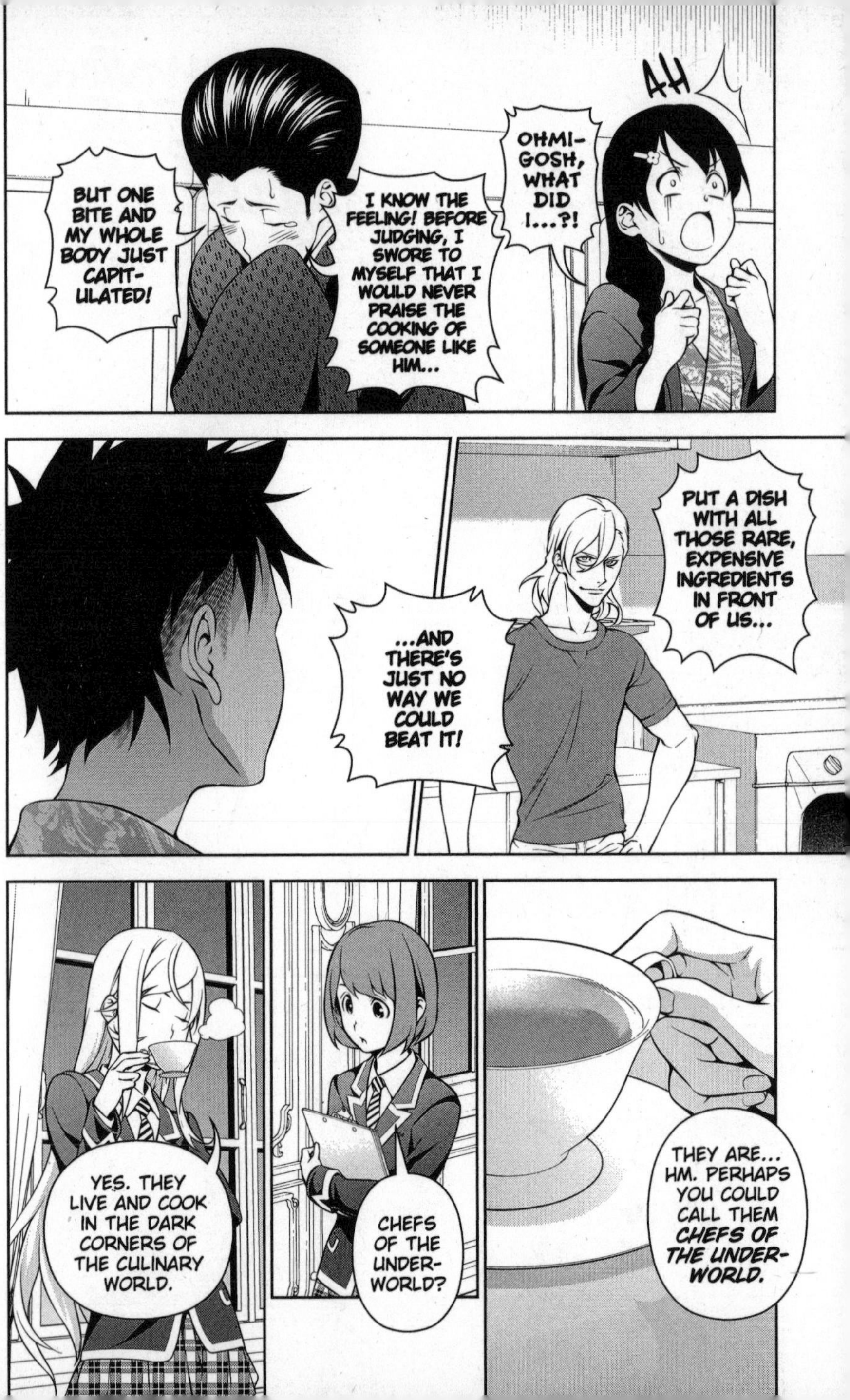
AH
OHMI-GOSH, WHAT DID I...?!
I KNOW THE FEELING! BEFORE JUDGING, I SWORE TO MYSELF THAT I WOULD NEVER PRAISE THE COOKING OF SOMEONE LIKE HIM...
BUT ONE BITE AND MY WHOLE BODY JUST CAPIT-ULATED!
PUT A DISH WITH ALL THOSE RARE, EXPENSIVE INGREDIENTS IN FRONT OF US...
...AND THERE'S JUST NO WAY WE COULD BEAT IT!
THEY ARE... HM. PERHAPS YOU COULD CALL THEM *CHEFS OF THE UNDER-WORLD.*
CHEFS OF THE UNDER-WORLD?
YES. THEY LIVE AND COOK IN THE DARK CORNERS OF THE CULINARY WORLD.

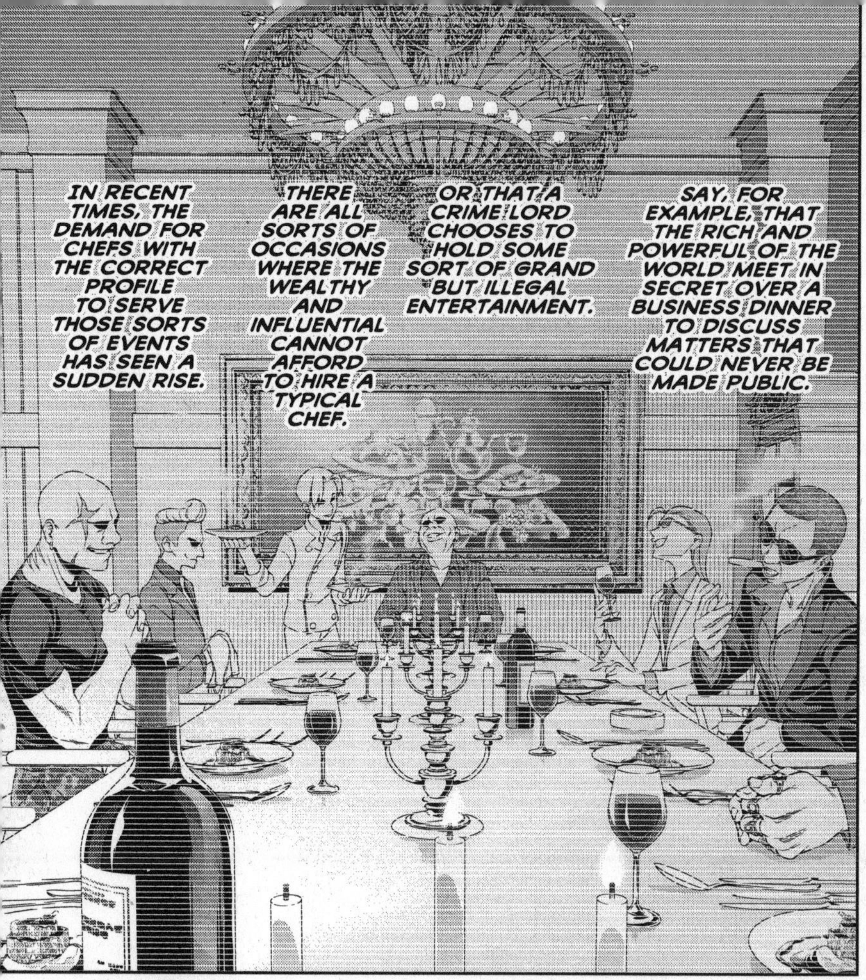
SAY, FOR EXAMPLE, THAT THE RICH AND POWERFUL OF THE WORLD MEET IN SECRET OVER A BUSINESS DINNER TO DISCUSS MATTERS THAT COULD NEVER BE MADE PUBLIC.
OR THAT A CRIME LORD CHOOSES TO HOLD SOME SORT OF GRAND BUT ILLEGAL ENTERTAINMENT.
THERE ARE ALL SORTS OF OCCASIONS WHERE THE WEALTHY AND INFLUENTIAL CANNOT AFFORD TO HIRE A TYPICAL CHEF.
IN RECENT TIMES, THE DEMAND FOR CHEFS WITH THE CORRECT PROFILE TO SERVE THOSE SORTS OF EVENTS HAS SEEN A SUDDEN RISE.

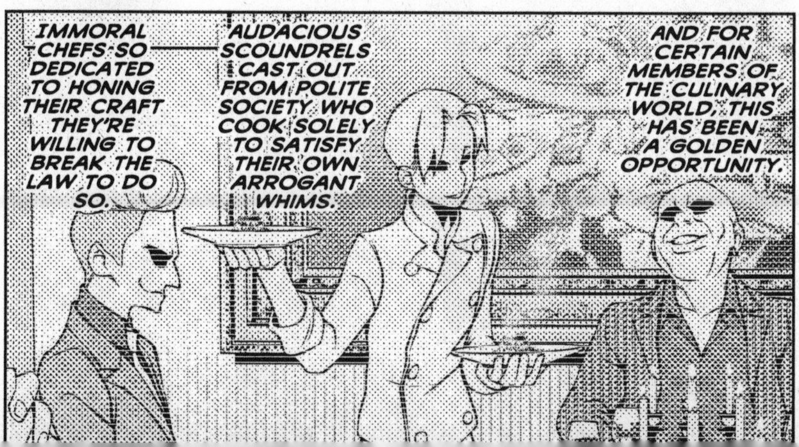
AND FOR CERTAIN MEMBERS OF THE CULINARY WORLD, THIS HAS BEEN A GOLDEN OPPORTUNITY.
AUDACIOUS SCOUNDRELS CAST OUT FROM POLITE SOCIETY WHO COOK SOLELY TO SATISFY THEIR OWN ARROGANT WHIMS.
IMMORAL CHEFS SO DEDICATED TO HONING THEIR CRAFT THEY'RE WILLING TO BREAK THE LAW TO DO SO.

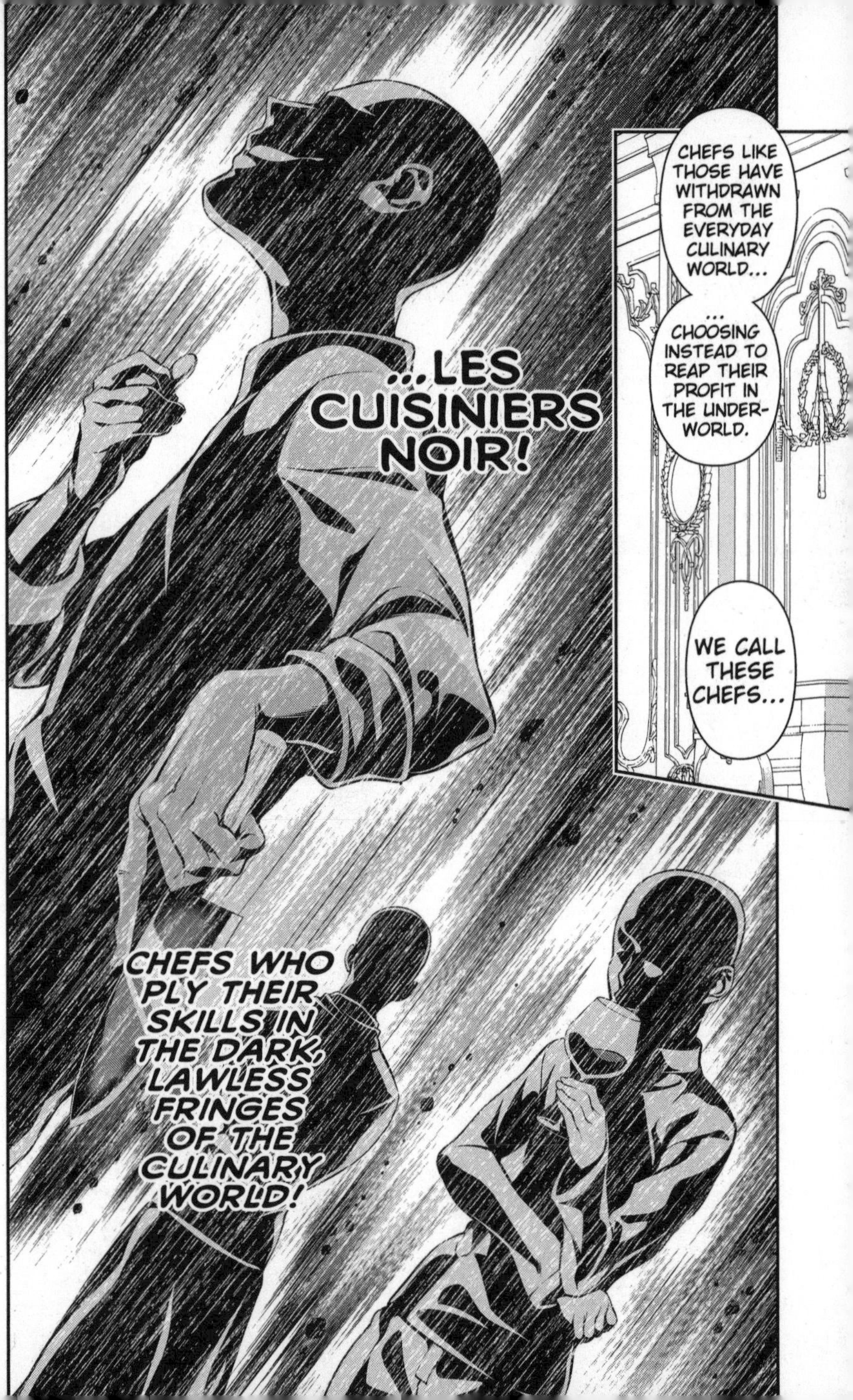
CHEFS LIKE THOSE HAVE WITHDRAWN FROM THE EVERYDAY CULINARY WORLD...
...CHOOSING INSTEAD TO REAP THEIR PROFIT IN THE UNDER-WORLD.
WE CALL THESE CHEFS...
...LES CUISINIERS NOIR!
CHEFS WHO PLY THEIR SKILLS IN THE DARK, LAWLESS FRINGES OF THE CULINARY WORLD!

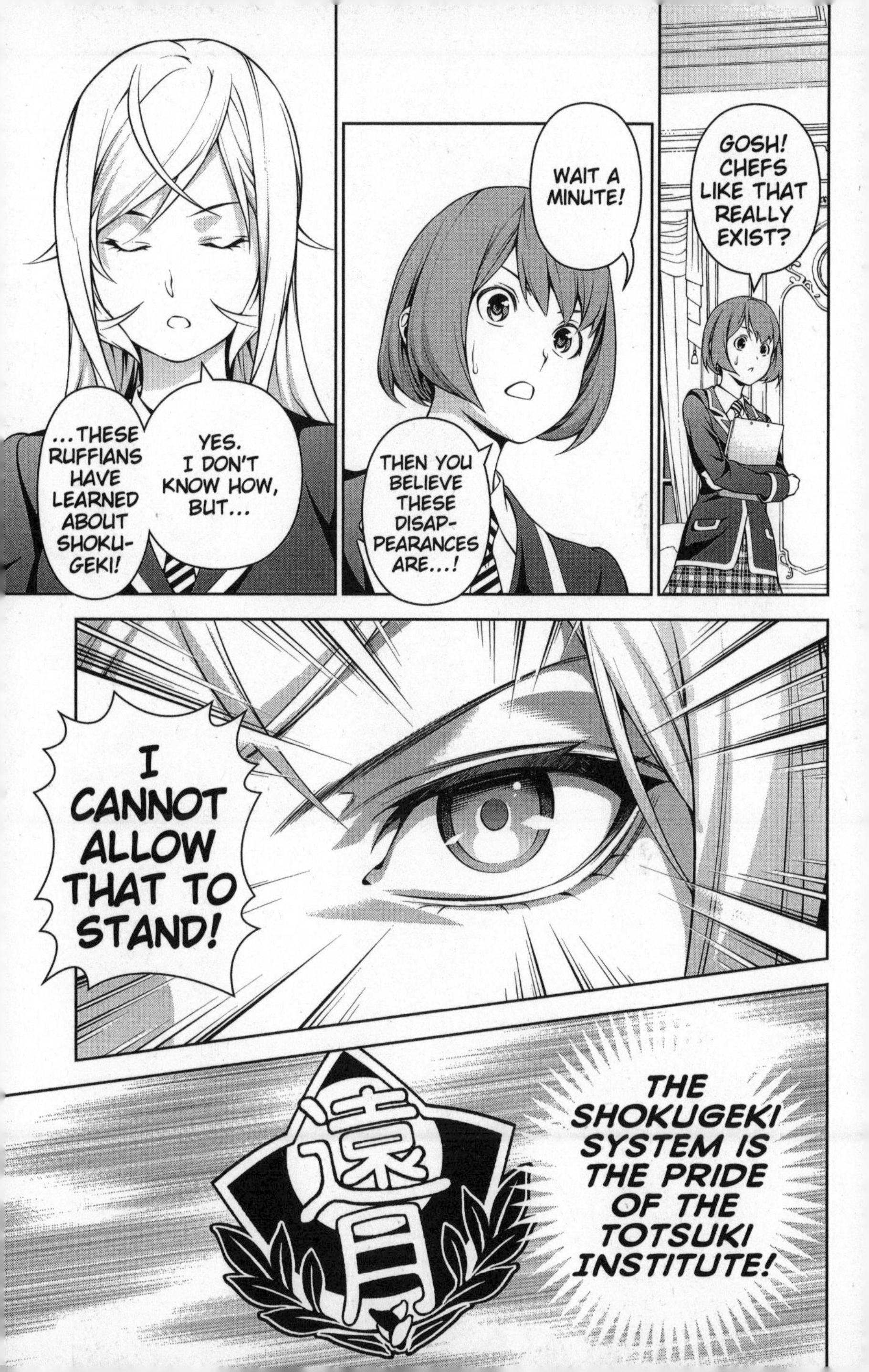
GOSH! CHEFS LIKE THAT REALLY EXIST?
WAIT A MINUTE!
THEN YOU BELIEVE THESE DISAP-PEARANCES ARE...!
YES. I DON'T KNOW HOW, BUT...
...THESE RUFFIANS HAVE LEARNED ABOUT SHOKU-GEKI!
I CANNOT ALLOW THAT TO STAND!
遠月
THE SHOKUGEKI SYSTEM IS THE PRIDE OF THE TOTSUKI INSTITUTE!

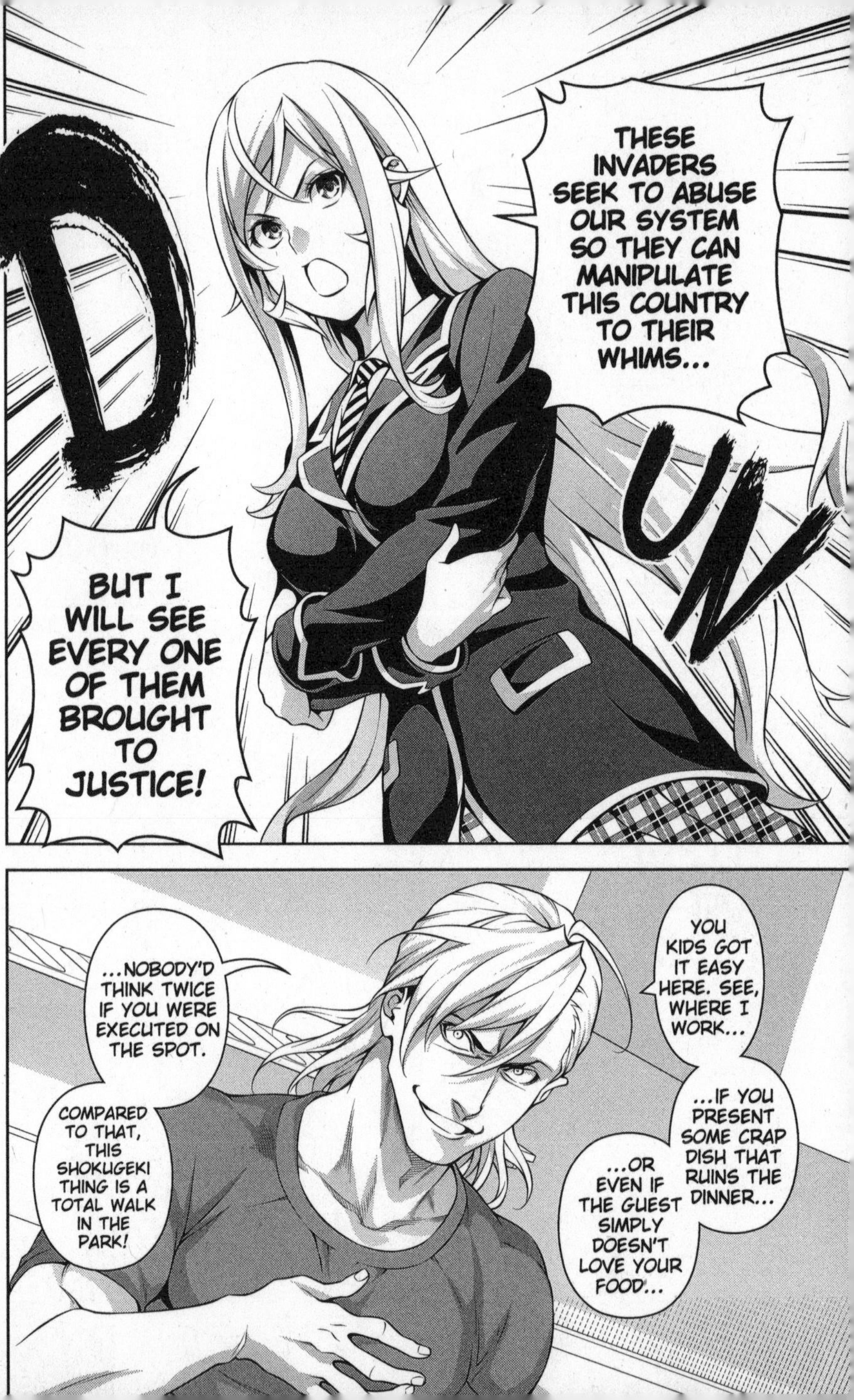
THESE INVADERS SEEK TO ABUSE OUR SYSTEM SO THEY CAN MANIPULATE THIS COUNTRY TO THEIR WHIMS...
DUN
BUT I WILL SEE EVERY ONE OF THEM BROUGHT TO JUSTICE!
YOU KIDS GOT IT EASY HERE. SEE, WHERE I WORK...
...IF YOU PRESENT SOME CRAP DISH THAT RUINS THE DINNER...
...OR EVEN IF THE GUEST SIMPLY DOESN'T LOVE YOUR FOOD...
...NOBODY'D THINK TWICE IF YOU WERE EXECUTED ON THE SPOT.
COMPARED TO THAT, THIS SHOKUGEKI THING IS A TOTAL WALK IN THE PARK!

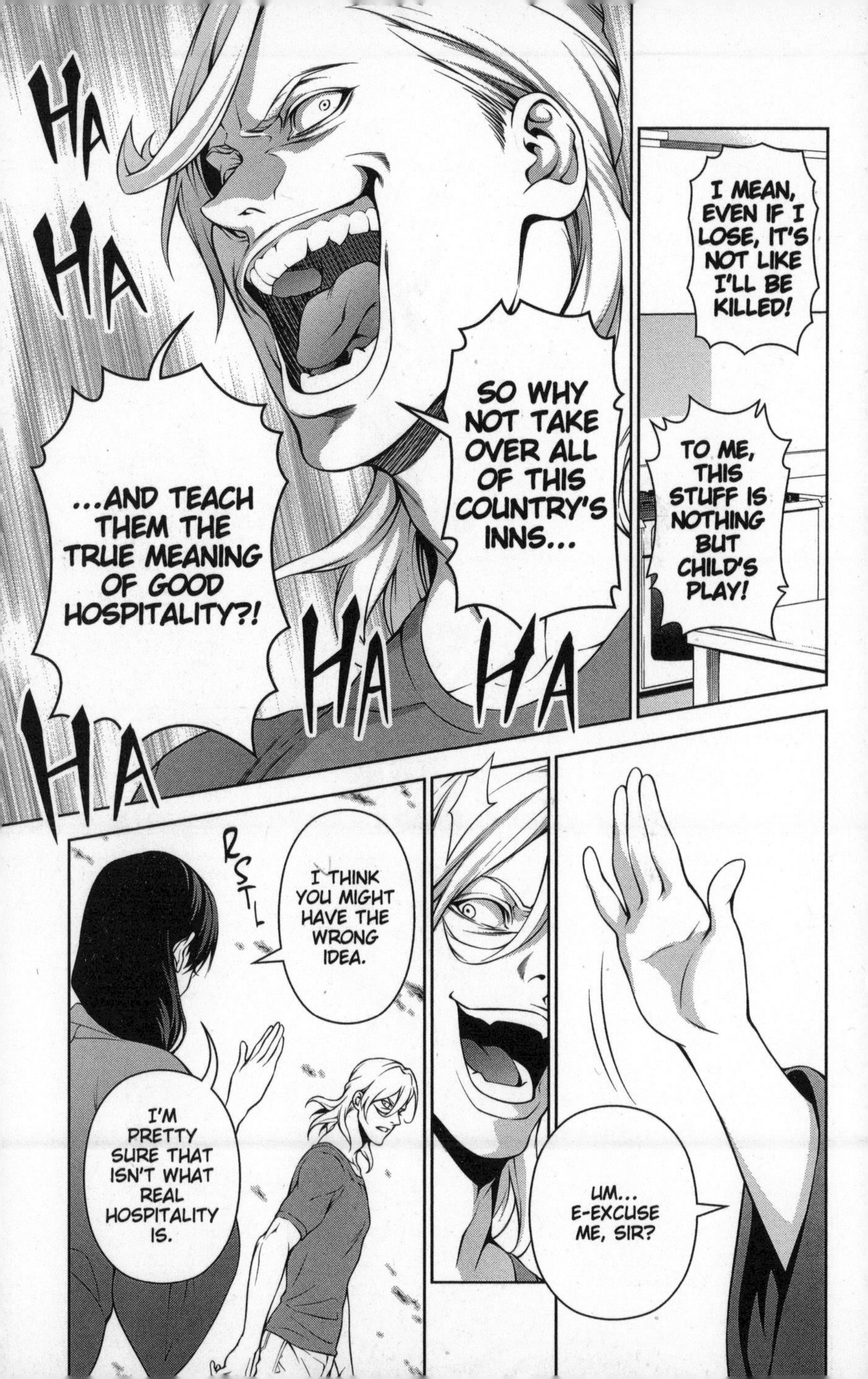
I MEAN, EVEN IF I LOSE, IT'S NOT LIKE I'LL BE KILLED!
TO ME, THIS STUFF IS NOTHING BUT CHILD'S PLAY!
HA HA HA
SO WHY NOT TAKE OVER ALL OF THIS COUNTRY'S INNS...
...AND TEACH THEM THE TRUE MEANING OF GOOD HOSPITALITY?!
HA HA HA
UM... E-EXCUSE ME, SIR?
RSTL
I THINK YOU MIGHT HAVE THE WRONG IDEA.
I'M PRETTY SURE THAT ISN'T WHAT REAL HOSPITALITY IS.

THE CASE OF MISS ALICE

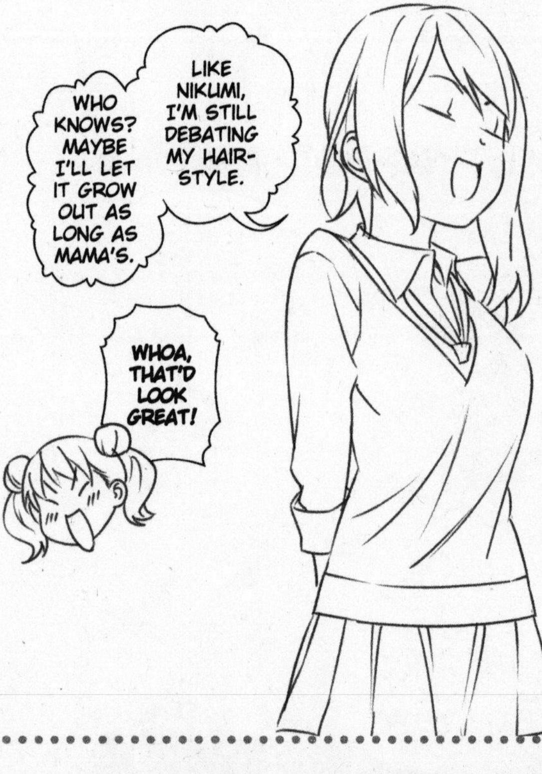
LIKE NIKUMI, I'M STILL DEBATING MY HAIR-STYLE.
WHO KNOWS? MAYBE I'LL LET IT GROW OUT AS LONG AS MAMA'S.
WHOA, THAT'D LOOK GREAT!

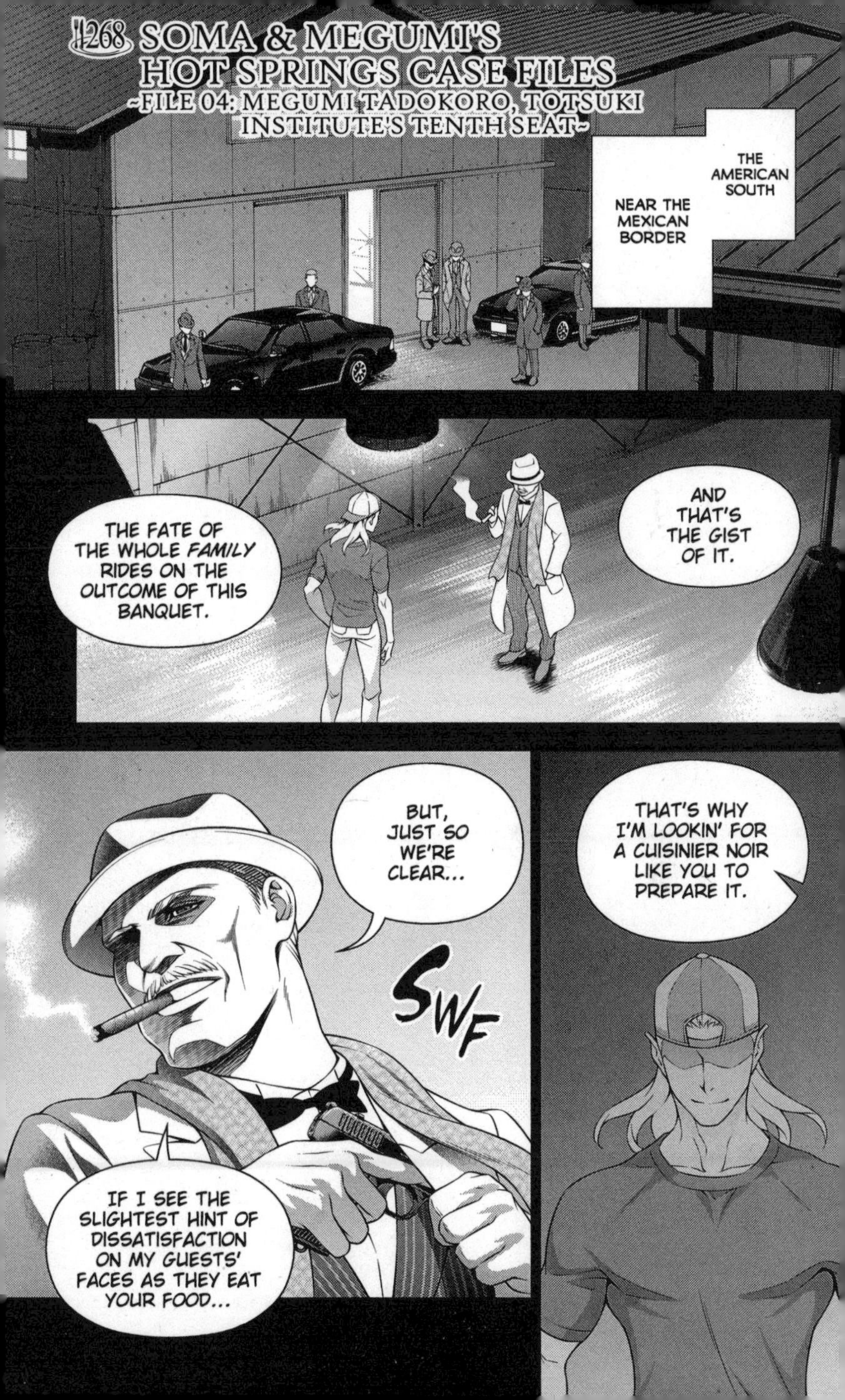

#268 SOMA & MEGUMI'S HOT SPRINGS CASE FILES
~FILE 04: MEGUMI TADOKORO, TOTSUKI INSTITUTE'S TENTH SEAT~
THE AMERICAN SOUTH
NEAR THE MEXICAN BORDER
AND THAT'S THE GIST OF IT.
THE FATE OF THE WHOLE *FAMILY* RIDES ON THE OUTCOME OF THIS BANQUET.
THAT'S WHY I'M LOOKIN' FOR A CUISINIER NOIR LIKE YOU TO PREPARE IT.
BUT, JUST SO WE'RE CLEAR...
SWF
IF I SEE THE SLIGHTEST HINT OF DISSATISFACTION ON MY GUESTS' FACES AS THEY EAT YOUR FOOD...

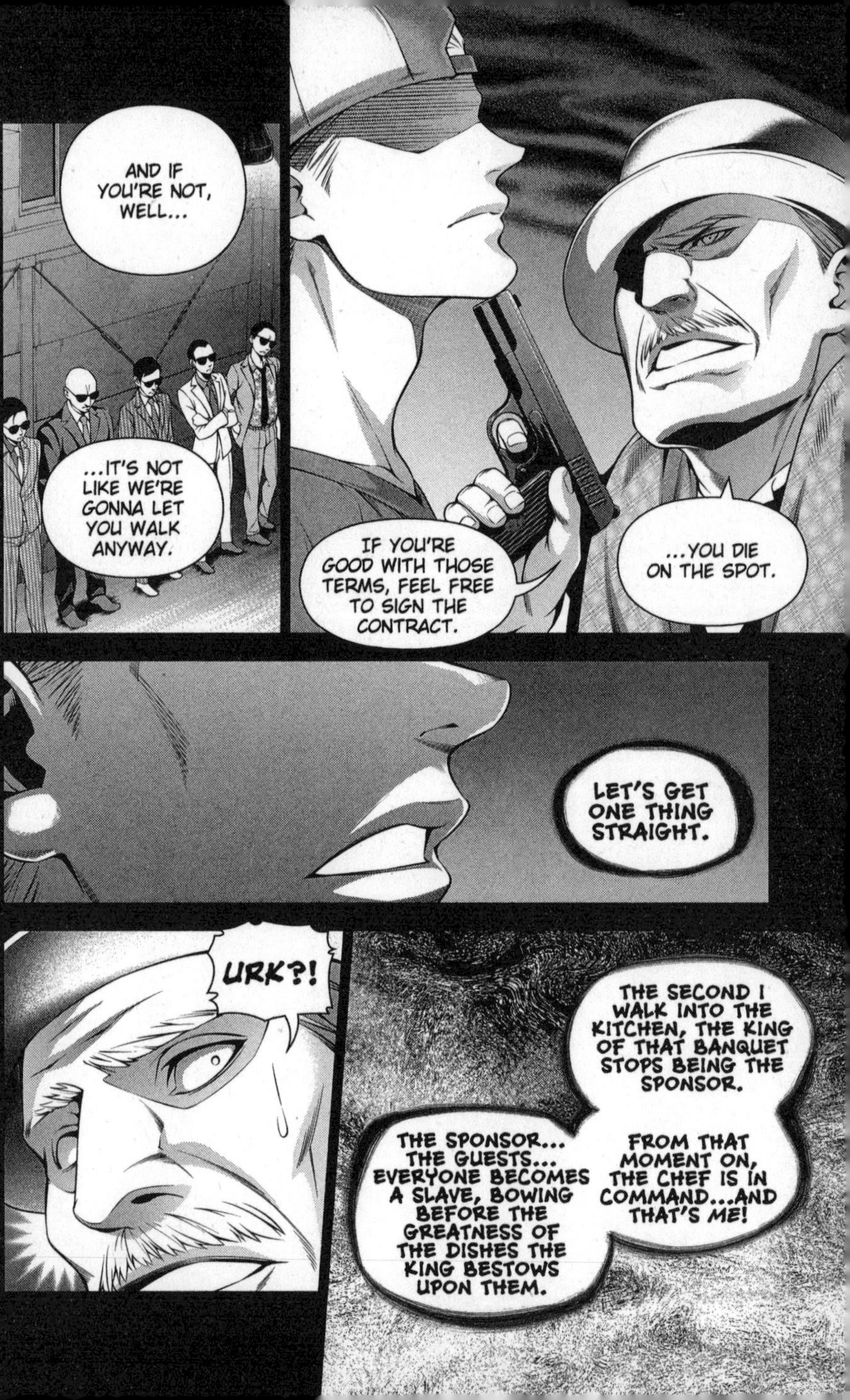
...YOU DIE ON THE SPOT.
IF YOU'RE GOOD WITH THOSE TERMS, FEEL FREE TO SIGN THE CONTRACT.
AND IF YOU'RE NOT, WELL...
...IT'S NOT LIKE WE'RE GONNA LET YOU WALK ANYWAY.
LET'S GET ONE THING STRAIGHT.
THE SECOND I WALK INTO THE KITCHEN, THE KING OF THAT BANQUET STOPS BEING THE SPONSOR.
FROM THAT MOMENT ON, THE CHEF IS IN COMMAND...AND THAT'S ME!
THE SPONSOR... THE GUESTS... EVERYONE BECOMES A SLAVE, BOWING BEFORE THE GREATNESS OF THE DISHES THE KING BESTOWS UPON THEM.
URK?!

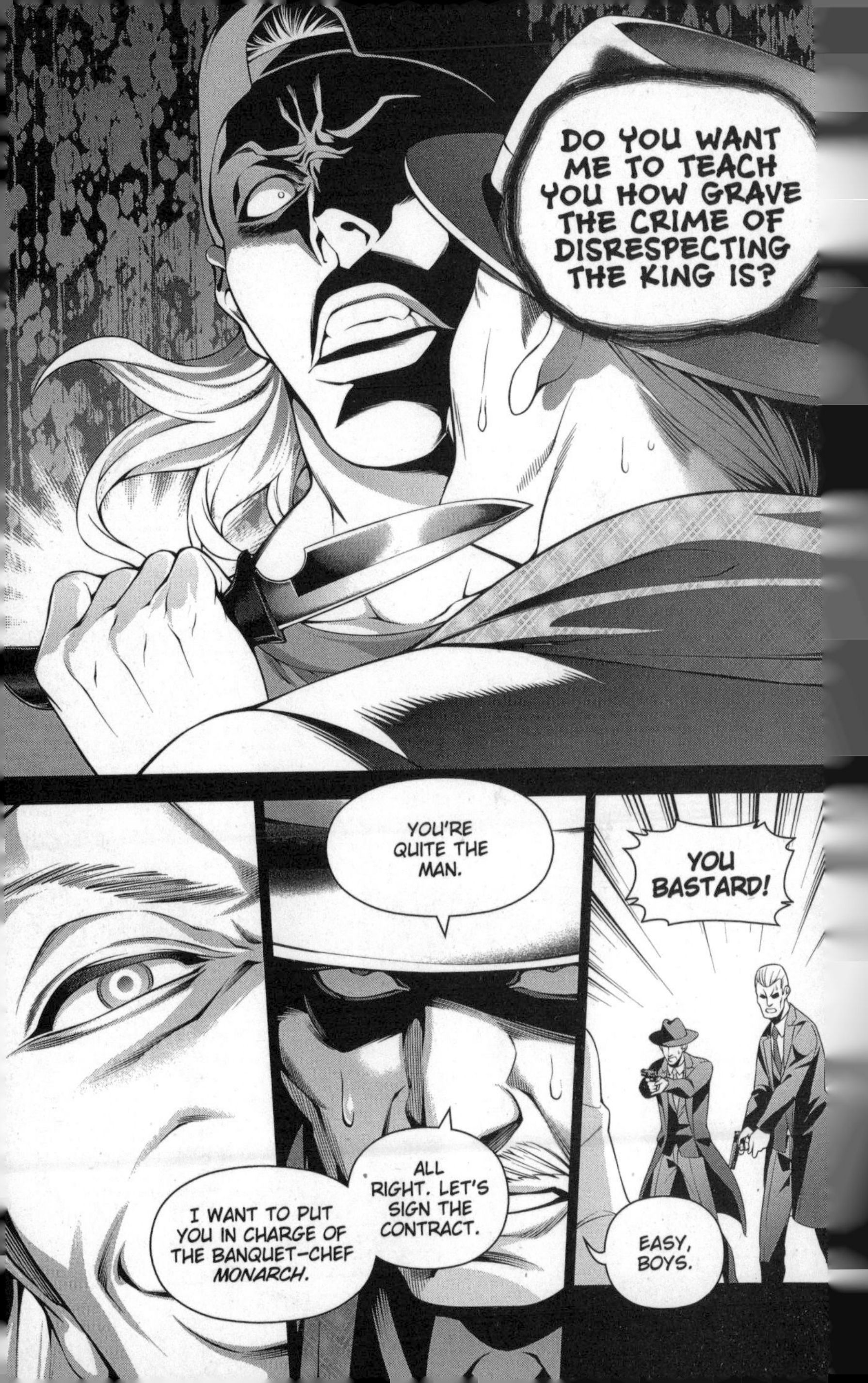
DO YOU WANT ME TO TEACH YOU HOW GRAVE THE CRIME OF DISRESPECTING THE KING IS?
YOU BASTARD!
EASY, BOYS.
YOU'RE QUITE THE MAN.
ALL RIGHT. LET'S SIGN THE CONTRACT.
I WANT TO PUT YOU IN CHARGE OF THE BANQUET-CHEF *MONARCH*.

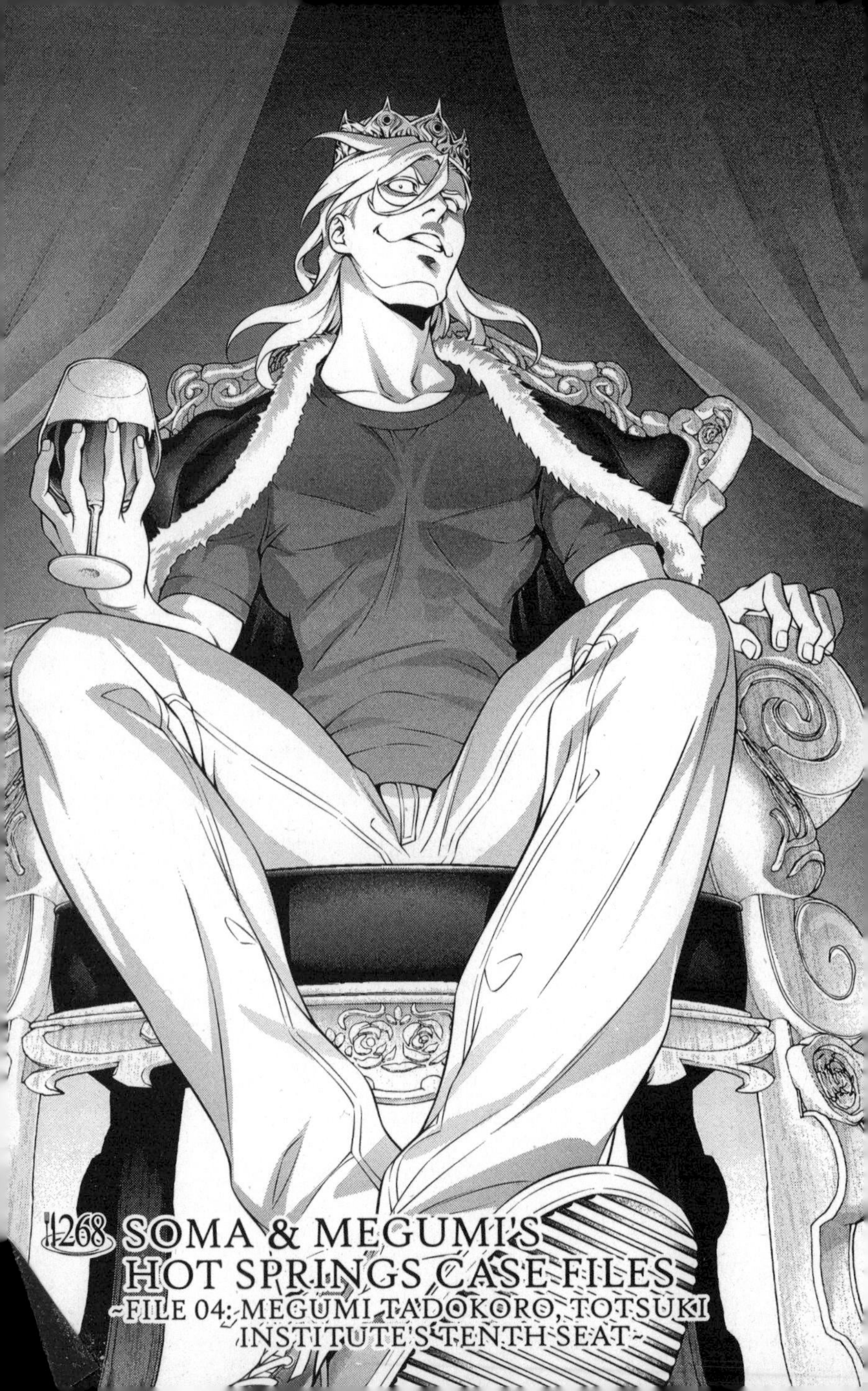

268
SOMA & MEGUMI'S HOT SPRINGS CASE FILES
~FILE 04: MEGUMI TADOKORO, TOTSUKI INSTITUTE'S TENTH SEAT~

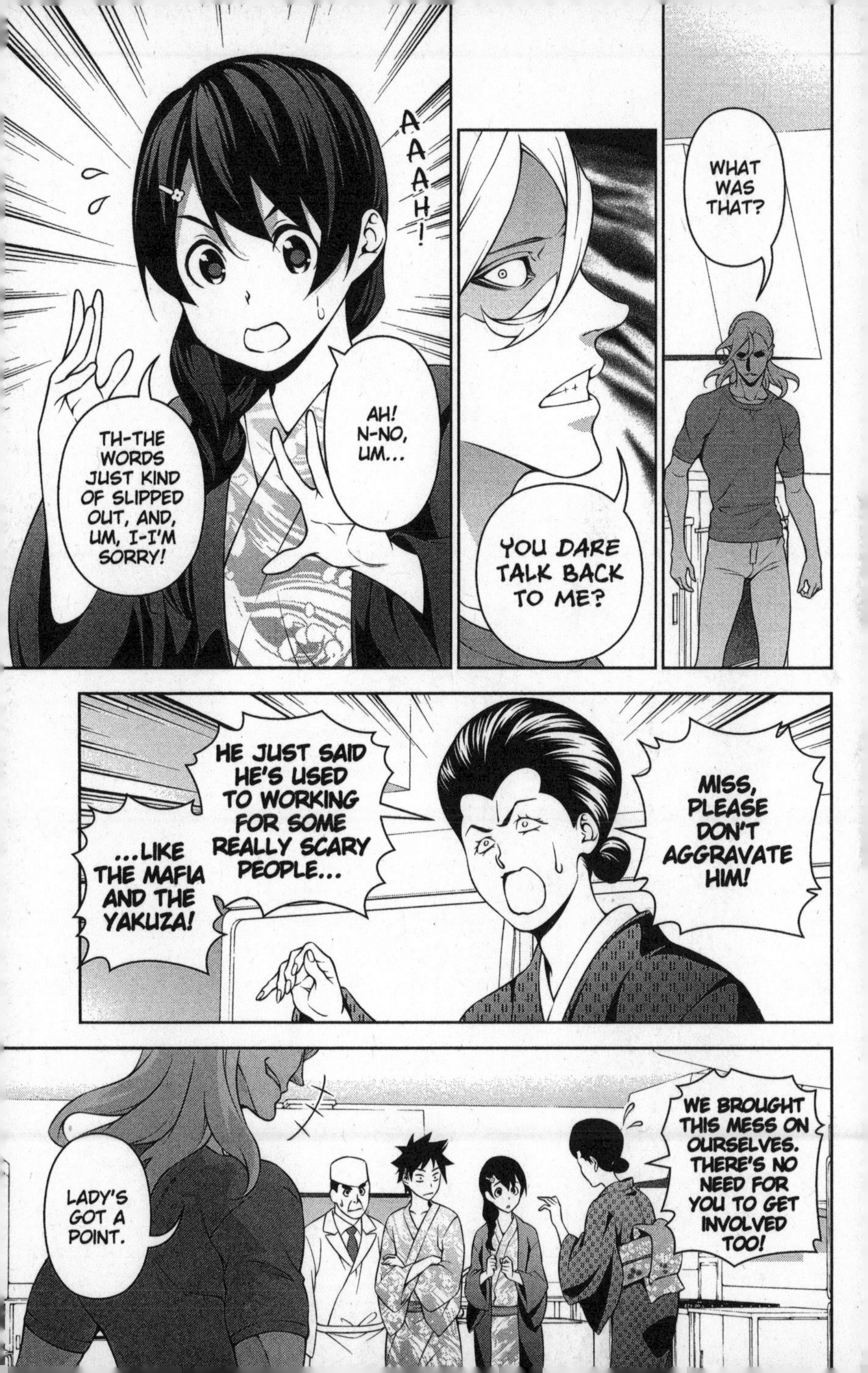
WHAT WAS THAT?
YOU DARE TALK BACK TO ME?
AAAAH!
AH! N-NO, UM...
TH-THE WORDS JUST KIND OF SLIPPED OUT, AND, UM, I-I'M SORRY!
MISS, PLEASE DON'T AGGRAVATE HIM!
HE JUST SAID HE'S USED TO WORKING FOR SOME REALLY SCARY PEOPLE...
...LIKE THE MAFIA AND THE YAKUZA!
WE BROUGHT THIS MESS ON OURSELVES. THERE'S NO NEED FOR YOU TO GET INVOLVED TOO!
LADY'S GOT A POINT.

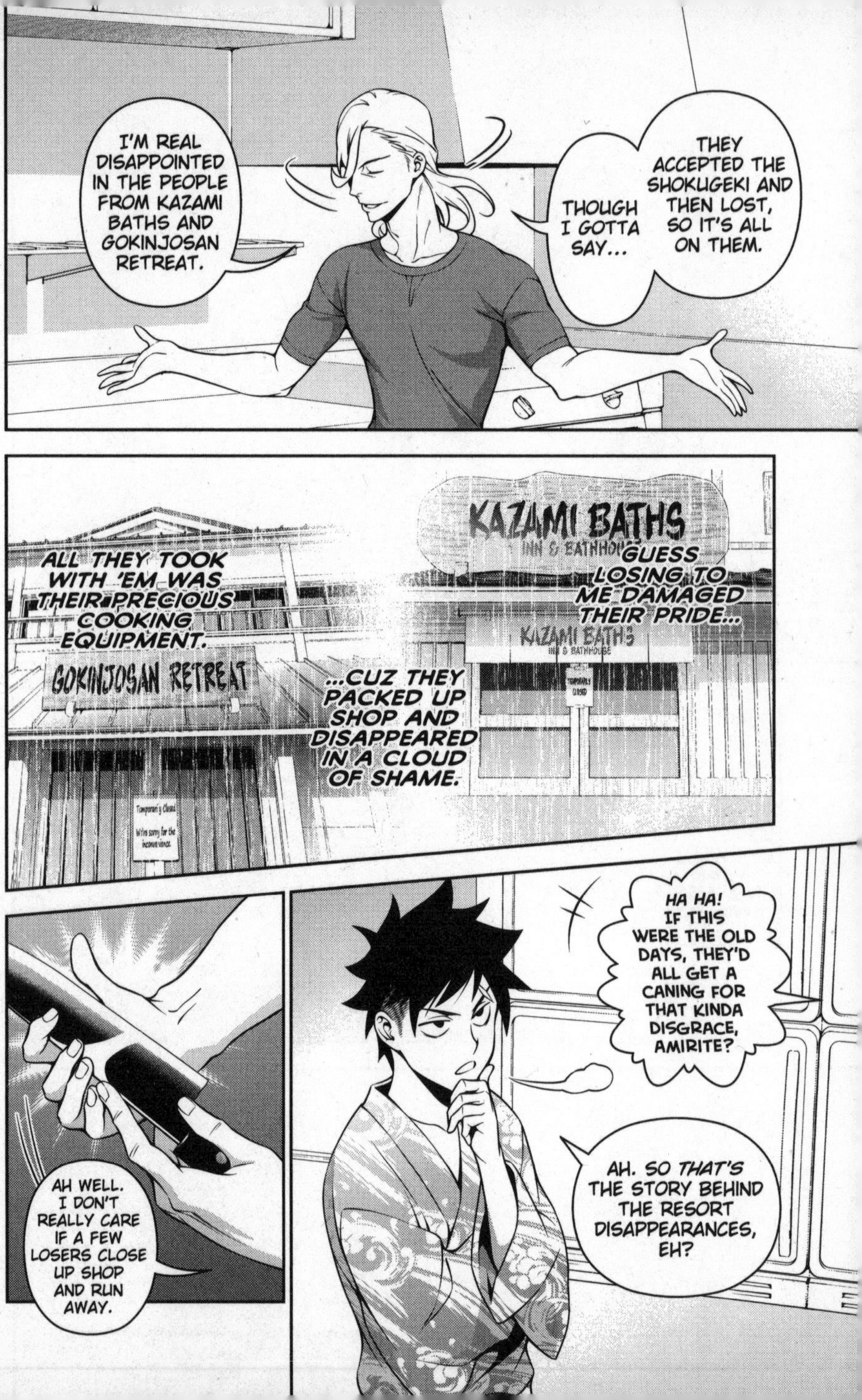
THEY ACCEPTED THE SHOKUGEKI AND THEN LOST, SO IT'S ALL ON THEM.
THOUGH I GOTTA SAY...
I'M REAL DISAPPOINTED IN THE PEOPLE FROM KAZAMI BATHS AND GOKINJOSAN RETREAT.
KAZAMI BATHS
INN & BATHHOUSE
GUESS LOSING TO ME DAMAGED THEIR PRIDE...
KAZAMI BATHS
INN & BATHHOUSE
...CUZ THEY PACKED UP SHOP AND DISAPPEARED IN A CLOUD OF SHAME.
ALL THEY TOOK WITH 'EM WAS THEIR PRECIOUS COOKING EQUIPMENT.
GOKINJOSAN RETREAT
Temporarily Closed
We're sorry for the inconvenience.
HA HA! IF THIS WERE THE OLD DAYS, THEY'D ALL GET A CANING FOR THAT KINDA DISGRACE, AMIRITE?
AH. SO *THAT'S* THE STORY BEHIND THE RESORT DISAPPEARANCES, EH?
AH WELL. I DON'T REALLY CARE IF A FEW LOSERS CLOSE UP SHOP AND RUN AWAY.

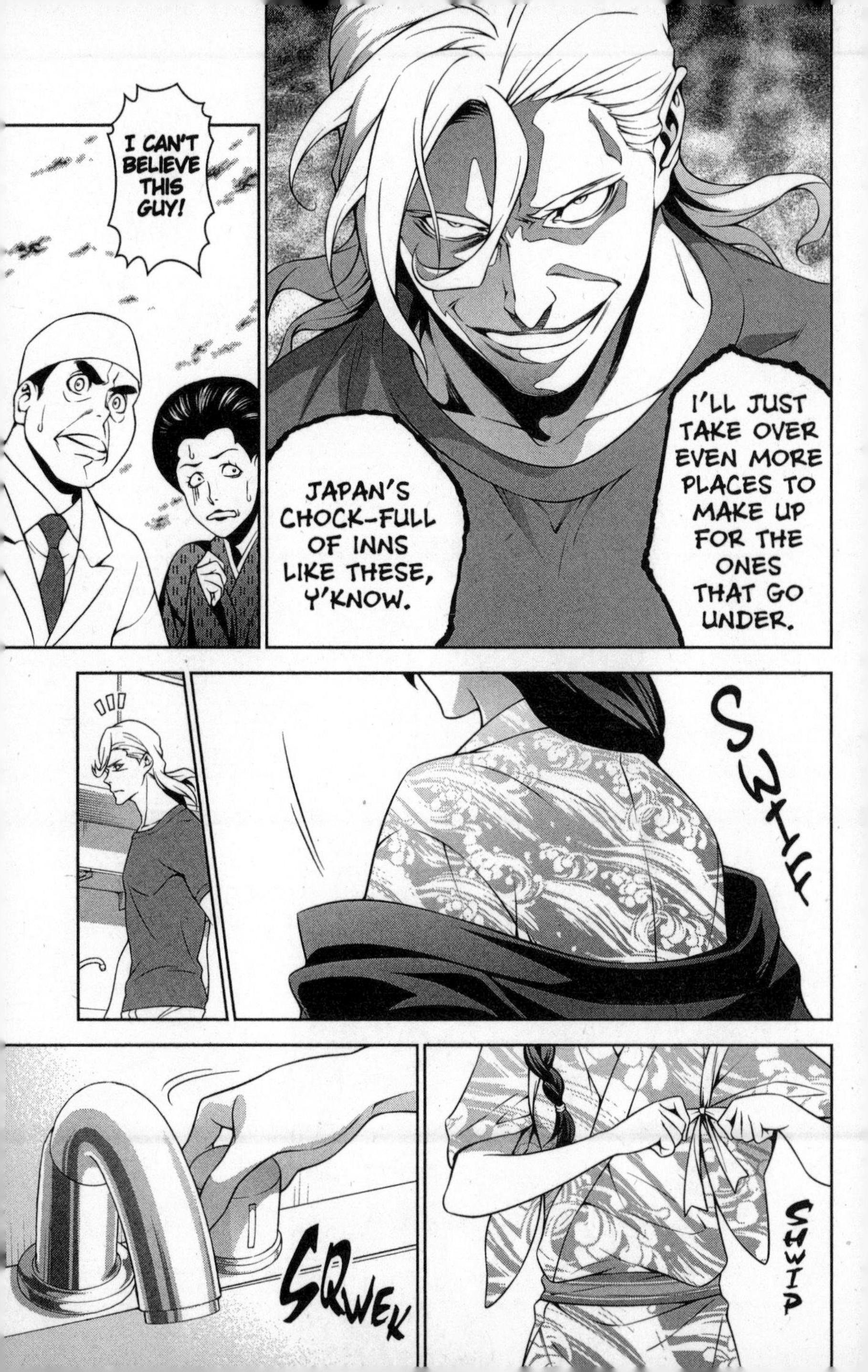
I'LL JUST TAKE OVER EVEN MORE PLACES TO MAKE UP FOR THE ONES THAT GO UNDER.
JAPAN'S CHOCK-FULL OF INNS LIKE THESE, Y'KNOW.
I CAN'T BELIEVE THIS GUY!
SWIII
SHWIP
SQWEK

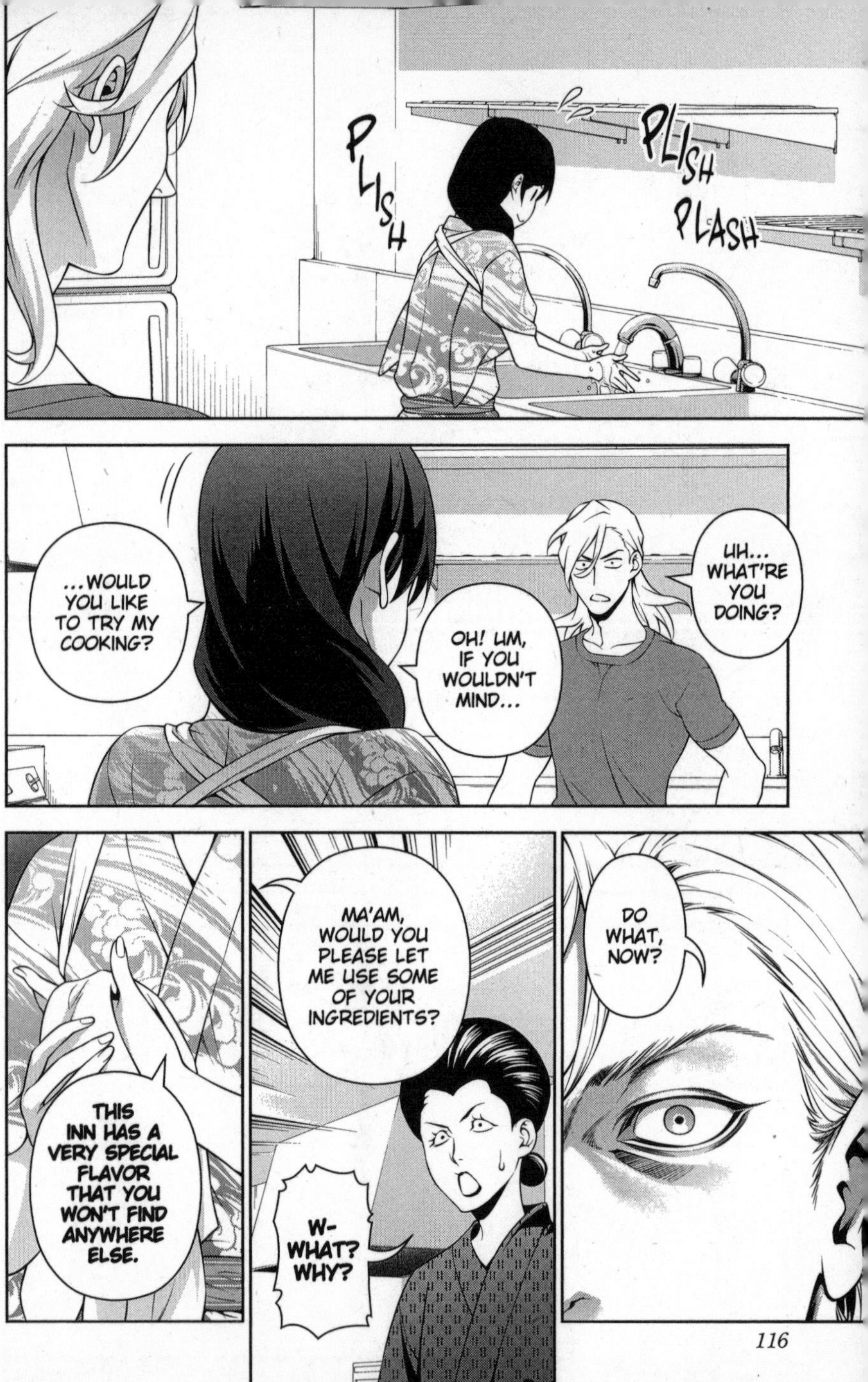
PLISH
PLASH
PLISH
UH... WHAT'RE YOU DOING?
...WOULD YOU LIKE TO TRY MY COOKING?
OH! UM, IF YOU WOULDN'T MIND...
DO WHAT, NOW?
MA'AM, WOULD YOU PLEASE LET ME USE SOME OF YOUR INGREDIENTS?
W- WHAT? WHY?
THIS INN HAS A VERY SPECIAL FLAVOR THAT YOU WON'T FIND ANYWHERE ELSE.

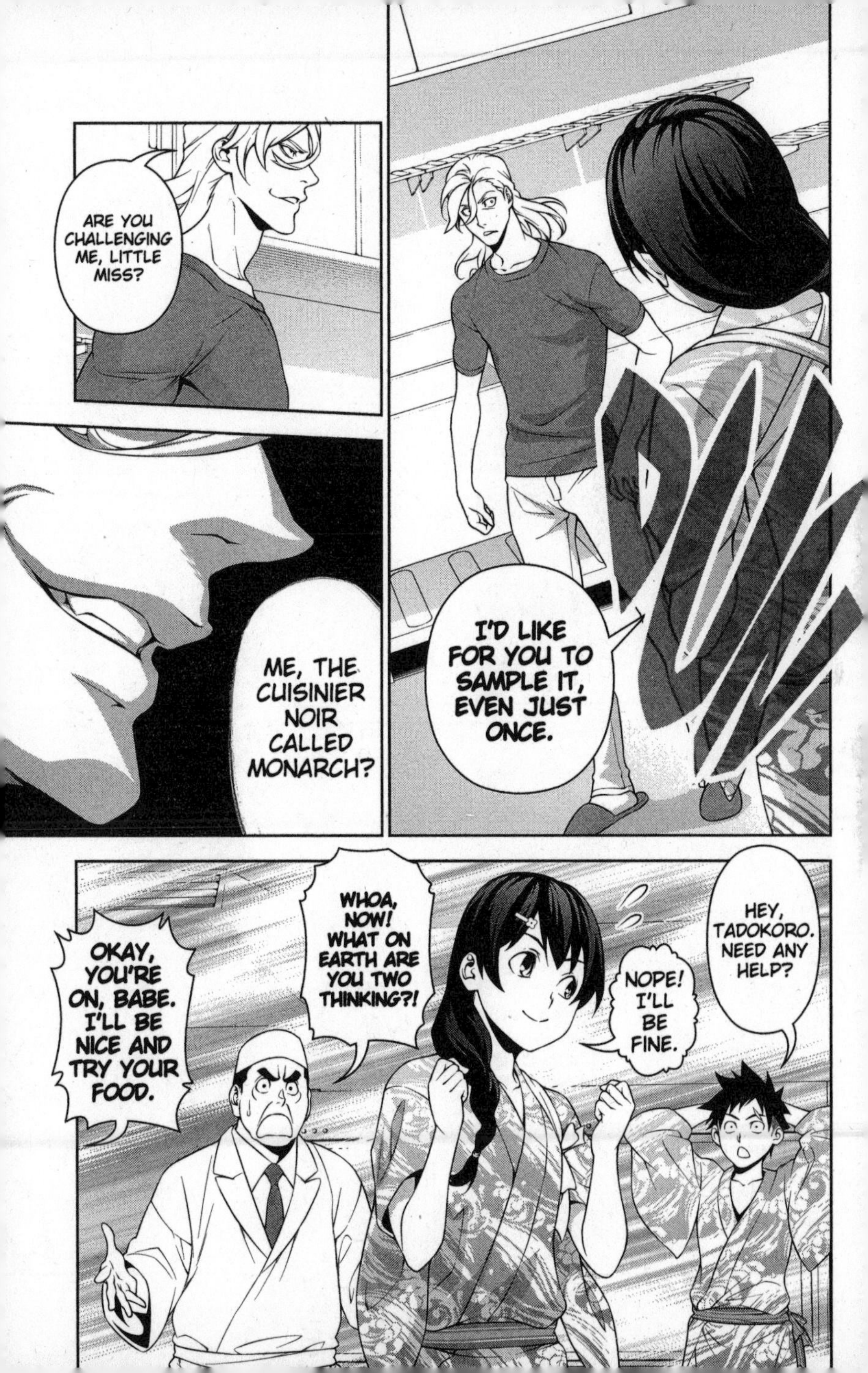
I'D LIKE FOR YOU TO SAMPLE IT, EVEN JUST ONCE.
ARE YOU CHALLENGING ME, LITTLE MISS?
ME, THE CUISINIER NOIR CALLED MONARCH?
HEY, TADOKORO. NEED ANY HELP?
NOPE! I'LL BE FINE.
WHOA, NOW! WHAT ON EARTH ARE YOU TWO THINKING?!
OKAY, YOU'RE ON, BABE. I'LL BE NICE AND TRY YOUR FOOD.

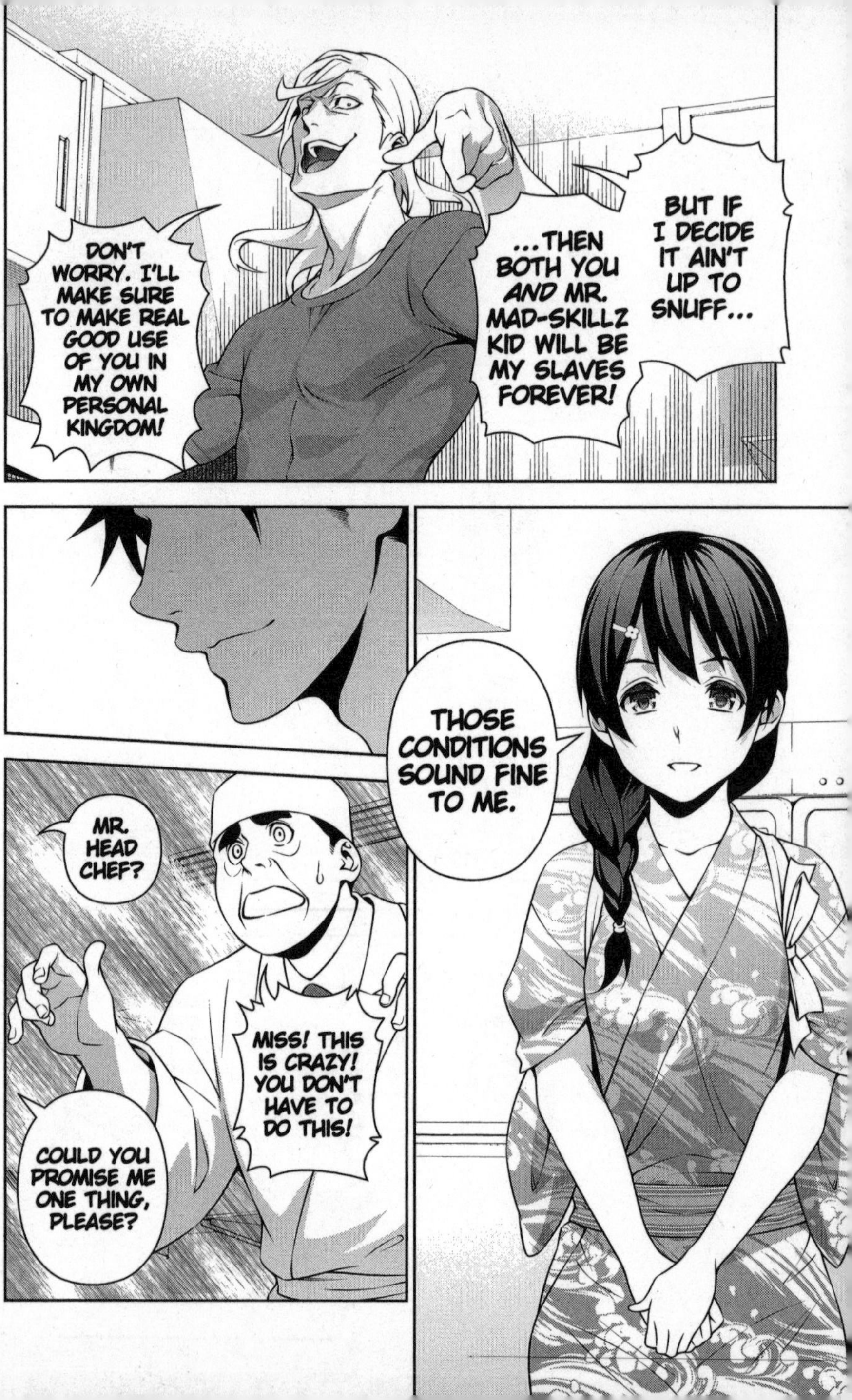
BUT IF I DECIDE IT AIN'T UP TO SNUFF...
...THEN BOTH YOU AND MR. MAD-SKILLZ KID WILL BE MY SLAVES FOREVER!
DON'T WORRY. I'LL MAKE SURE TO MAKE REAL GOOD USE OF YOU IN MY OWN PERSONAL KINGDOM!
THOSE CONDITIONS SOUND FINE TO ME.
MR. HEAD CHEF?
MISS! THIS IS CRAZY! YOU DON'T HAVE TO DO THIS!
COULD YOU PROMISE ME ONE THING, PLEASE?

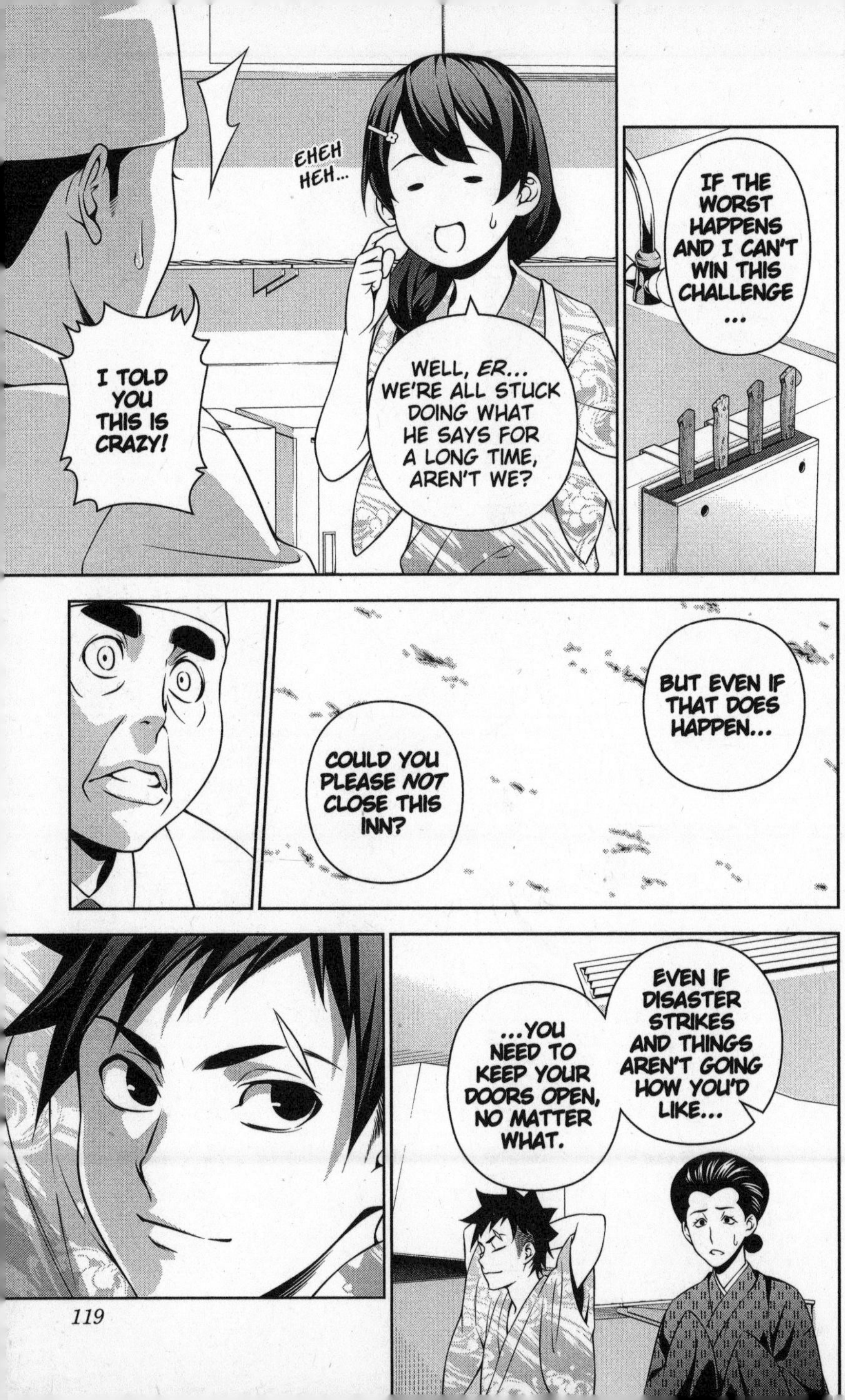
I TOLD YOU THIS IS CRAZY!
EHEH HEH...
WELL, *ER*... WE'RE ALL STUCK DOING WHAT HE SAYS FOR A LONG TIME, AREN'T WE?
IF THE WORST HAPPENS AND I CAN'T WIN THIS CHALLENGE ...
BUT EVEN IF THAT DOES HAPPEN...
COULD YOU PLEASE *NOT* CLOSE THIS INN?
EVEN IF DISASTER STRIKES AND THINGS AREN'T GOING HOW YOU'D LIKE...
...YOU NEED TO KEEP YOUR DOORS OPEN, NO MATTER WHAT.

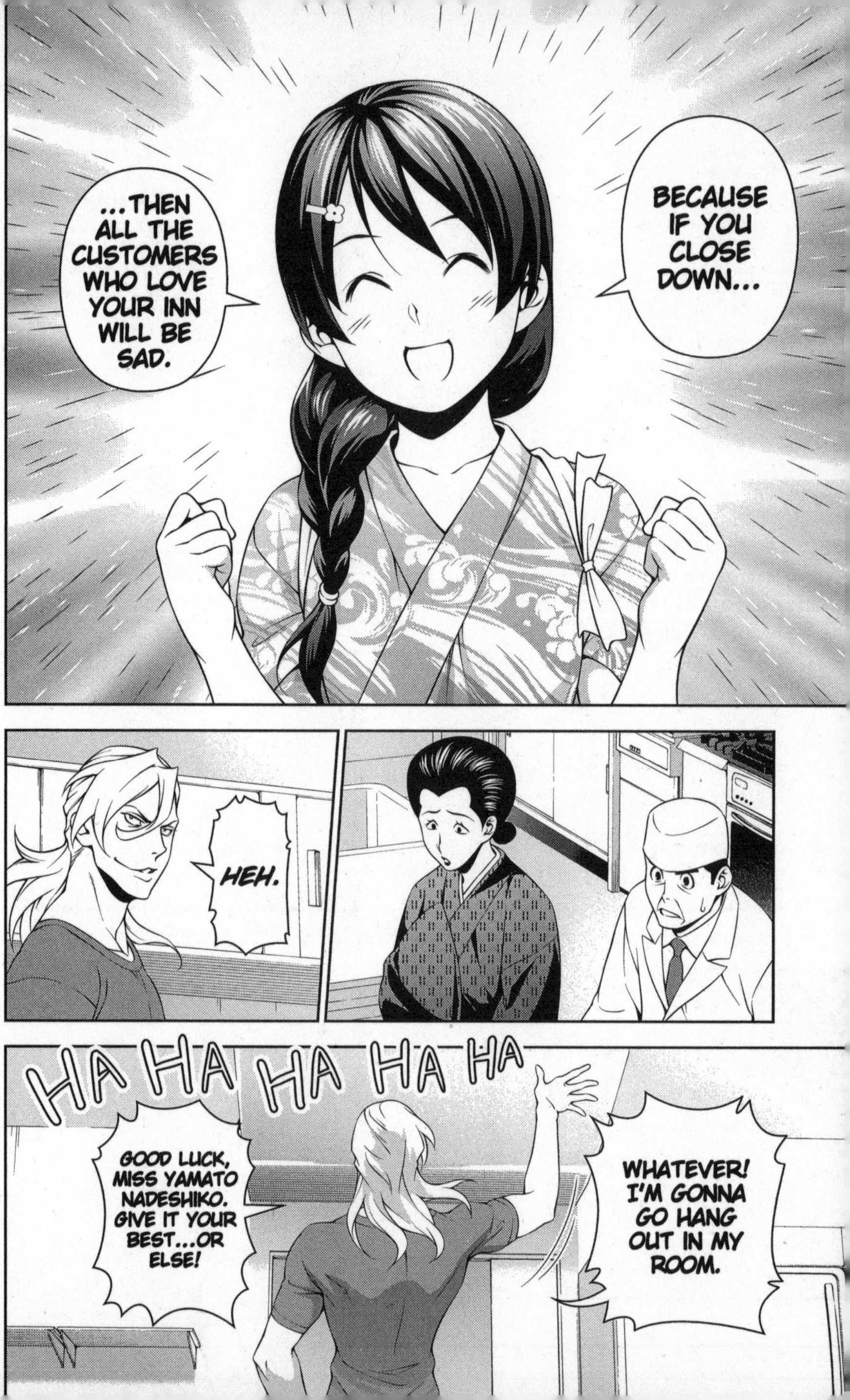
BECAUSE IF YOU CLOSE DOWN...
...THEN ALL THE CUSTOMERS WHO LOVE YOUR INN WILL BE SAD.
HEH.
HA HA HA HA HA
WHATEVER! I'M GONNA GO HANG OUT IN MY ROOM.
GOOD LUCK, MISS YAMATO NADESHIKO. GIVE IT YOUR BEST...OR ELSE!

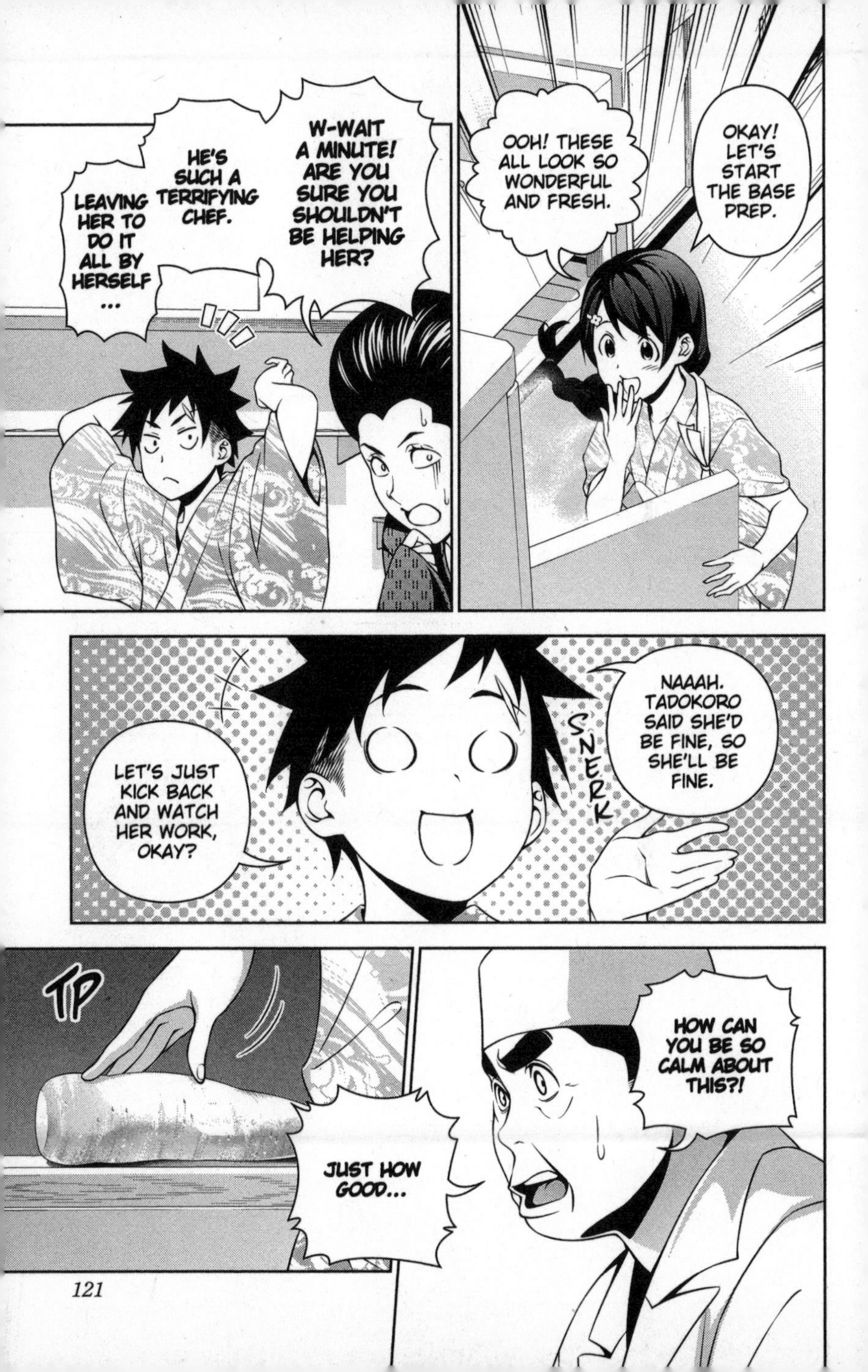
OKAY! LET'S START THE BASE PREP.
OOH! THESE ALL LOOK SO WONDERFUL AND FRESH.
W-WAIT A MINUTE! ARE YOU SURE YOU SHOULDN'T BE HELPING HER?
HE'S SUCH A TERRIFYING CHEF.
LEAVING HER TO DO IT ALL BY HERSELF...
NAAAH. TADOKORO SAID SHE'D BE FINE, SO SHE'LL BE FINE.
SNERK
LET'S JUST KICK BACK AND WATCH HER WORK, OKAY?
HOW CAN YOU BE SO CALM ABOUT THIS?!
JUST HOW GOOD...
TP

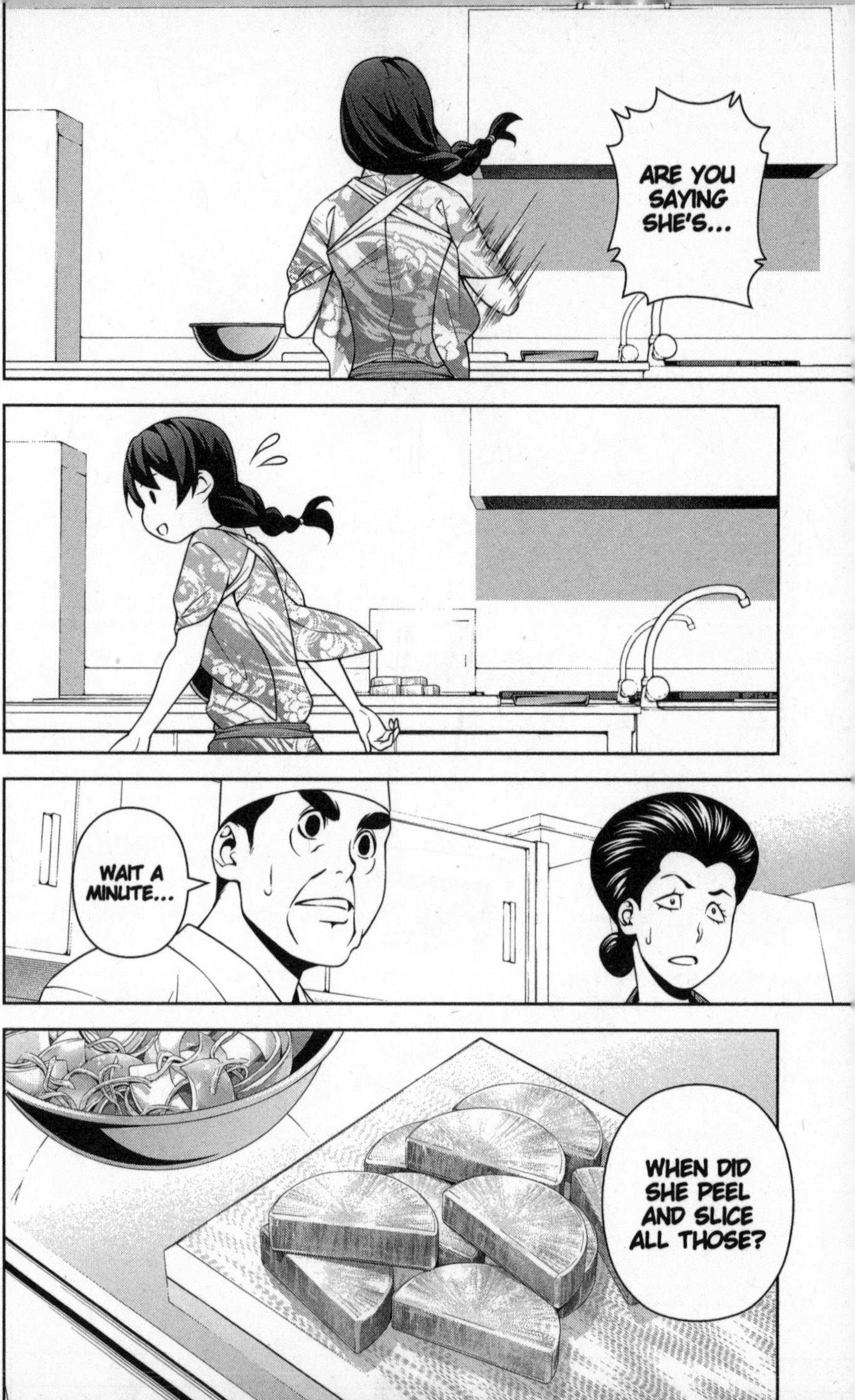
ARE YOU SAYING SHE'S...
WAIT A MINUTE...
WHEN DID SHE PEEL AND SLICE ALL THOSE?

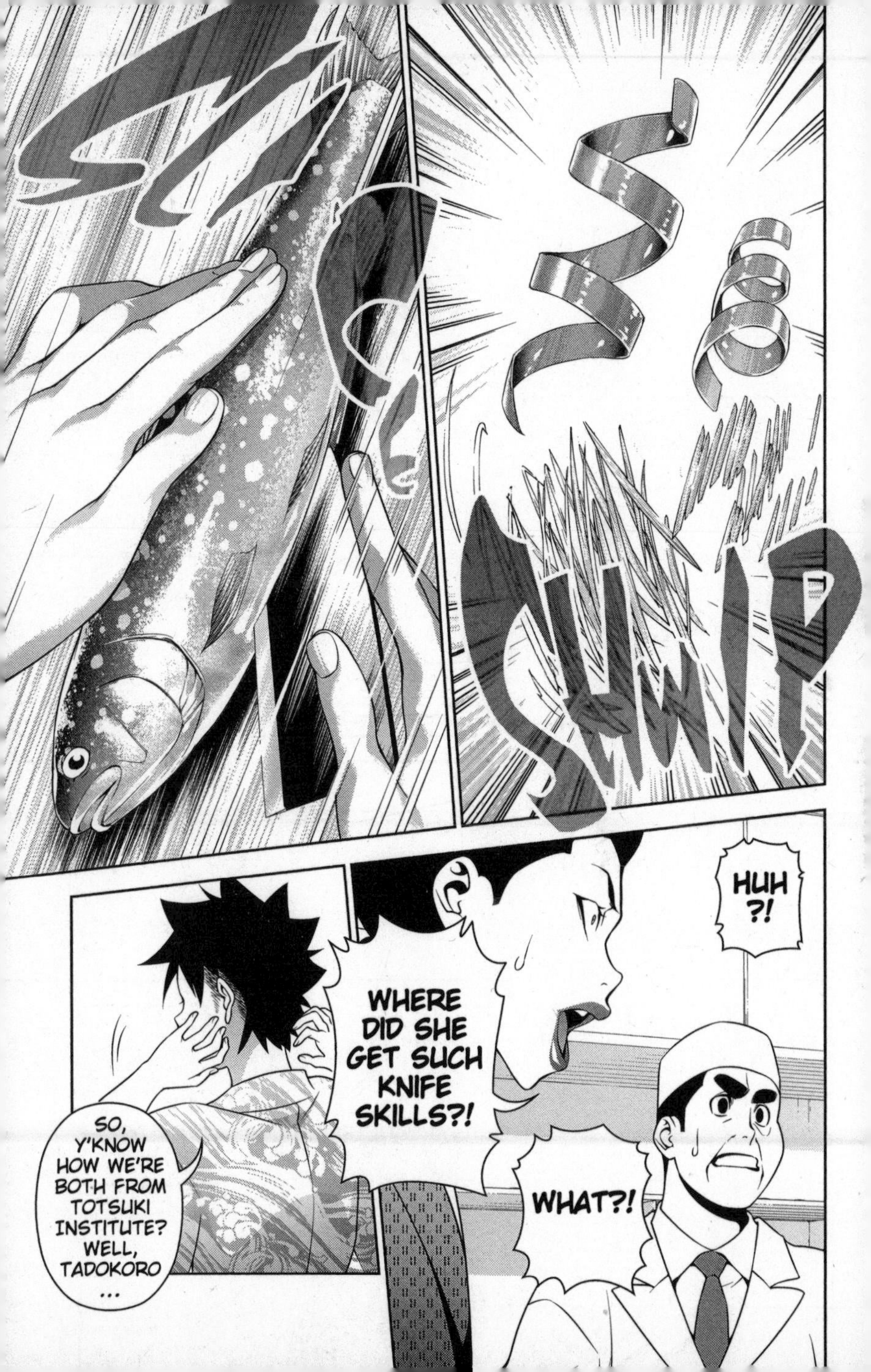
SWIP
HUH?!
WHERE DID SHE GET SUCH KNIFE SKILLS?!
WHAT?!
SO, Y'KNOW HOW WE'RE BOTH FROM TOTSUKI INSTITUTE? WELL, TADOKORO...

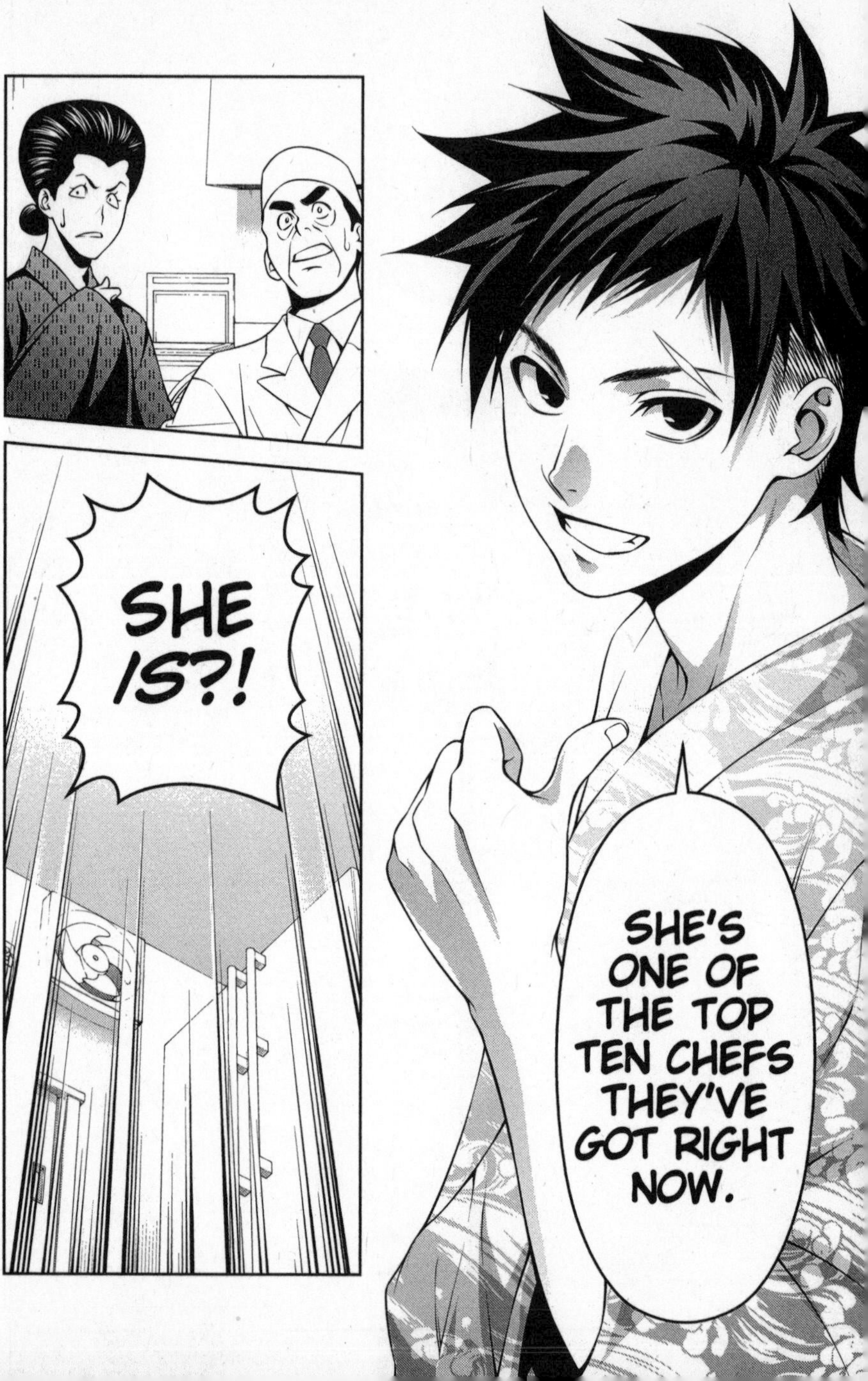
SHE'S ONE OF THE TOP TEN CHEFS THEY'VE GOT RIGHT NOW.
SHE IS?!

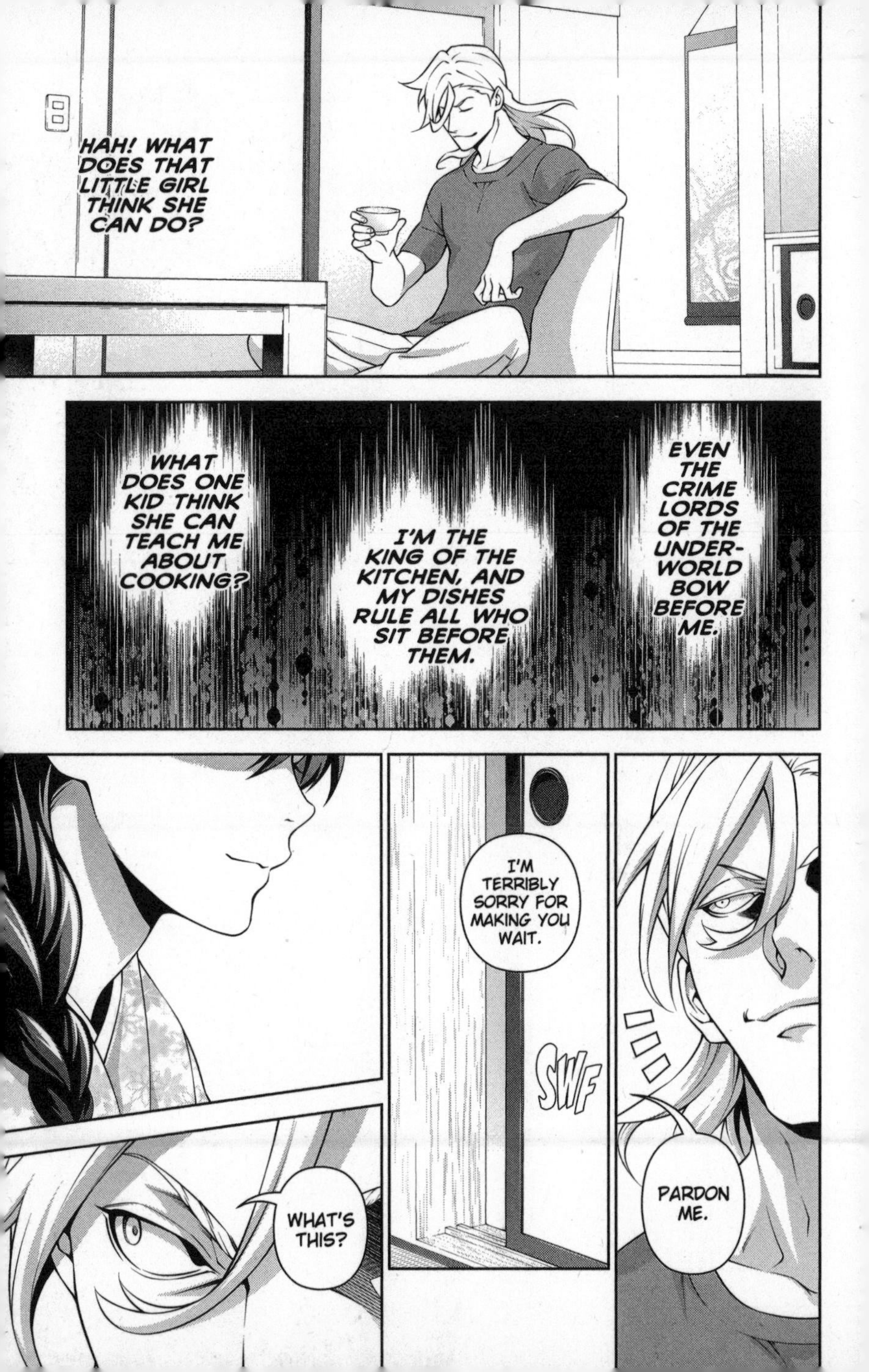
HAH! WHAT DOES THAT LITTLE GIRL THINK SHE CAN DO?
EVEN THE CRIME LORDS OF THE UNDER-WORLD BOW BEFORE ME.
I'M THE KING OF THE KITCHEN, AND MY DISHES RULE ALL WHO SIT BEFORE THEM.
WHAT DOES ONE KID THINK SHE CAN TEACH ME ABOUT COOKING?
PARDON ME.
I'M TERRIBLY SORRY FOR MAKING YOU WAIT.
SWF
WHAT'S THIS?

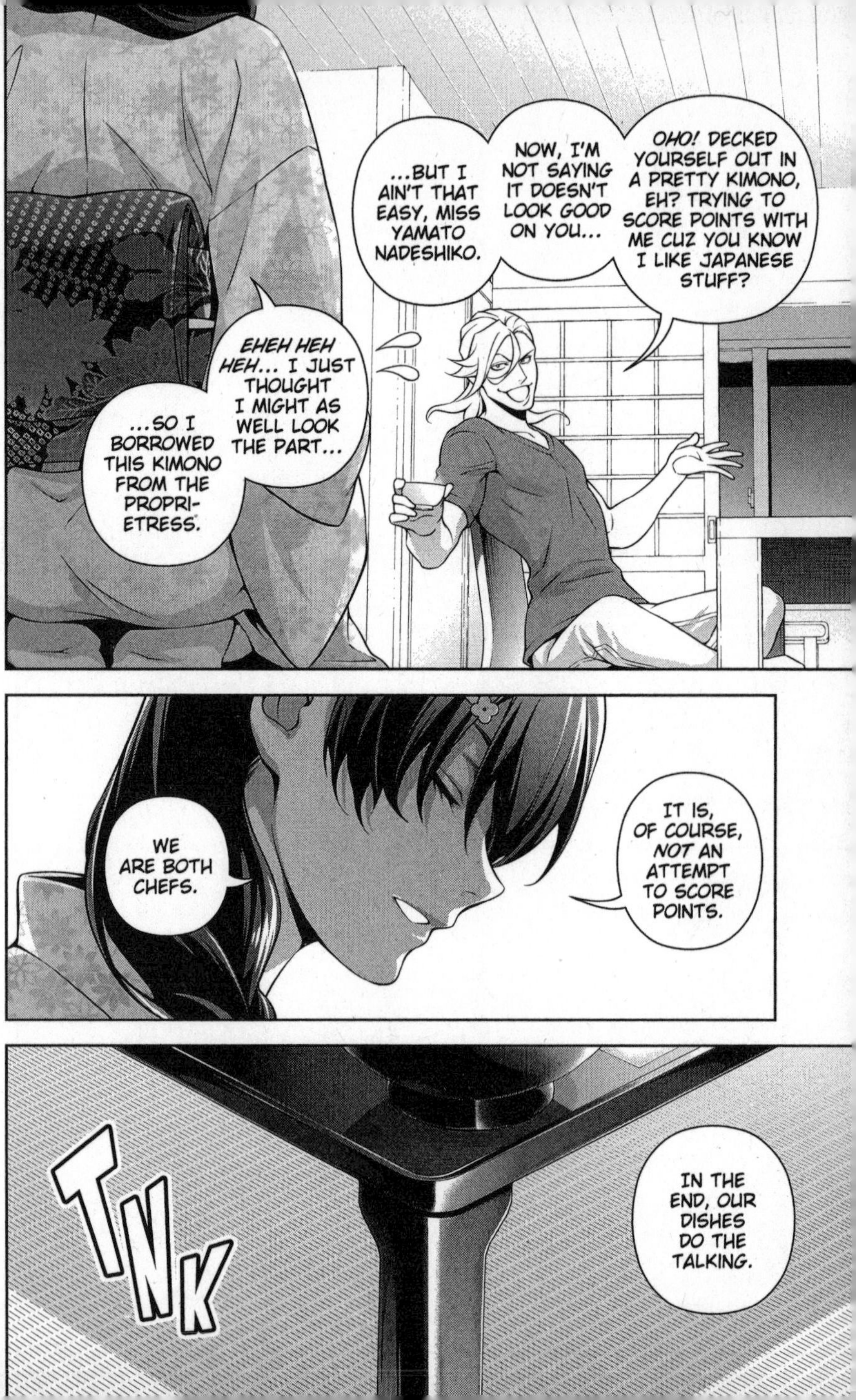
OHO! DECKED YOURSELF OUT IN A PRETTY KIMONO, EH? TRYING TO SCORE POINTS WITH ME CUZ YOU KNOW I LIKE JAPANESE STUFF?
NOW, I'M NOT SAYING IT DOESN'T LOOK GOOD ON YOU...
...BUT I AIN'T THAT EASY, MISS YAMATO NADESHIKO.
EHEH HEH HEH... I JUST THOUGHT I MIGHT AS WELL LOOK THE PART...
...SO I BORROWED THIS KIMONO FROM THE PROPRIETRESS.
IT IS, OF COURSE, NOT AN ATTEMPT TO SCORE POINTS.
WE ARE BOTH CHEFS.
IN THE END, OUR DISHES DO THE TALKING.
TNK

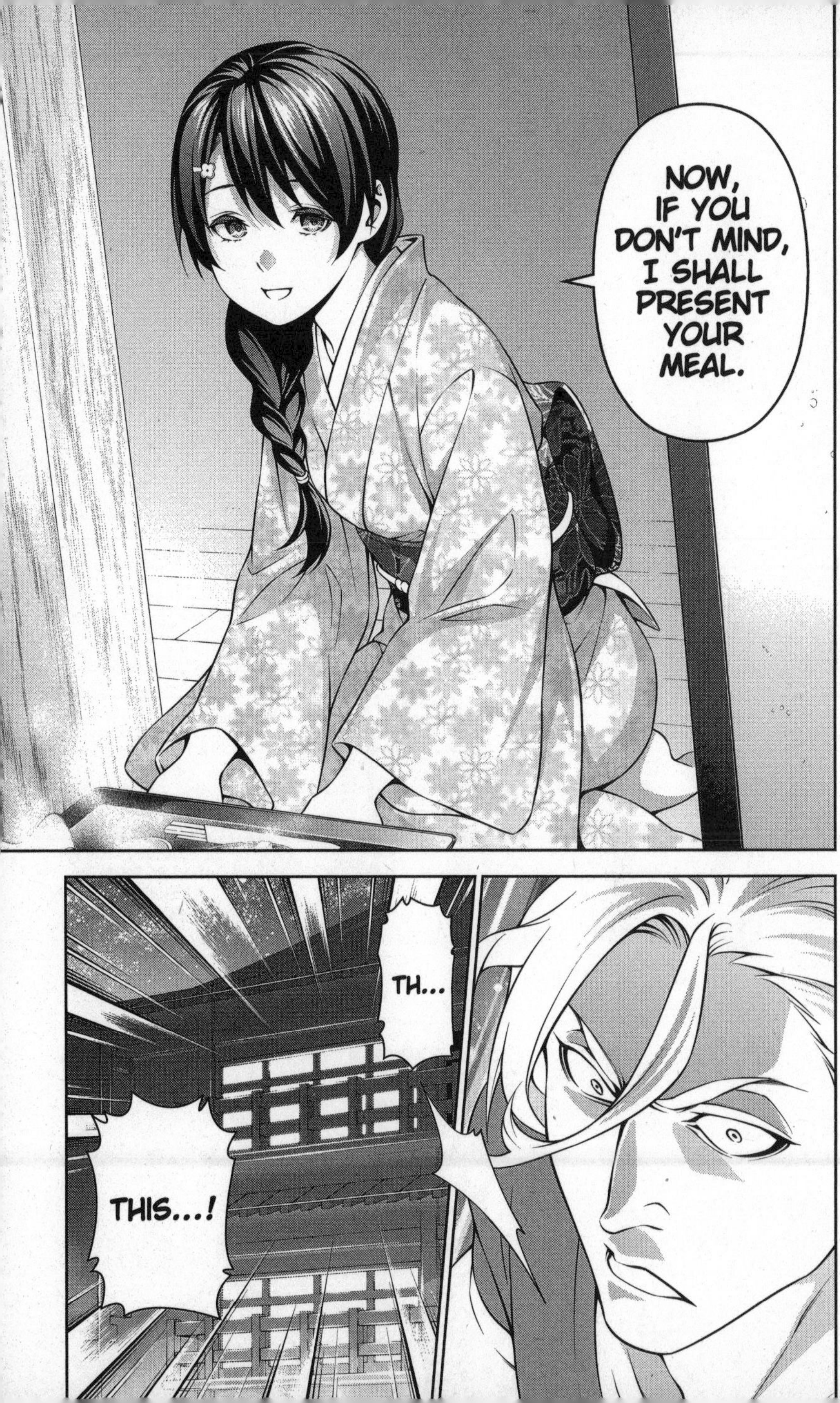
NOW, IF YOU DON'T MIND, I SHALL PRESENT YOUR MEAL.
TH...
THIS...!

THE CASE OF IBUSAKI

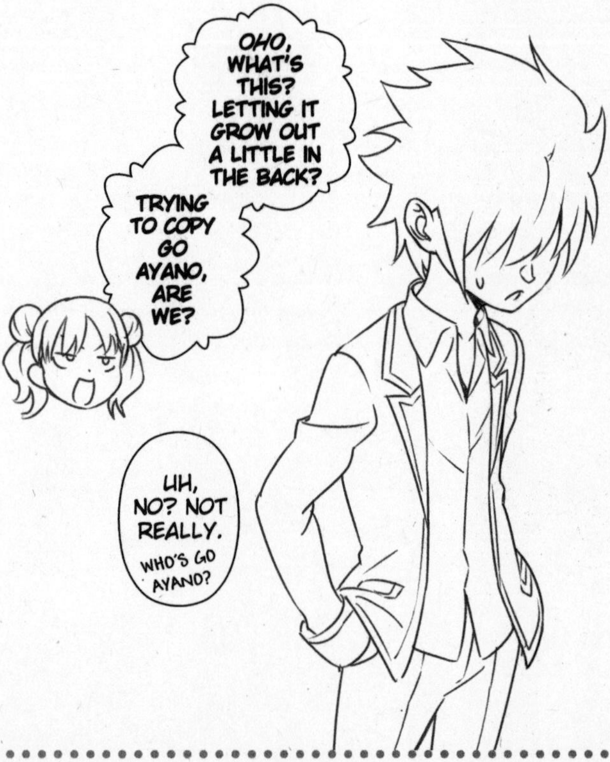
OHO, WHAT'S THIS? LETTING IT GROW OUT A LITTLE IN THE BACK?
TRYING TO COPY GO AYANO, ARE WE?
UH, NO? NOT REALLY.
WHO'S GO AYANO?

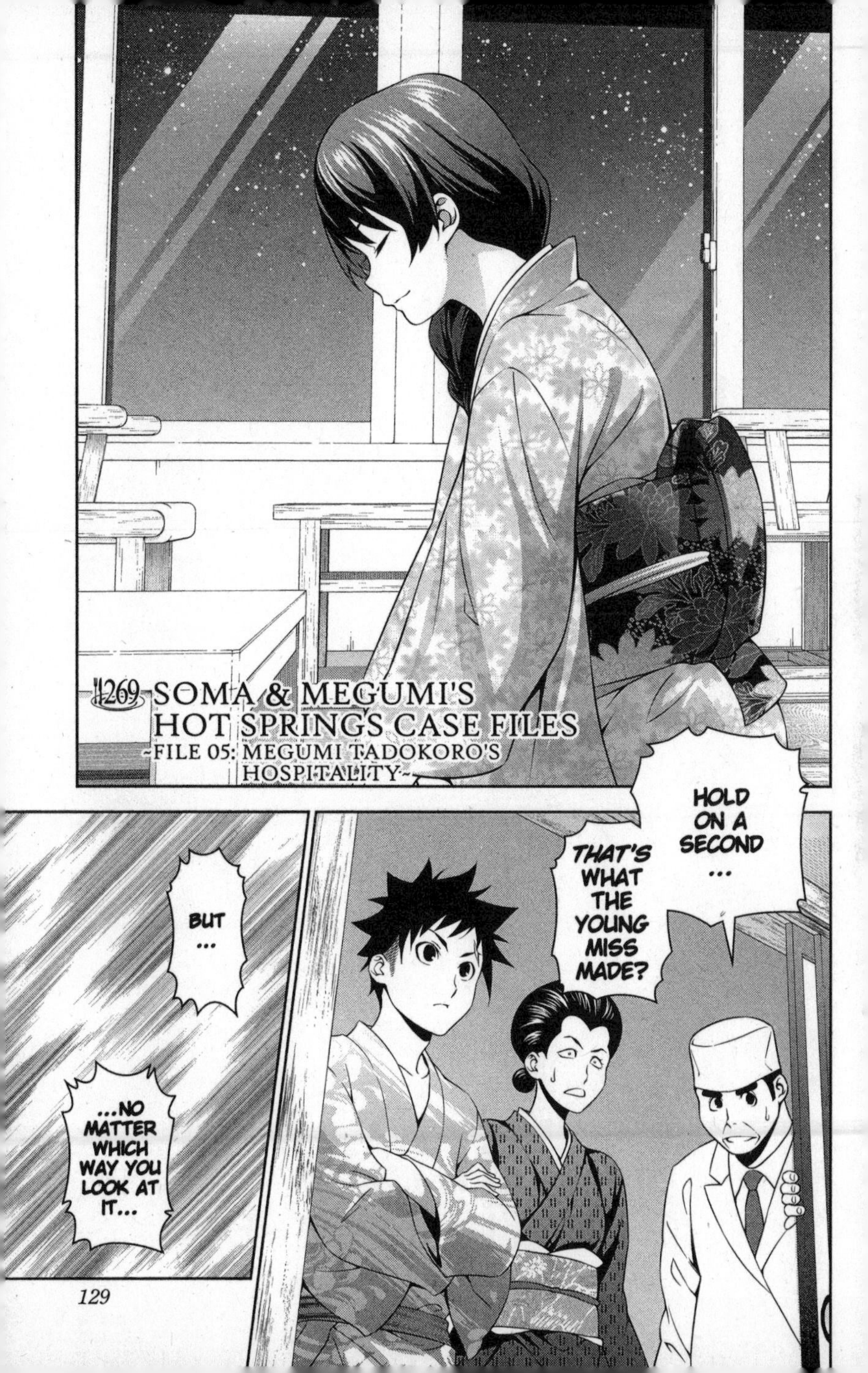

≣269 SOMA & MEGUMI'S HOT SPRINGS CASE FILES
~FILE 05: MEGUMI TADOKORO'S HOSPITALITY~
HOLD ON A SECOND ...
THAT'S WHAT THE YOUNG MISS MADE?
BUT ...
...NO MATTER WHICH WAY YOU LOOK AT IT...

TA-DAH!

#129 SOMA & MEGUMI'S HOT SPRINGS CASE FILES
~FILE 05: MEGUMI TADOKORO'S HOSPITALITY~

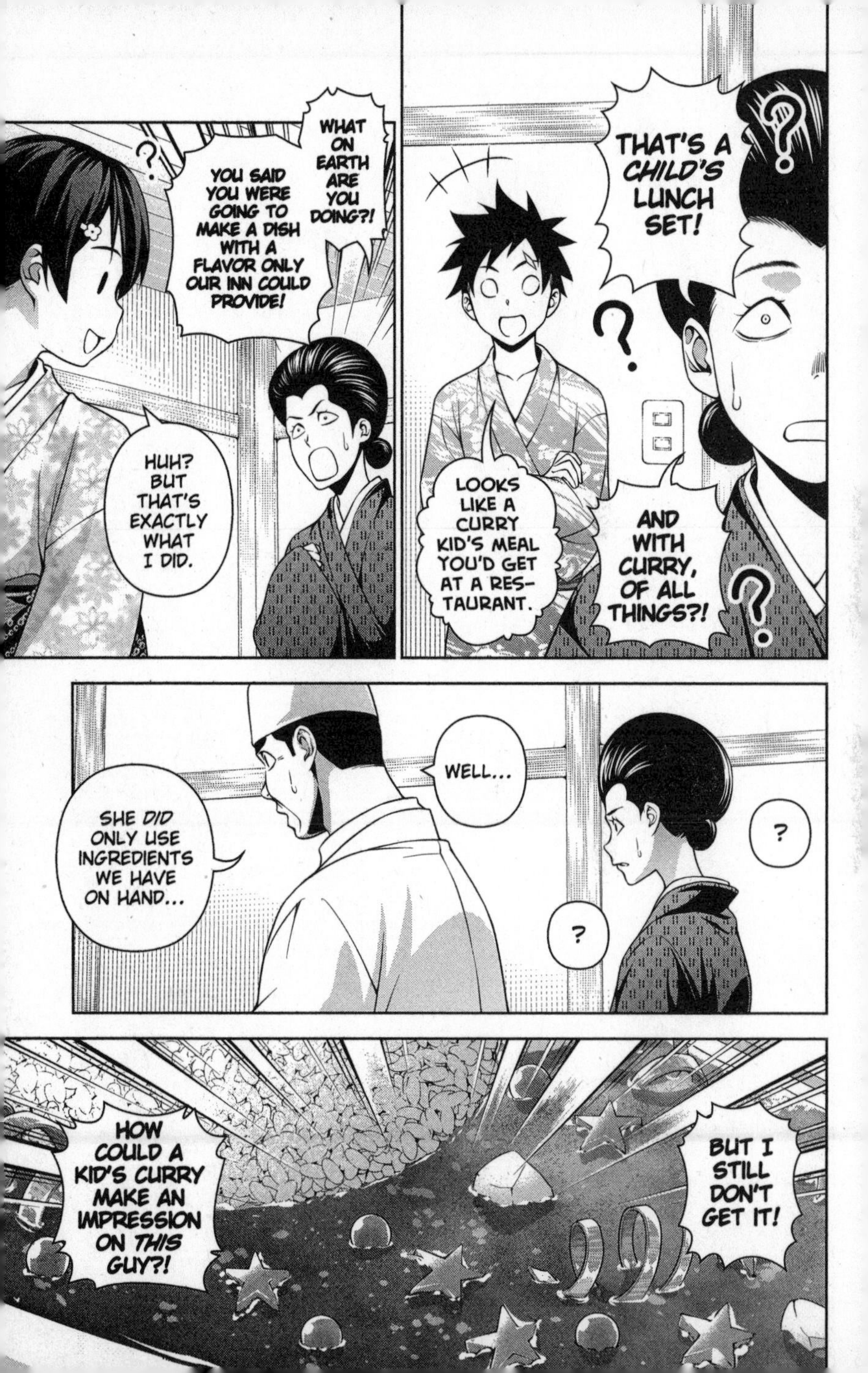
THAT'S A *CHILD'S* LUNCH SET!
AND WITH CURRY, OF ALL THINGS?!
LOOKS LIKE A CURRY KID'S MEAL YOU'D GET AT A RES-TAURANT.
WHAT ON EARTH ARE YOU DOING?!
YOU SAID YOU WERE GOING TO MAKE A DISH WITH A FLAVOR ONLY OUR INN COULD PROVIDE!
HUH? BUT THAT'S EXACTLY WHAT I DID.
?
WELL...
?
SHE *DID* ONLY USE INGREDIENTS WE HAVE ON HAND...
BUT I STILL DON'T GET IT!
HOW COULD A KID'S CURRY MAKE AN IMPRESSION ON *THIS* GUY?!

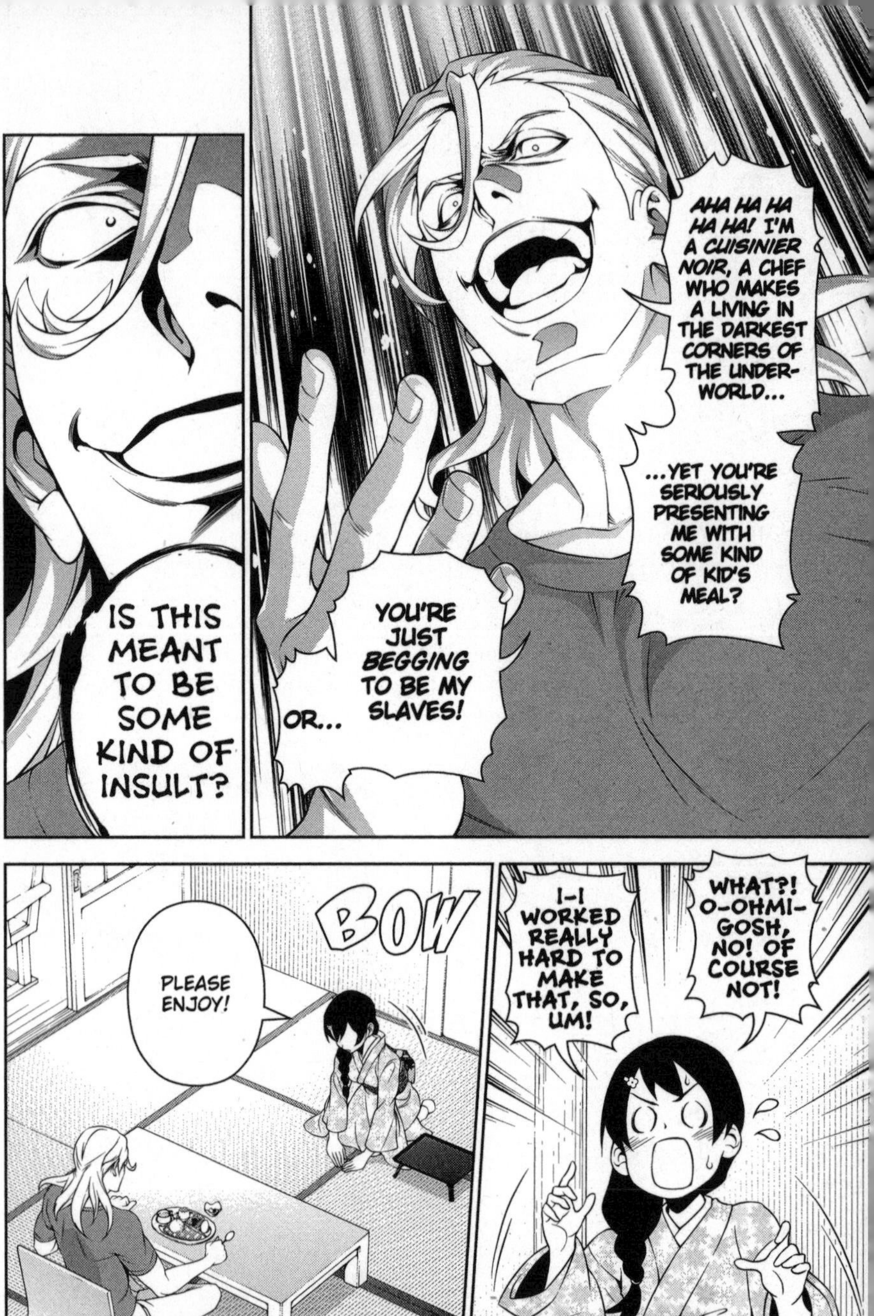
AHA HA HA HA HA! I'M A CUISINIER NOIR, A CHEF WHO MAKES A LIVING IN THE DARKEST CORNERS OF THE UNDER-WORLD...
...YET YOU'RE SERIOUSLY PRESENTING ME WITH SOME KIND OF KID'S MEAL?
YOU'RE JUST BEGGING TO BE MY SLAVES!
OR...
IS THIS MEANT TO BE SOME KIND OF INSULT?
WHAT?! O-OHMI-GOSH, NO! OF COURSE NOT!
I-I WORKED REALLY HARD TO MAKE THAT, SO, UM!
BOW
PLEASE ENJOY!

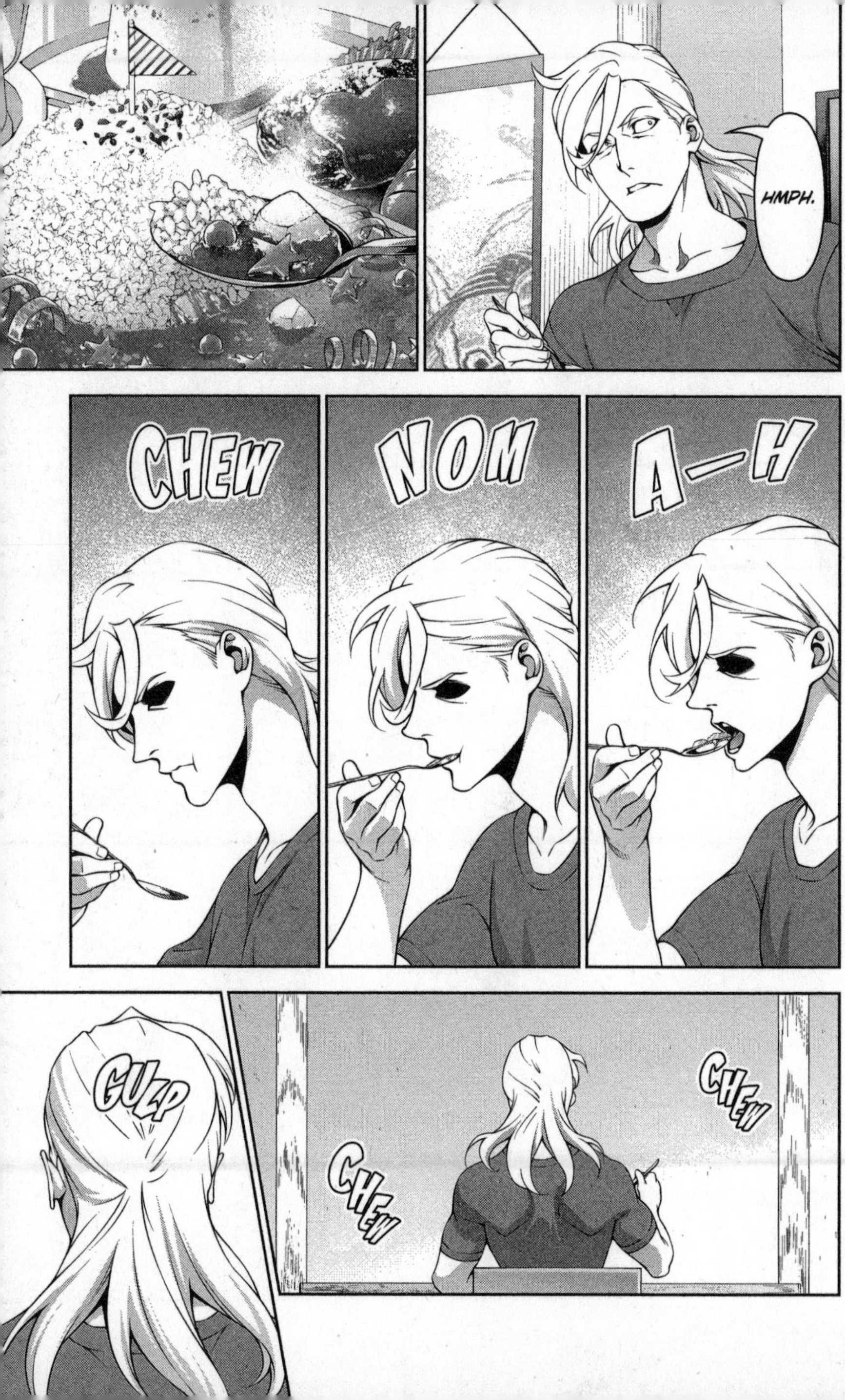
HMPH.
A—H
NOM
CHEW
CHEW
CHEW
GULP

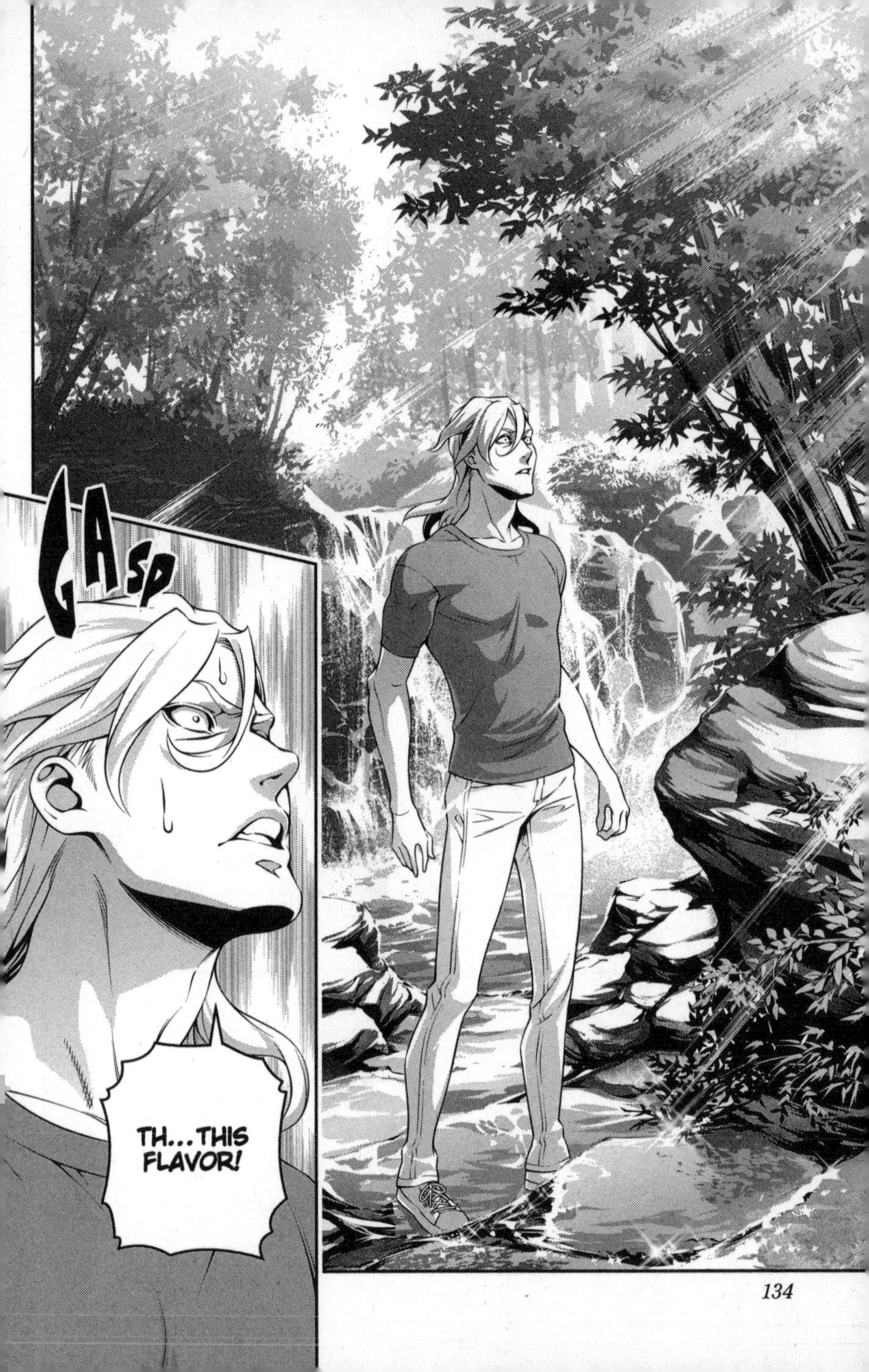
GASP
TH...THIS FLAVOR!

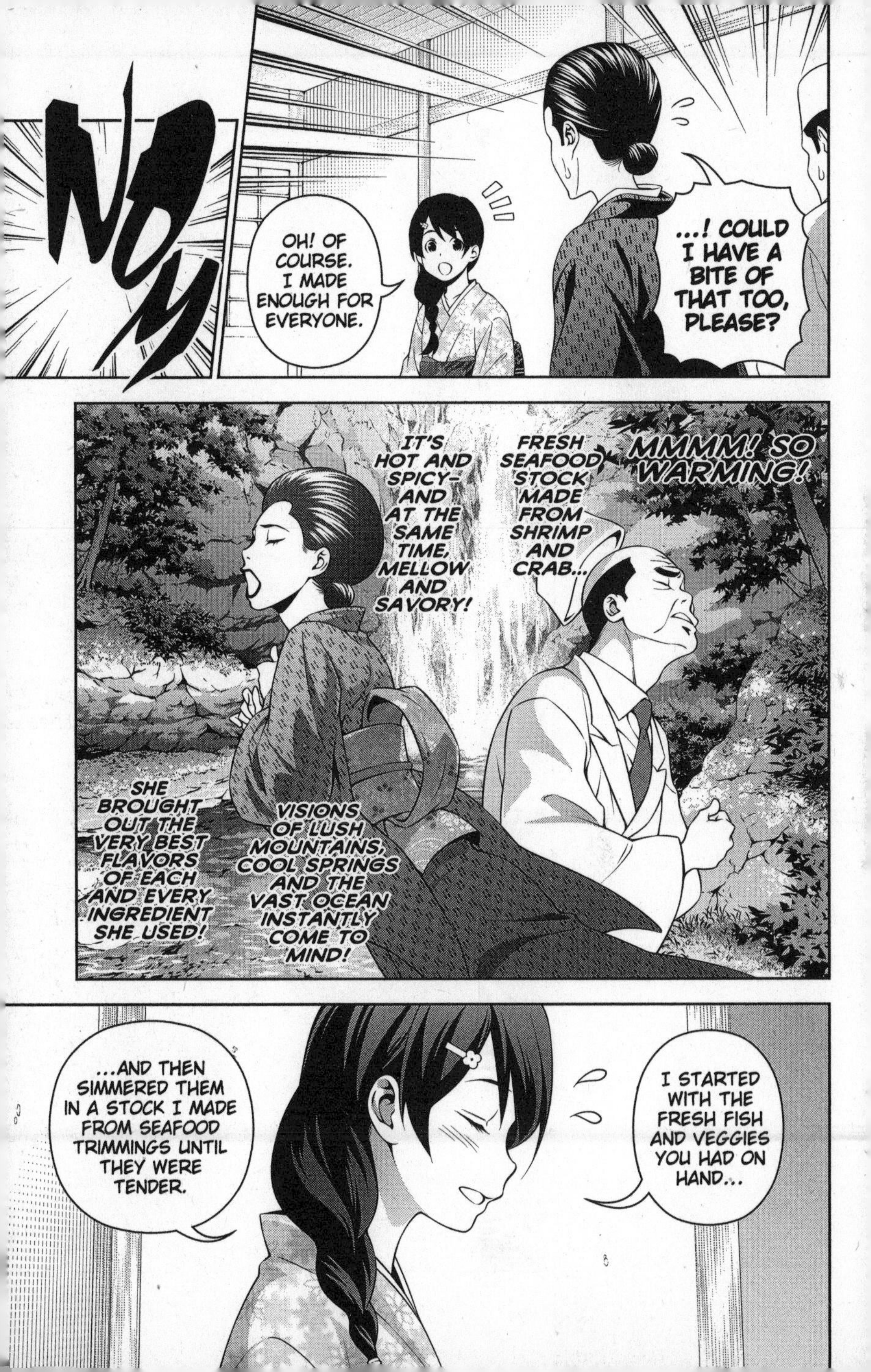
...! COULD I HAVE A BITE OF THAT TOO, PLEASE?
OH! OF COURSE. I MADE ENOUGH FOR EVERYONE.
NOM
MMMM! SO WARMING!
FRESH SEAFOOD STOCK MADE FROM SHRIMP AND CRAB...
IT'S HOT AND SPICY-AND AT THE SAME TIME, MELLOW AND SAVORY!
VISIONS OF LUSH MOUNTAINS, COOL SPRINGS AND THE VAST OCEAN INSTANTLY COME TO MIND!
SHE BROUGHT OUT THE VERY BEST FLAVORS OF EACH AND EVERY INGREDIENT SHE USED!
I STARTED WITH THE FRESH FISH AND VEGGIES YOU HAD ON HAND...
...AND THEN SIMMERED THEM IN A STOCK I MADE FROM SEAFOOD TRIMMINGS UNTIL THEY WERE TENDER.

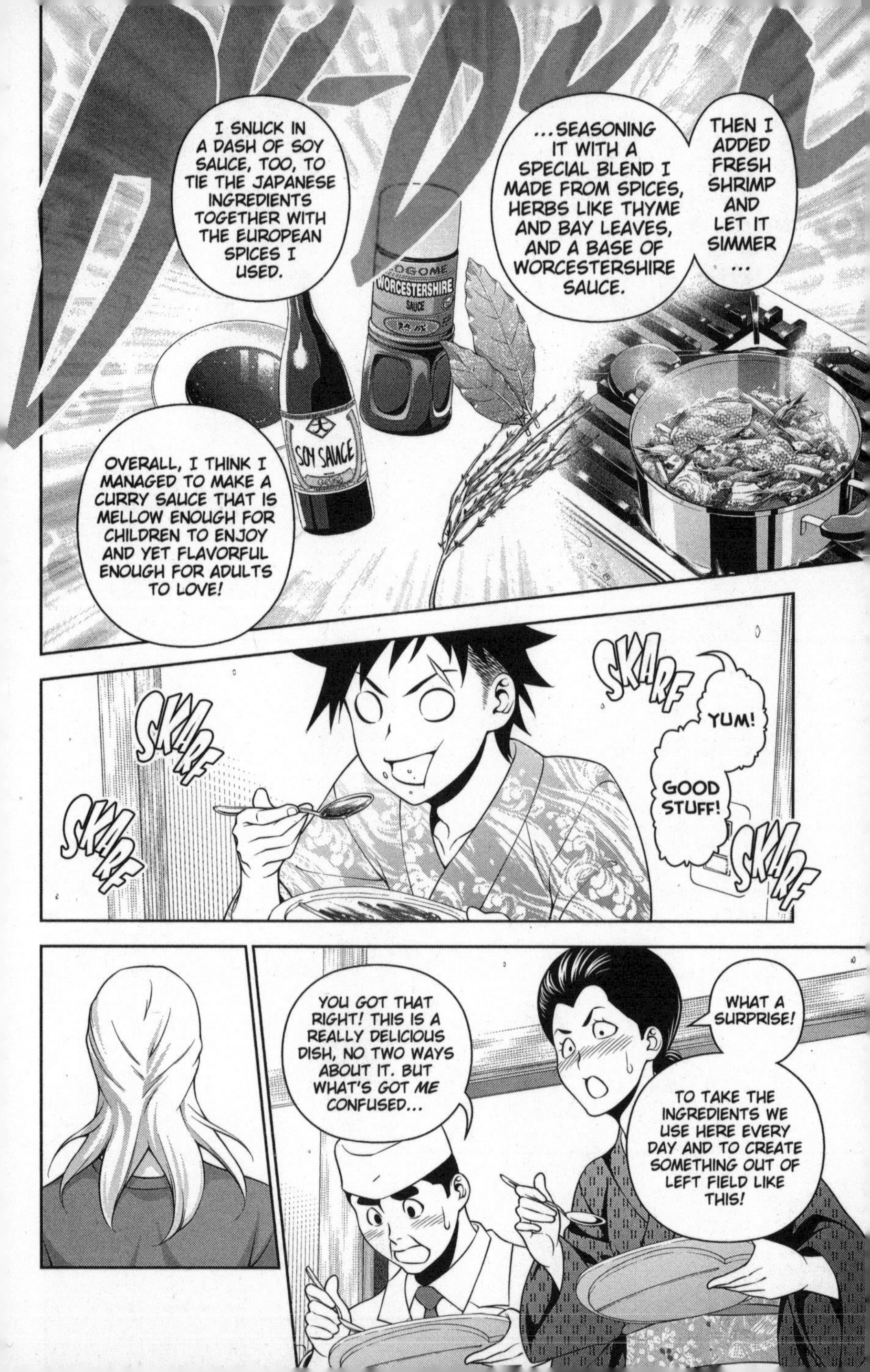
THEN I ADDED FRESH SHRIMP AND LET IT SIMMER...
...SEASONING IT WITH A SPECIAL BLEND I MADE FROM SPICES, HERBS LIKE THYME AND BAY LEAVES, AND A BASE OF WORCESTERSHIRE SAUCE.
I SNUCK IN A DASH OF SOY SAUCE, TOO, TO TIE THE JAPANESE INGREDIENTS TOGETHER WITH THE EUROPEAN SPICES I USED.
WORCESTERSHIRE
SAUCE
SOY SAUCE
OVERALL, I THINK I MANAGED TO MAKE A CURRY SAUCE THAT IS MELLOW ENOUGH FOR CHILDREN TO ENJOY AND YET FLAVORFUL ENOUGH FOR ADULTS TO LOVE!
SKARF
YUM!
GOOD STUFF!
SKARF
SKARF
SKARF
WHAT A SURPRISE!
TO TAKE THE INGREDIENTS WE USE HERE EVERY DAY AND TO CREATE SOMETHING OUT OF LEFT FIELD LIKE THIS!
YOU GOT THAT RIGHT! THIS IS A REALLY DELICIOUS DISH, NO TWO WAYS ABOUT IT. BUT WHAT'S GOT *ME* CONFUSED...

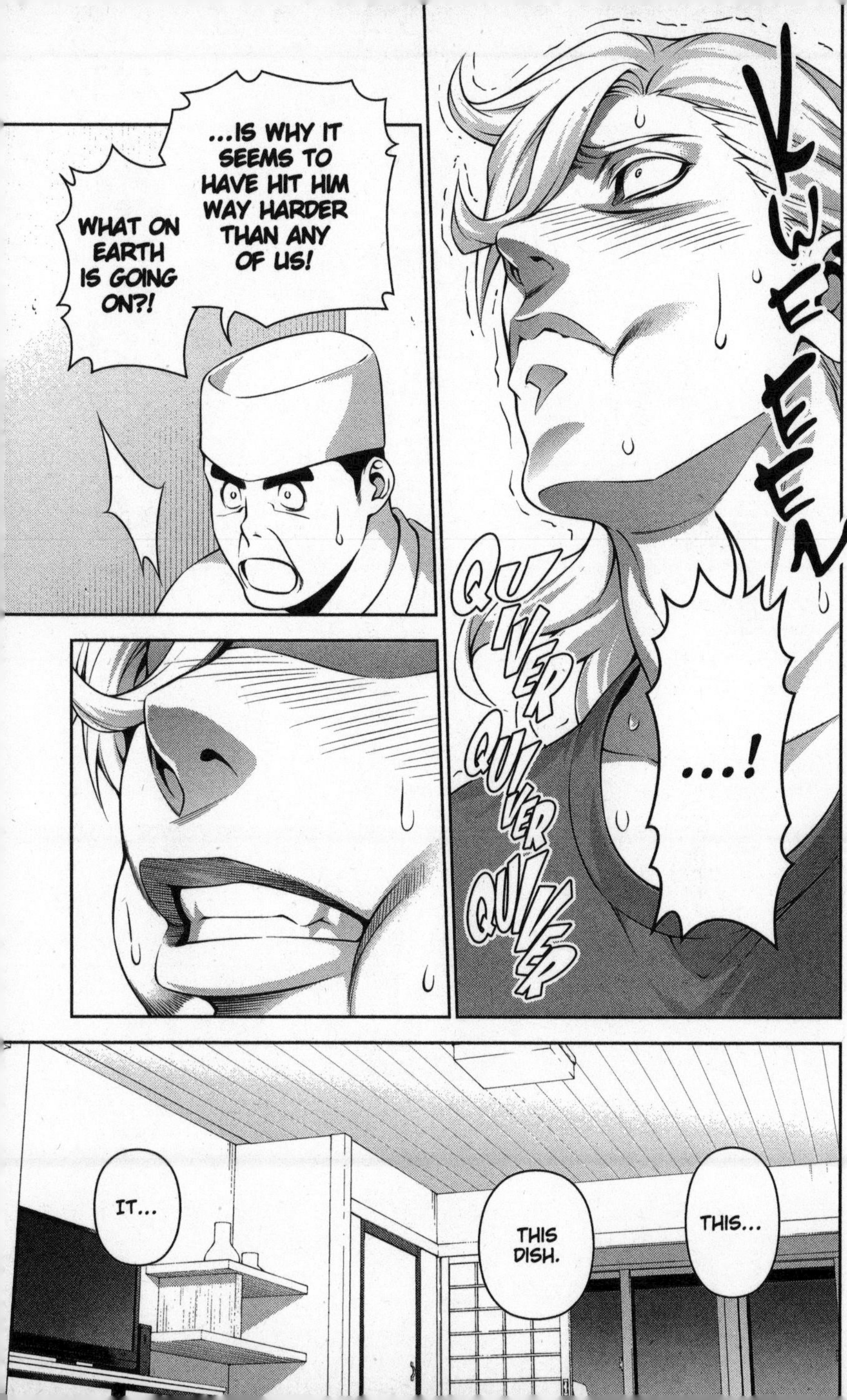
KWEEEEN
QUIVER QUIVER QUIVER
...!
...IS WHY IT SEEMS TO HAVE HIT HIM WAY HARDER THAN ANY OF US!
WHAT ON EARTH IS GOING ON?!
THIS...
THIS DISH.
IT...

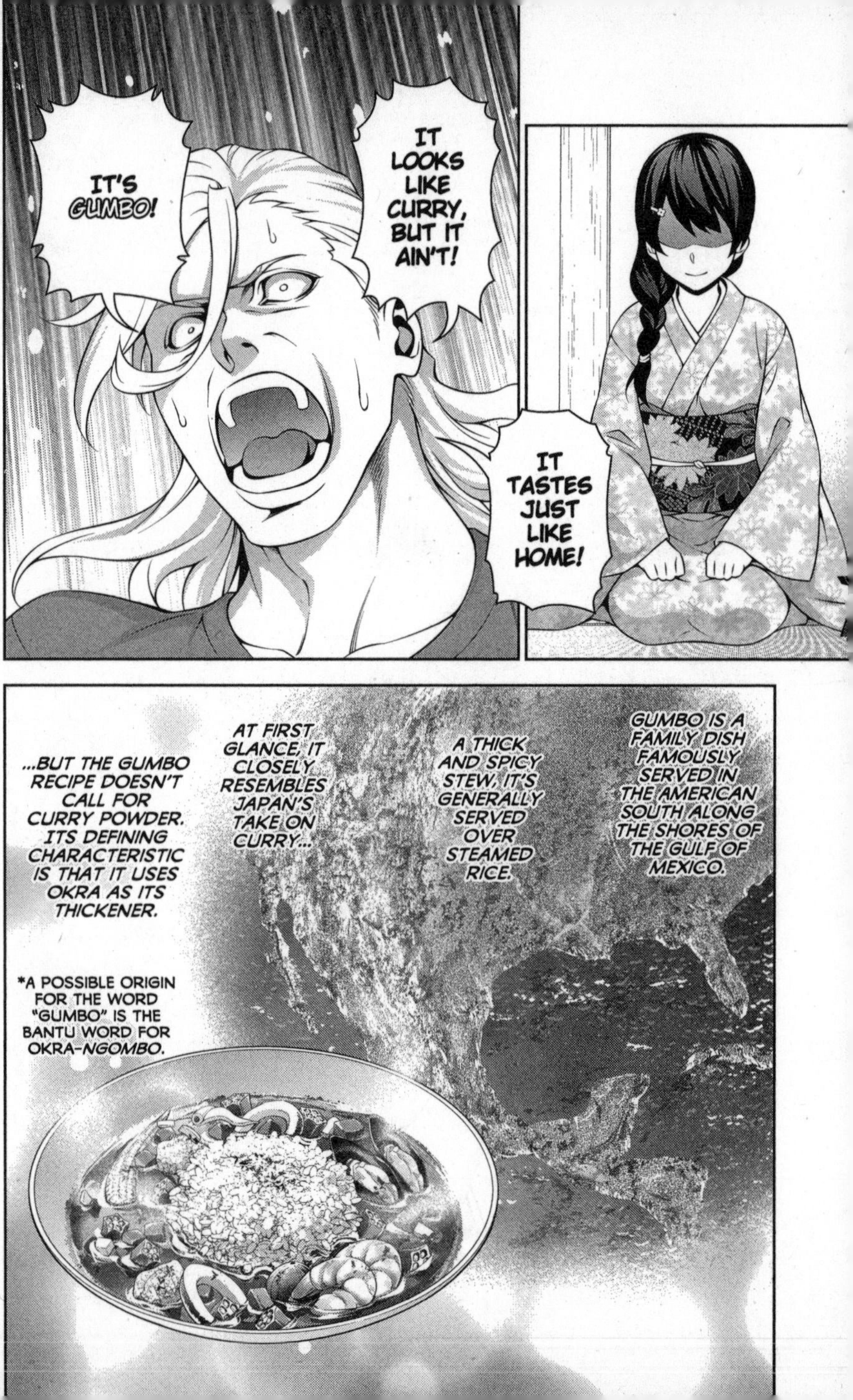
IT LOOKS LIKE CURRY, BUT IT AIN'T!
IT'S GUMBO!
IT TASTES JUST LIKE HOME!
GUMBO IS A FAMILY DISH FAMOUSLY SERVED IN THE AMERICAN SOUTH ALONG THE SHORES OF THE GULF OF MEXICO.
A THICK AND SPICY STEW, IT'S GENERALLY SERVED OVER STEAMED RICE.
AT FIRST GLANCE, IT CLOSELY RESEMBLES JAPAN'S TAKE ON CURRY...
...BUT THE GUMBO RECIPE DOESN'T CALL FOR CURRY POWDER. ITS DEFINING CHARACTERISTIC IS THAT IT USES OKRA AS ITS THICKENER.
*A POSSIBLE ORIGIN FOR THE WORD "GUMBO" IS THE BANTU WORD FOR OKRA-NGOMBO.

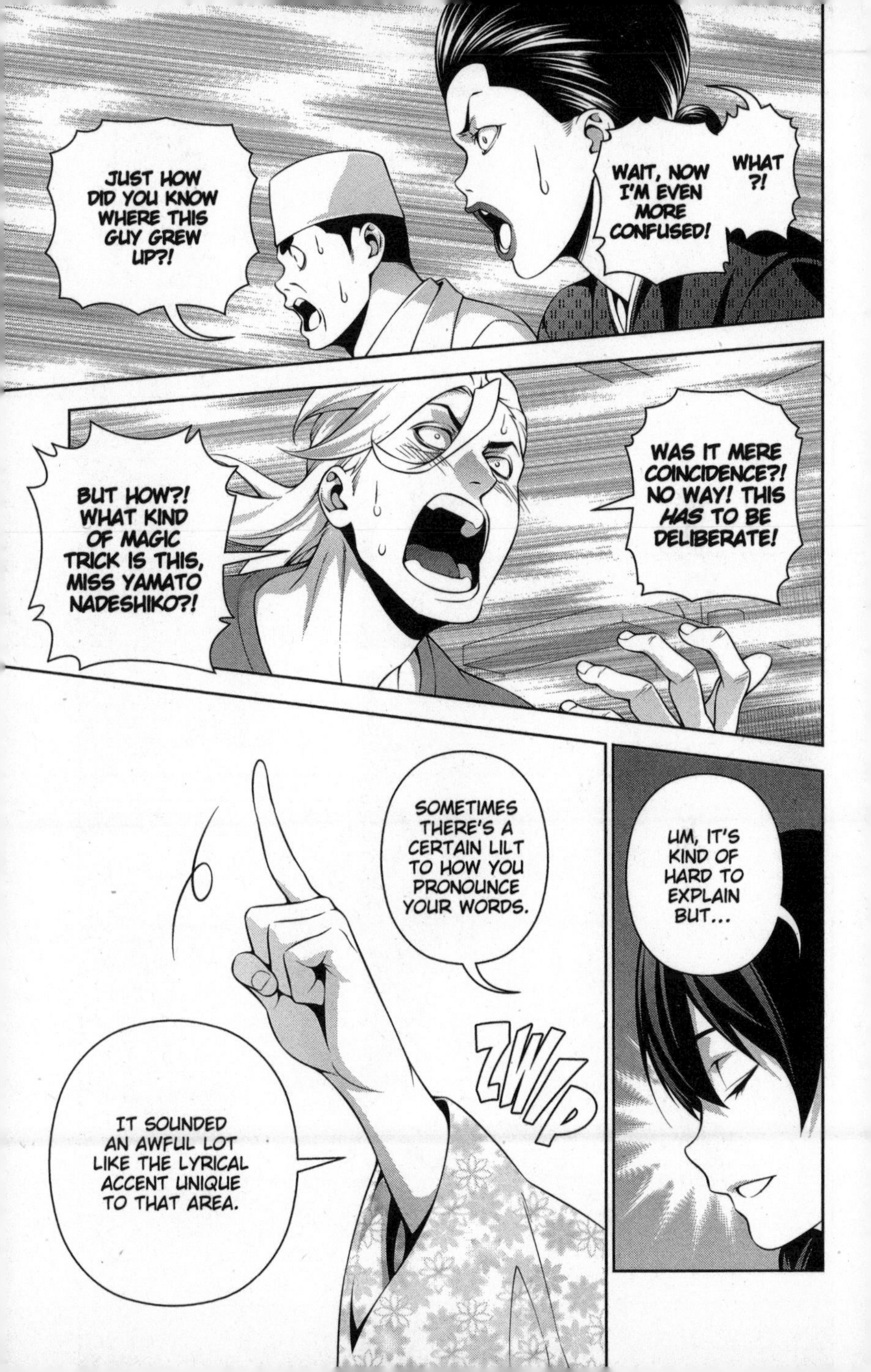
WHAT ?!
WAIT, NOW I'M EVEN MORE CONFUSED!
JUST HOW DID YOU KNOW WHERE THIS GUY GREW UP?!
WAS IT MERE COINCIDENCE?! NO WAY! THIS *HAS* TO BE DELIBERATE!
BUT HOW?! WHAT KIND OF MAGIC TRICK IS THIS, MISS YAMATO NADESHIKO?!
UM, IT'S KIND OF HARD TO EXPLAIN BUT...
SOMETIMES THERE'S A CERTAIN LILT TO HOW YOU PRONOUNCE YOUR WORDS.
ZWIP
IT SOUNDED AN AWFUL LOT LIKE THE LYRICAL ACCENT UNIQUE TO THAT AREA.

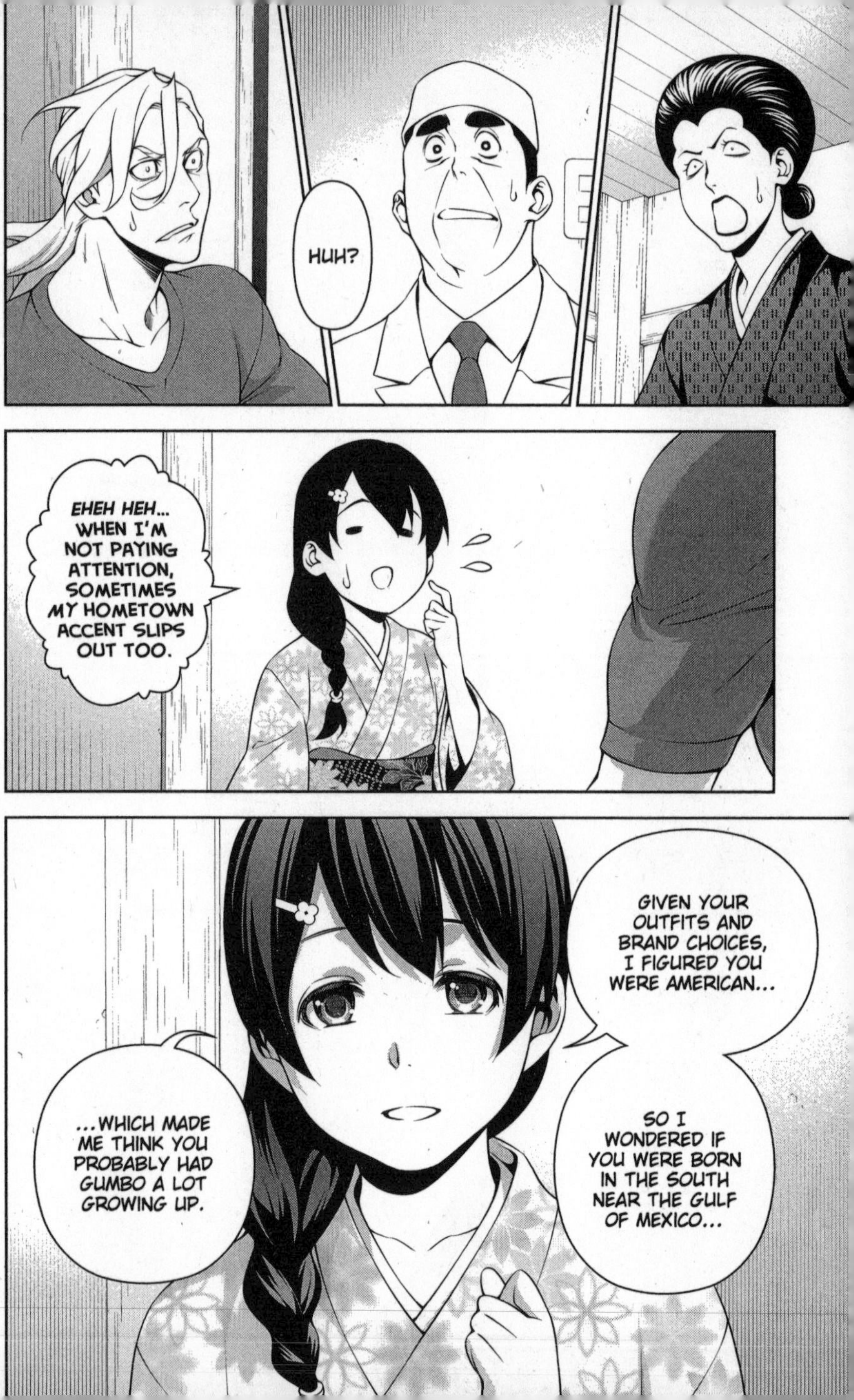
HUH?
EHEH HEH... WHEN I'M NOT PAYING ATTENTION, SOMETIMES MY HOMETOWN ACCENT SLIPS OUT TOO.
GIVEN YOUR OUTFITS AND BRAND CHOICES, I FIGURED YOU WERE AMERICAN...
SO I WONDERED IF YOU WERE BORN IN THE SOUTH NEAR THE GULF OF MEXICO...
...WHICH MADE ME THINK YOU PROBABLY HAD GUMBO A LOT GROWING UP.

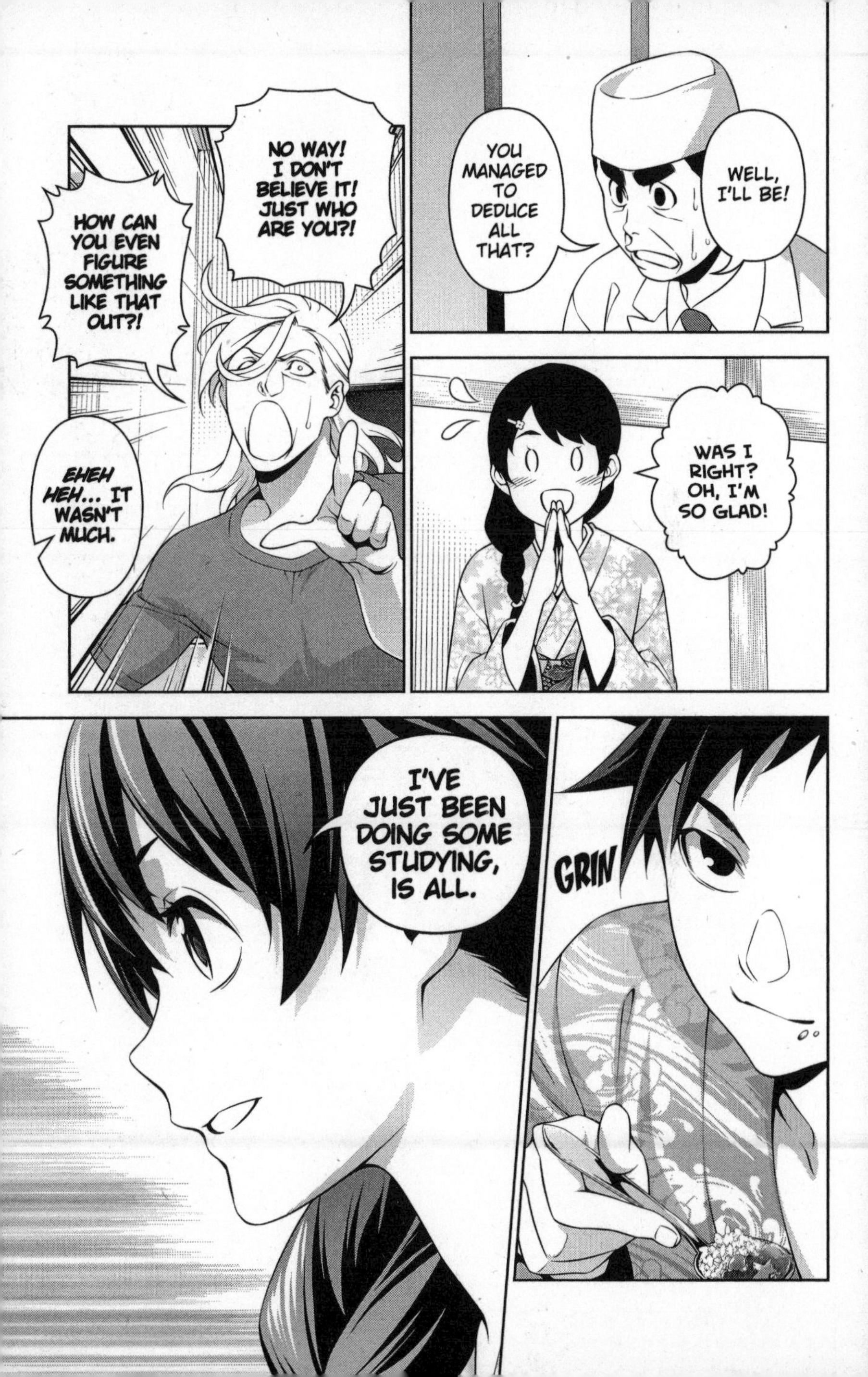
WELL, I'LL BE!
YOU MANAGED TO DEDUCE ALL THAT?
WAS I RIGHT? OH, I'M SO GLAD!
NO WAY! I DON'T BELIEVE IT! JUST WHO ARE YOU?!
HOW CAN YOU EVEN FIGURE SOMETHING LIKE THAT OUT?!
EHEH HEH... IT WASN'T MUCH.
GRIN
I'VE JUST BEEN DOING SOME STUDYING, IS ALL.

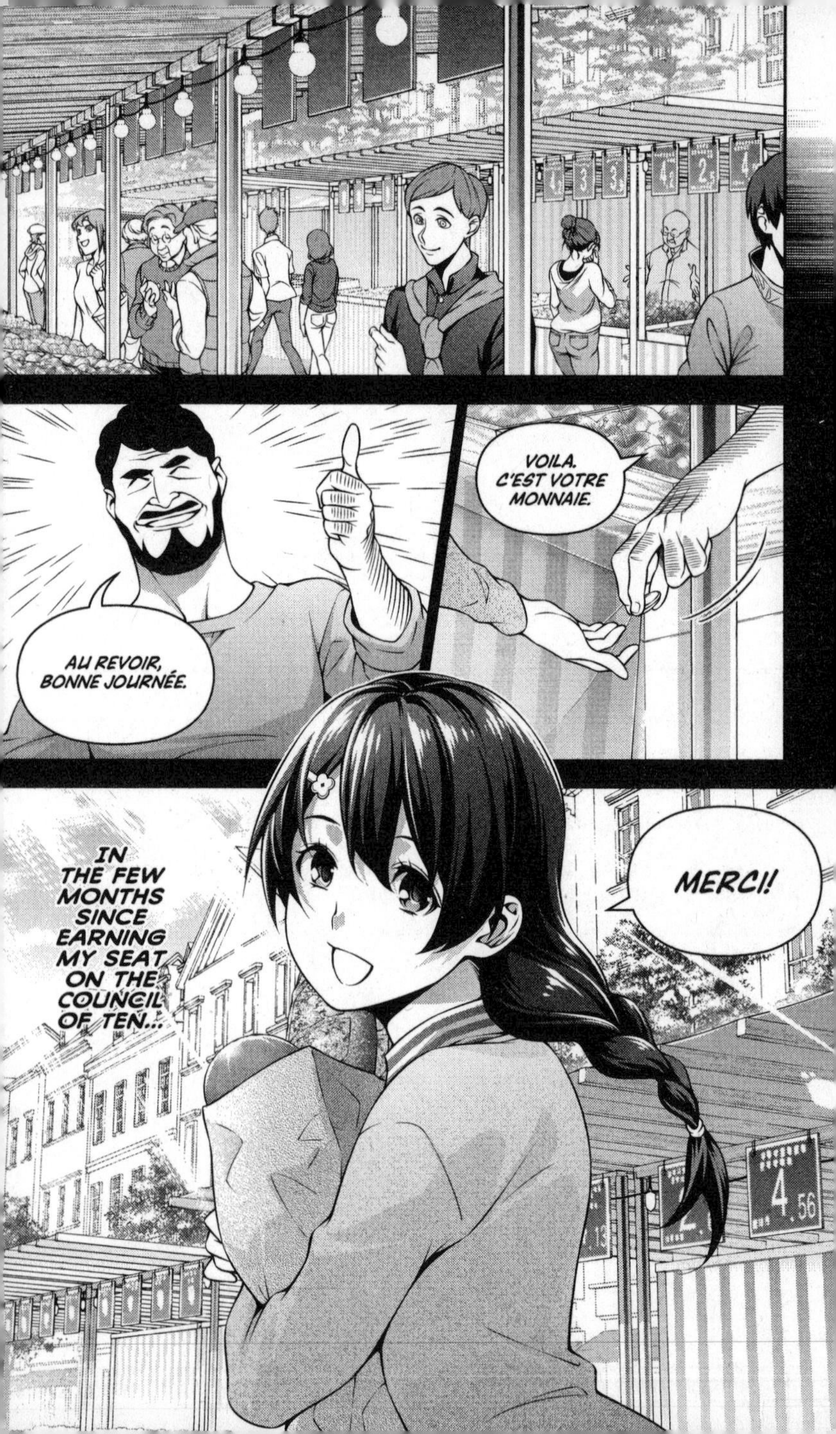
VOILA. C'EST VOTRE MONNAIE.
AU REVOIR, BONNE JOURNÉE.
MERCI!
IN THE FEW MONTHS SINCE EARNING MY SEAT ON THE COUNCIL OF TEN...

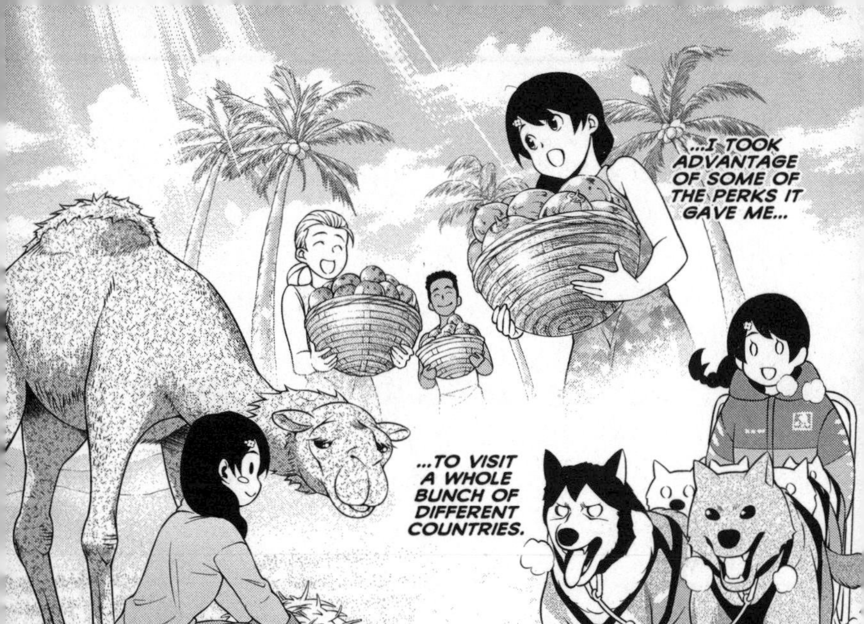
...I TOOK ADVANTAGE OF SOME OF THE PERKS IT GAVE ME...
...TO VISIT A WHOLE BUNCH OF DIFFERENT COUNTRIES.
I WENT TO ALL KINDS OF REGIONS AND MET ALL KINDS OF PEOPLE...
...LEARNING FIRSTHAND WHAT IT FEELS LIKE TO LIVE AND THRIVE THERE.
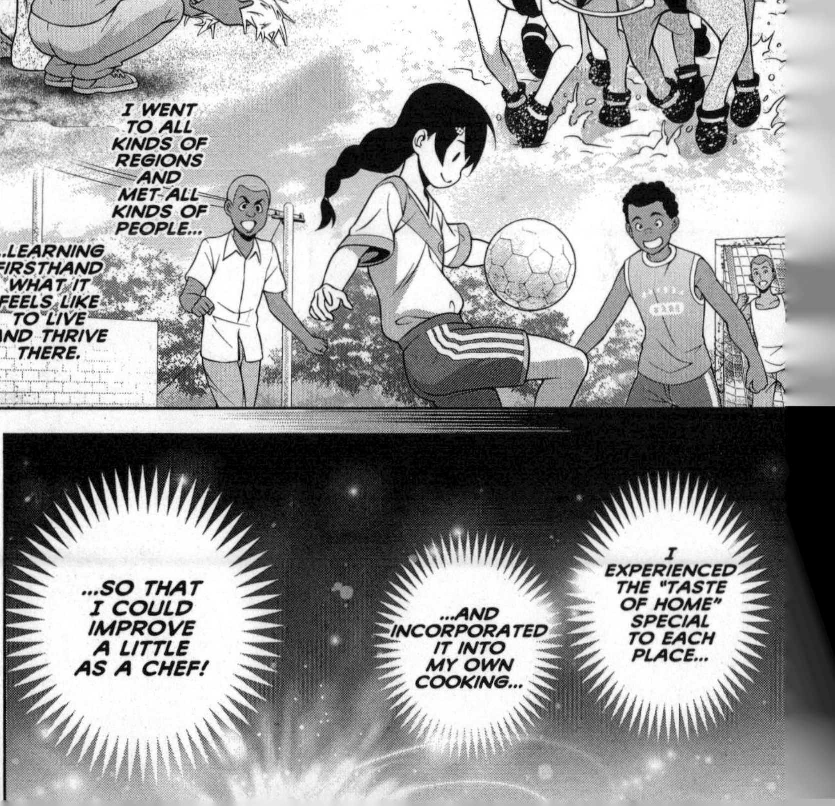
I EXPERIENCED THE "TASTE OF HOME" SPECIAL TO EACH PLACE...
...AND INCORPORATED IT INTO MY OWN COOKING...
...SO THAT I COULD IMPROVE A LITTLE AS A CHEF!

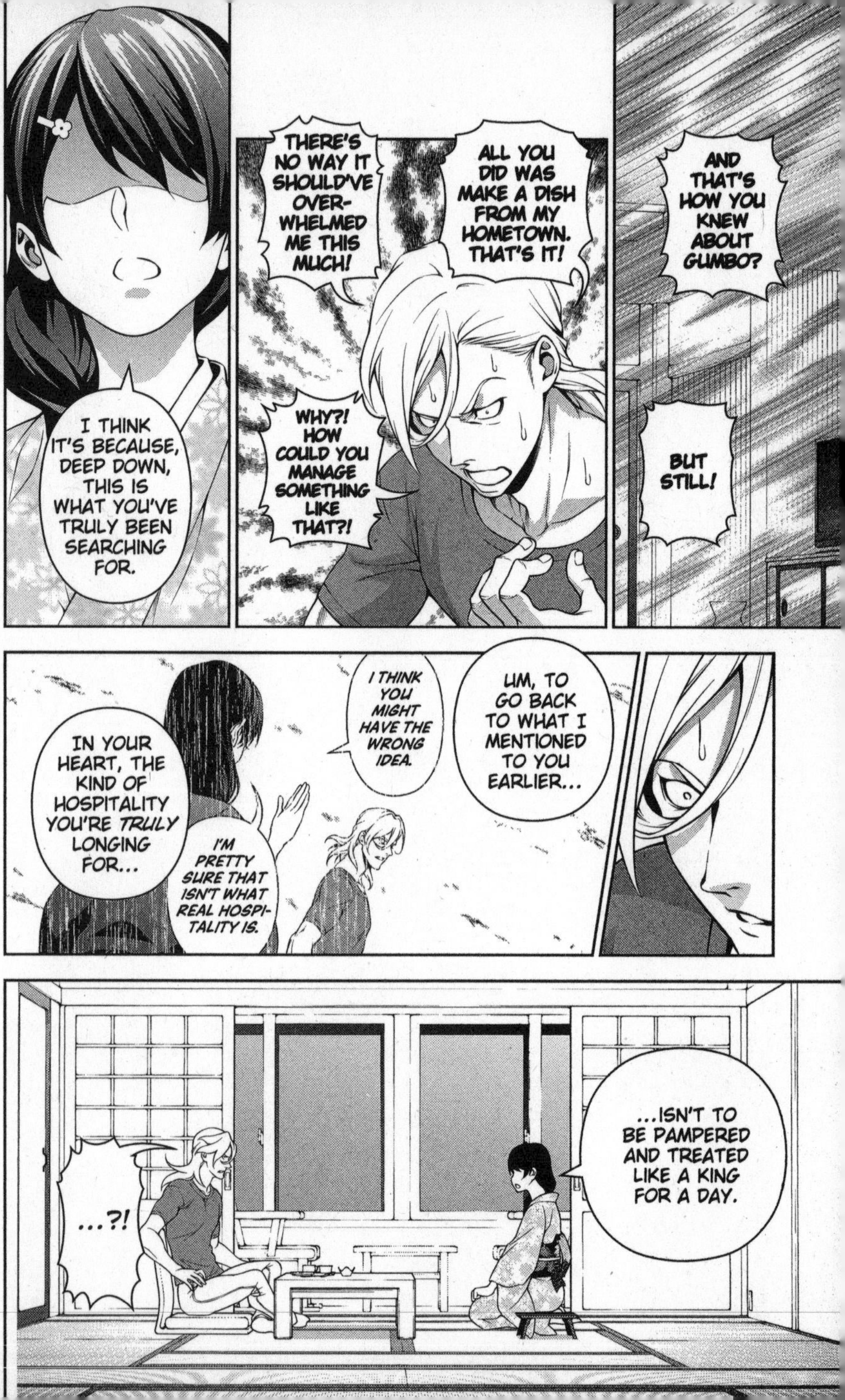
AND THAT'S HOW YOU KNEW ABOUT GUMBO?
BUT STILL!
ALL YOU DID WAS MAKE A DISH FROM MY HOMETOWN. THAT'S IT!
THERE'S NO WAY IT SHOULD'VE OVER-WHELMED ME THIS MUCH!
WHY?! HOW COULD YOU MANAGE SOMETHING LIKE THAT?!
I THINK IT'S BECAUSE, DEEP DOWN, THIS IS WHAT YOU'VE TRULY BEEN SEARCHING FOR.
UM, TO GO BACK TO WHAT I MENTIONED TO YOU EARLIER...
I THINK YOU MIGHT HAVE THE WRONG IDEA.
IN YOUR HEART, THE KIND OF HOSPITALITY YOU'RE *TRULY* LONGING FOR...
I'M PRETTY SURE THAT ISN'T WHAT REAL HOSPI-TALITY IS.
...ISN'T TO BE PAMPERED AND TREATED LIKE A KING FOR A DAY.
...?!

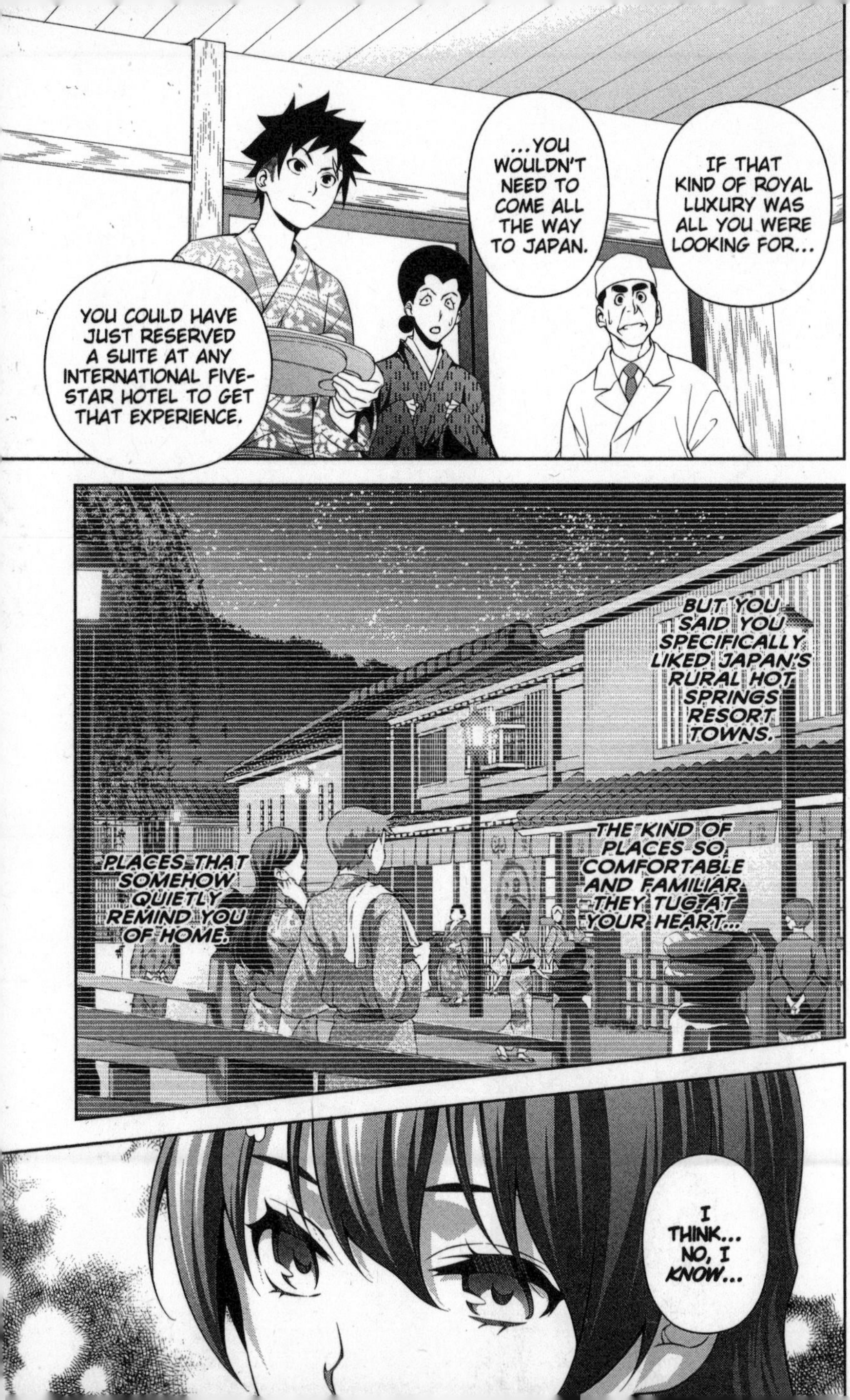
IF THAT KIND OF ROYAL LUXURY WAS ALL YOU WERE LOOKING FOR...
...YOU WOULDN'T NEED TO COME ALL THE WAY TO JAPAN.
YOU COULD HAVE JUST RESERVED A SUITE AT ANY INTERNATIONAL FIVE-STAR HOTEL TO GET THAT EXPERIENCE.
BUT YOU SAID YOU SPECIFICALLY LIKED JAPAN'S RURAL HOT SPRINGS RESORT TOWNS.
THE KIND OF PLACES SO COMFORTABLE AND FAMILIAR THEY TUG AT YOUR HEART...
PLACES THAT SOMEHOW QUIETLY REMIND YOU OF HOME.
I THINK... NO, I KNOW...

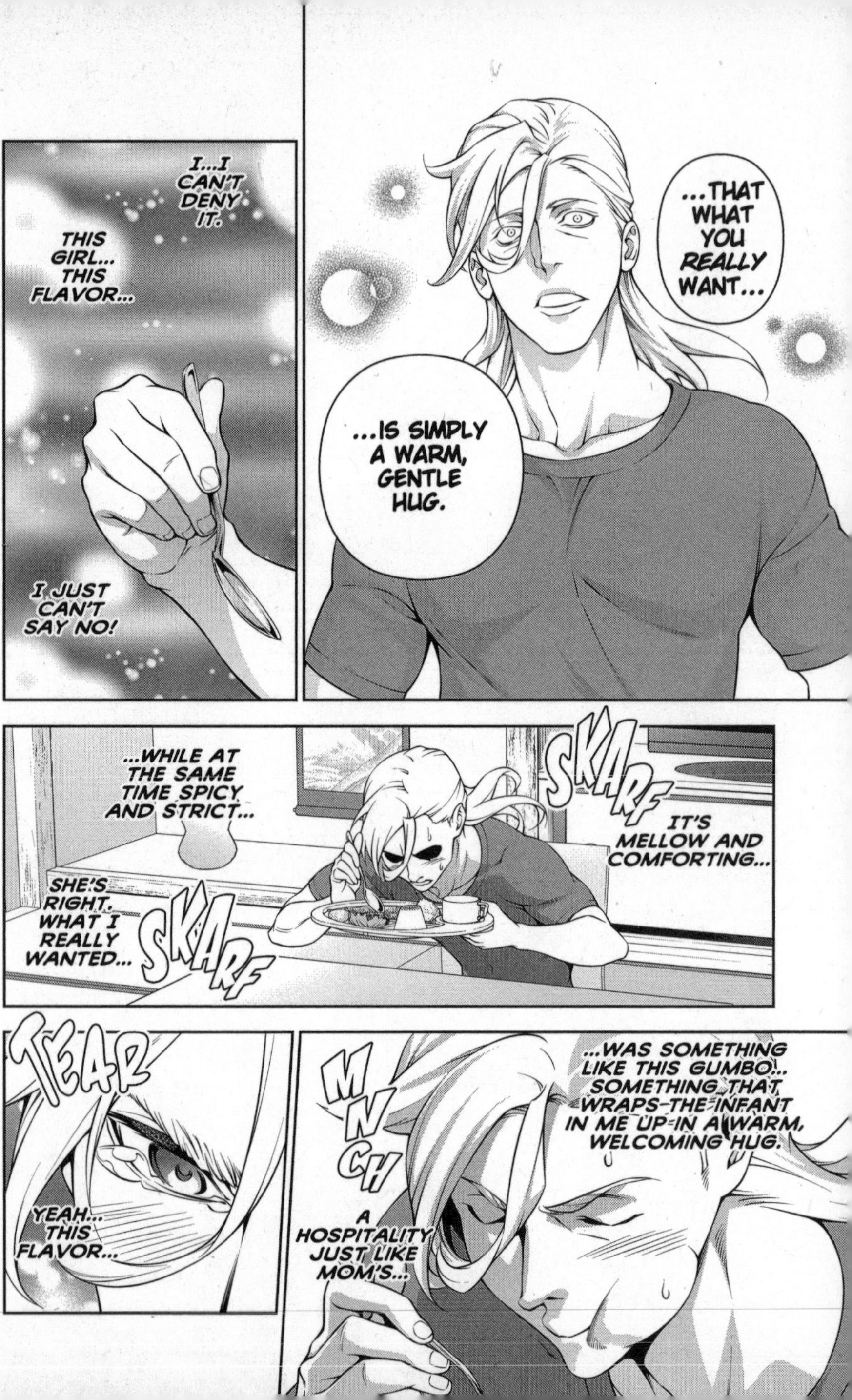
...THAT WHAT YOU REALLY WANT...
...IS SIMPLY A WARM, GENTLE HUG.
I...I CAN'T DENY IT.
THIS GIRL... THIS FLAVOR...
I JUST CAN'T SAY NO!
SKARF
IT'S MELLOW AND COMFORTING...
...WHILE AT THE SAME TIME SPICY AND STRICT...
SKARF
SHE'S RIGHT. WHAT I REALLY WANTED...
MNCH
...WAS SOMETHING LIKE THIS GUMBO... SOMETHING THAT WRAPS THE INFANT IN ME UP IN A WARM, WELCOMING HUG.
A HOSPITALITY JUST LIKE MOM'S...
TEAR
YEAH... THIS FLAVOR...

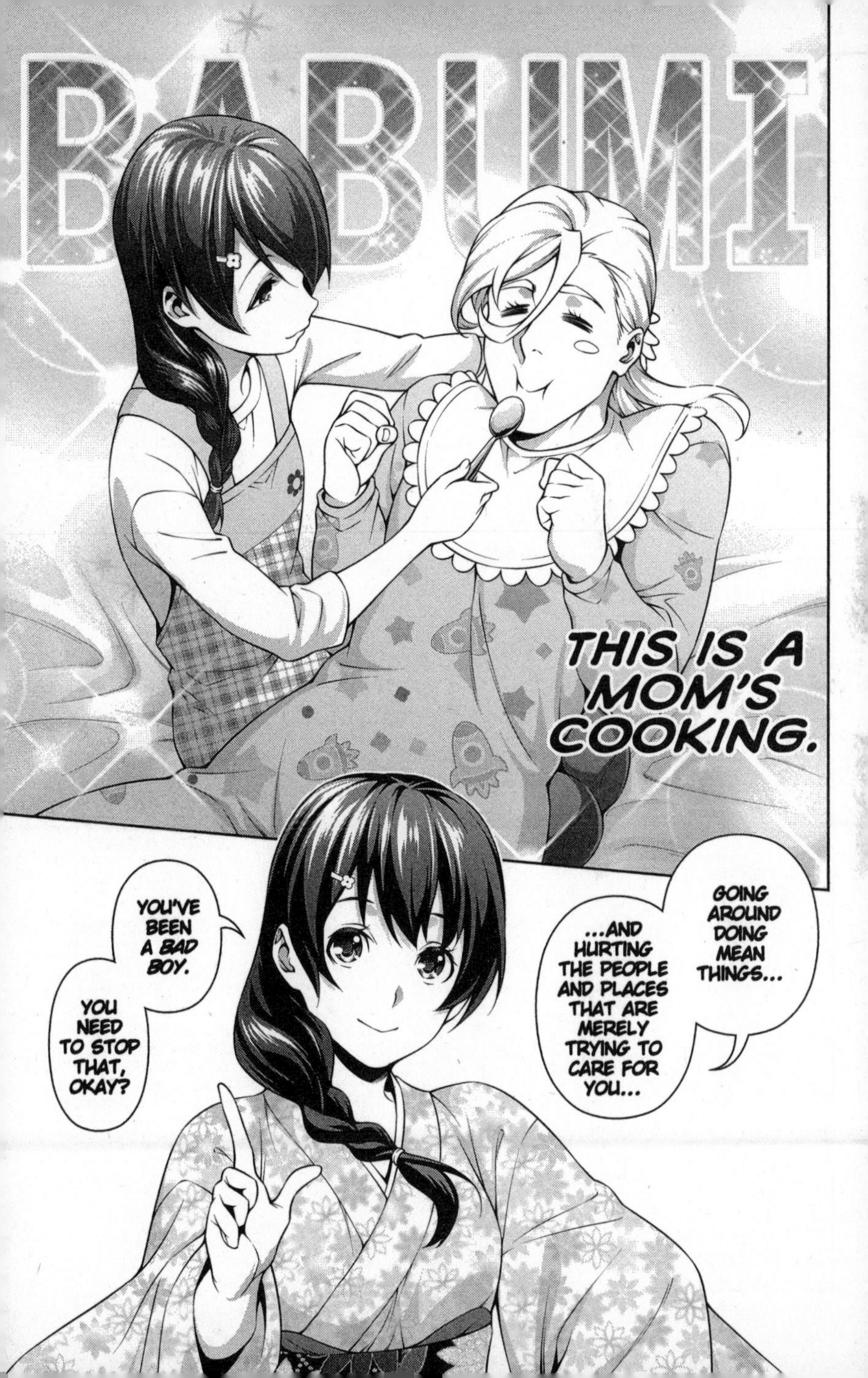
BABUMI
THIS IS A MOM'S COOKING.
GOING AROUND DOING MEAN THINGS...
...AND HURTING THE PEOPLE AND PLACES THAT ARE MERELY TRYING TO CARE FOR YOU...
YOU'VE BEEN A *BAD* BOY.
YOU NEED TO STOP THAT, OKAY?

THE CASE OF MISS ERINA

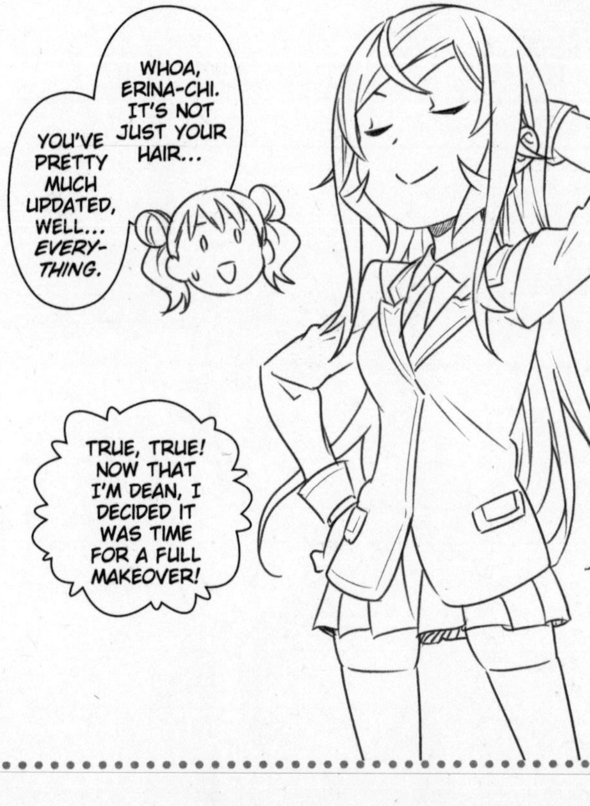
WHOA, ERINA-CHI. IT'S NOT JUST YOUR HAIR...
YOU'VE PRETTY MUCH UPDATED, WELL... *EVERYTHING.*
TRUE, TRUE! NOW THAT I'M DEAN, I DECIDED IT WAS TIME FOR A FULL MAKEOVER!

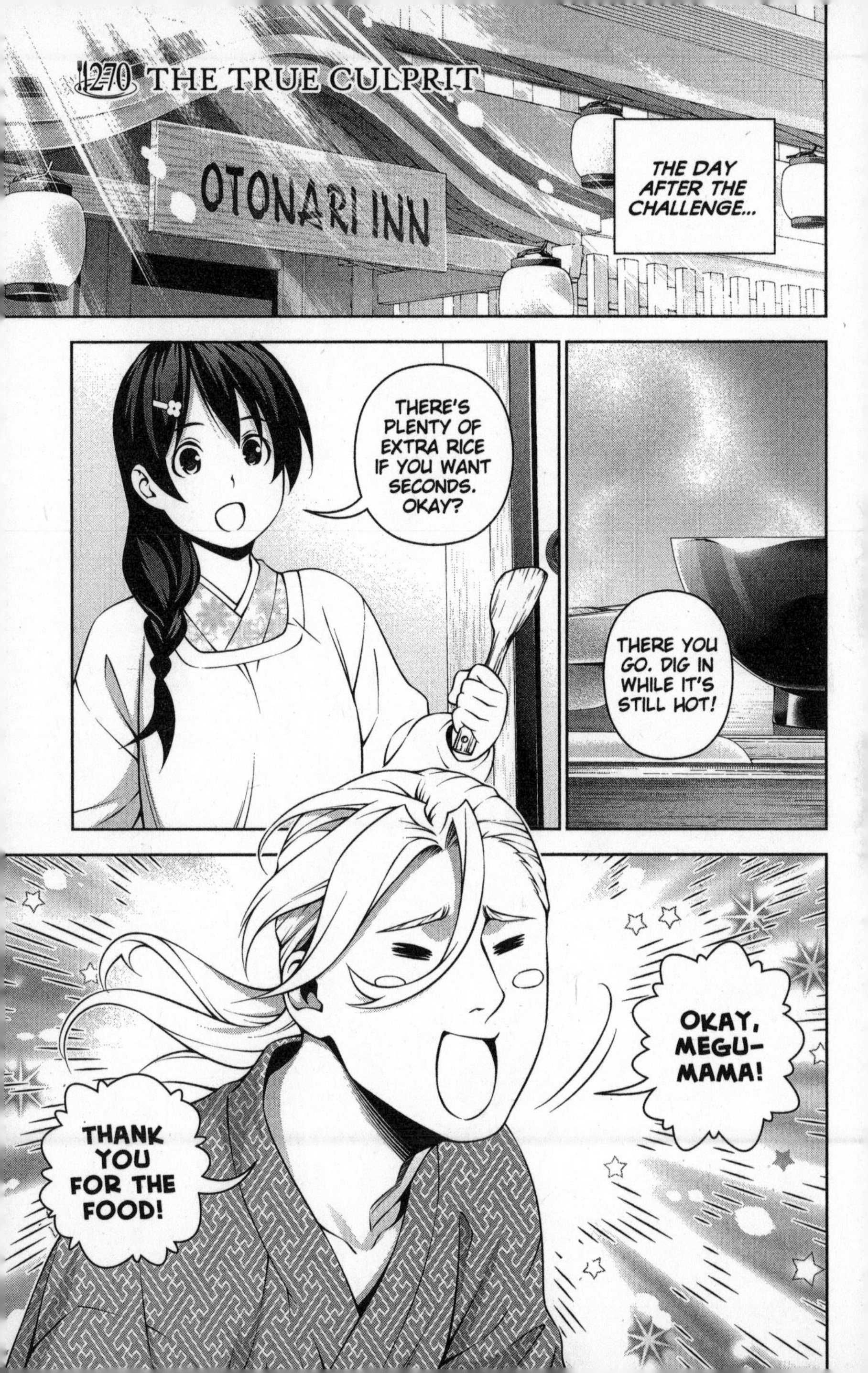
270 THE TRUE CULPRIT
OTONARI INN
THE DAY AFTER THE CHALLENGE...
THERE YOU GO. DIG IN WHILE IT'S STILL HOT!
THERE'S PLENTY OF EXTRA RICE IF YOU WANT SECONDS. OKAY?
OKAY, MEGU-MAMA!
THANK YOU FOR THE FOOD!

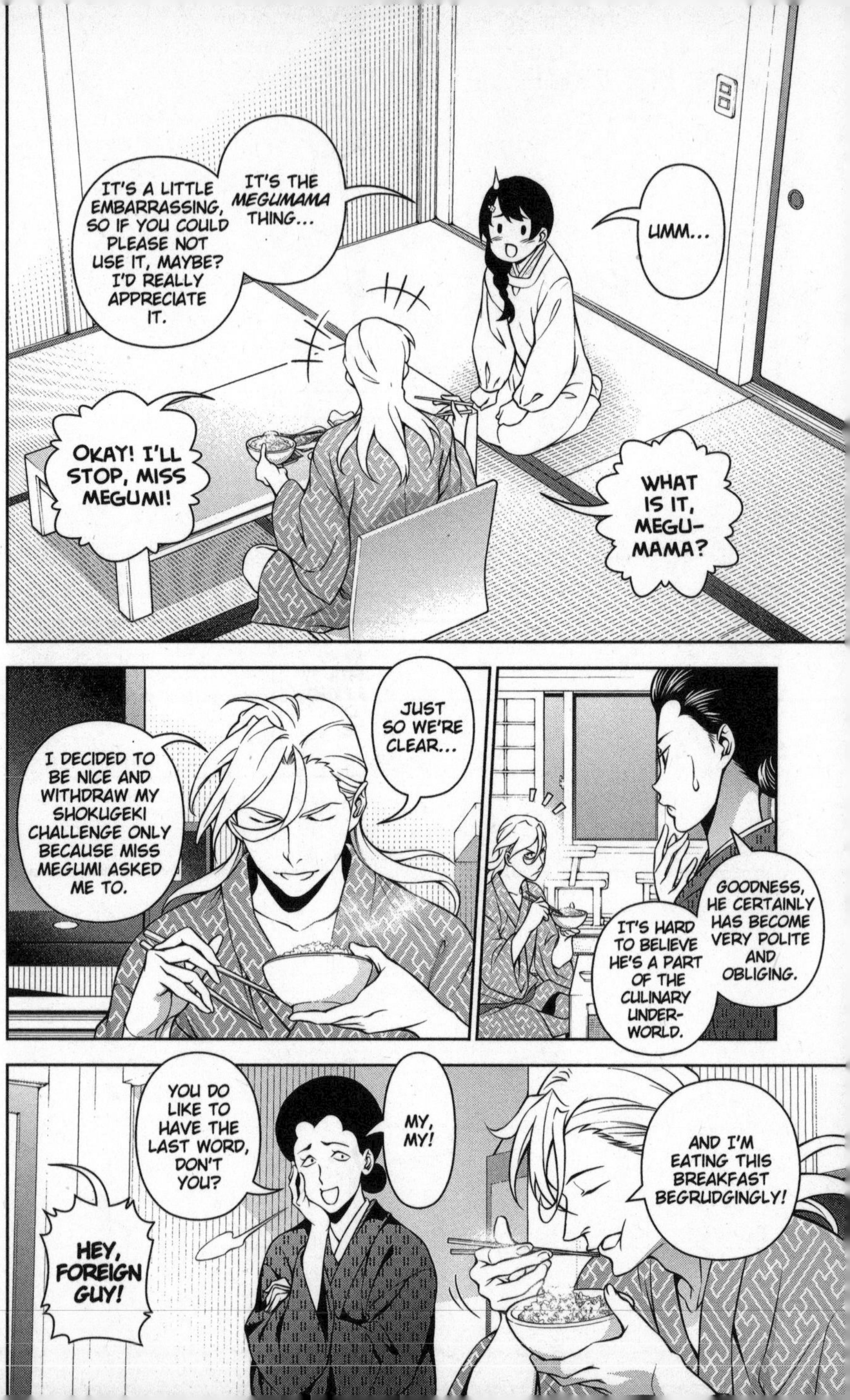
UMM...
WHAT IS IT, MEGU-MAMA?
IT'S THE *MEGUMAMA* THING...
IT'S A LITTLE EMBARRASSING, SO IF YOU COULD PLEASE NOT USE IT, MAYBE? I'D REALLY APPRECIATE IT.
OKAY! I'LL STOP, MISS MEGUMI!
GOODNESS, HE CERTAINLY HAS BECOME VERY POLITE AND OBLIGING.
IT'S HARD TO BELIEVE HE'S A PART OF THE CULINARY UNDER-WORLD.
JUST SO WE'RE CLEAR...
I DECIDED TO BE NICE AND WITHDRAW MY SHOKUGEKI CHALLENGE ONLY BECAUSE MISS MEGUMI ASKED ME TO.
AND I'M EATING THIS BREAKFAST BEGRUDGINGLY!
MY, MY!
YOU DO LIKE TO HAVE THE LAST WORD, DON'T YOU?
HEY, FOREIGN GUY!

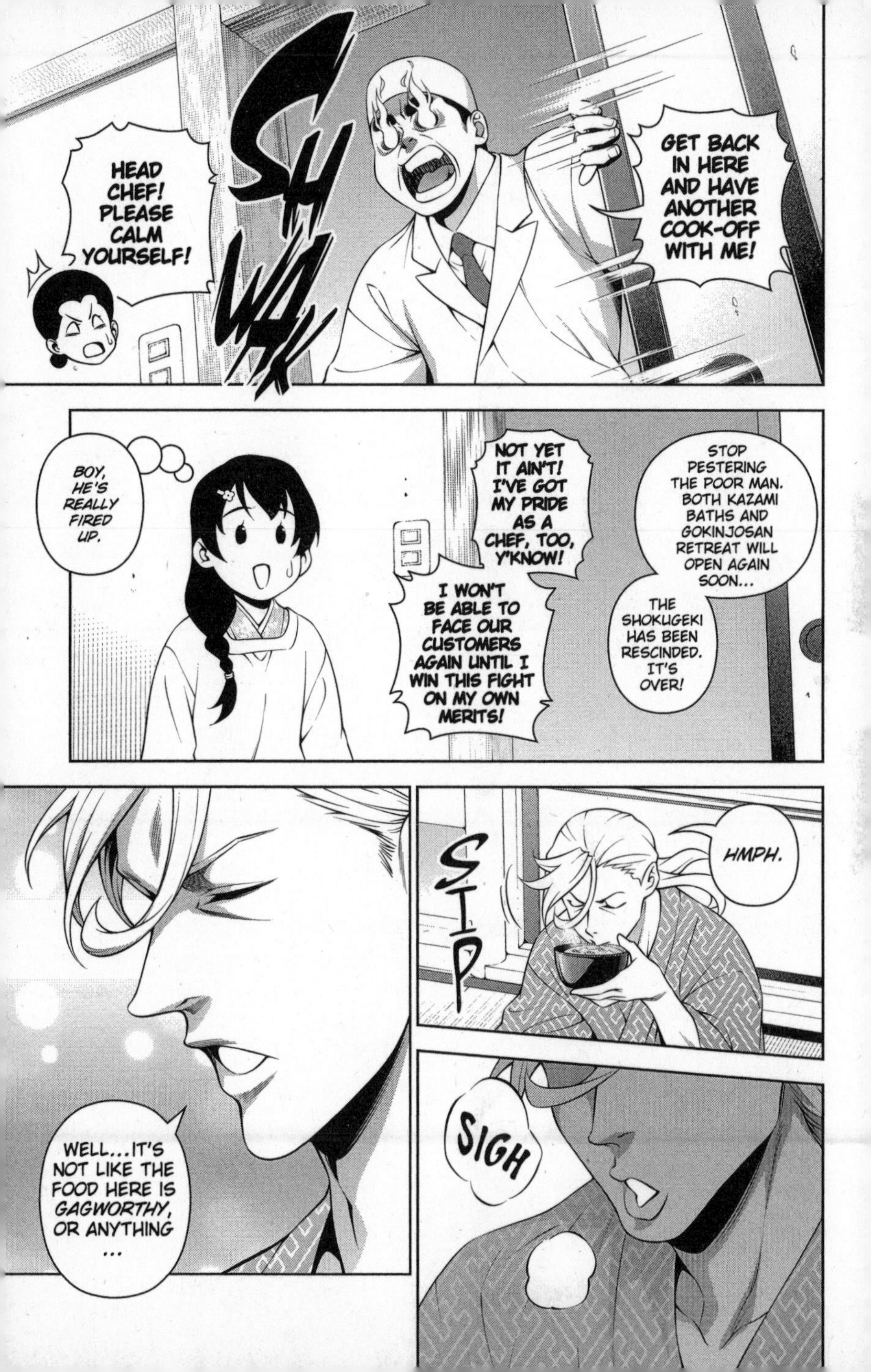
GET BACK IN HERE AND HAVE ANOTHER COOK-OFF WITH ME!
SHWAK
HEAD CHEF! PLEASE CALM YOURSELF!
STOP PESTERING THE POOR MAN. BOTH KAZAMI BATHS AND GOKINJOSAN RETREAT WILL OPEN AGAIN SOON...
THE SHOKUGEKI HAS BEEN RESCINDED. IT'S OVER!
NOT YET IT AIN'T! I'VE GOT MY PRIDE AS A CHEF, TOO, Y'KNOW!
I WON'T BE ABLE TO FACE OUR CUSTOMERS AGAIN UNTIL I WIN THIS FIGHT ON MY OWN MERITS!
BOY, HE'S REALLY FIRED UP.
HMPH.
SIP
SIGH
WELL...IT'S NOT LIKE THE FOOD HERE IS GAGWORTHY, OR ANYTHING...

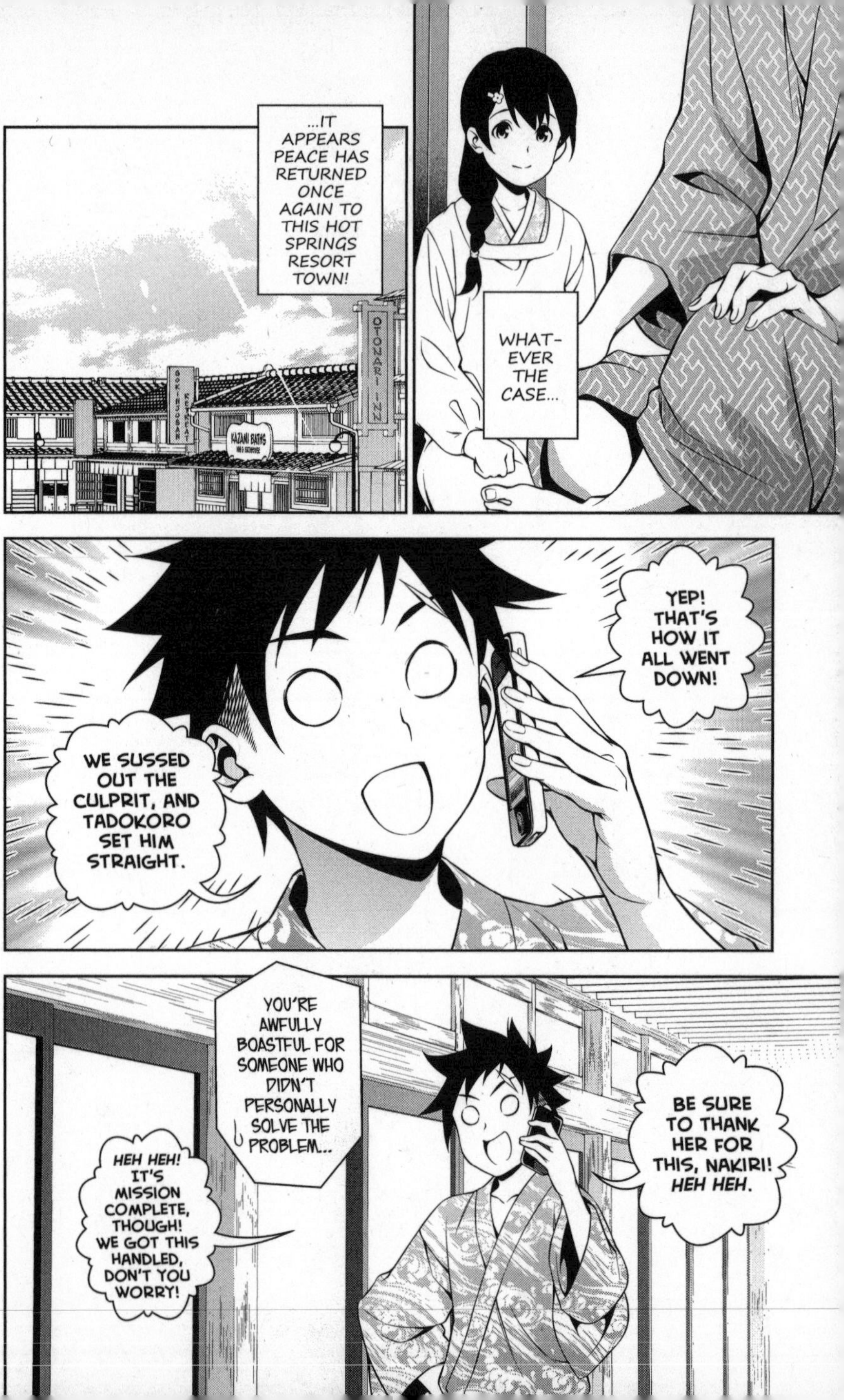
WHAT-EVER THE CASE...
...IT APPEARS PEACE HAS RETURNED ONCE AGAIN TO THIS HOT SPRINGS RESORT TOWN!
OTONARI INN
KAZAMI BATHS
YEP! THAT'S HOW IT ALL WENT DOWN!
WE SUSSED OUT THE CULPRIT, AND TADOKORO SET HIM STRAIGHT.
BE SURE TO THANK HER FOR THIS, NAKIRI! HEH HEH.
YOU'RE AWFULLY BOASTFUL FOR SOMEONE WHO DIDN'T PERSONALLY SOLVE THE PROBLEM...
HEH HEH! IT'S MISSION COMPLETE, THOUGH! WE GOT THIS HANDLED, DON'T YOU WORRY!

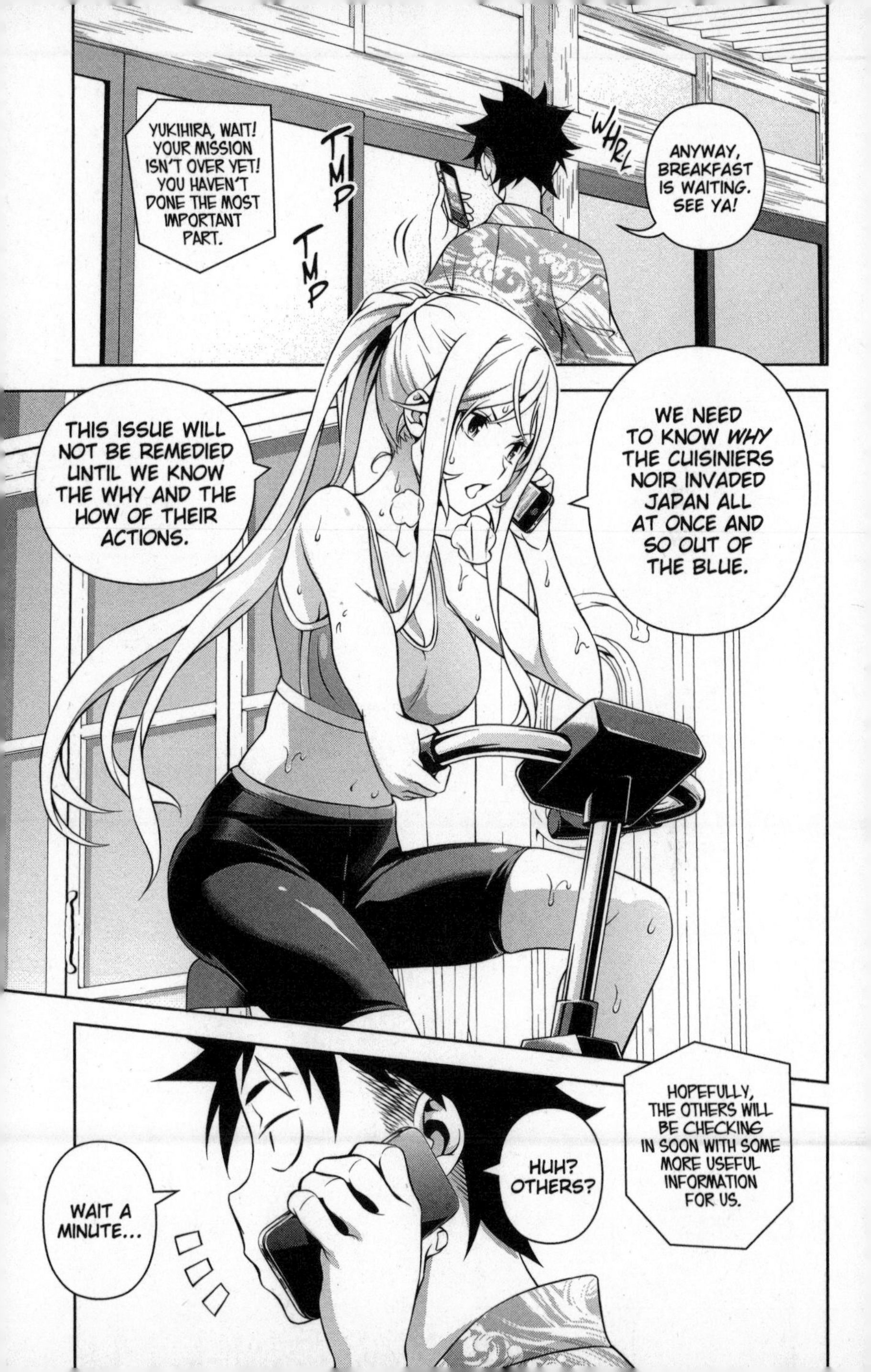
ANYWAY, BREAKFAST IS WAITING. SEE YA!
WHRL
TMP
TMP
YUKIHIRA, WAIT! YOUR MISSION ISN'T OVER YET! YOU HAVEN'T DONE THE MOST IMPORTANT PART.
WE NEED TO KNOW *WHY* THE CUISINIERS NOIR INVADED JAPAN ALL AT ONCE AND SO OUT OF THE BLUE.
THIS ISSUE WILL NOT BE REMEDIED UNTIL WE KNOW THE WHY AND THE HOW OF THEIR ACTIONS.
HOPEFULLY, THE OTHERS WILL BE CHECKING IN SOON WITH SOME MORE USEFUL INFORMATION FOR US.
HUH? OTHERS?
WAIT A MINUTE...

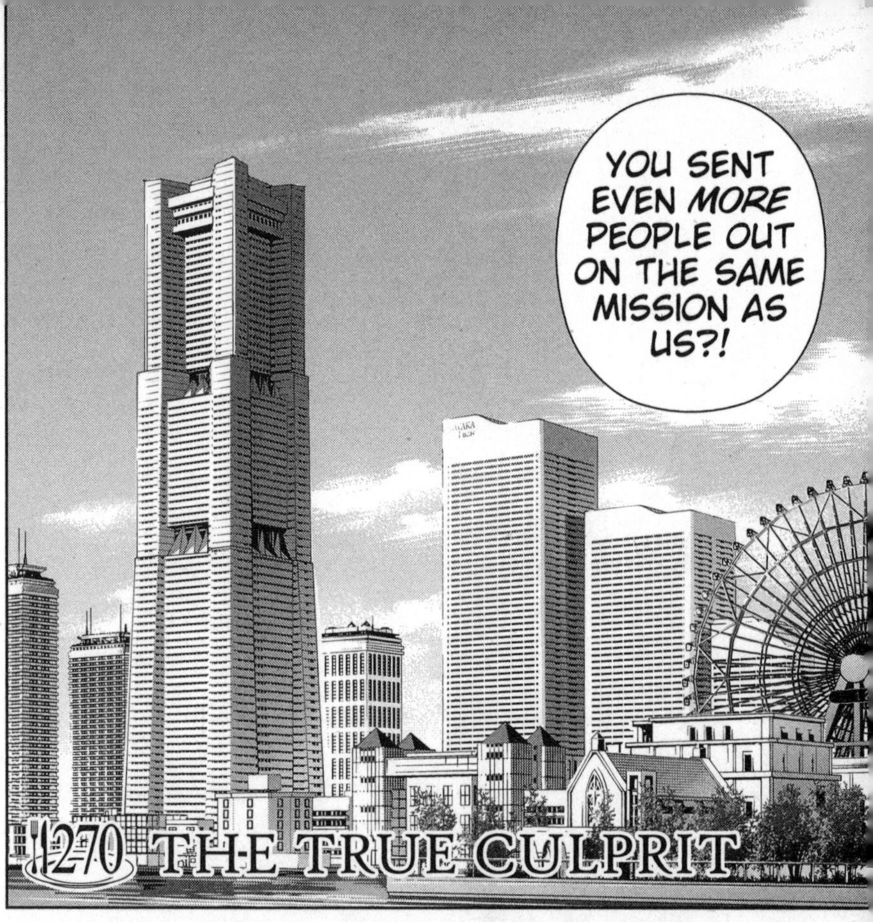
YOU SENT EVEN *MORE* PEOPLE OUT ON THE SAME MISSION AS US?!
270 THE TRUE CULPRIT

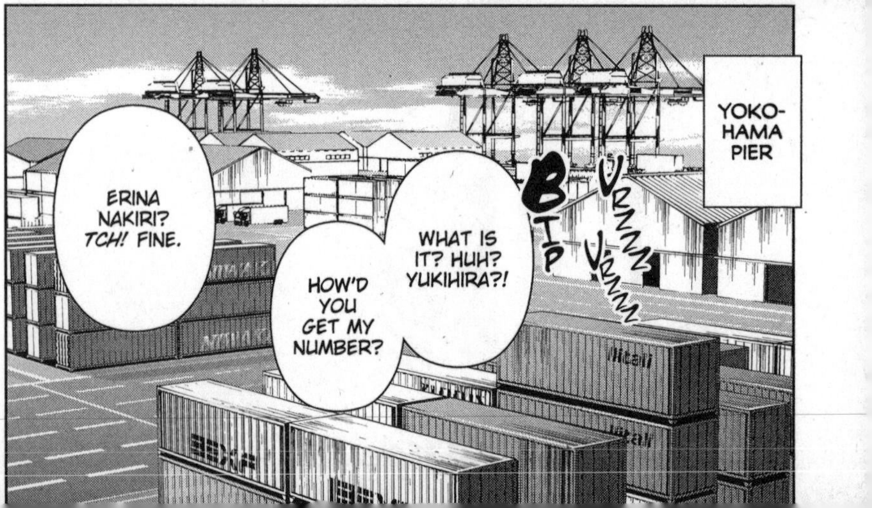
YOKO-HAMA PIER
VRZZZ VRZZZ
BIP
WHAT IS IT? HUH? YUKIHIRA?!
HOW'D YOU GET MY NUMBER?
ERINA NAKIRI? *TCH!* FINE.

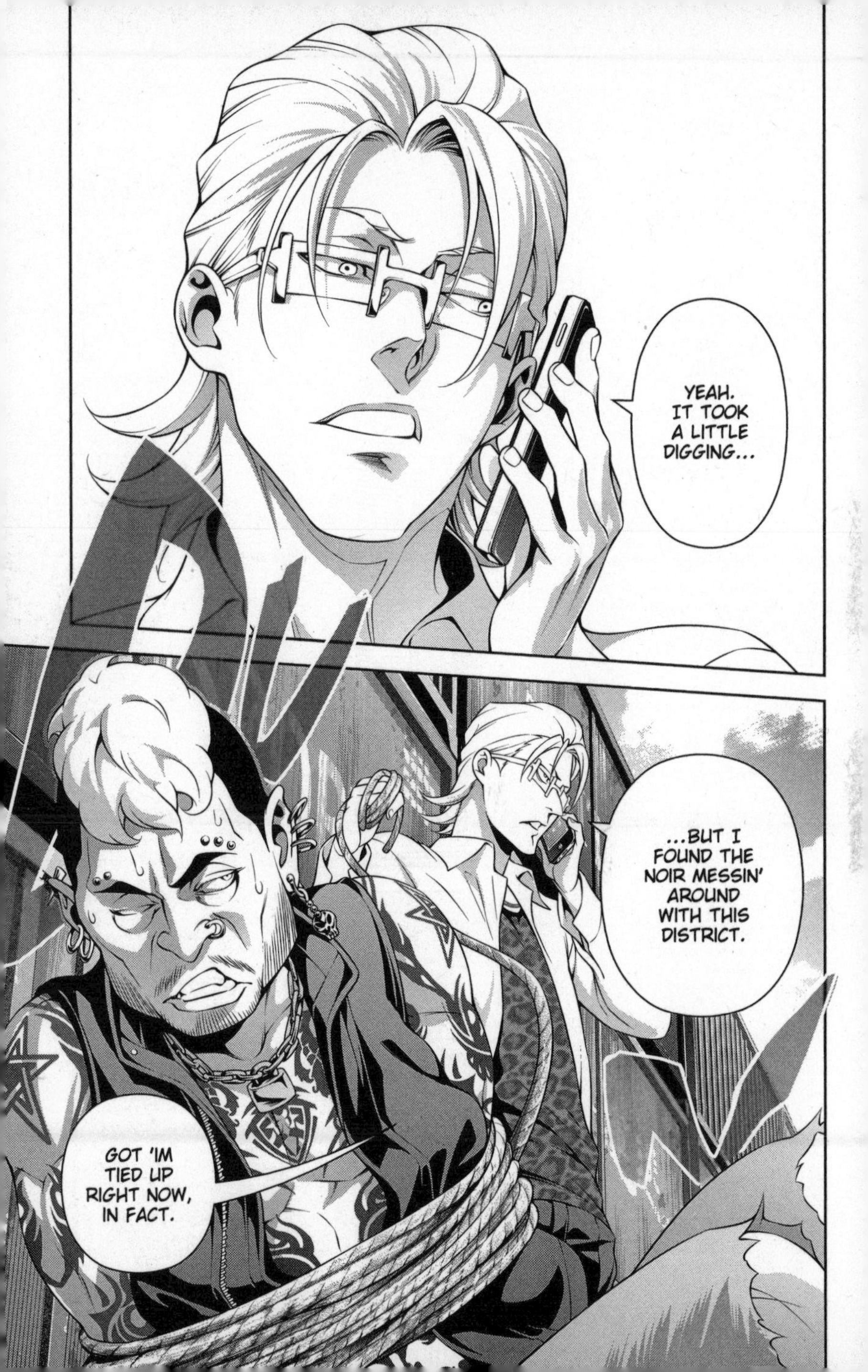
YEAH. IT TOOK A LITTLE DIGGING...
...BUT I FOUND THE NOIR MESSIN' AROUND WITH THIS DISTRICT.
GOT 'IM TIED UP RIGHT NOW, IN FACT.

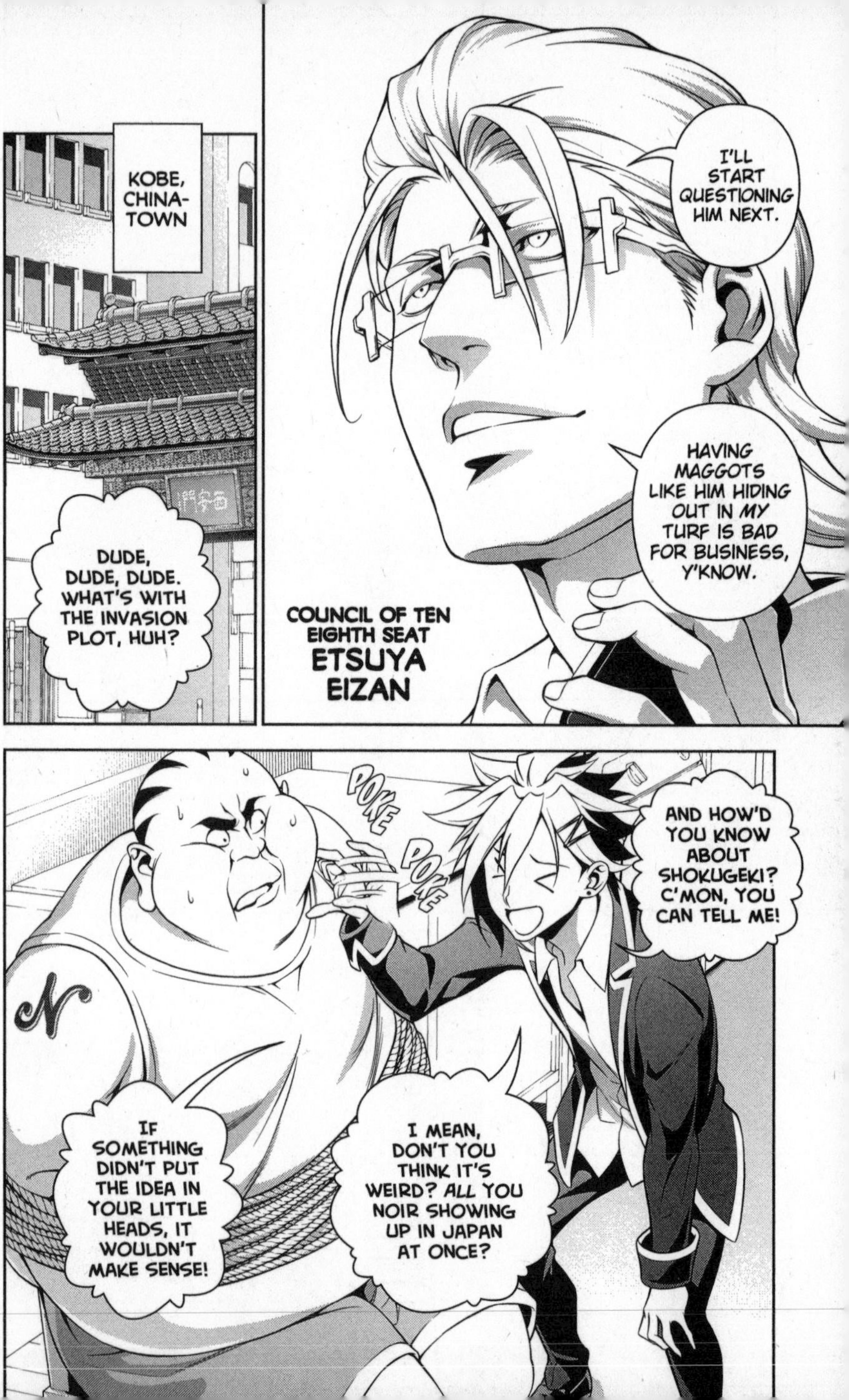
I'LL START QUESTIONING HIM NEXT.
HAVING MAGGOTS LIKE HIM HIDING OUT IN *MY* TURF IS BAD FOR BUSINESS, Y'KNOW.
COUNCIL OF TEN EIGHTH SEAT ETSUYA EIZAN
KOBE, CHINA-TOWN
DUDE, DUDE, DUDE. WHAT'S WITH THE INVASION PLOT, HUH?
POKE
POKE
AND HOW'D YOU KNOW ABOUT SHOKUGEKI? C'MON, YOU CAN TELL ME!
I MEAN, DON'T YOU THINK IT'S WEIRD? *ALL* YOU NOIR SHOWING UP IN JAPAN AT ONCE?
IF SOMETHING DIDN'T PUT THE IDEA IN YOUR LITTLE HEADS, IT WOULDN'T MAKE SENSE!

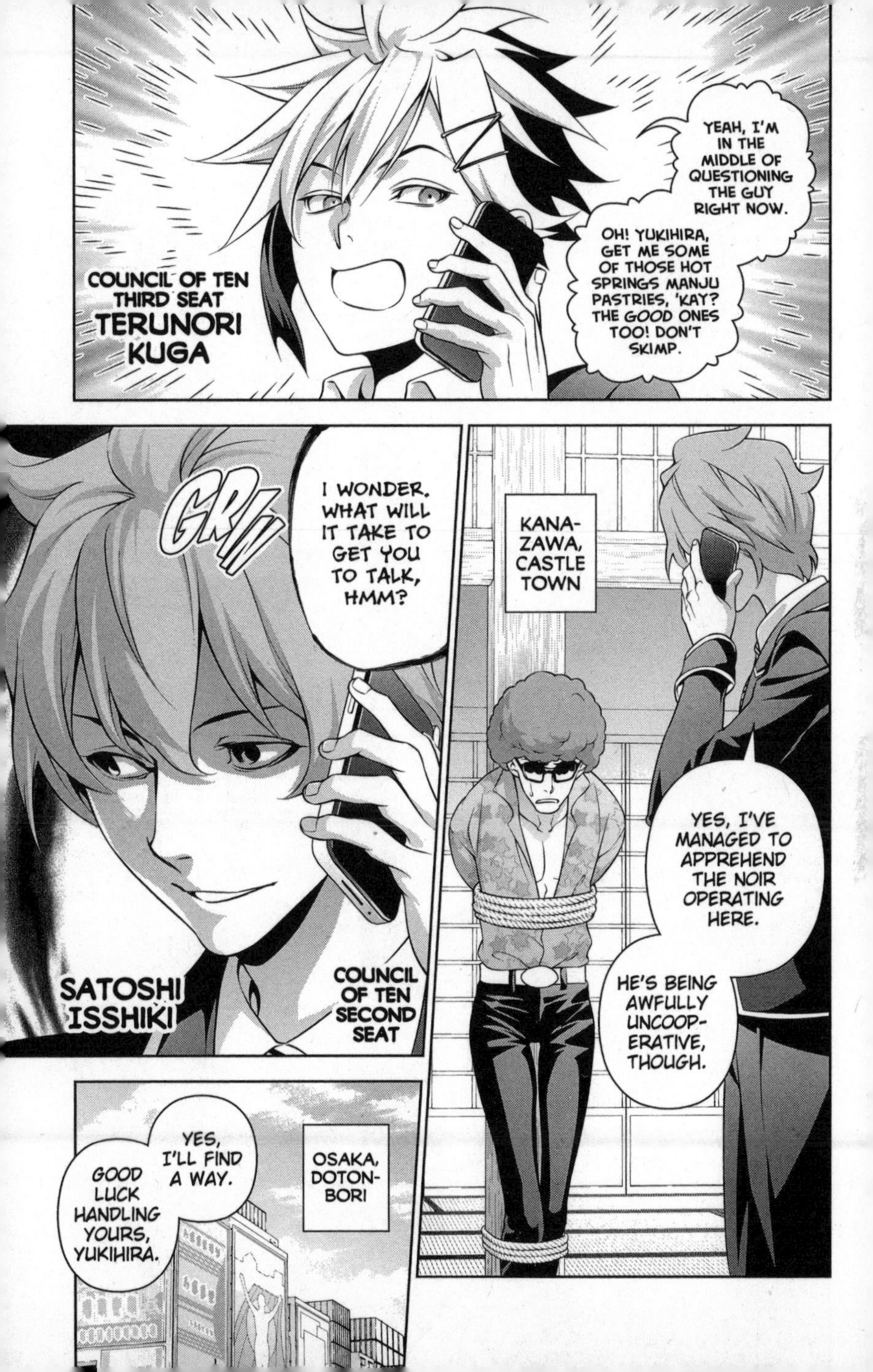
YEAH, I'M IN THE MIDDLE OF QUESTIONING THE GUY RIGHT NOW.
OH! YUKIHIRA, GET ME SOME OF THOSE HOT SPRINGS MANJU PASTRIES, 'KAY? THE *GOOD* ONES TOO! DON'T SKIMP.
COUNCIL OF TEN THIRD SEAT TERUNORI KUGA
KANA-ZAWA, CASTLE TOWN
YES, I'VE MANAGED TO APPREHEND THE NOIR OPERATING HERE.
HE'S BEING AWFULLY UNCOOP-ERATIVE, THOUGH.
I WONDER. WHAT WILL IT TAKE TO GET YOU TO TALK, HMM?
COUNCIL OF TEN SECOND SEAT
SATOSHI ISSHIKI
OSAKA, DOTON-BORI
YES, I'LL FIND A WAY.
GOOD LUCK HANDLING YOURS, YUKIHIRA.

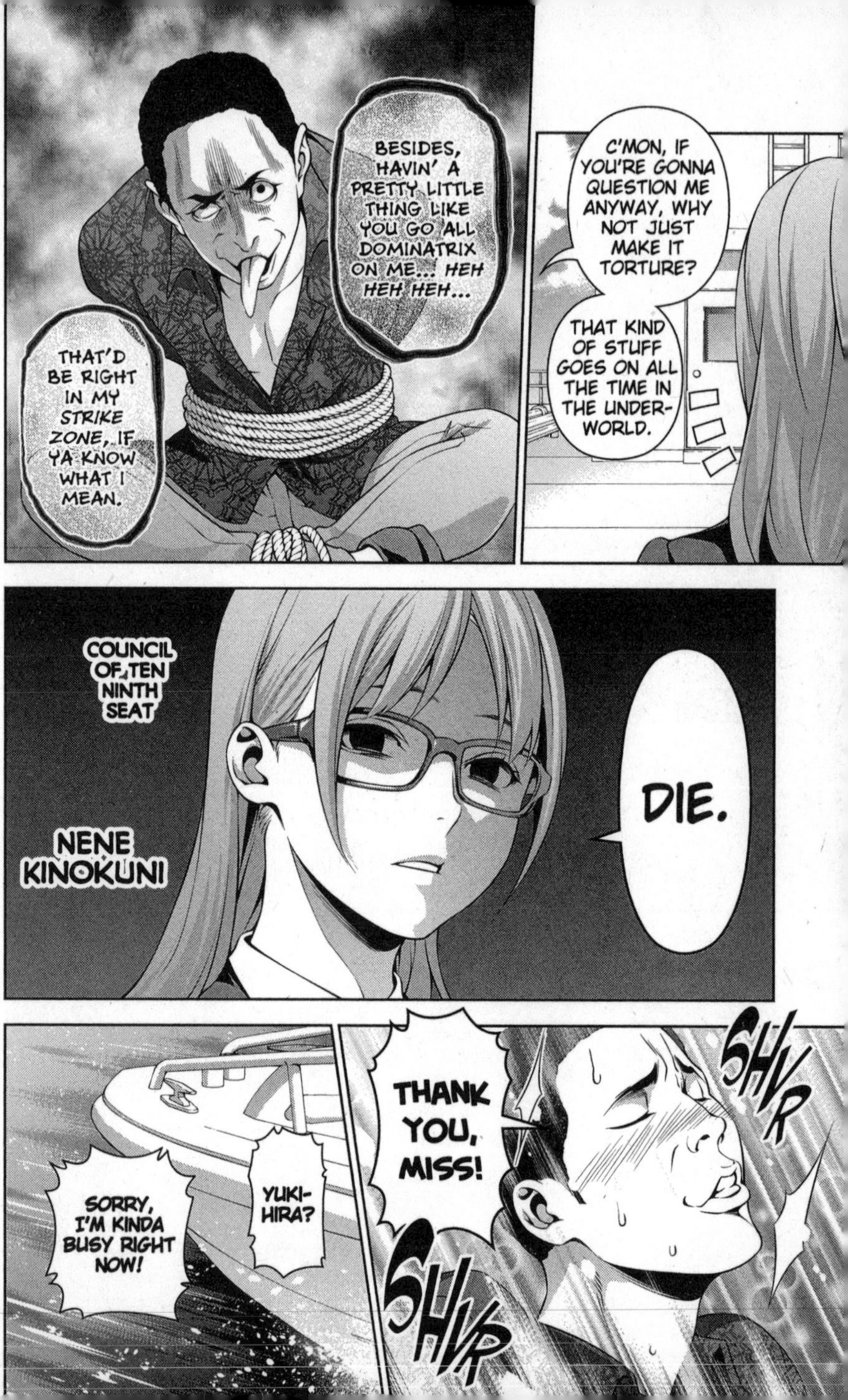
C'MON, IF YOU'RE GONNA QUESTION ME ANYWAY, WHY NOT JUST MAKE IT TORTURE?
THAT KIND OF STUFF GOES ON ALL THE TIME IN THE UNDER-WORLD.
BESIDES, HAVIN' A PRETTY LITTLE THING LIKE YOU GO ALL DOMINATRIX ON ME... HEH HEH HEH...
THAT'D BE RIGHT IN MY STRIKE ZONE, IF YA KNOW WHAT I MEAN.
DIE.
COUNCIL OF TEN NINTH SEAT
NENE KINOKUNI
SHVR
THANK YOU, MISS!
SHVR
YUKI-HIRA?
SORRY, I'M KINDA BUSY RIGHT NOW!

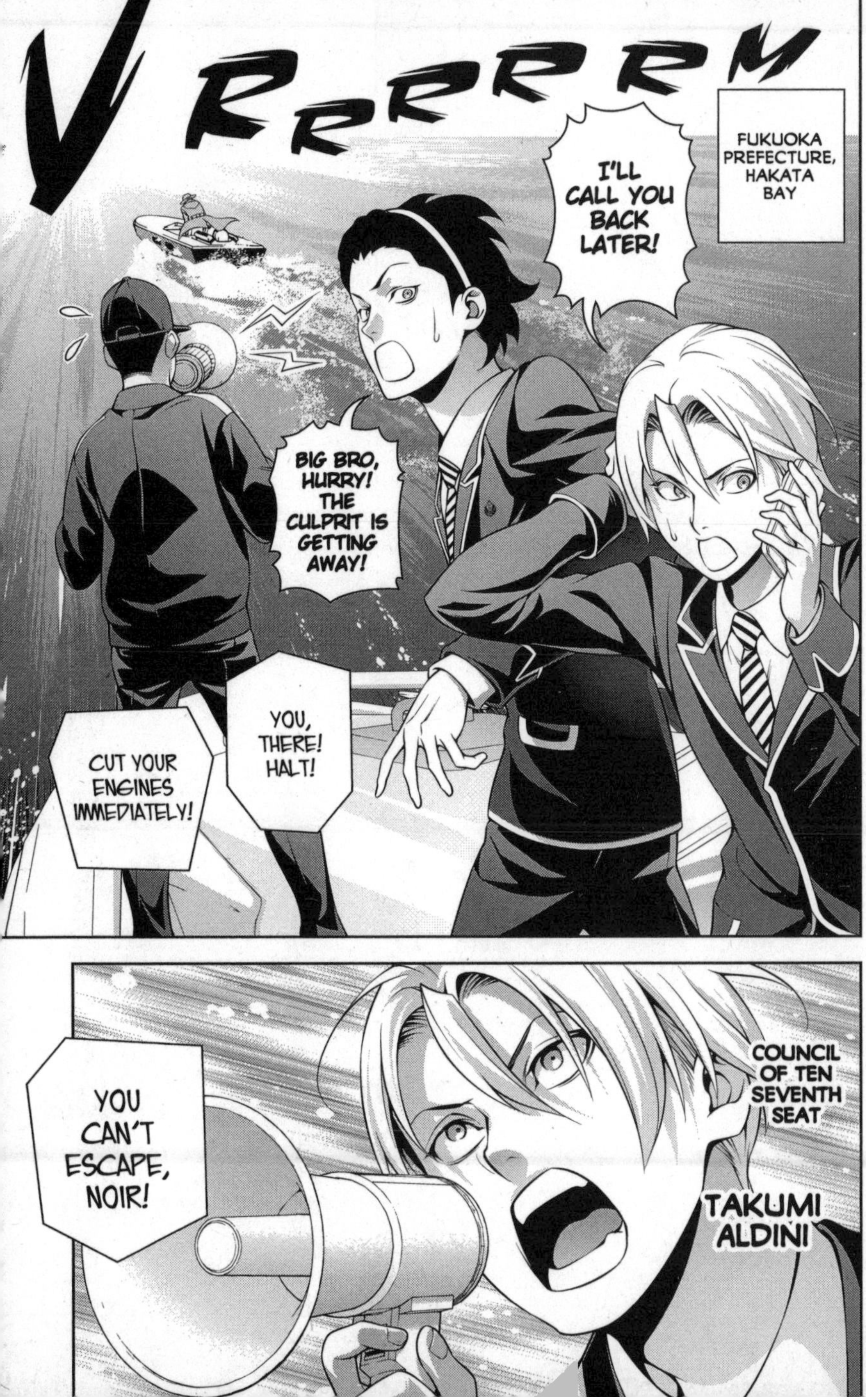
VRRRRRM
FUKUOKA PREFECTURE, HAKATA BAY
I'LL CALL YOU BACK LATER!
BIG BRO, HURRY! THE CULPRIT IS GETTING AWAY!
YOU, THERE! HALT!
CUT YOUR ENGINES IMMEDIATELY!
COUNCIL OF TEN SEVENTH SEAT
TAKUMI ALDINI
YOU CAN'T ESCAPE, NOIR!

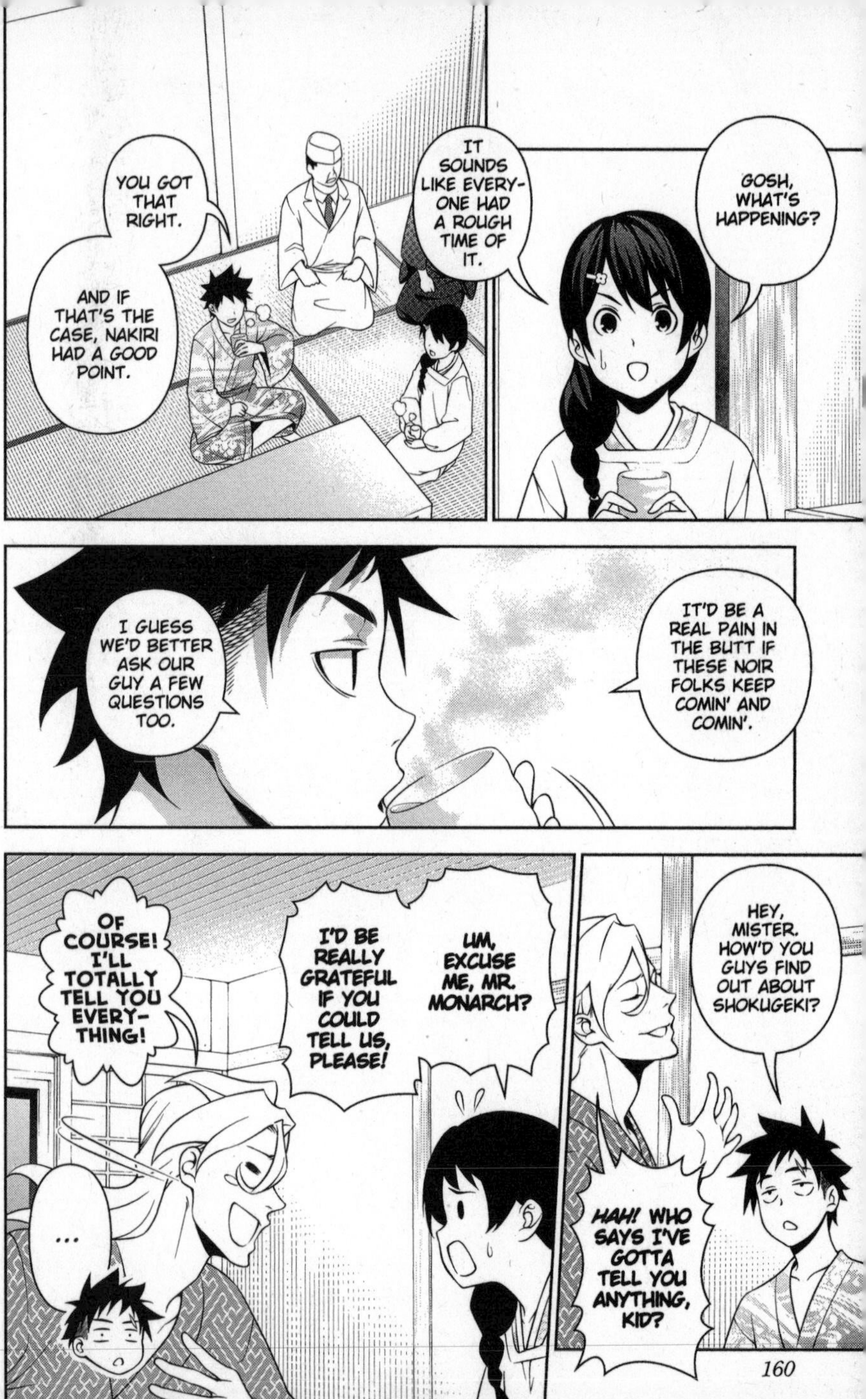
GOSH, WHAT'S HAPPENING?
IT SOUNDS LIKE EVERY-ONE HAD A ROUGH TIME OF IT.
YOU GOT THAT RIGHT.
AND IF THAT'S THE CASE, NAKIRI HAD A GOOD POINT.
IT'D BE A REAL PAIN IN THE BUTT IF THESE NOIR FOLKS KEEP COMIN' AND COMIN'.
I GUESS WE'D BETTER ASK OUR GUY A FEW QUESTIONS TOO.
HEY, MISTER. HOW'D YOU GUYS FIND OUT ABOUT SHOKUGEKI?
HAH! WHO SAYS I'VE GOTTA TELL YOU ANYTHING, KID?
UM, EXCUSE ME, MR. MONARCH?
I'D BE REALLY GRATEFUL IF YOU COULD TELL US, PLEASE!
OF COURSE! I'LL TOTALLY TELL YOU EVERY-THING!
...

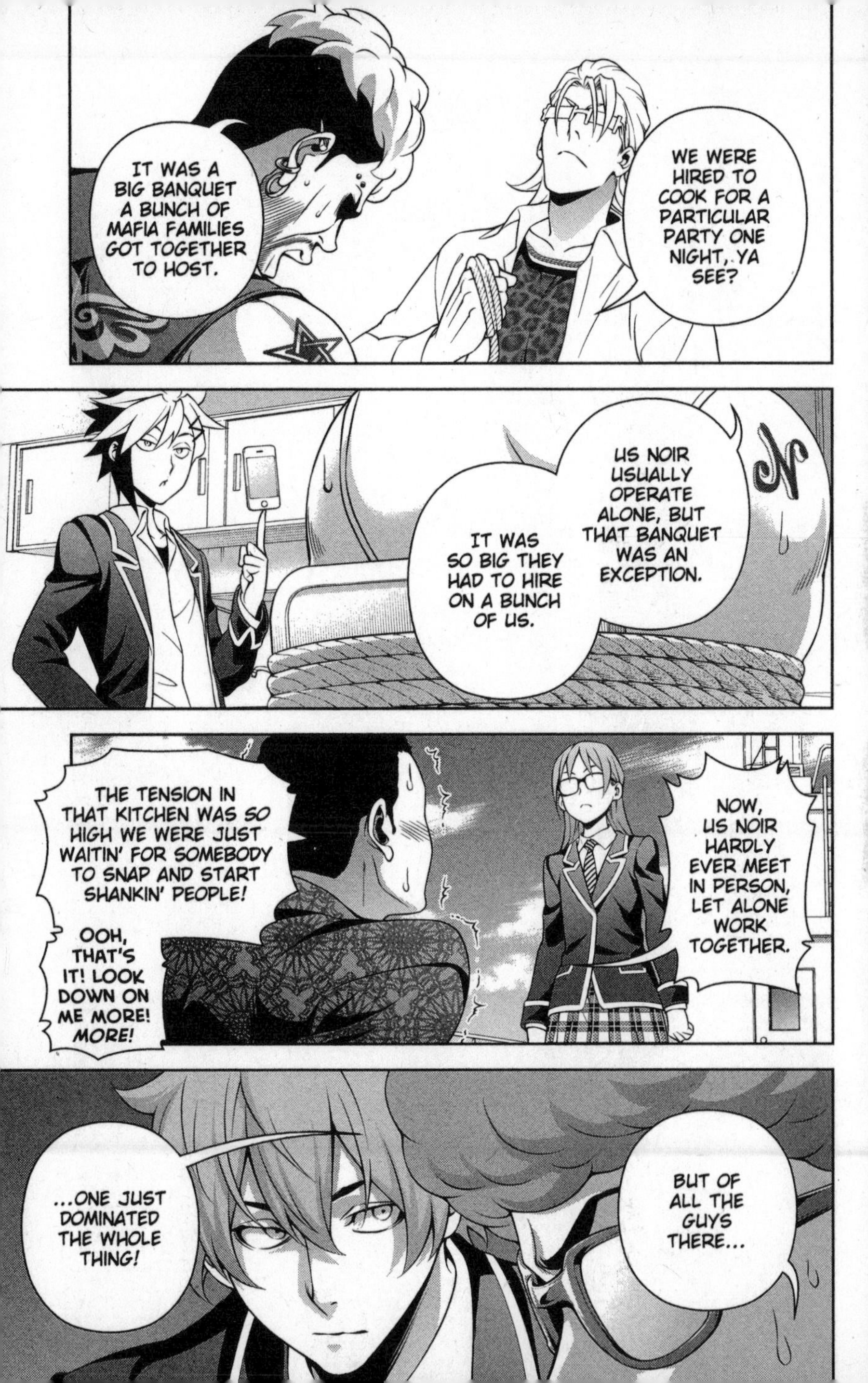
WE WERE HIRED TO COOK FOR A PARTICULAR PARTY ONE NIGHT, YA SEE?
IT WAS A BIG BANQUET A BUNCH OF MAFIA FAMILIES GOT TOGETHER TO HOST.
US NOIR USUALLY OPERATE ALONE, BUT THAT BANQUET WAS AN EXCEPTION.
IT WAS SO BIG THEY HAD TO HIRE ON A BUNCH OF US.
NOW, US NOIR HARDLY EVER MEET IN PERSON, LET ALONE WORK TOGETHER.
THE TENSION IN THAT KITCHEN WAS SO HIGH WE WERE JUST WAITIN' FOR SOMEBODY TO SNAP AND START SHANKIN' PEOPLE!
OOH, THAT'S IT! LOOK DOWN ON ME MORE! MORE!
BUT OF ALL THE GUYS THERE...
...ONE JUST DOMINATED THE WHOLE THING!

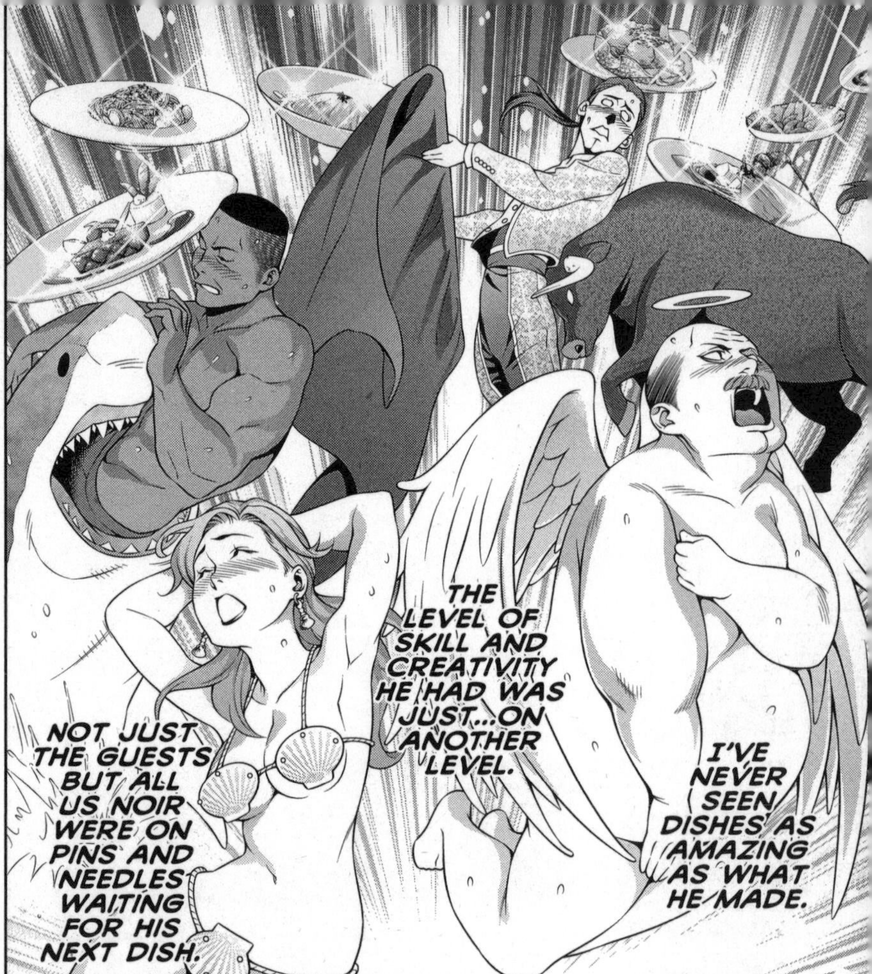
I'VE NEVER SEEN DISHES AS AMAZING AS WHAT HE MADE.
THE LEVEL OF SKILL AND CREATIVITY HE HAD WAS JUST...ON ANOTHER LEVEL.
NOT JUST THE GUESTS BUT ALL US NOIR WERE ON PINS AND NEEDLES WAITING FOR HIS NEXT DISH.
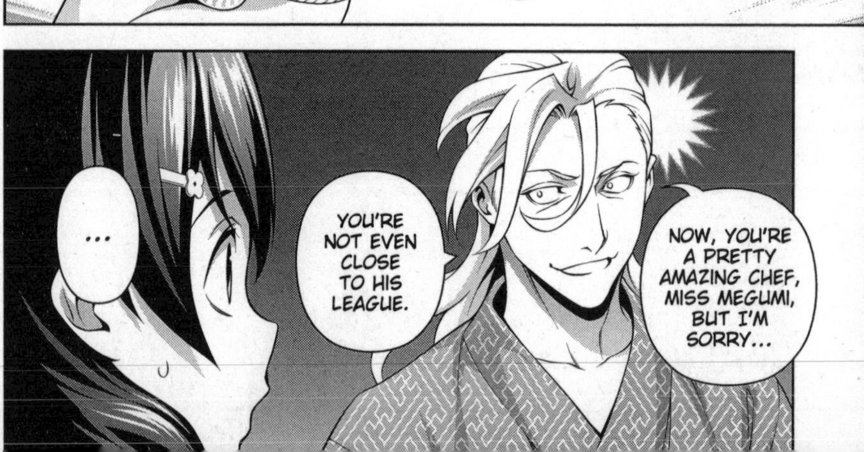
NOW, YOU'RE A PRETTY AMAZING CHEF, MISS MEGUMI, BUT I'M SORRY...
YOU'RE NOT EVEN CLOSE TO HIS LEAGUE.
...

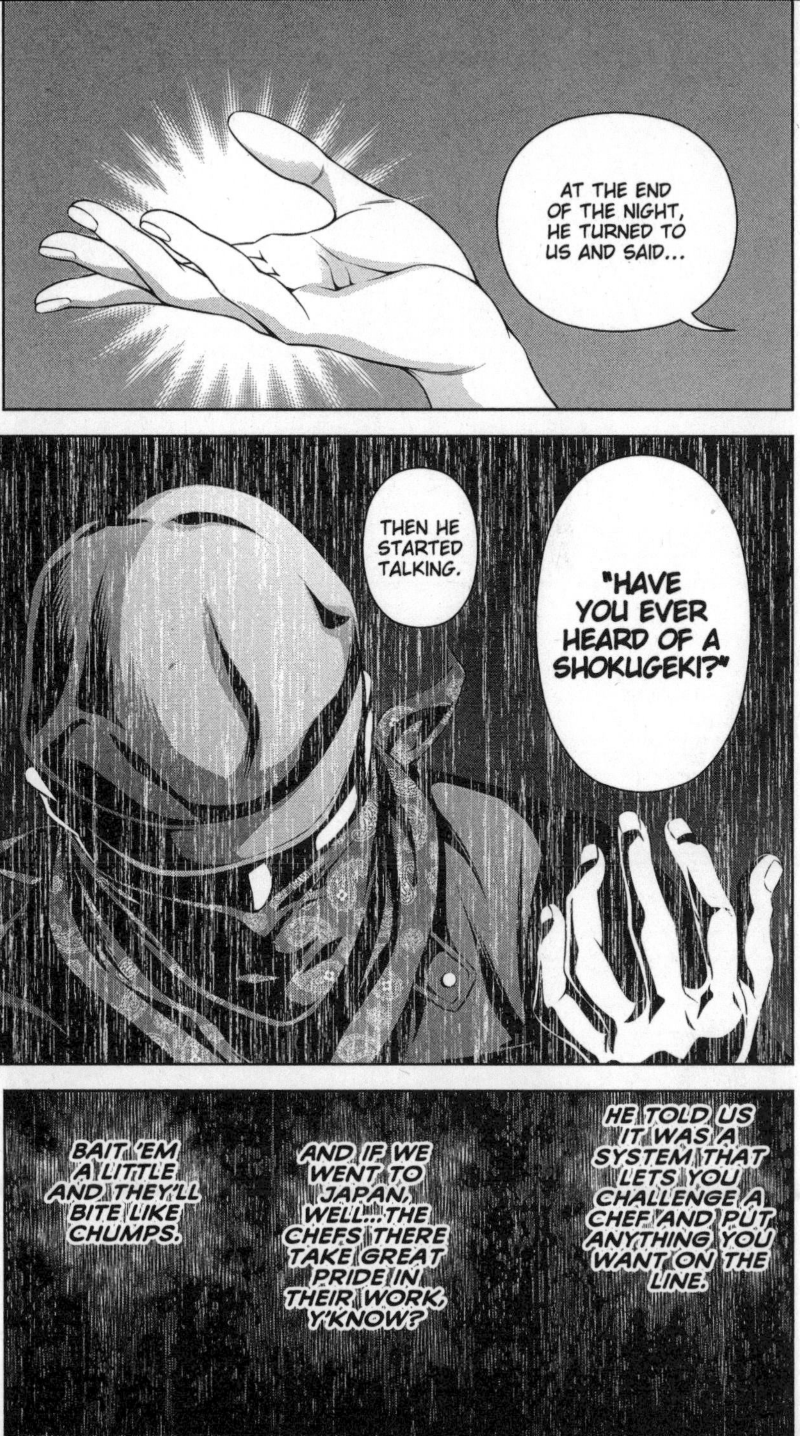
AT THE END OF THE NIGHT, HE TURNED TO US AND SAID...
"HAVE YOU EVER HEARD OF A SHOKUGEKI?"
THEN HE STARTED TALKING.
HE TOLD US IT WAS A SYSTEM THAT LETS YOU CHALLENGE A CHEF AND PUT ANYTHING YOU WANT ON THE LINE.
AND IF WE WENT TO JAPAN, WELL... THE CHEFS THERE TAKE GREAT PRIDE IN THEIR WORK, Y'KNOW?
BAIT 'EM A LITTLE AND THEY'LL BITE LIKE CHUMPS.

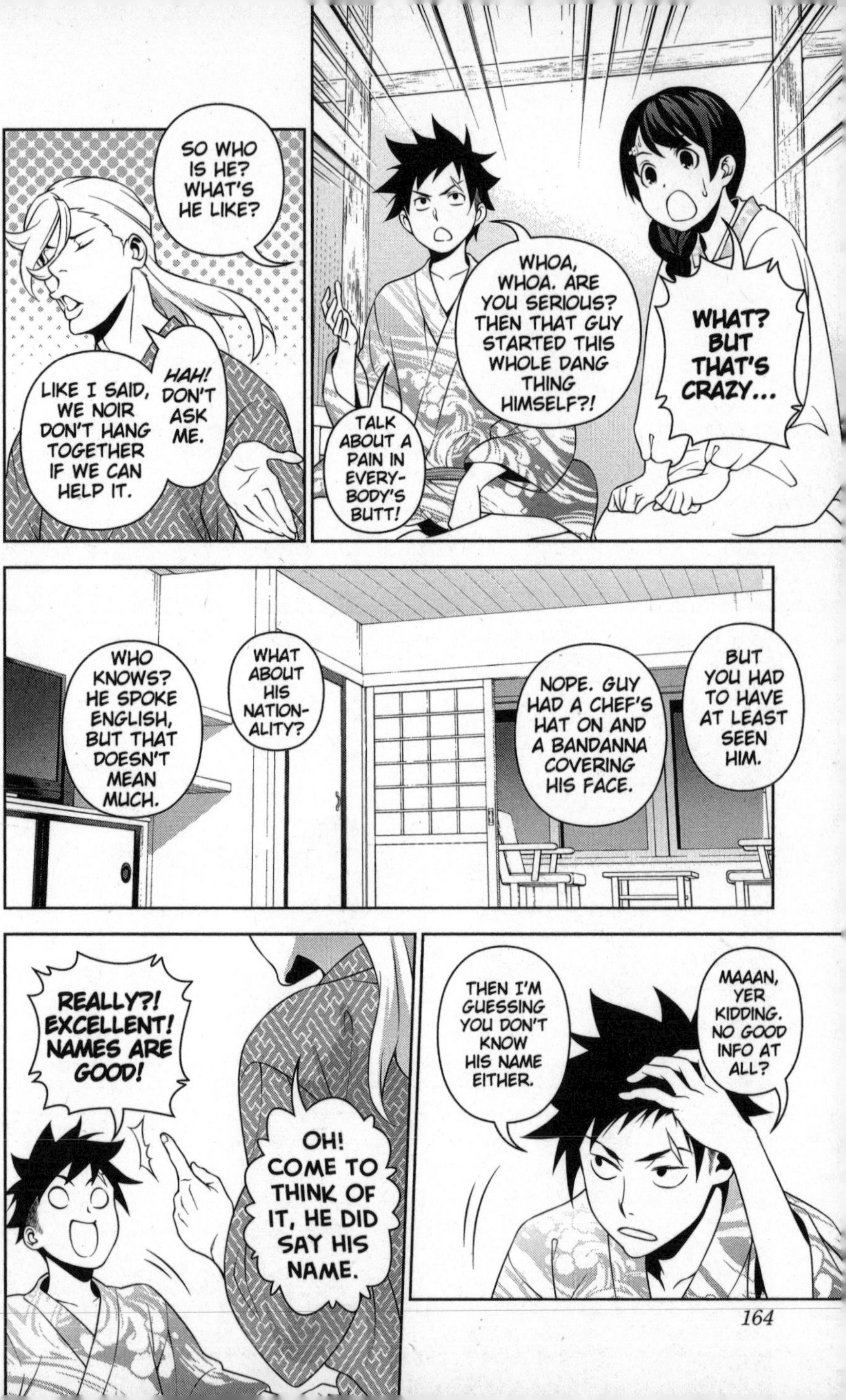
WHAT? BUT THAT'S CRAZY...
WHOA, WHOA. ARE YOU SERIOUS? THEN THAT GUY STARTED THIS WHOLE DANG THING HIMSELF?!
TALK ABOUT A PAIN IN EVERY-BODY'S BUTT!
SO WHO IS HE? WHAT'S HE LIKE?
HAH! DON'T ASK ME.
LIKE I SAID, WE NOIR DON'T HANG TOGETHER IF WE CAN HELP IT.
BUT YOU HAD TO HAVE AT LEAST SEEN HIM.
NOPE. GUY HAD A CHEF'S HAT ON AND A BANDANNA COVERING HIS FACE.
WHAT ABOUT HIS NATION-ALITY?
WHO KNOWS? HE SPOKE ENGLISH, BUT THAT DOESN'T MEAN MUCH.
MAAAN, YER KIDDING. NO GOOD INFO AT ALL?
THEN I'M GUESSING YOU DON'T KNOW HIS NAME EITHER.
OH! COME TO THINK OF IT, HE DID SAY HIS NAME.
REALLY?! EXCELLENT! NAMES ARE GOOD!

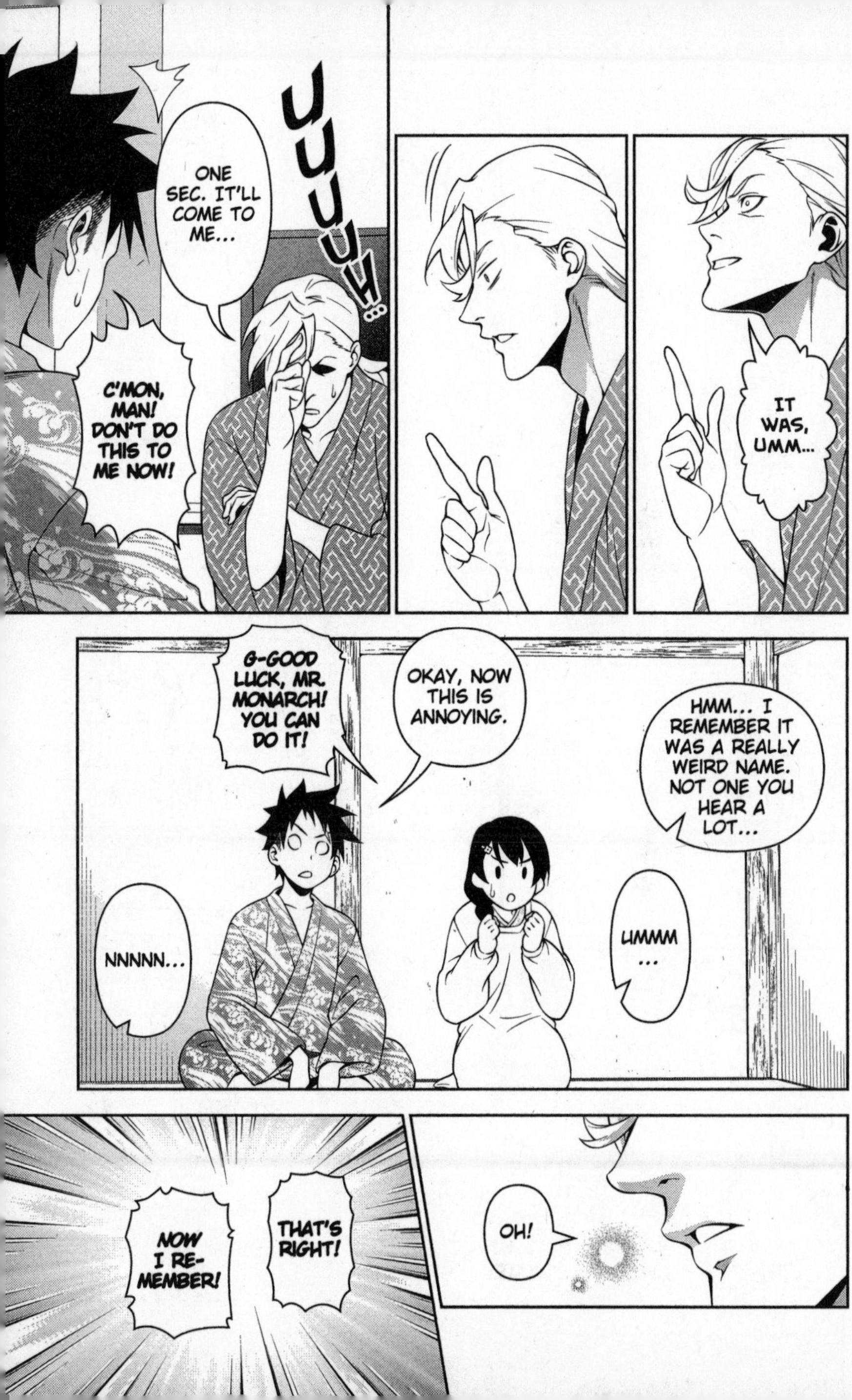
IT WAS, UMM...
UUUUUH!!
ONE SEC. IT'LL COME TO ME...
C'MON, MAN! DON'T DO THIS TO ME NOW!
HMM... I REMEMBER IT WAS A REALLY WEIRD NAME. NOT ONE YOU HEAR A LOT...
OKAY, NOW THIS IS ANNOYING.
G-GOOD LUCK, MR. MONARCH! YOU CAN DO IT!
UMMM...
NNNNN...
OH!
THAT'S RIGHT!
NOW I RE-MEMBER!

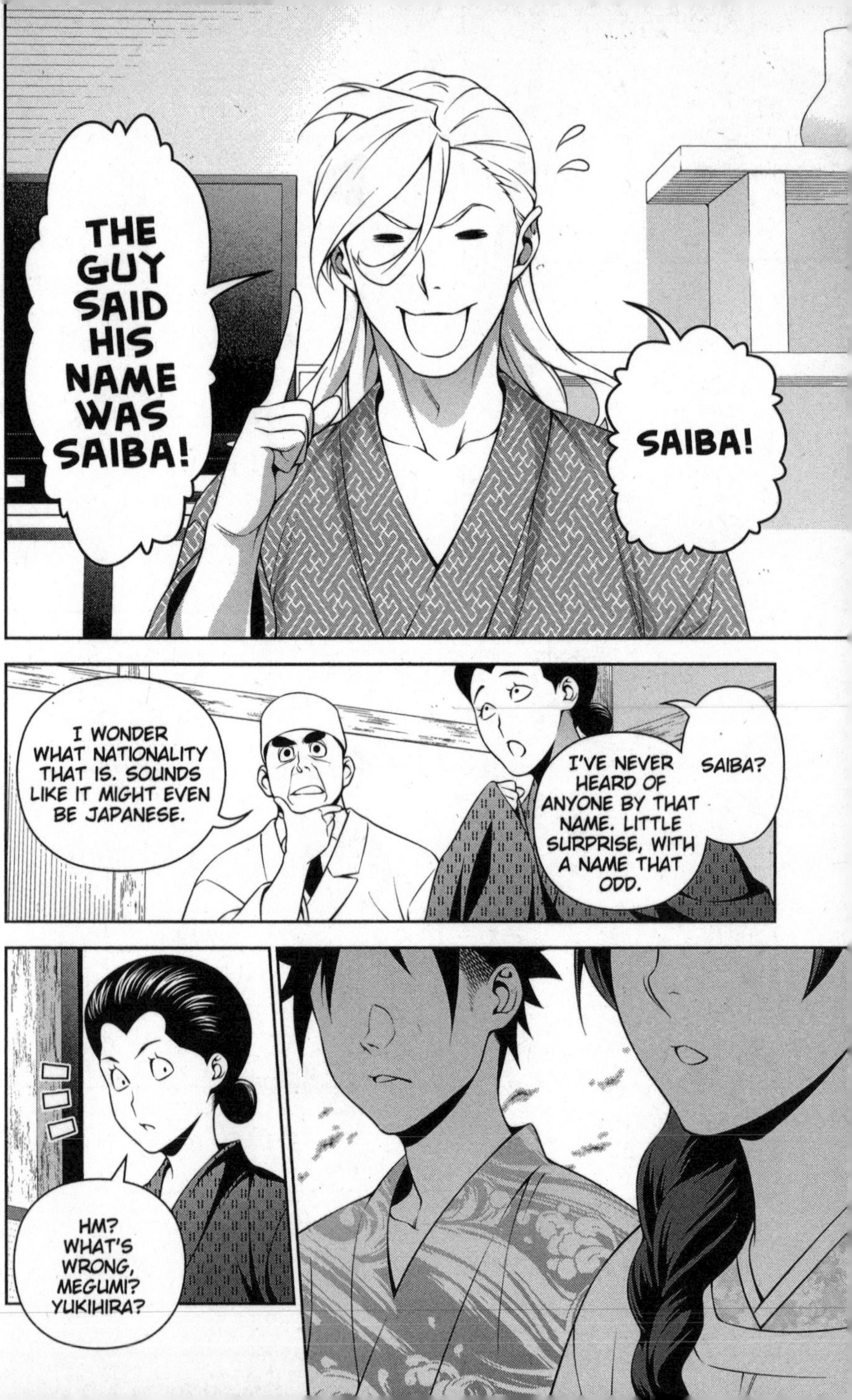

THE GUY SAID HIS NAME WAS SAIBA!
SAIBA!
SAIBA?
I'VE NEVER HEARD OF ANYONE BY THAT NAME. LITTLE SURPRISE, WITH A NAME THAT ODD.
I WONDER WHAT NATIONALITY THAT IS. SOUNDS LIKE IT MIGHT EVEN BE JAPANESE.
HM? WHAT'S WRONG, MEGUMI? YUKIHIRA?

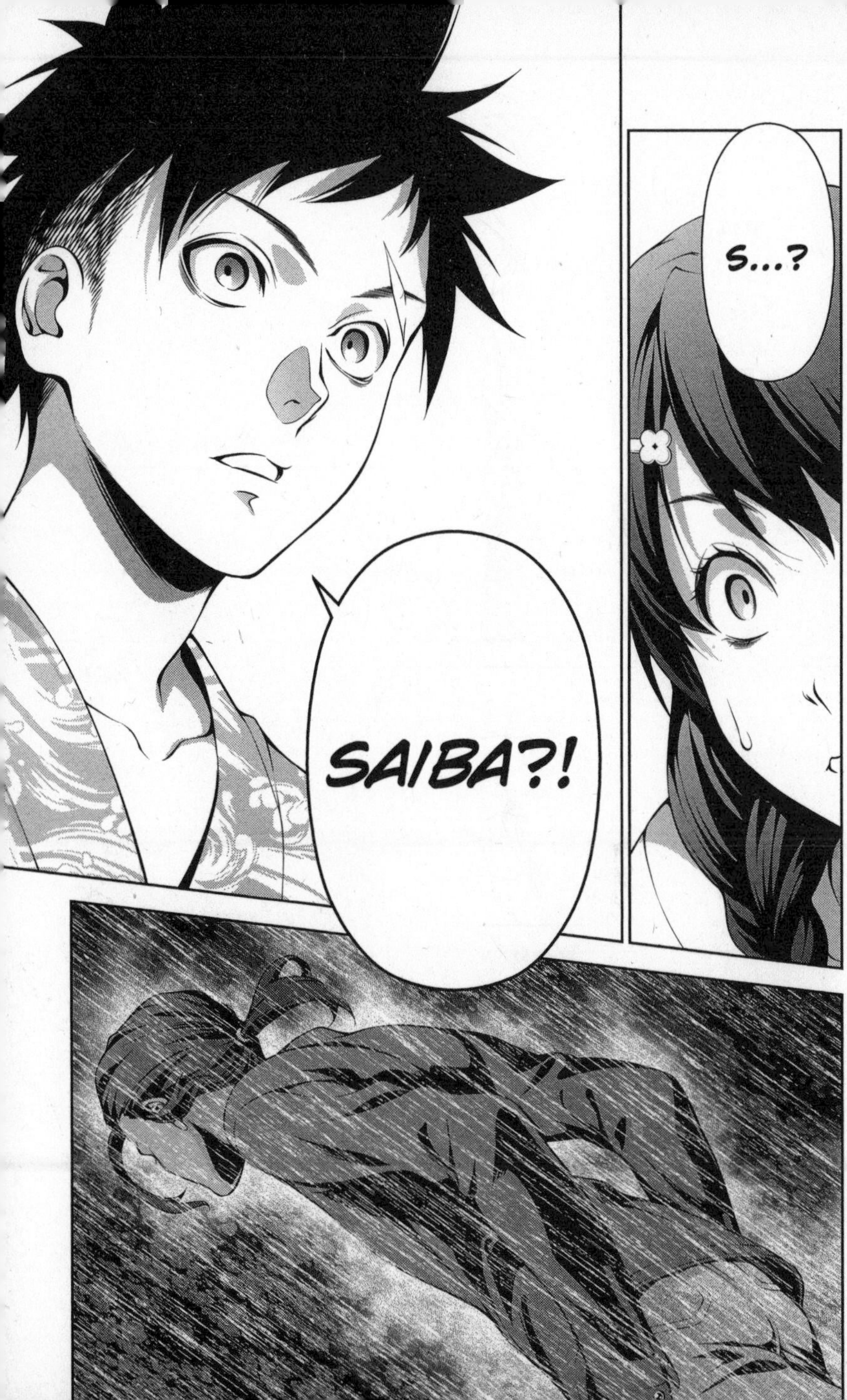
S...?
SAIBA?!

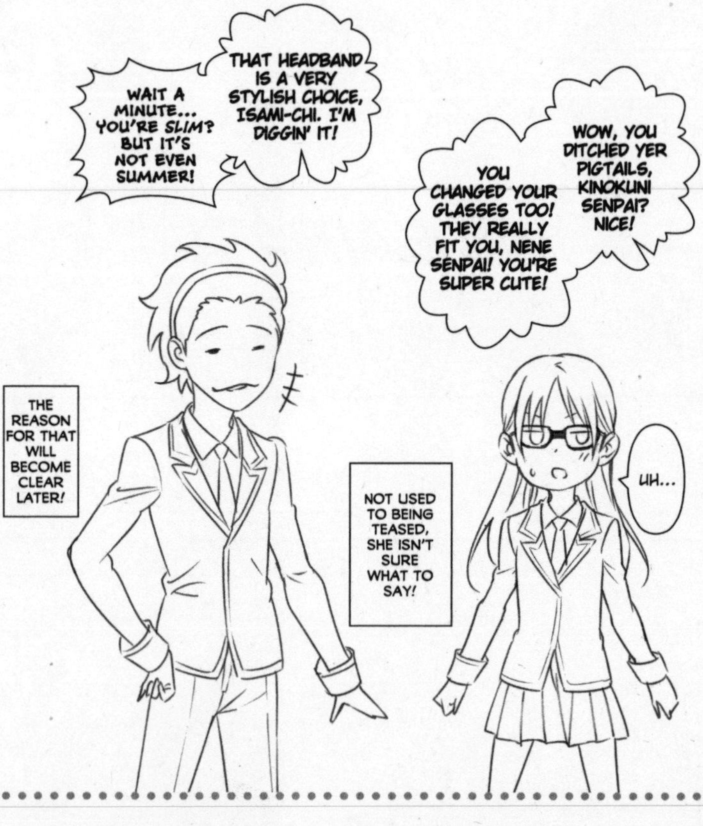
WOW, YOU DITCHED YER PIGTAILS, KINOKUNI SENPAI? NICE!
YOU CHANGED YOUR GLASSES TOO! THEY REALLY FIT YOU, NENE SENPAI! YOU'RE SUPER CUTE!
THAT HEADBAND IS A VERY STYLISH CHOICE, ISAMI-CHI. I'M DIGGIN' IT!
WAIT A MINUTE... YOU'RE *SLIM*? BUT IT'S NOT EVEN SUMMER!
UH...
NOT USED TO BEING TEASED, SHE ISN'T SURE WHAT TO SAY!
THE REASON FOR THAT WILL BECOME CLEAR LATER!

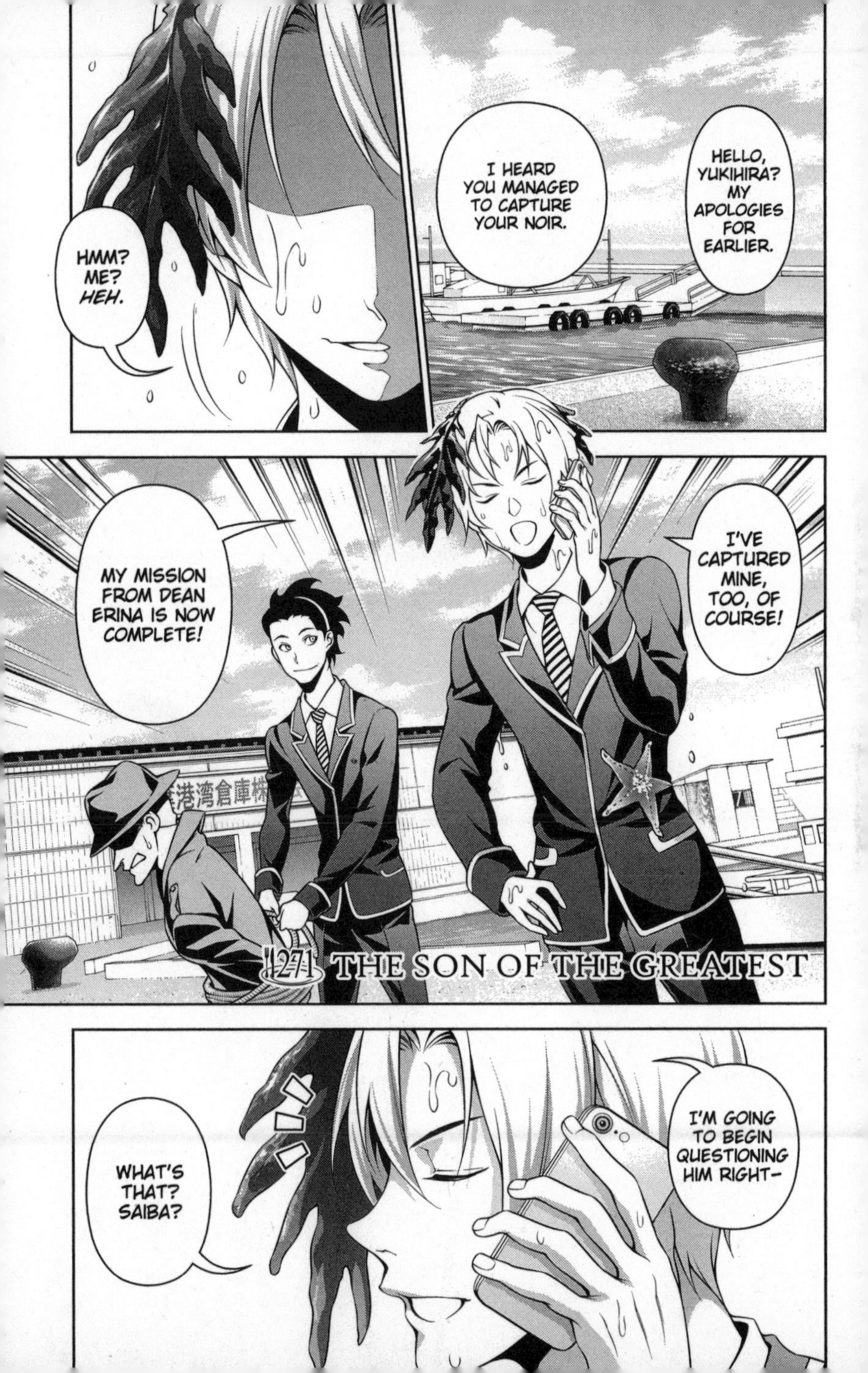
HELLO, YUKIHIRA? MY APOLOGIES FOR EARLIER.
I HEARD YOU MANAGED TO CAPTURE YOUR NOIR.
HMM? ME? HEH.
I'VE CAPTURED MINE, TOO, OF COURSE!
MY MISSION FROM DEAN ERINA IS NOW COMPLETE!
271 THE SON OF THE GREATEST
I'M GOING TO BEGIN QUESTIONING HIM RIGHT—
WHAT'S THAT? SAIBA?

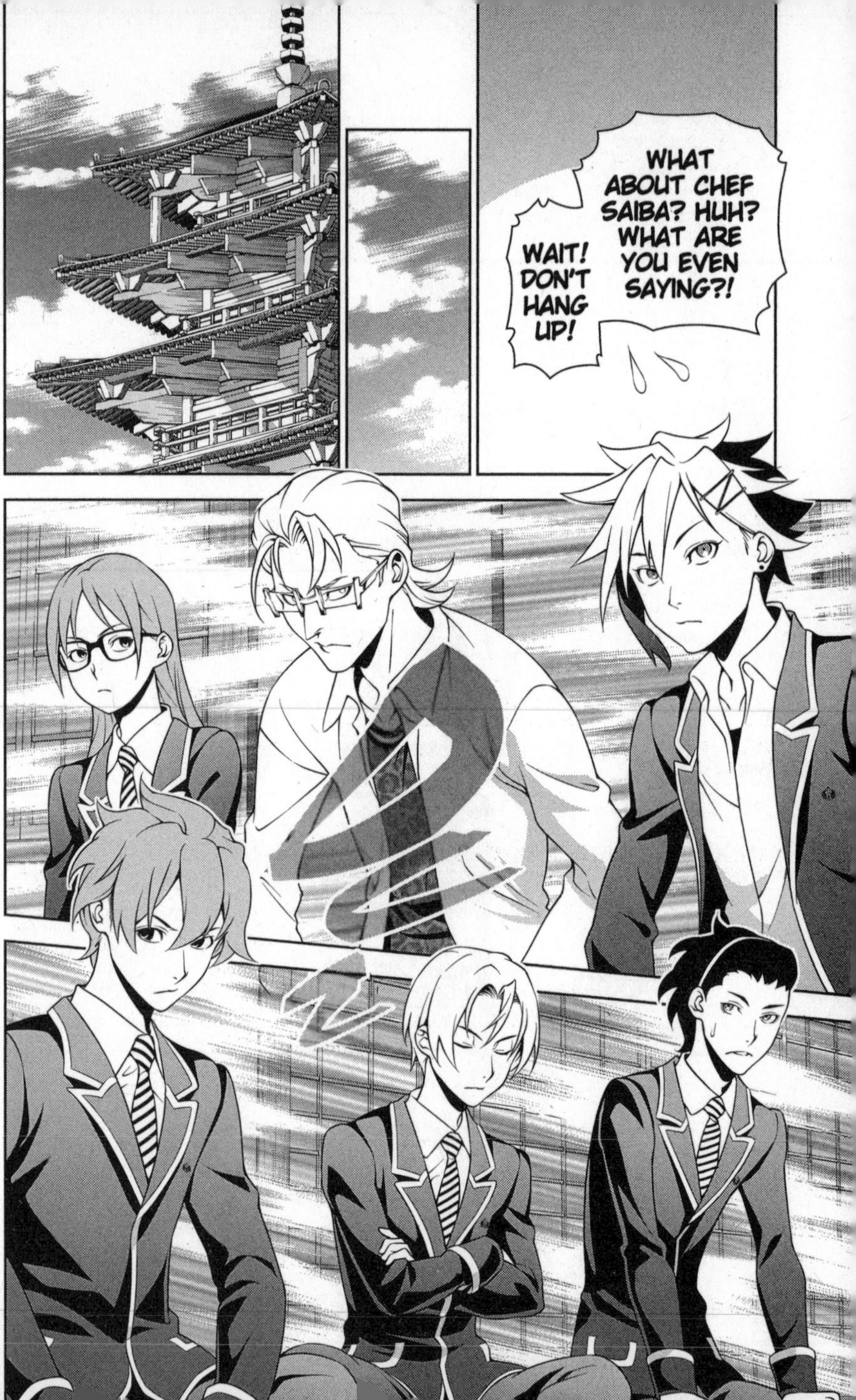
WHAT ABOUT CHEF SAIBA? HUH? WHAT ARE YOU EVEN SAYING?!
WAIT! DON'T HANG UP!

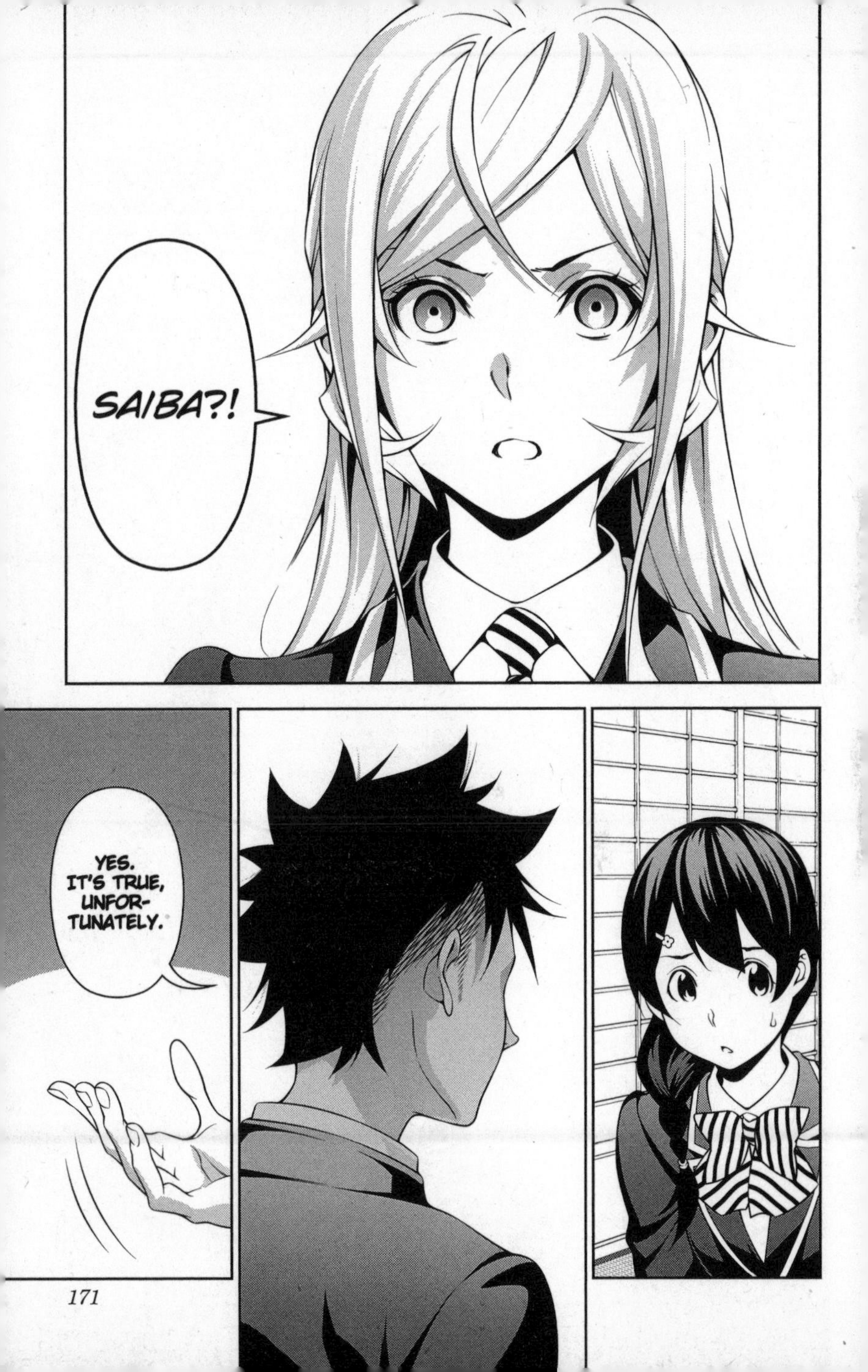
SAIBA?!
YES. IT'S TRUE, UNFOR-TUNATELY.

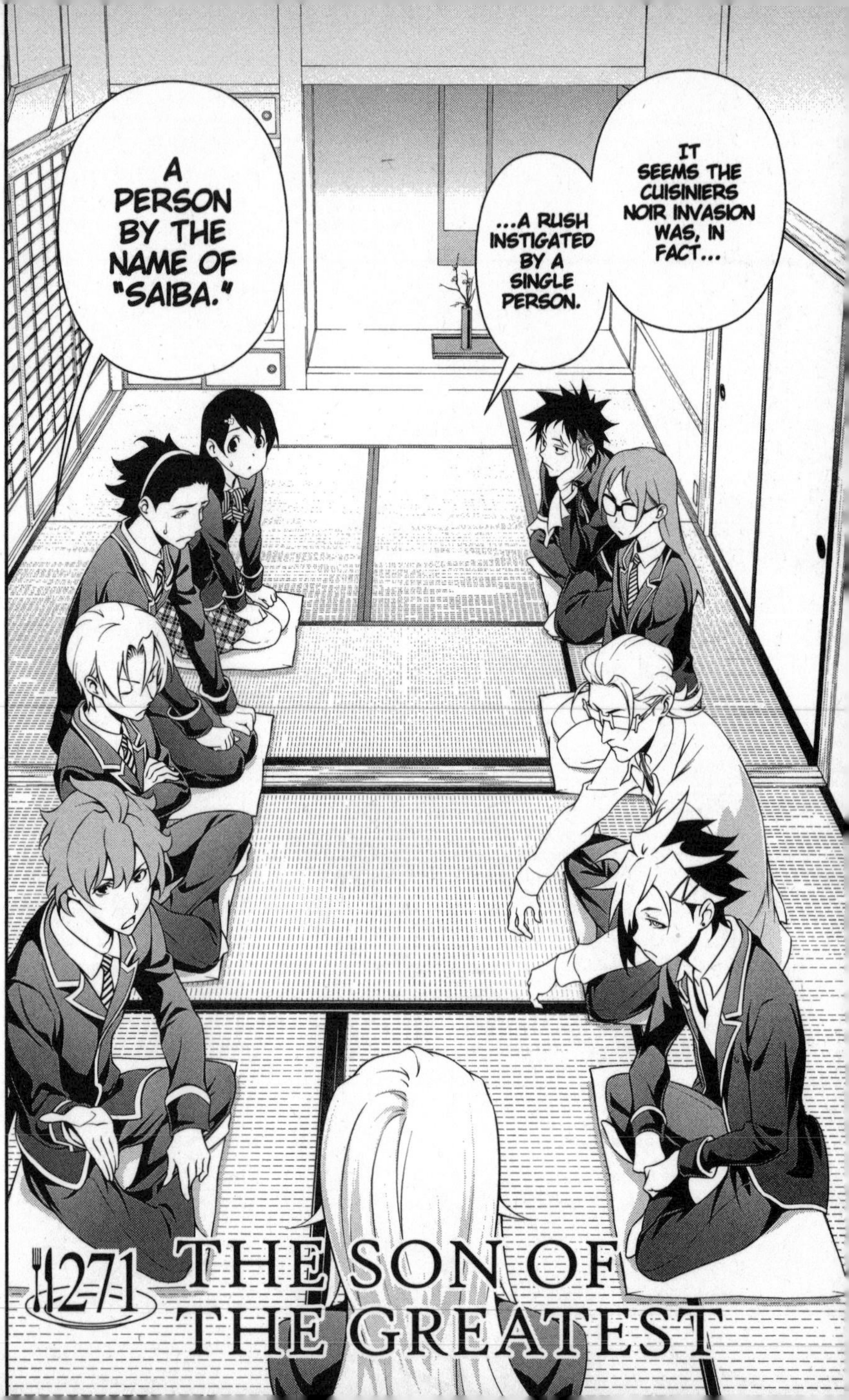
IT SEEMS THE CUISINIERS NOIR INVASION WAS, IN FACT...
...A RUSH INSTIGATED BY A SINGLE PERSON.
A PERSON BY THE NAME OF "SAIBA."
271
THE SON OF THE GREATEST

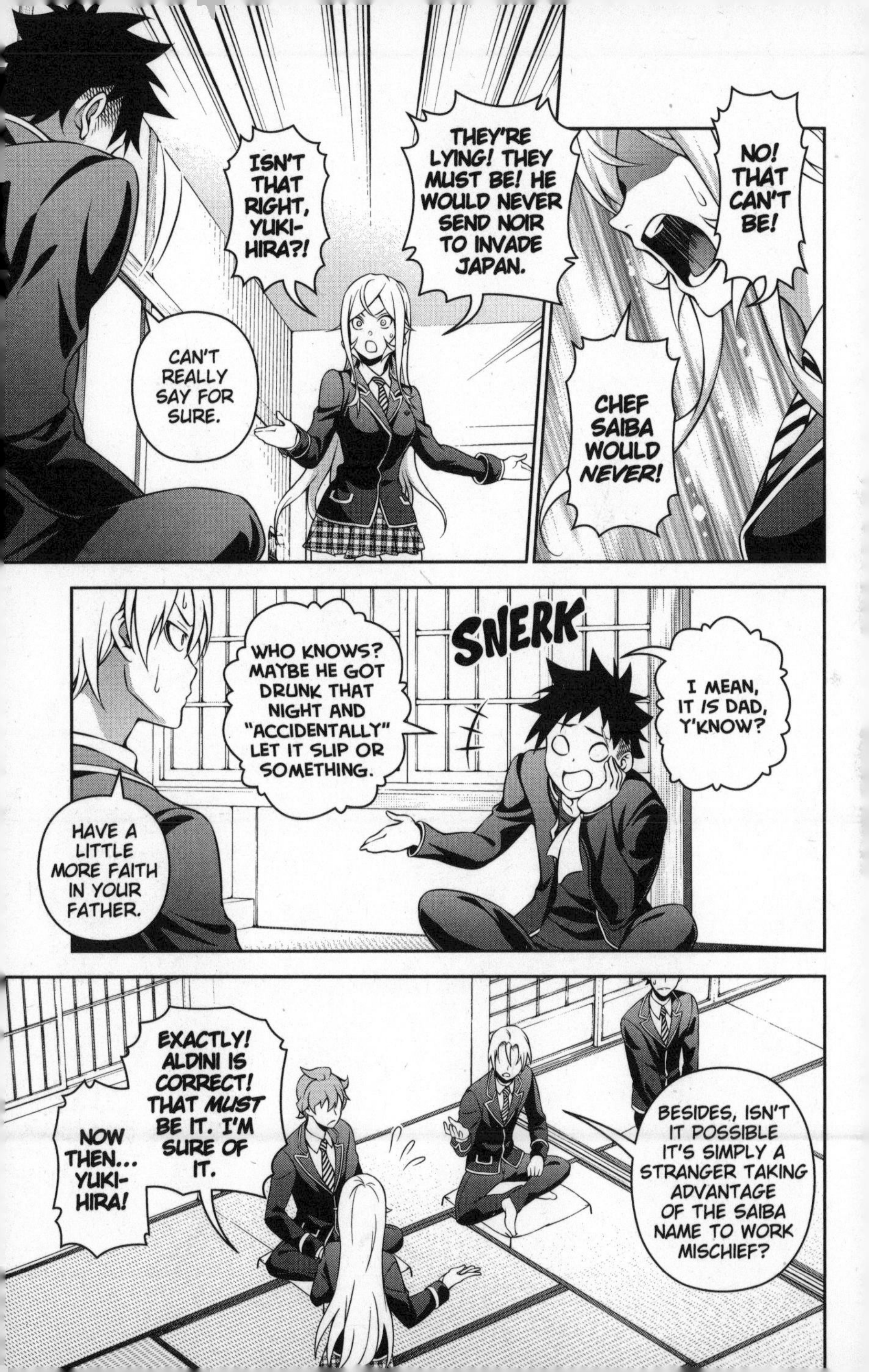
NO! THAT CAN'T BE!
CHEF SAIBA WOULD *NEVER*!
THEY'RE LYING! THEY MUST BE! HE WOULD NEVER SEND NOIR TO INVADE JAPAN.
ISN'T THAT RIGHT, YUKI-HIRA?!
CAN'T REALLY SAY FOR SURE.
SNERK
I MEAN, IT *IS* DAD, Y'KNOW?
WHO KNOWS? MAYBE HE GOT DRUNK THAT NIGHT AND "ACCIDENTALLY" LET IT SLIP OR SOMETHING.
HAVE A LITTLE MORE FAITH IN YOUR FATHER.
BESIDES, ISN'T IT POSSIBLE IT'S SIMPLY A STRANGER TAKING ADVANTAGE OF THE SAIBA NAME TO WORK MISCHIEF?
EXACTLY! ALDINI IS CORRECT! THAT *MUST* BE IT. I'M SURE OF IT.
NOW THEN... YUKI-HIRA!

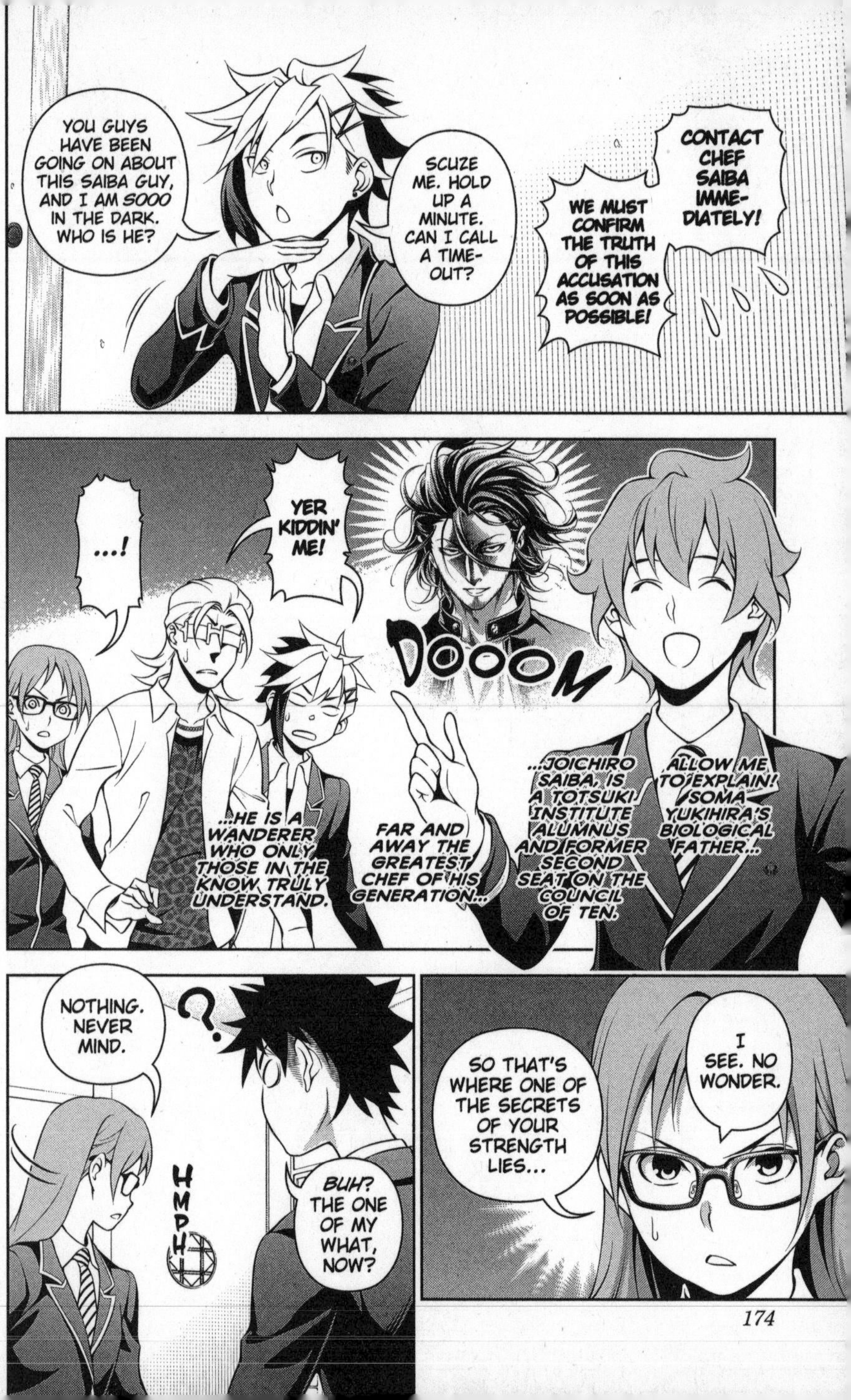
CONTACT CHEF SAIBA IMMEDIATELY!
WE MUST CONFIRM THE TRUTH OF THIS ACCUSATION AS SOON AS POSSIBLE!
SCUZE ME. HOLD UP A MINUTE. CAN I CALL A TIME-OUT?
YOU GUYS HAVE BEEN GOING ON ABOUT THIS SAIBA GUY, AND I AM *SOOO* IN THE DARK. WHO IS HE?
ALLOW ME TO EXPLAIN! SOMA YUKIHIRA'S BIOLOGICAL FATHER...
...JOICHIRO SAIBA, IS A TOTSUKI INSTITUTE ALUMNUS AND FORMER SECOND SEAT ON THE COUNCIL OF TEN.
FAR AND AWAY THE GREATEST CHEF OF HIS GENERATION...
...HE IS A WANDERER WHO ONLY THOSE IN THE KNOW TRULY UNDERSTAND.
DOOOM
YER KIDDIN' ME!
...!
I SEE. NO WONDER.
SO THAT'S WHERE ONE OF THE SECRETS OF YOUR STRENGTH LIES...
?
BUH? THE ONE OF MY WHAT, NOW?
HMPH
NOTHING. NEVER MIND.

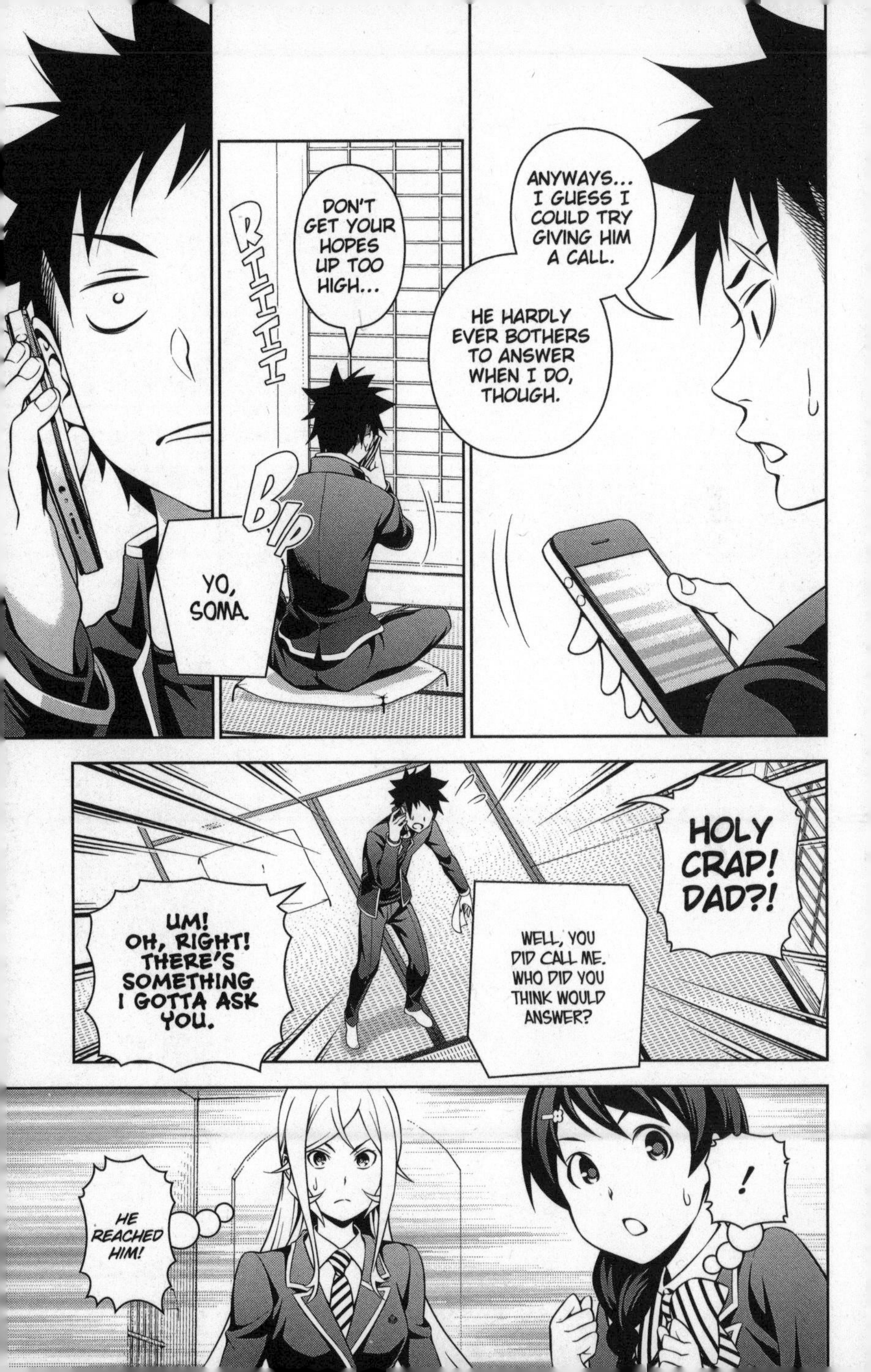
ANYWAYS... I GUESS I COULD TRY GIVING HIM A CALL.
HE HARDLY EVER BOTHERS TO ANSWER WHEN I DO, THOUGH.
DON'T GET YOUR HOPES UP TOO HIGH...
RIIIII
BIP
YO, SOMA.
HOLY CRAP! DAD?!
WELL, YOU DID CALL ME. WHO DID YOU THINK WOULD ANSWER?
UM! OH, RIGHT! THERE'S SOMETHING I GOTTA ASK YOU.
!
HE REACHED HIM!

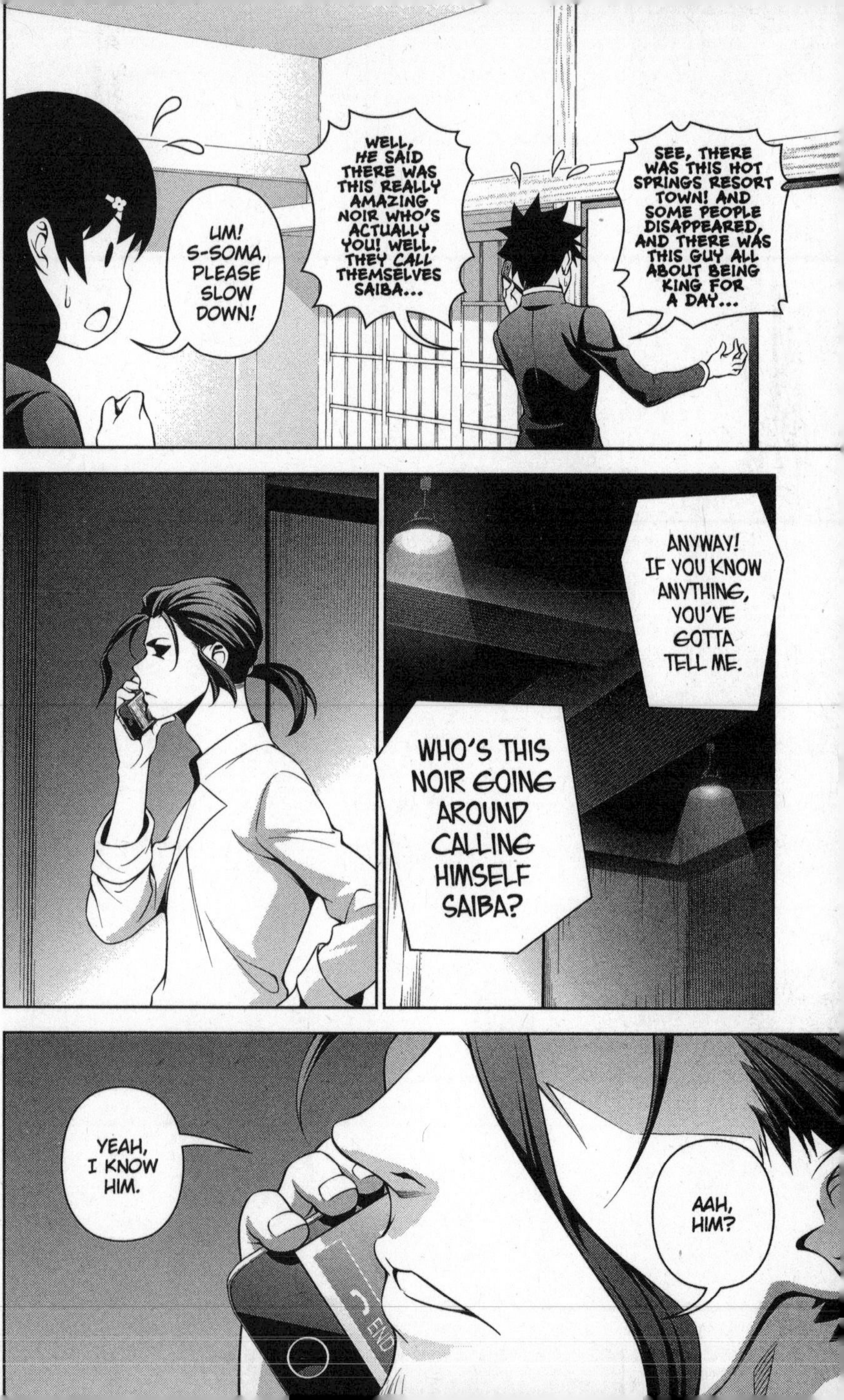
SEE, THERE WAS THIS HOT SPRINGS RESORT TOWN! AND SOME PEOPLE DISAPPEARED, AND THERE WAS THIS GUY ALL ABOUT BEING KING FOR A DAY...
WELL, HE SAID THERE WAS THIS REALLY AMAZING NOIR WHO'S ACTUALLY YOU! WELL, THEY CALL THEMSELVES SAIBA...
UM! S-SOMA, PLEASE SLOW DOWN!
ANYWAY! IF YOU KNOW ANYTHING, YOU'VE GOTTA TELL ME.
WHO'S THIS NOIR GOING AROUND CALLING HIMSELF SAIBA?
AAH, HIM?
YEAH, I KNOW HIM.
END

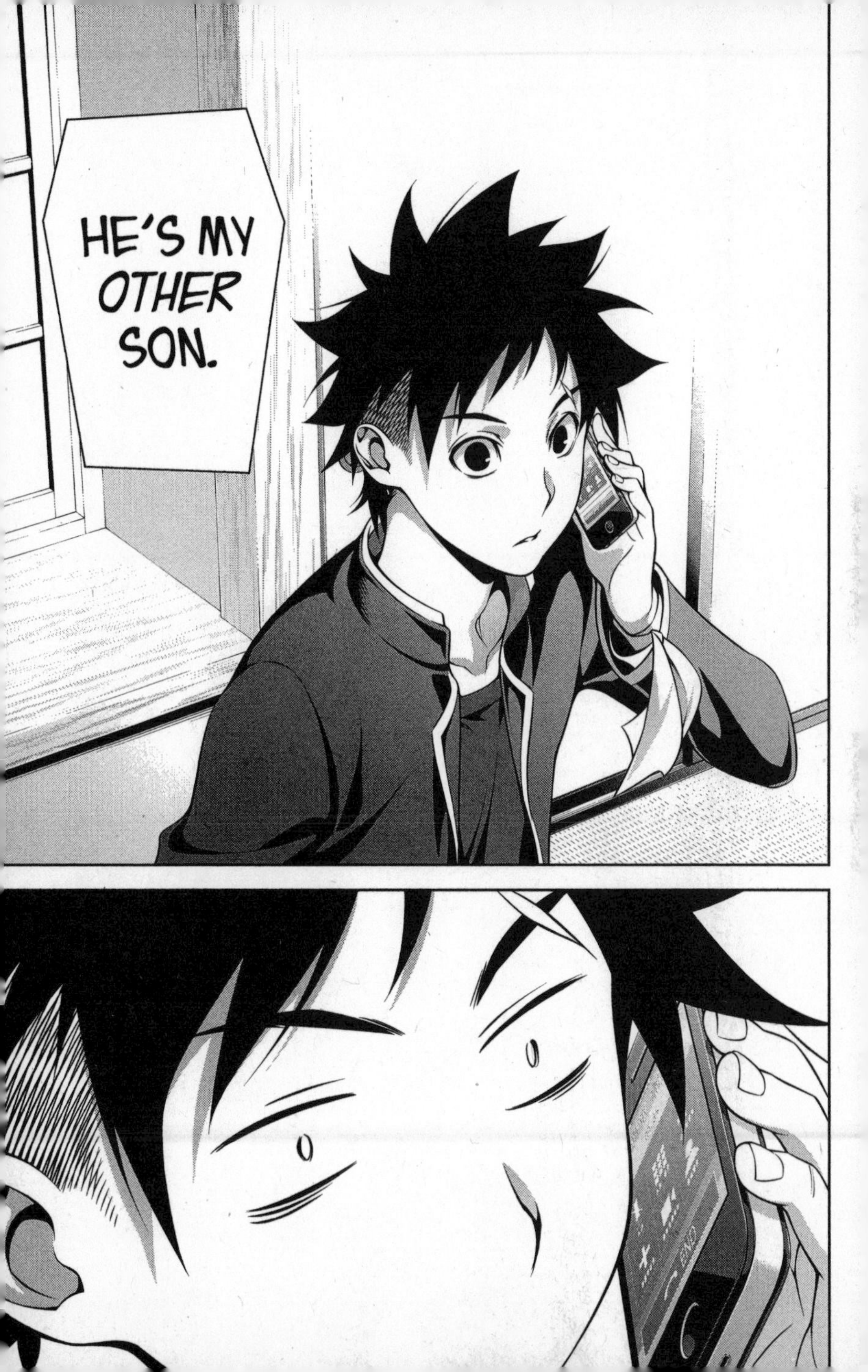
HE'S MY OTHER SON.

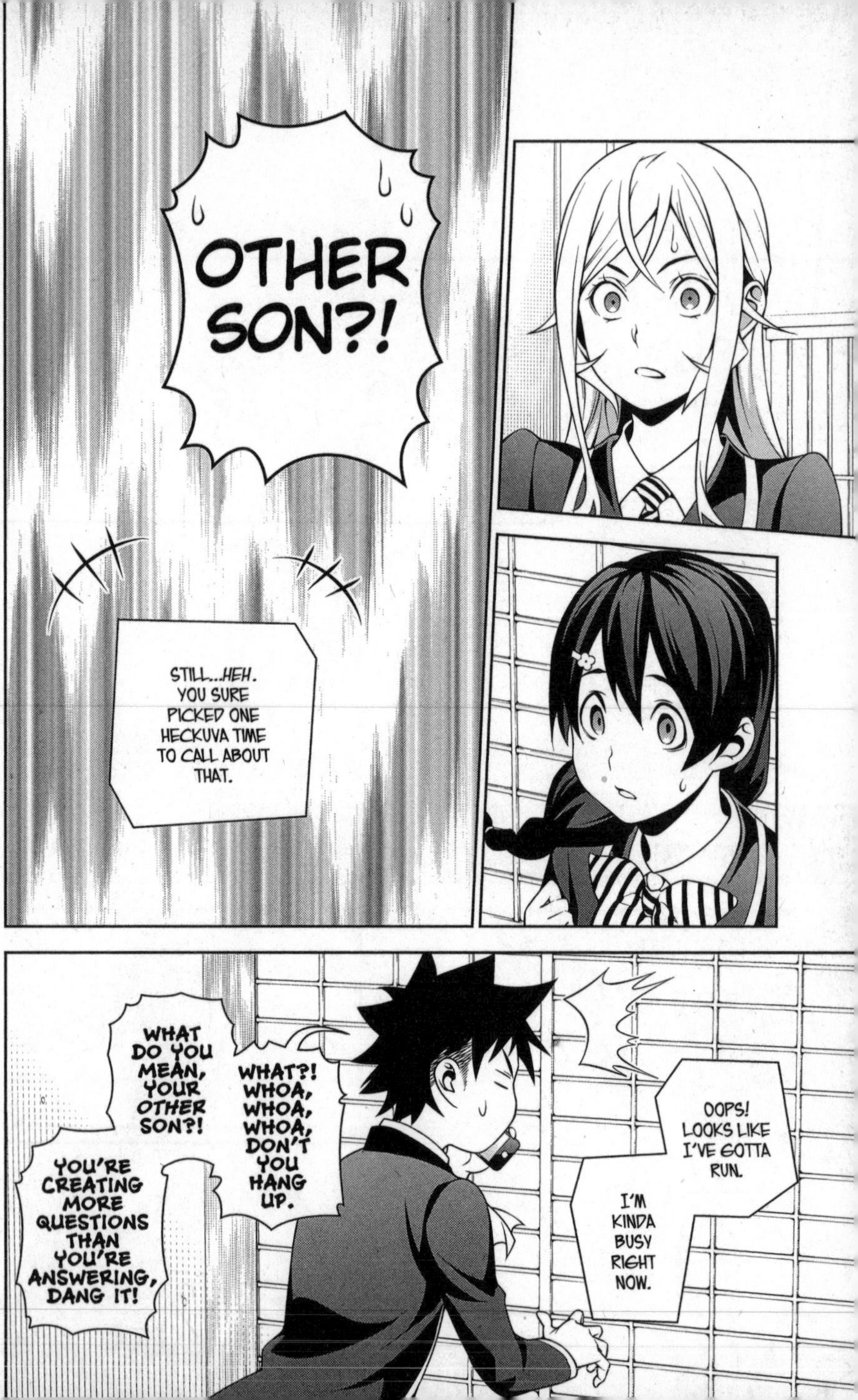
OTHER SON?!
STILL...HEH. YOU SURE PICKED ONE HECKUVA TIME TO CALL ABOUT THAT.
OOPS! LOOKS LIKE I'VE GOTTA RUN.
I'M KINDA BUSY RIGHT NOW.
WHAT?! WHOA, WHOA, WHOA, DON'T YOU HANG UP.
WHAT DO YOU MEAN, YOUR OTHER SON?!
YOU'RE CREATING MORE QUESTIONS THAN YOU'RE ANSWERING, DANG IT!

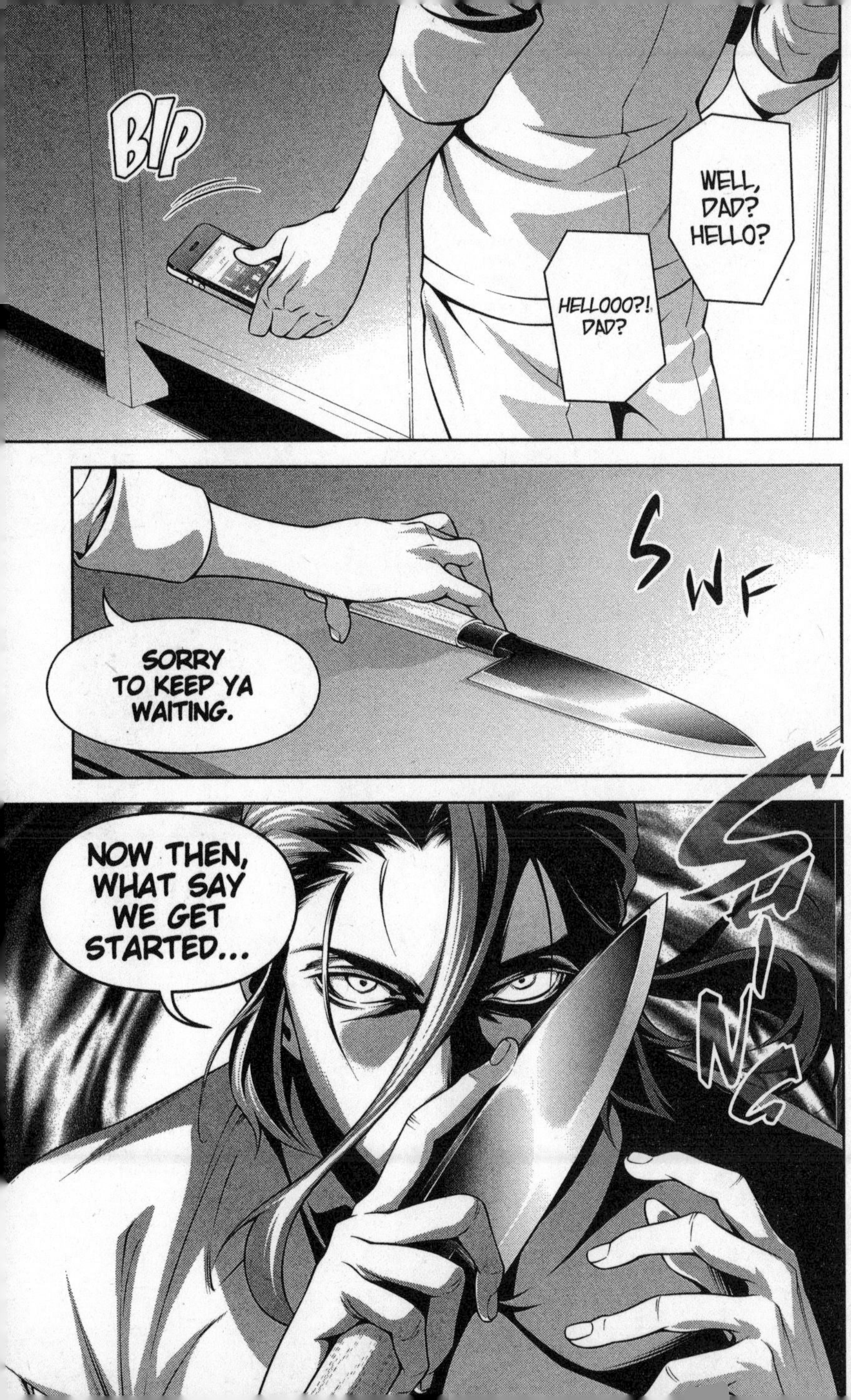
WELL, DAD? HELLO?
HELLOOO?! DAD?
BIP
SWF
SORRY TO KEEP YA WAITING.
NOW THEN, WHAT SAY WE GET STARTED...

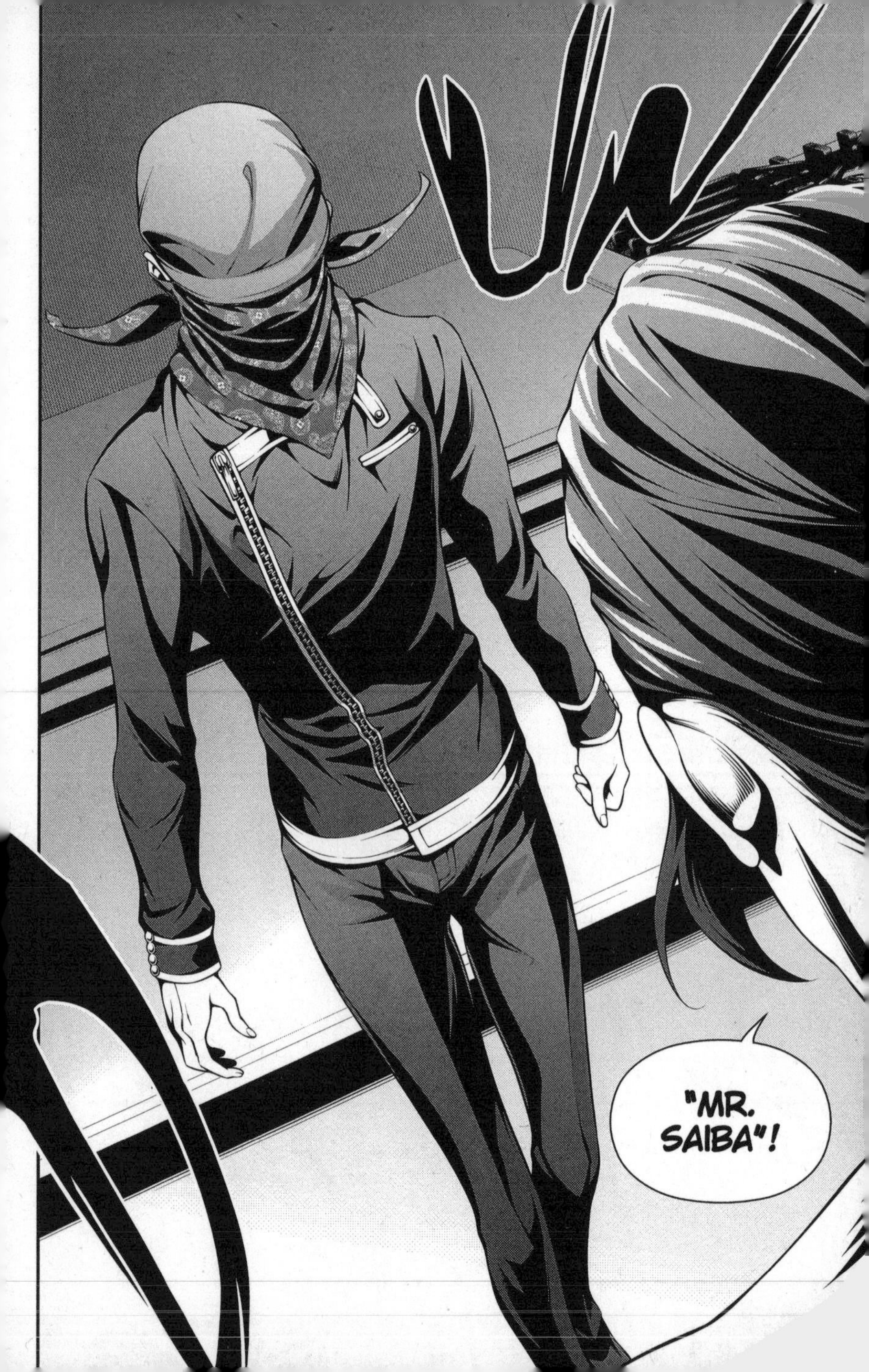
"MR. SAIBA"!

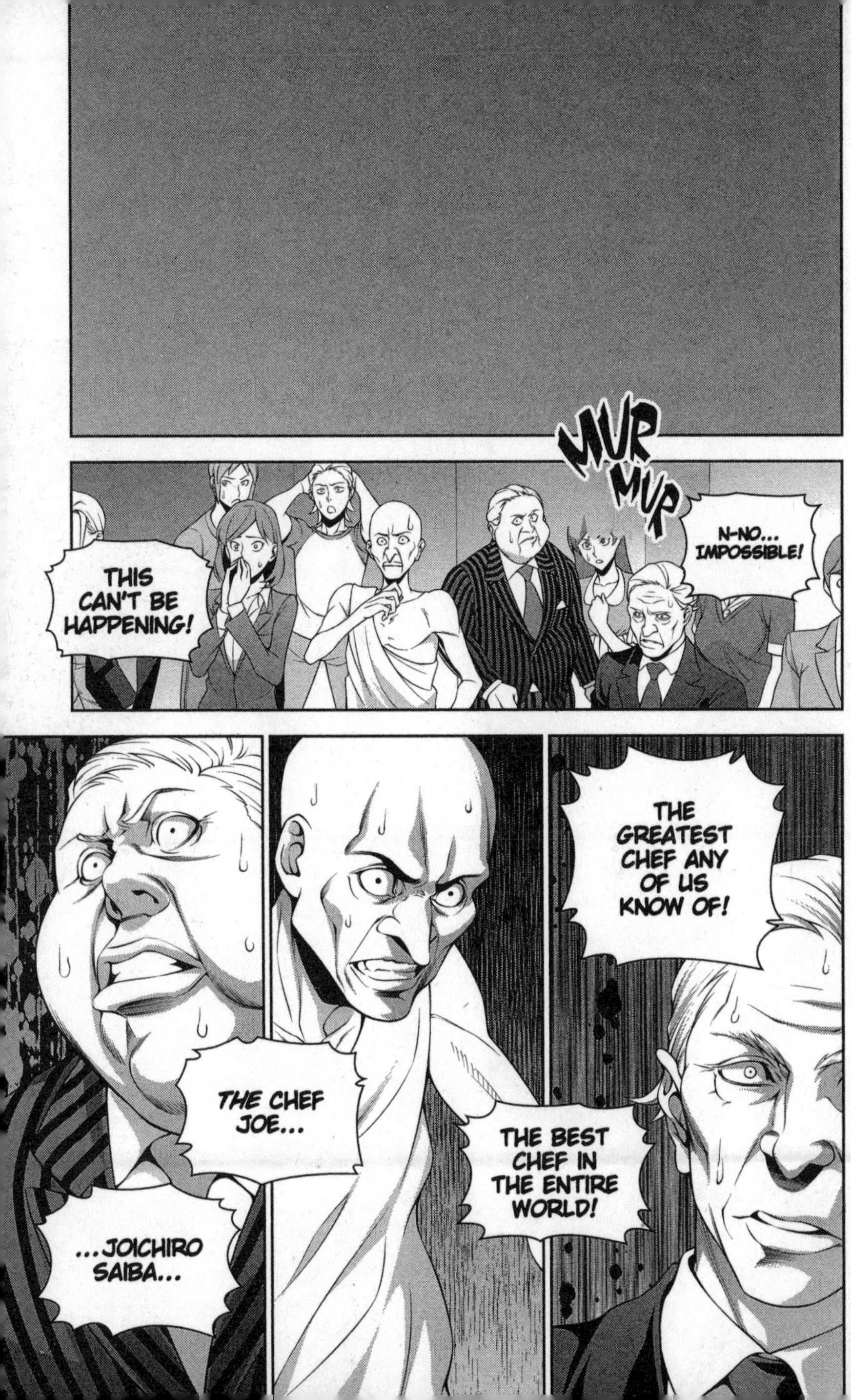
MUR MUR
N-NO... IMPOSSIBLE!
THIS CAN'T BE HAPPENING!
THE GREATEST CHEF ANY OF US KNOW OF!
THE BEST CHEF IN THE ENTIRE WORLD!
THE CHEF JOE...
...JOICHIRO SAIBA...

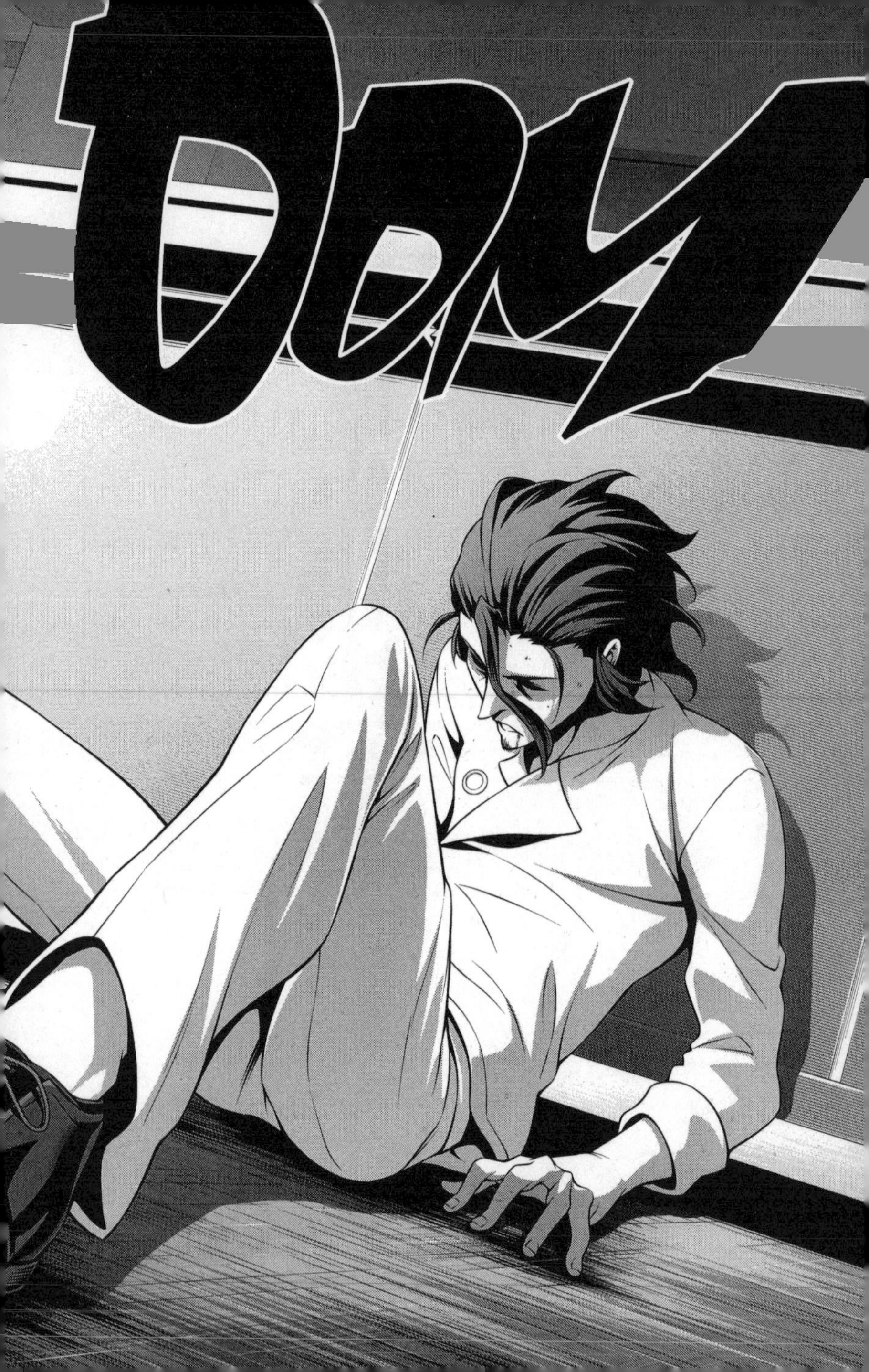
DOM

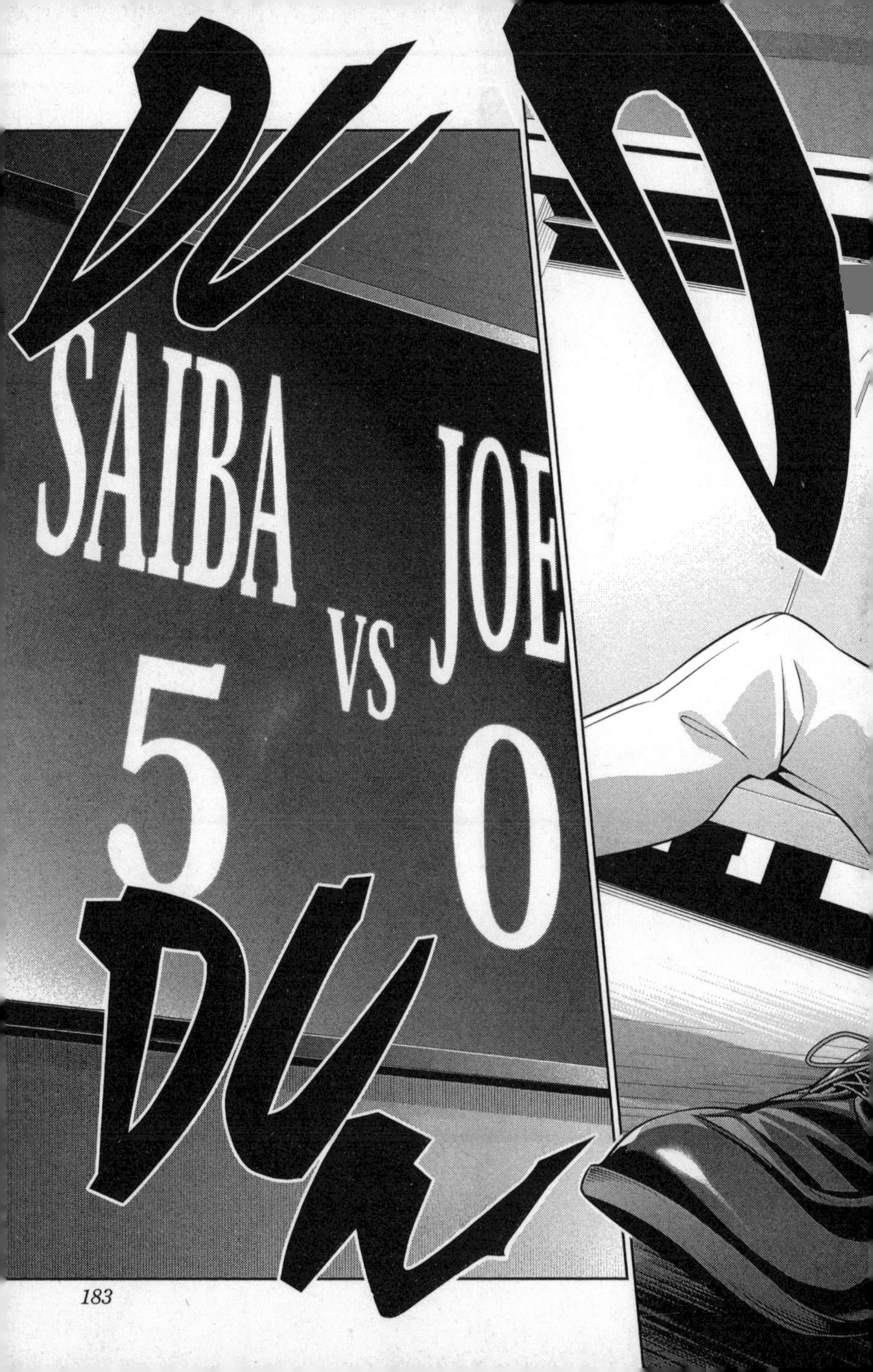
SAIBA
VS
JOE
5
0

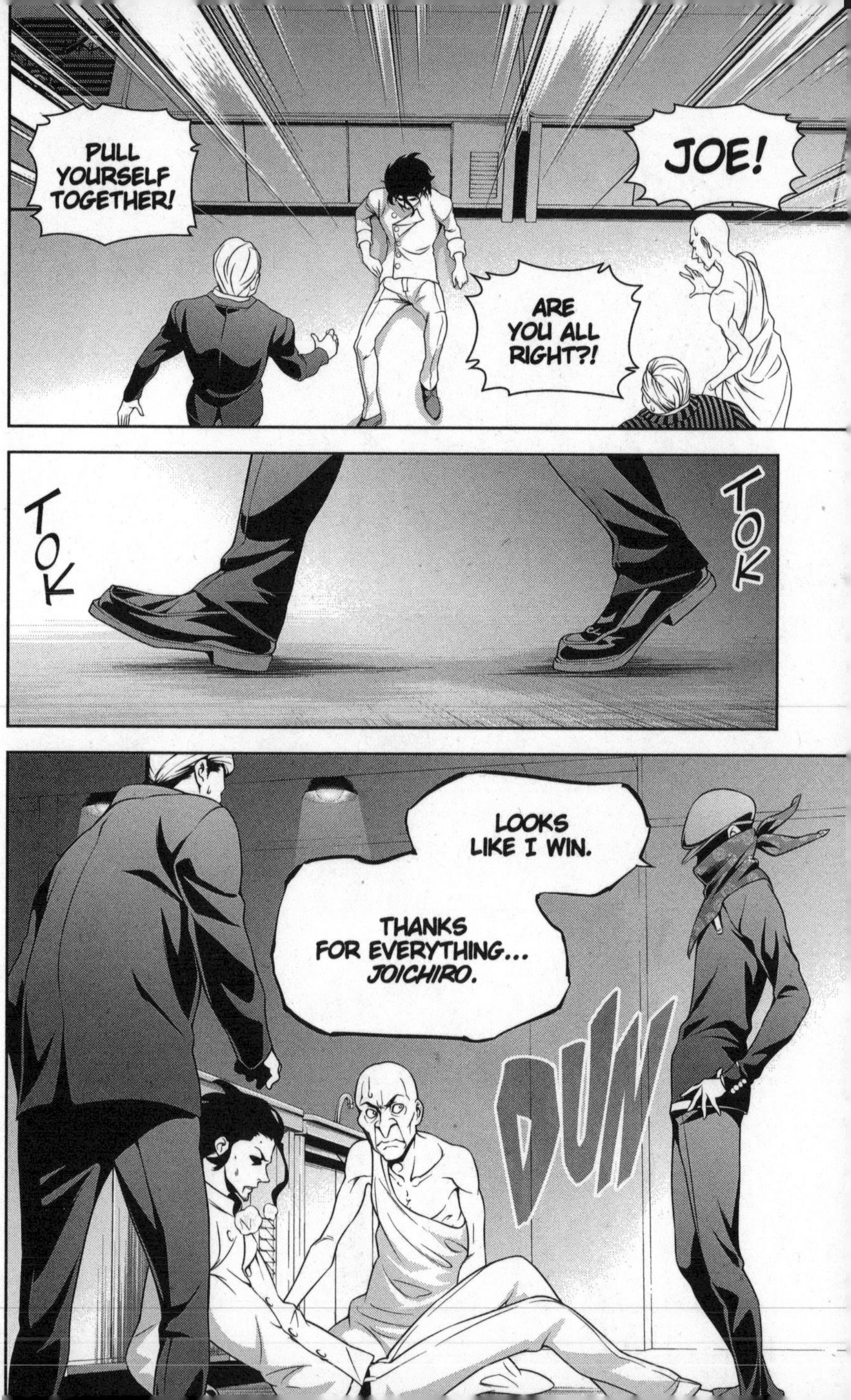
JOE!
ARE YOU ALL RIGHT?!
PULL YOURSELF TOGETHER!
TOK
TOK
LOOKS LIKE I WIN.
THANKS FOR EVERYTHING... JOICHIRO.
DUN

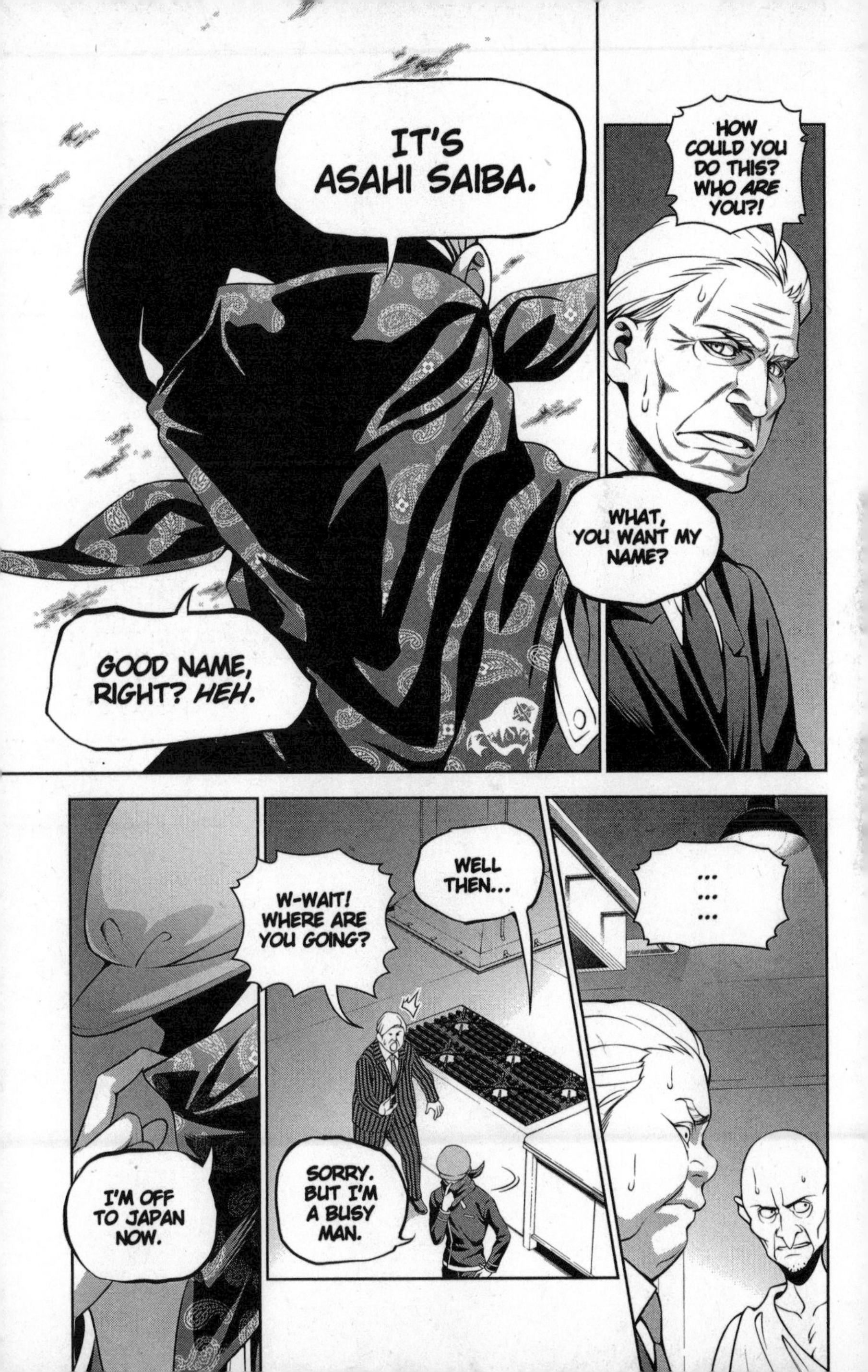
HOW COULD YOU DO THIS? WHO ARE YOU?!
WHAT, YOU WANT MY NAME?
IT'S ASAHI SAIBA.
GOOD NAME, RIGHT? HEH.
...
...
...
WELL THEN...
W-WAIT! WHERE ARE YOU GOING?
SORRY. BUT I'M A BUSY MAN.
I'M OFF TO JAPAN NOW.

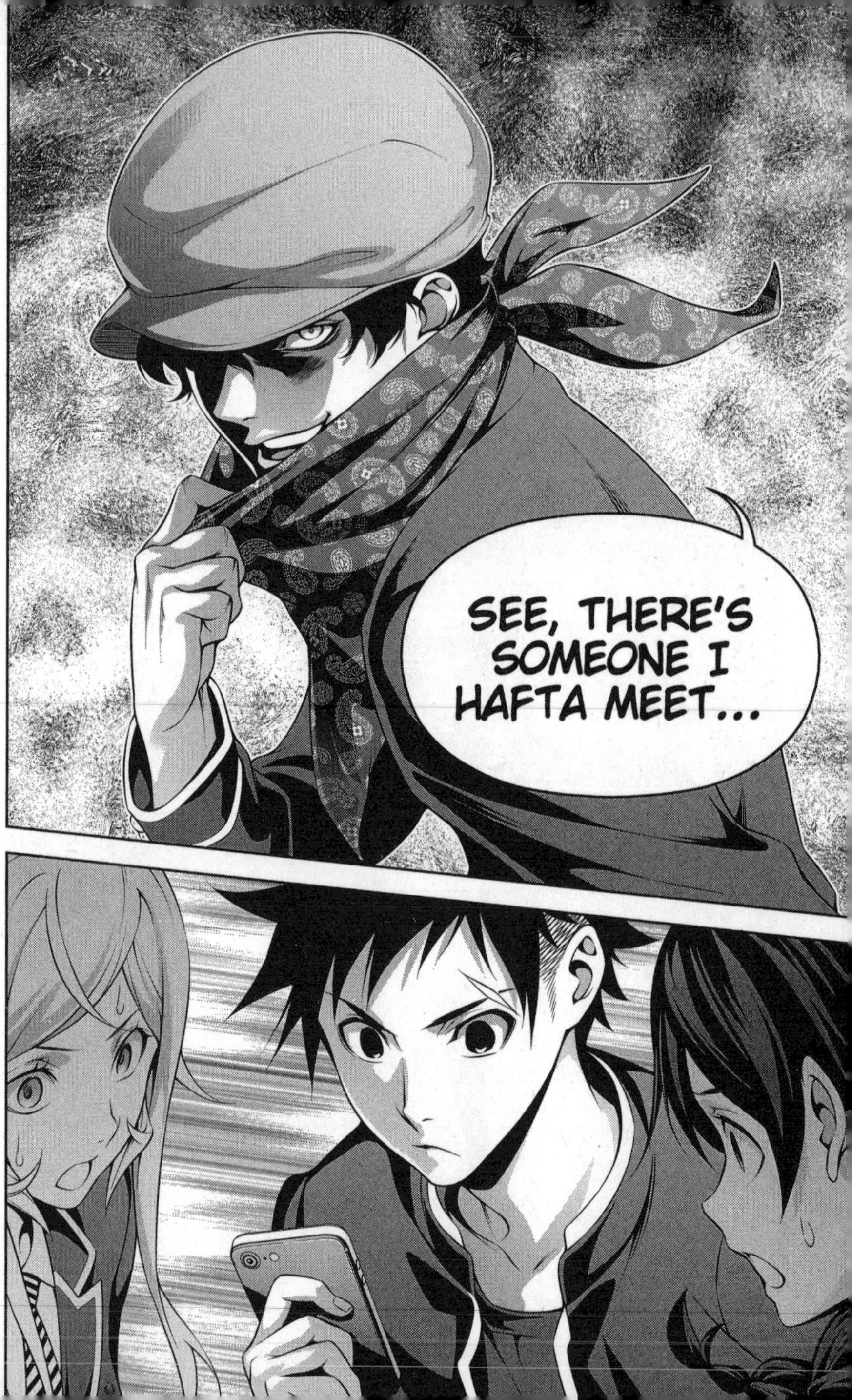
SEE, THERE'S SOMEONE I HAFTA MEET...

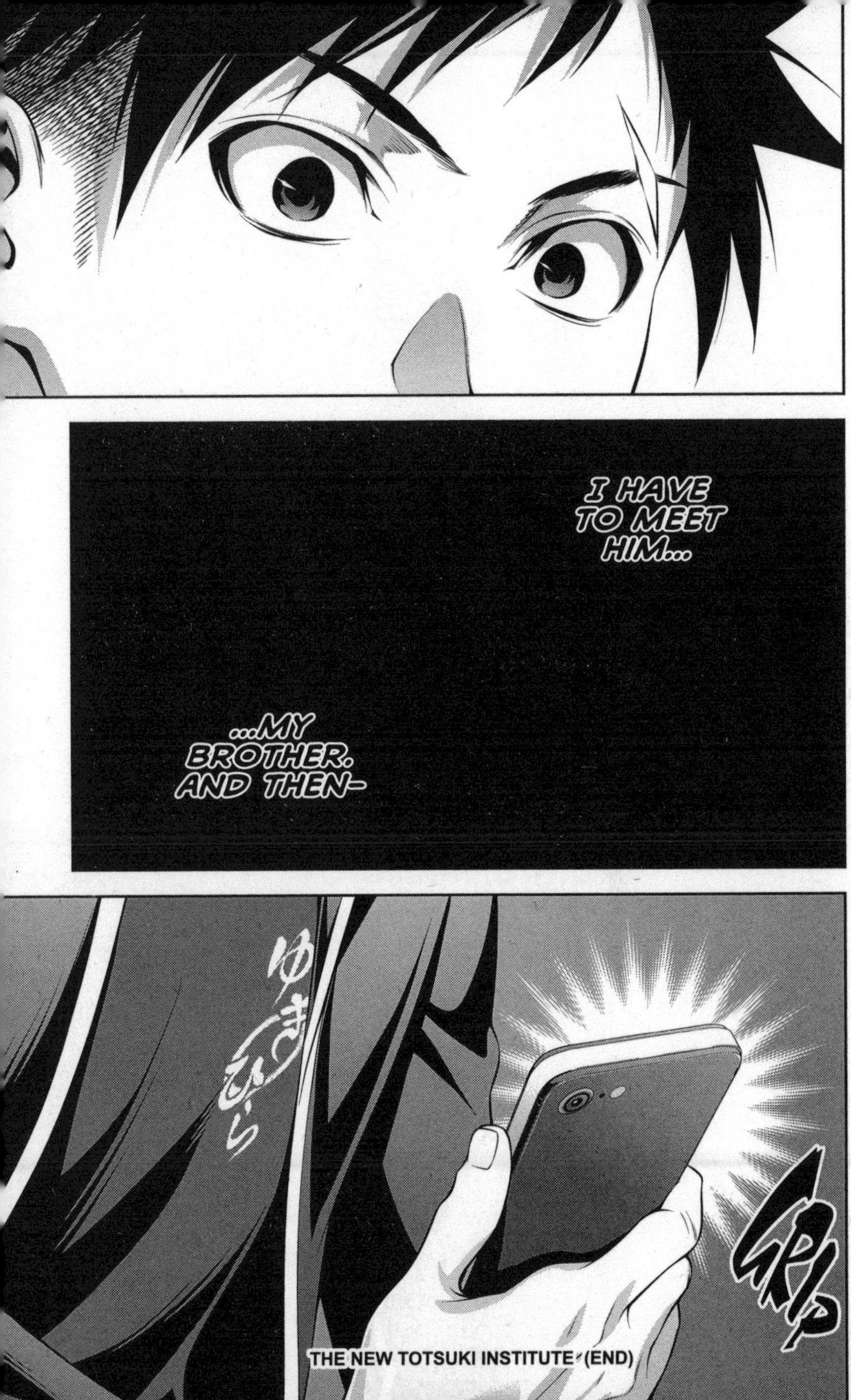
I HAVE TO MEET HIM...
...MY BROTHER. AND THEN-
ゆきひら
GRIP
THE NEW TOTSUKI INSTITUTE (END)

ON THE NEXT PAGE
BEGINS A SPECIAL ONE-
SHOT STORY THAT RAN
IN 2015 IN THE #22-23
COMBINED ISSUE OF
WEEKLY SHONEN JUMP.

SOMETIME BEFORE
ERINA BECAME DEAN
OF THE INSTITUTE,
SHE HELD A SPECIAL
DINNER BANQUET FOR
A CERTAIN GROUP OF
VERY SPECIAL GUESTS...

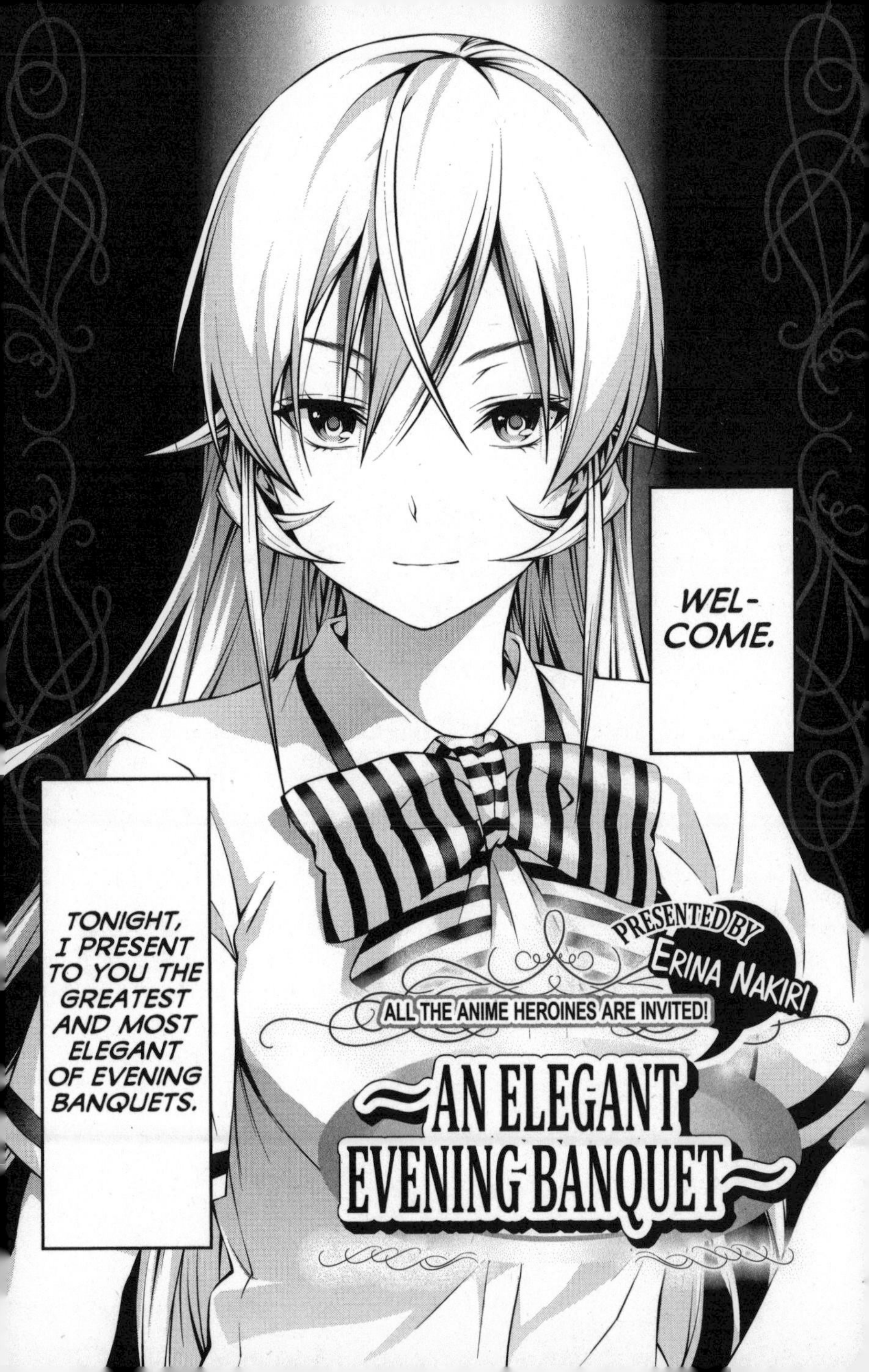
WEL-COME.
TONIGHT, I PRESENT TO YOU THE GREATEST AND MOST ELEGANT OF EVENING BANQUETS.
PRESENTED BY ERINA NAKIRI
ALL THE ANIME HEROINES ARE INVITED!
~AN ELEGANT EVENING BANQUET~

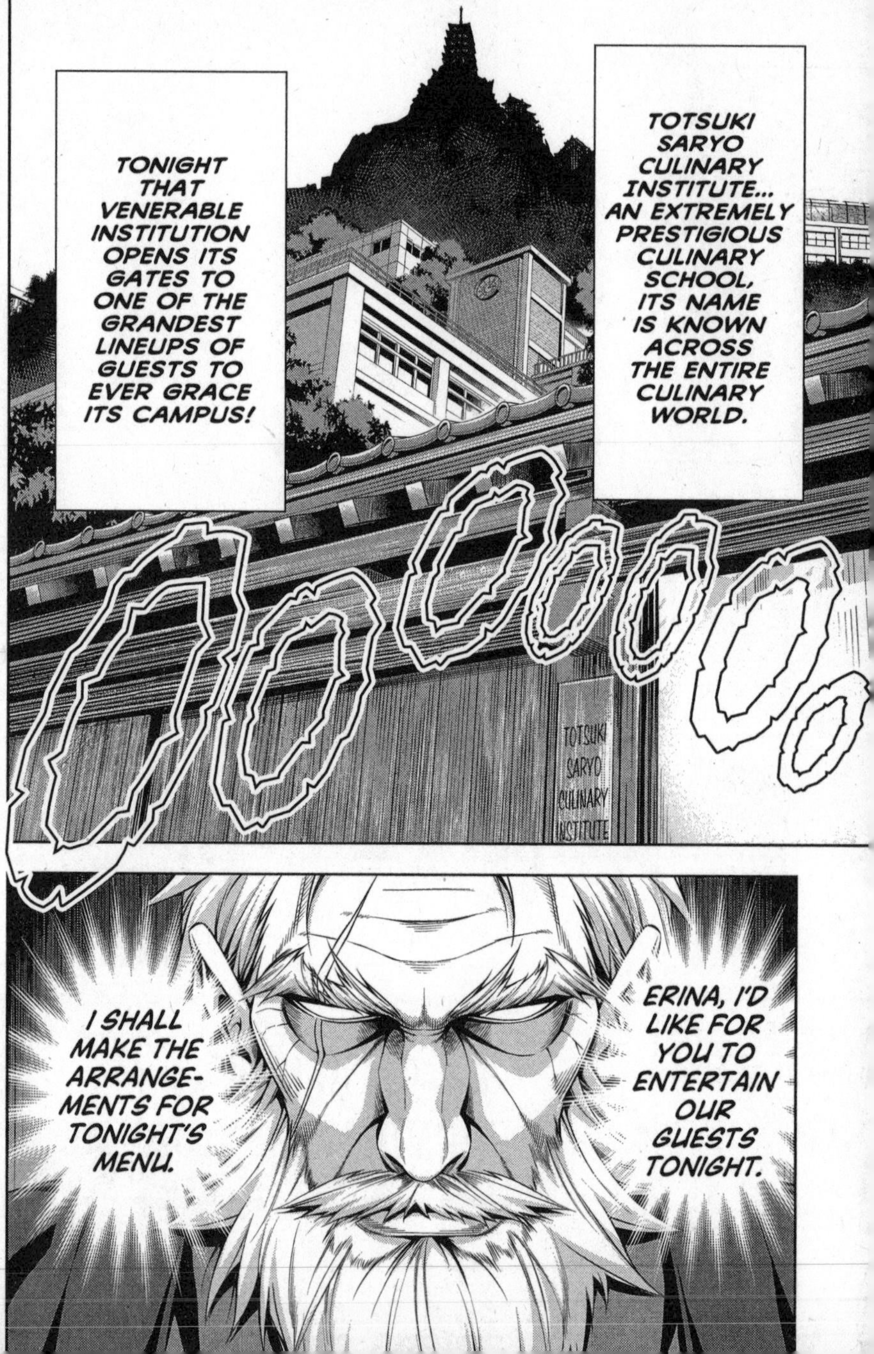
TOTSUKI SARYO CULINARY INSTITUTE... AN EXTREMELY PRESTIGIOUS CULINARY SCHOOL, ITS NAME IS KNOWN ACROSS THE ENTIRE CULINARY WORLD.
TONIGHT THAT VENERABLE INSTITUTION OPENS ITS GATES TO ONE OF THE GRANDEST LINEUPS OF GUESTS TO EVER GRACE ITS CAMPUS!
TOTSUKI SARYO CULINARY INSTITUTE
ERINA, I'D LIKE FOR YOU TO ENTERTAIN OUR GUESTS TONIGHT.
I SHALL MAKE THE ARRANGE-MENTS FOR TONIGHT'S MENU.

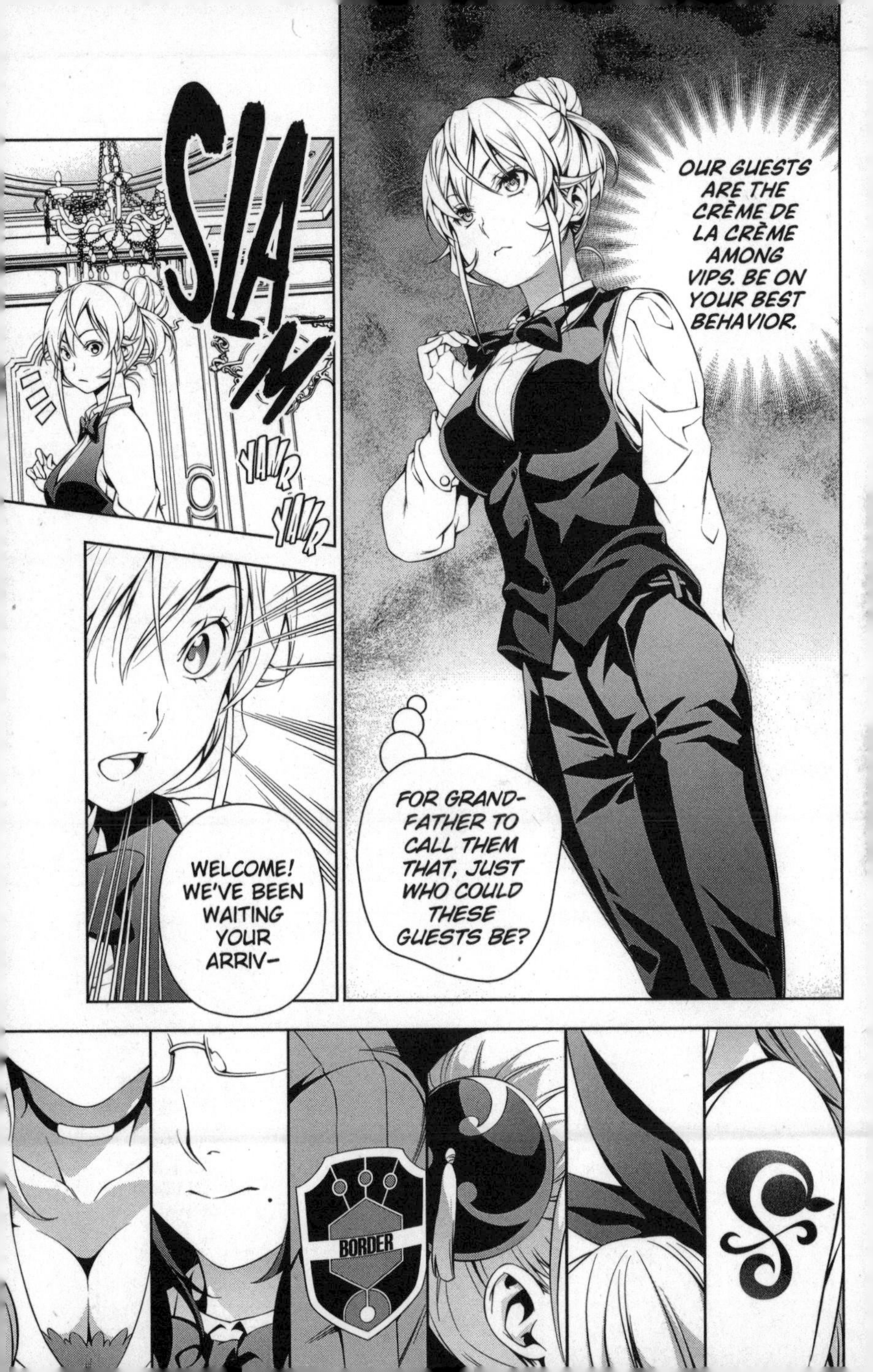
OUR GUESTS ARE THE CRÈME DE LA CRÈME AMONG VIPS. BE ON YOUR BEST BEHAVIOR.
FOR GRAND-FATHER TO CALL THEM THAT, JUST WHO COULD THESE GUESTS BE?
SLAM
YAWR
YAWR
...
WELCOME! WE'VE BEEN WAITING YOUR ARRIV-
BORDER

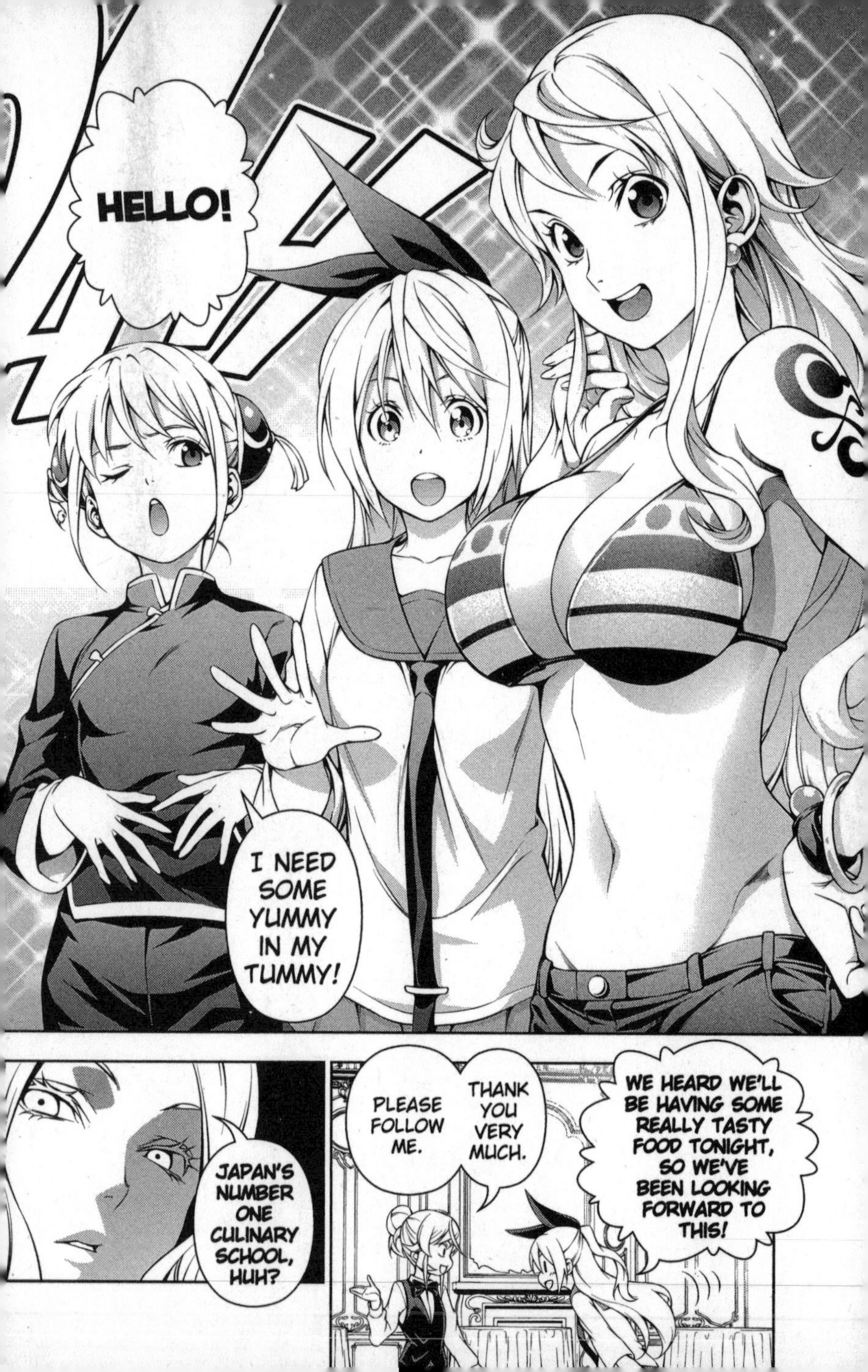
HELLO!
I NEED SOME YUMMY IN MY TUMMY!
WE HEARD WE'LL BE HAVING SOME REALLY TASTY FOOD TONIGHT, SO WE'VE BEEN LOOKING FORWARD TO THIS!
THANK YOU VERY MUCH.
PLEASE FOLLOW ME.
JAPAN'S NUMBER ONE CULINARY SCHOOL, HUH?

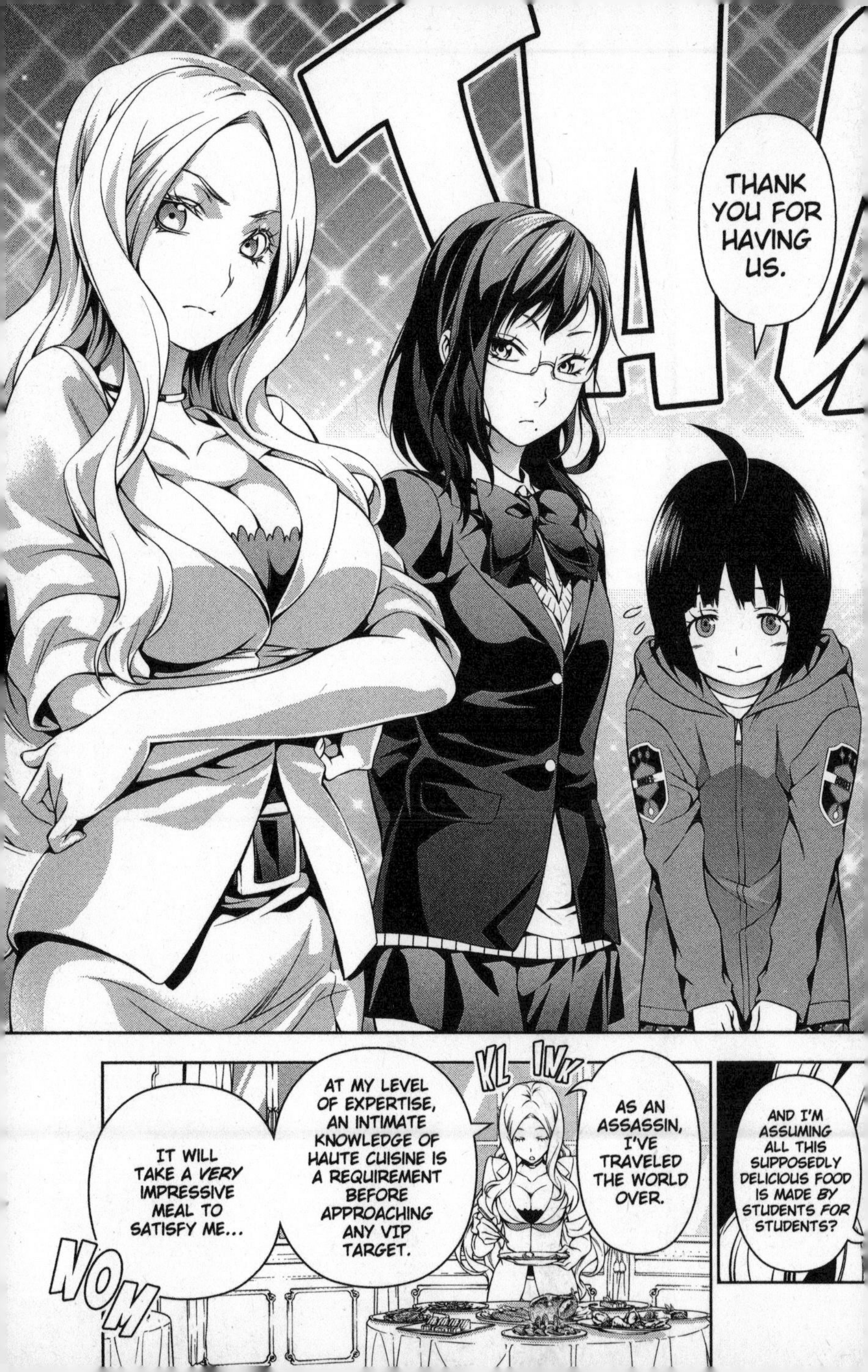
THANK YOU FOR HAVING US.
AND I'M ASSUMING ALL THIS SUPPOSEDLY DELICIOUS FOOD IS MADE BY STUDENTS FOR STUDENTS?
KLINK
AS AN ASSASSIN, I'VE TRAVELED THE WORLD OVER.
AT MY LEVEL OF EXPERTISE, AN INTIMATE KNOWLEDGE OF HAUTE CUISINE IS A REQUIREMENT BEFORE APPROACHING ANY VIP TARGET.
IT WILL TAKE A VERY IMPRESSIVE MEAL TO SATISFY ME...
NOM

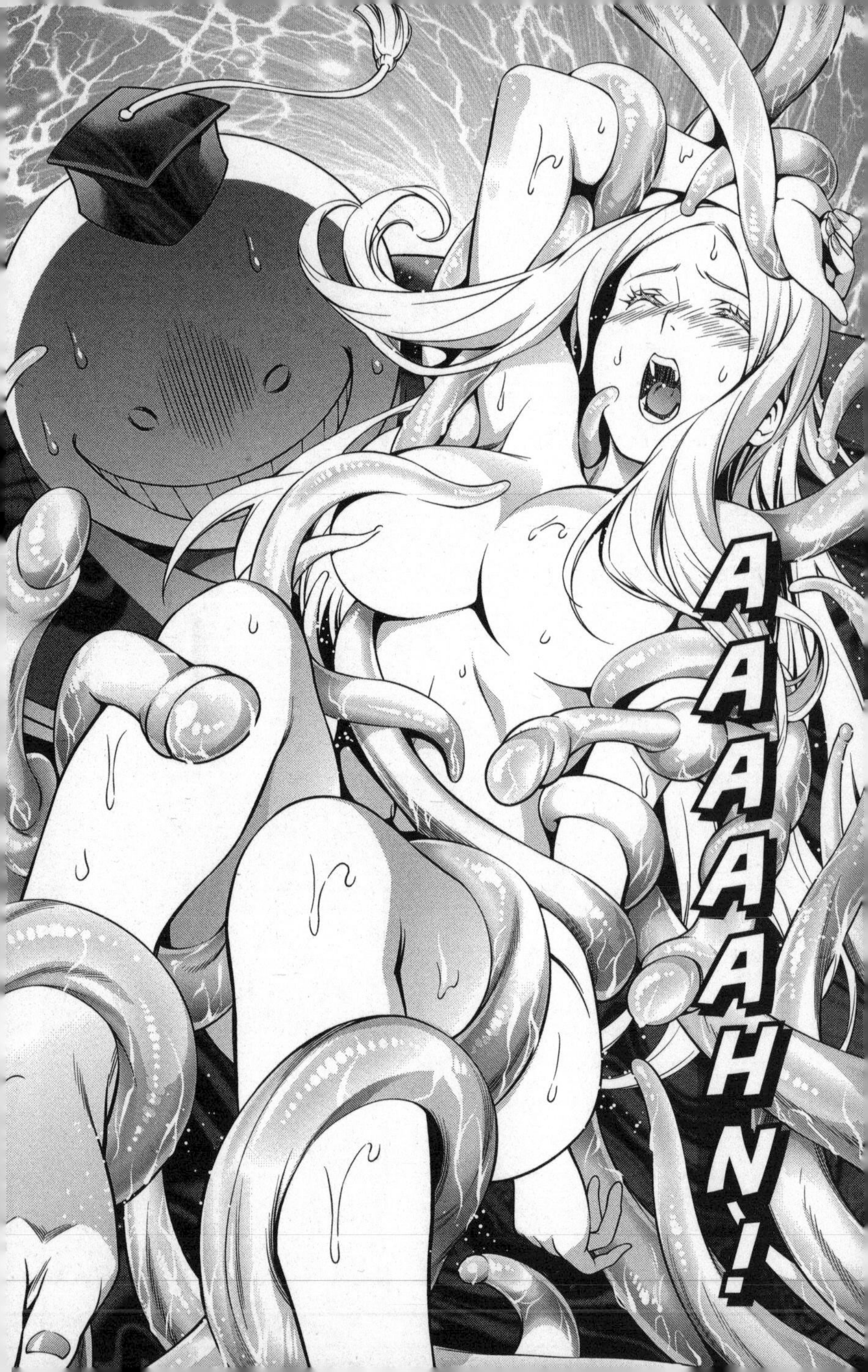
AAAAAHN!!

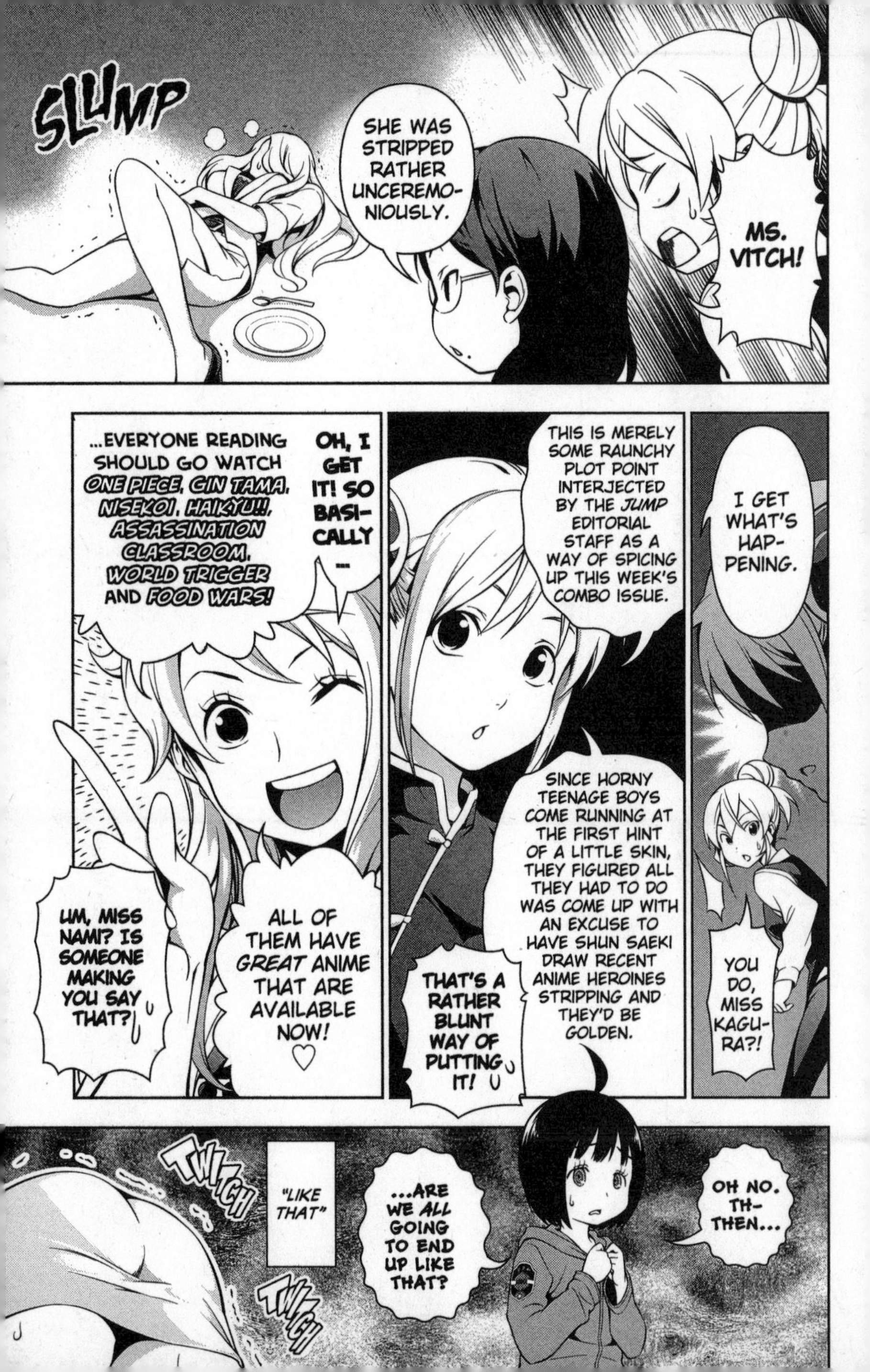
MS. VITCH!
SHE WAS STRIPPED RATHER UNCEREMONIOUSLY.
SLUMP
I GET WHAT'S HAPPENING.
YOU DO, MISS KAGURA?!
THIS IS MERELY SOME RAUNCHY PLOT POINT INTERJECTED BY THE *JUMP* EDITORIAL STAFF AS A WAY OF SPICING UP THIS WEEK'S COMBO ISSUE.
SINCE HORNY TEENAGE BOYS COME RUNNING AT THE FIRST HINT OF A LITTLE SKIN, THEY FIGURED ALL THEY HAD TO DO WAS COME UP WITH AN EXCUSE TO HAVE SHUN SAEKI DRAW RECENT ANIME HEROINES STRIPPING AND THEY'D BE GOLDEN.
THAT'S A RATHER BLUNT WAY OF PUTTING IT!
OH, I GET IT! SO BASICALLY...
...EVERYONE READING SHOULD GO WATCH *ONE PIECE*, *GIN TAMA*, *NISEKOI*, *HAIKYU!!*, *ASSASSINATION CLASSROOM*, *WORLD TRIGGER* AND *FOOD WARS!*
ALL OF THEM HAVE *GREAT* ANIME THAT ARE AVAILABLE NOW! ♡
UM, MISS NAMI? IS SOMEONE MAKING YOU SAY THAT?!
OH NO. TH-THEN...
...ARE WE *ALL* GOING TO END UP LIKE THAT?
"LIKE THAT"
TWITCH
TWITCH

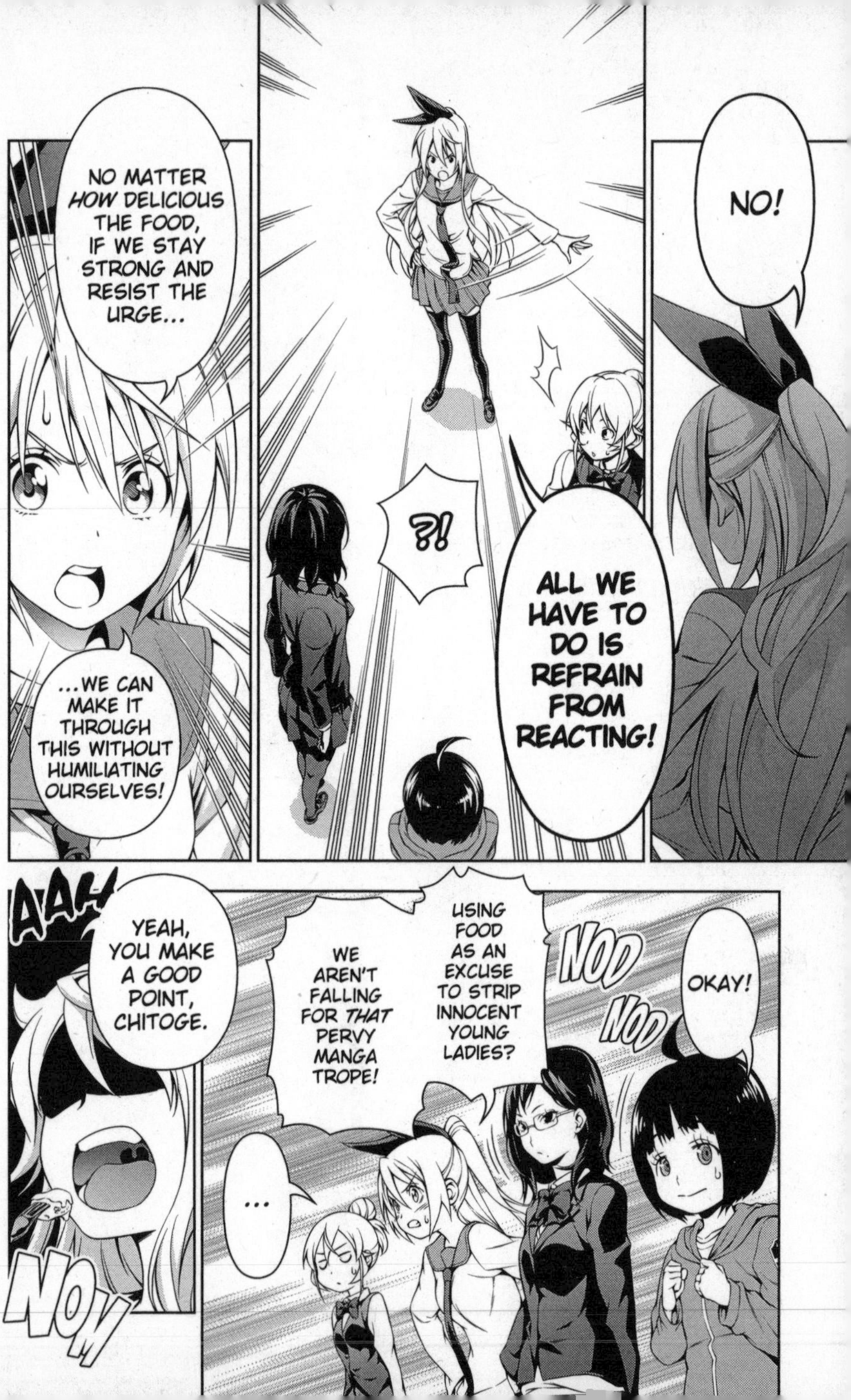
NO!
?!
ALL WE HAVE TO DO IS REFRAIN FROM REACTING!
NO MATTER *HOW* DELICIOUS THE FOOD, IF WE STAY STRONG AND RESIST THE URGE...
...WE CAN MAKE IT THROUGH THIS WITHOUT HUMILIATING OURSELVES!
OKAY!
NOD
NOD
USING FOOD AS AN EXCUSE TO STRIP INNOCENT YOUNG LADIES?
WE AREN'T FALLING FOR *THAT* PERVY MANGA TROPE!
...
YEAH, YOU MAKE A GOOD POINT, CHITOGE.
AAH
NOM

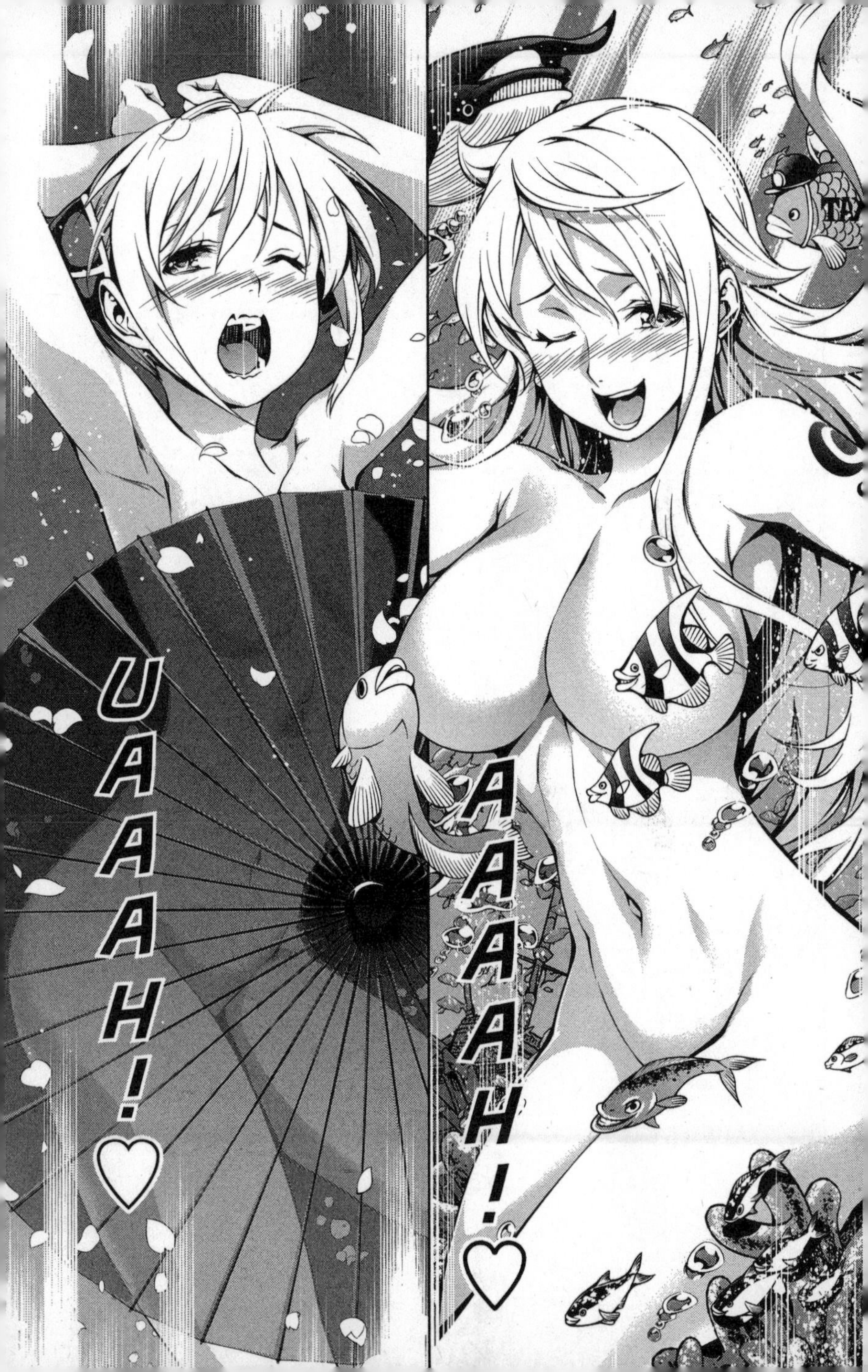
AAAAH!♡
UAAAH!♡

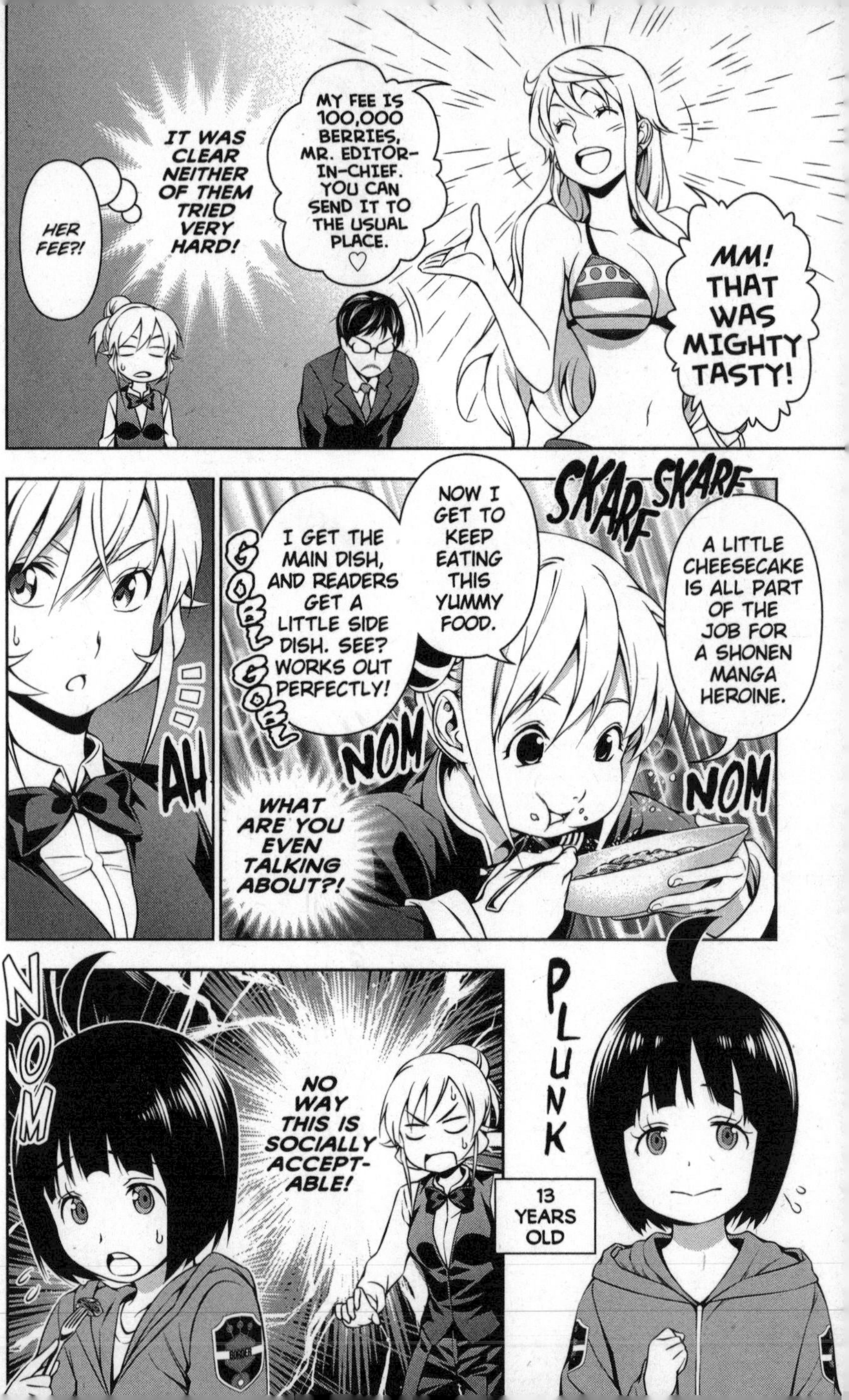
MM! THAT WAS MIGHTY TASTY!
MY FEE IS 100,000 BERRIES, MR. EDITOR-IN-CHIEF. YOU CAN SEND IT TO THE USUAL PLACE. ♡
IT WAS CLEAR NEITHER OF THEM TRIED VERY HARD!
HER FEE?!
SKARF SKARF
A LITTLE CHEESECAKE IS ALL PART OF THE JOB FOR A SHONEN MANGA HEROINE.
NOW I GET TO KEEP EATING THIS YUMMY FOOD.
NOM
I GET THE MAIN DISH, AND READERS GET A LITTLE SIDE DISH. SEE? WORKS OUT PERFECTLY!
GOBL GOBL
NOM
WHAT ARE YOU EVEN TALKING ABOUT?!
......
AH
PLUNK
13 YEARS OLD
NO WAY THIS IS SOCIALLY ACCEPT-ABLE!
NOM

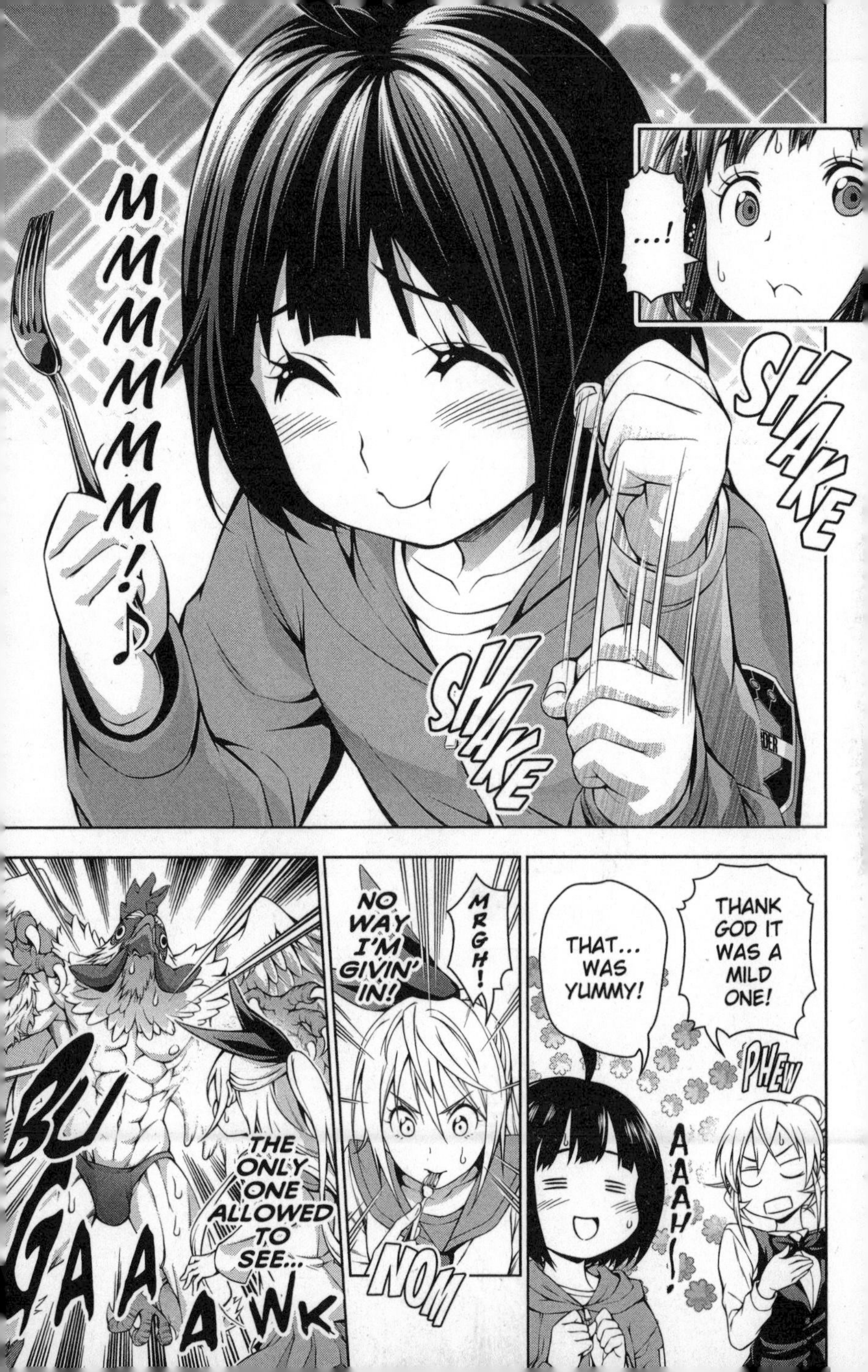

...!
SHAKE
MMMMMMMM!♪
SHAKE
THANK GOD IT WAS A MILD ONE!
PHEW
THAT... WAS YUMMY!
AAAH!
MRGH!
NO WAY I'M GIVIN' IN!
NOM
THE ONLY ONE ALLOWED TO SEE...
BUGAAAWK

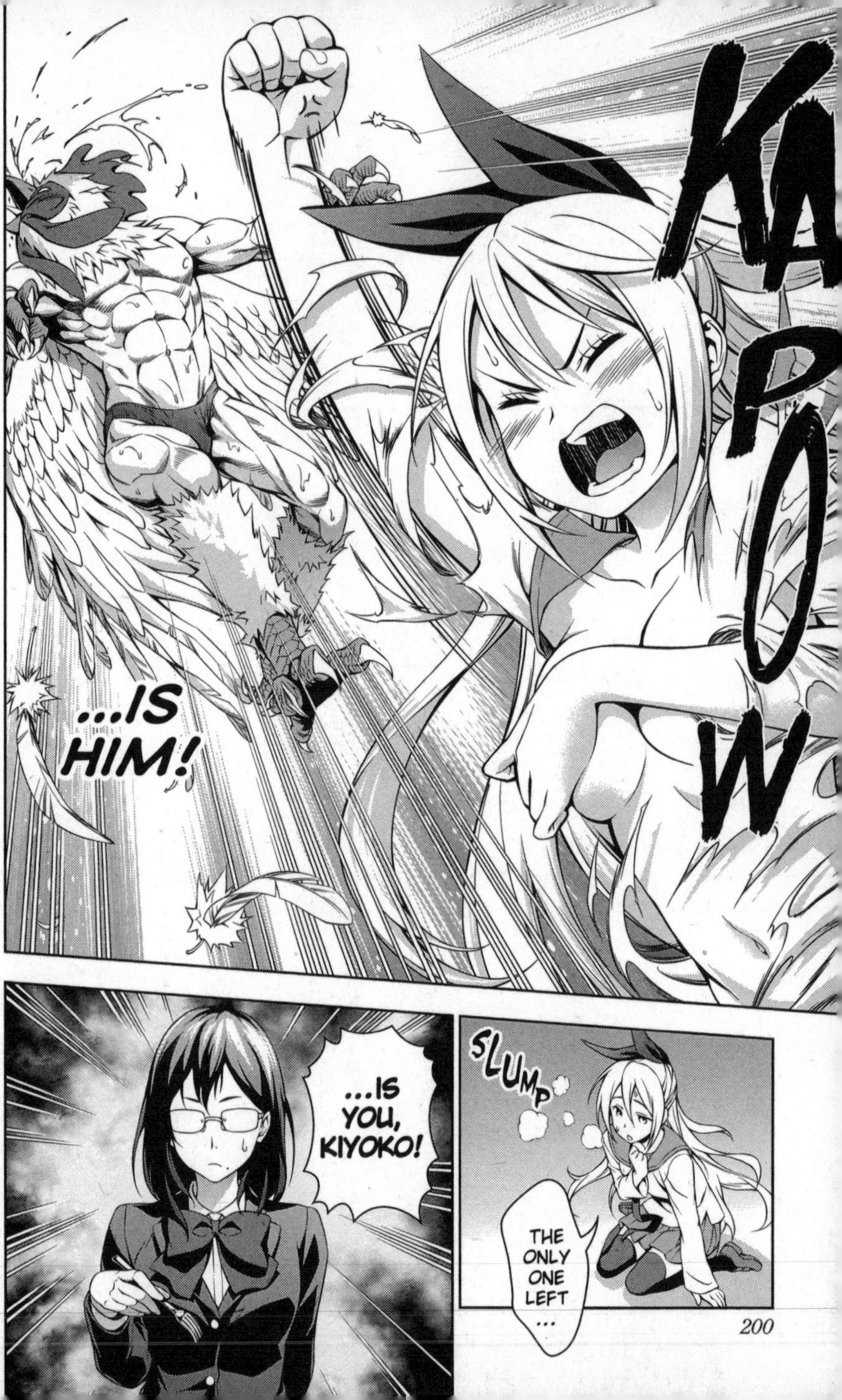
KAPOW
...IS HIM!
SLUMP
THE ONLY ONE LEFT ...
...IS YOU, KIYOKO!

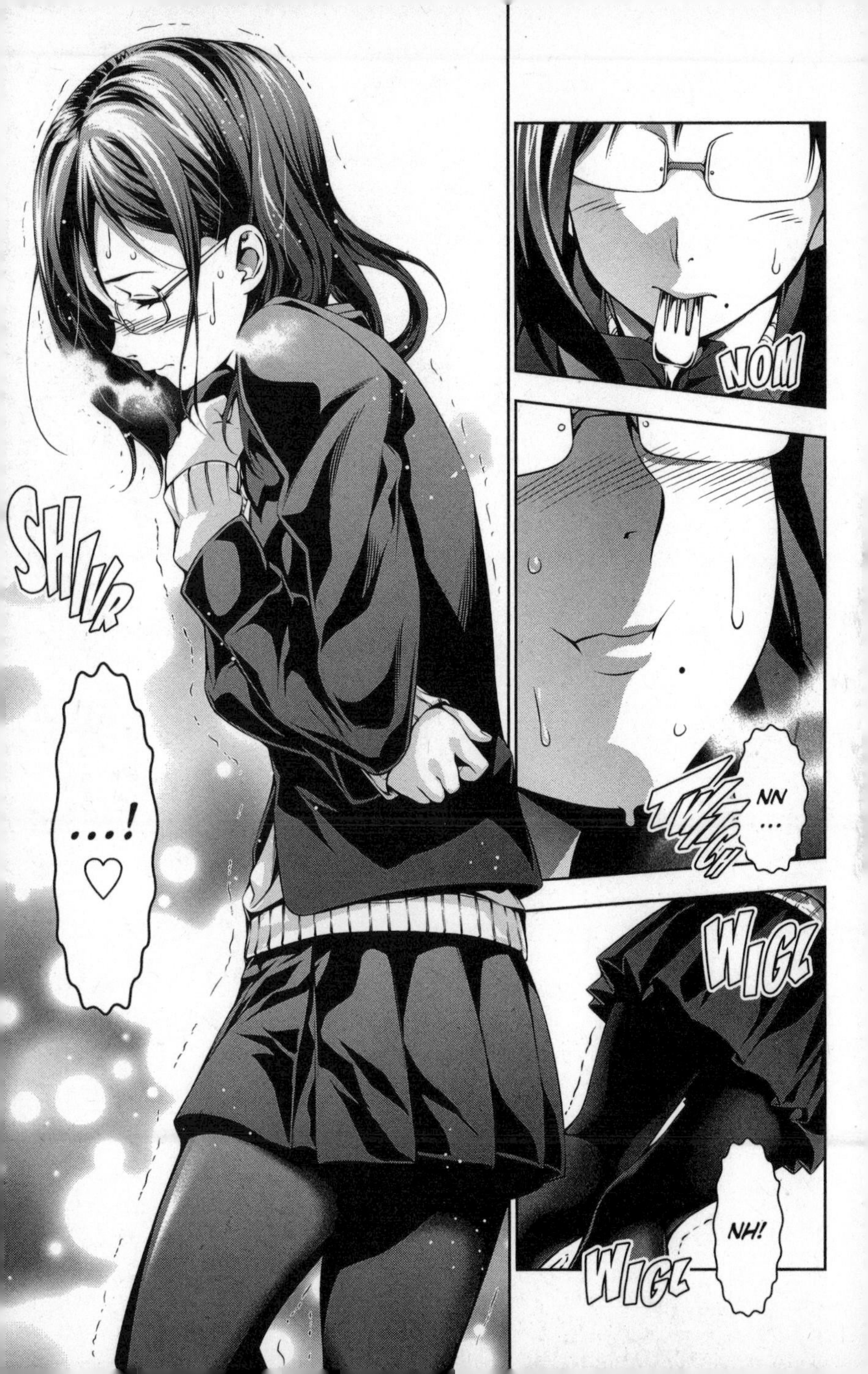
NOM
NN ...
TWITCH
WIGL
NH!
WIGL
SHIVR
...! ♥

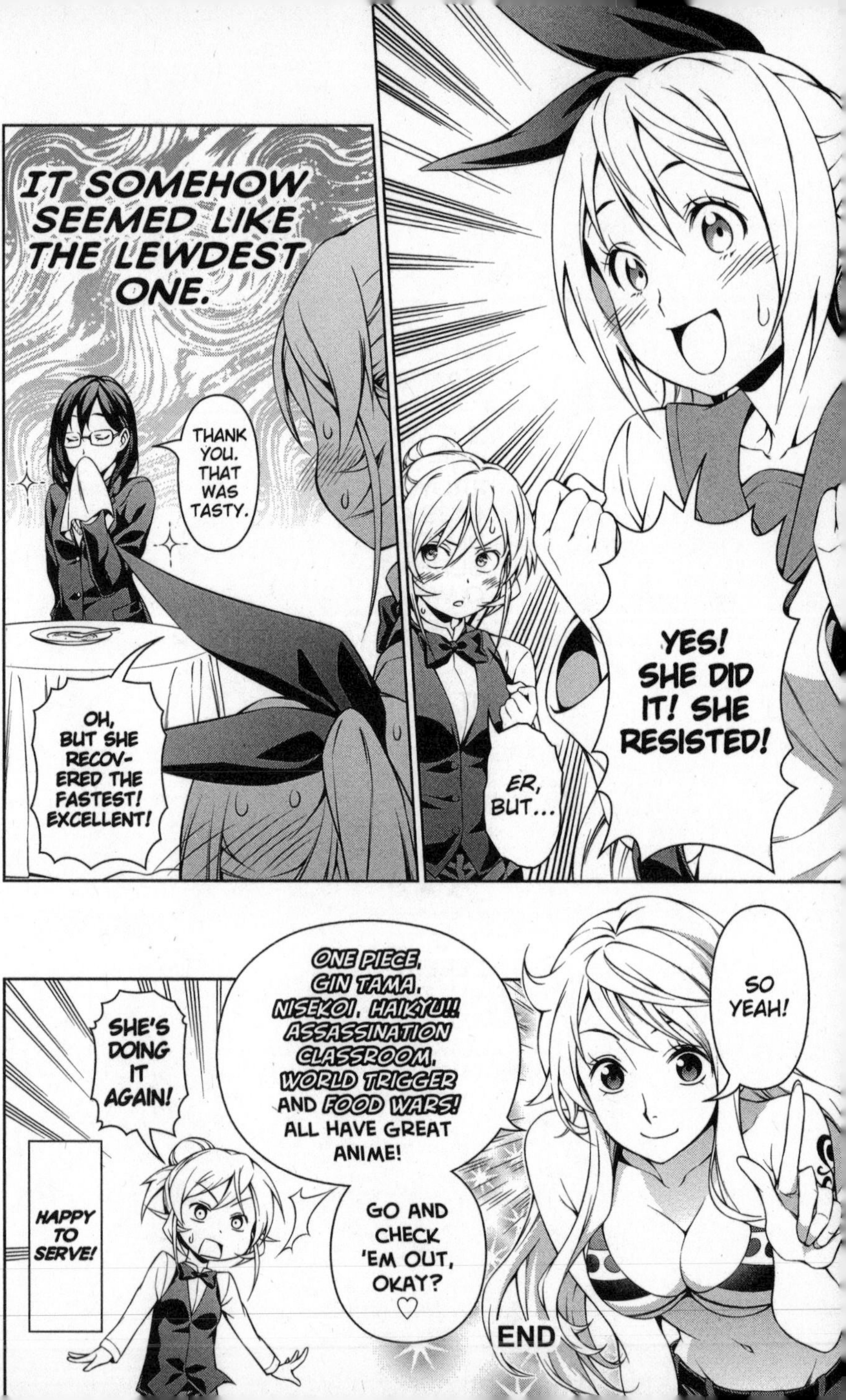
YES! SHE DID IT! SHE RESISTED!
ER, BUT...
IT SOMEHOW SEEMED LIKE THE LEWDEST ONE.
THANK YOU. THAT WAS TASTY.
OH, BUT SHE RECOVERED THE FASTEST! EXCELLENT!
SO YEAH!
ONE PIECE, GIN TAMA, NISEKOI, HAIKYU!! ASSASSINATION CLASSROOM, WORLD TRIGGER AND FOOD WARS! ALL HAVE GREAT ANIME!
GO AND CHECK 'EM OUT, OKAY? ♡
SHE'S DOING IT AGAIN!
HAPPY TO SERVE!
END

DID YOU ALL ENJOY
"AN ELEGANT EVENING
BANQUET"?

SINCE IT WAS A SPECIAL
ONE-SHOT THAT
BORROWED A LOT OF
FAMOUS CHARACTERS
FROM OTHER SERIES,
I FIGURED THERE WAS
NO WAY IT COULD
MAKE IT INTO THE
VOLUME...

BUT JUST IN CASE,
I DECIDED TO BRING
THE IDEA UP TO THE
OTHER CREATORS,
AND SURPRISINGLY,
THEY ALL SAID YES!
AND THAT'S HOW IT
MADE IT IN!

I'D LIKE TO OFFER MY
SINCEREST GRATITUDE
TO ALL THE CREATORS
AND EDITORS FOR
ALLOWING THIS TO
HAPPEN! THANK YOU
VERY MUCH!

ARTIST: YUTO TSUKUDA RECIPE BY: YUKI MORISAKI

VOLUME 31
SPECIAL SUPPLEMENT!

PRACTICAL RECIPE #1

MONARCH'S CHAUDFROID

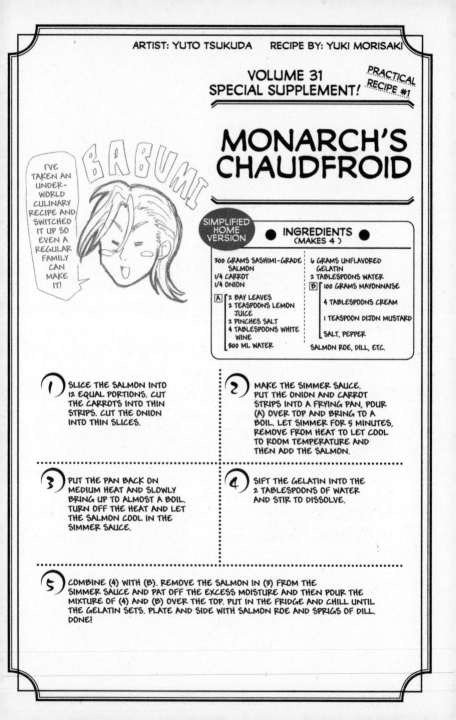

BABUM!
I'VE TAKEN AN UNDER-WORLD CULINARY RECIPE AND SWITCHED IT UP SO EVEN A REGULAR FAMILY CAN MAKE IT!

SIMPLIFIED HOME VERSION

● INGREDIENTS ●
(MAKES 4)

- 300 GRAMS SASHIMI-GRADE SALMON
- 1/4 CARROT
- 1/4 ONION
- [A]
  - 2 BAY LEAVES
  - 2 TEASPOONS LEMON JUICE
  - 2 PINCHES SALT
  - 4 TABLESPOONS WHITE WINE
  - 800 ML WATER
- 6 GRAMS UNFLAVORED GELATIN
- 2 TABLESPOONS WATER
- [B]
  - 100 GRAMS MAYONNAISE
  - 4 TABLESPOONS CREAM
  - 1 TEASPOON DIJON MUSTARD
  - SALT, PEPPER
- SALMON ROE, DILL, ETC.

1. SLICE THE SALMON INTO 12 EQUAL PORTIONS. CUT THE CARROTS INTO THIN STRIPS. CUT THE ONION INTO THIN SLICES.

2. MAKE THE SIMMER SAUCE. PUT THE ONION AND CARROT STRIPS INTO A FRYING PAN, POUR (A) OVER TOP AND BRING TO A BOIL. LET SIMMER FOR 5 MINUTES, REMOVE FROM HEAT TO LET COOL TO ROOM TEMPERATURE AND THEN ADD THE SALMON.

3. PUT THE PAN BACK ON MEDIUM HEAT AND SLOWLY BRING UP TO ALMOST A BOIL. TURN OFF THE HEAT AND LET THE SALMON COOL IN THE SIMMER SAUCE.

4. SIFT THE GELATIN INTO THE 2 TABLESPOONS OF WATER AND STIR TO DISSOLVE.

5. COMBINE (4) WITH (B). REMOVE THE SALMON IN (3) FROM THE SIMMER SAUCE AND PAT OFF THE EXCESS MOISTURE AND THEN POUR THE MIXTURE OF (4) AND (B) OVER THE TOP. PUT IN THE FRIDGE AND CHILL UNTIL THE GELATIN SETS. PLATE AND SIDE WITH SALMON ROE AND SPRIGS OF DILL. DONE!

ARTIST: YUTO TSUKUDA   RECIPE BY: YUKI MORISAKI

VOLUME 31 SPECIAL SUPPLEMENT!

PRACTICAL RECIPE #2

MEGU-MAMA'S HOMEMADE GUMBO

WORLD-WIDE MEGUMI

● INGREDIENTS ●
(MAKES 4)

2 EACH ONIONS AND GREEN PEPPERS
1 RED BELL PEPPER
1 STALK OF CELERY
10 OKRA
8 VIENNA SAUSAGES
3 TABLESPOONS EACH BUTTER AND FLOUR
2 CLOVES GARLIC

B
1 CAN DICED TOMATOES
2 TEASPOONS GRANULATED CONSOMMÉ
2 CUPS WATER
1 SPRIG THYME
2 BAY LEAVES
1/2 TEASPOON CHILI PEPPER

200 GRAMS SEAFOOD MIX
1 TABLESPOON WORCESTERSHIRE SAUCE
COOKED RICE, SALT, PEPPER, SOY SAUCE

1 DICE THE ONIONS, CELERY, RED BELL PEPPER AND GREEN PEPPERS. SLICE THE OKRA AND VIENNA SAUSAGES INTO BITE-SIZE ROUNDS. MINCE THE GARLIC. SET THE SEAFOOD MIX OUT TO DEFROST.

2 HEAT THE BUTTER AND GARLIC IN A FRYING PAN. ONCE FRAGRANT, ADD THE ONIONS AND COOK UNTIL THEY ARE TENDER. ADD THE RED BELL PEPPER, GREEN PEPPERS, OKRA, CELERY AND SAUSAGES AND COOK UNTIL HEATED THROUGH.

3 SPRINKLE THE FLOUR OVER (2), STIR TO COMBINE AND THEN POUR IN (B). BRING TO A BOIL AND SIMMER OVER LOW HEAT FOR 30 MINUTES.

4 POUR IN THE DEFROSTED SEAFOOD MIX AND BRING BACK TO A BOIL. SIMMER FOR 5 MINUTES AND THEN SEASON TO TASTE WITH SALT, PEPPER AND SOY SAUCE.

5 PUT SOME COOKED RICE IN A BOWL, LADLE THE GUMBO OVER TOP AND DONE!

THE PROMISED NEVERLAND

STORY BY **KAIU SHIRAI**

ART BY **POSUKA DEMIZU**

mma, Norman and Ray are the brightest kids
the Grace Field House orphanage. And under
e care of the woman they refer to as "Mom,"
all the kids have enjoyed a comfortable life.
ood food, clean clothes and the perfect envi-
nment to learn—what more could an orphan
sk for? One day, though, Emma and Norman
uncover the dark truth of the outside world
they are forbidden from seeing.

VIZ
viz.com

RATED T+ OLDER TEEN

YAKUSOKU NO NEVERLAND © 2016 by Kaiu Shirai, Posuka Demizu/Shueisha Inc.